What Today Withholds:
Autism and Human Rights in America

Megan McLaughlin

ISBN: 979-8-9885559-1-9

Cover Design by Adam Renvoize

Typesetting by Stewart Williams

DEDICATION

For Howard, for many, many years of support and love.
You always have been, and still are, the best.

Epigraph

A river of cringe is flowing through our collective sky.
It is like when your heart is hanging over
some tree line, large and ghostly as
an autumn moon before sundown.

Meanwhile we are doing
the same things once done by people
in an earlier present, only
for different reasons, reasons more our own.

There are always those of us in possession of
the skillset brief rain requires. The thing known as a river
is what it is, which is why we expect ourselves
to continue generalizing it to make it what it is. Like

a picturesque expanse, like a bouquet of fallen rain, like
the penury of mountains, like the allure of a skyscraper with its
panoply of windows
flashing, like a mother and grandmother caring for a smiling
infant, we are waiting for tomorrow to give us what today
withholds.

—NATHAN SPOON, "A History of Leaves"

Acknowledgements

This book has taken a long time to write, and I have incurred many debts along the way. As a neurotypical writer, I am especially grateful to the many autistic individuals who have provided me with the results of their research, their personal stories, general information, references to other sources, and new angles of perception. I am especially grateful to Nathan Spoon for allowing me to reproduce his beautiful poem "A History of Leaves" here, and for letting me use a phrase from the poem in the book's title. I also want to thank Zoe Gross for talking to me about the murder of autistic children by their parents and caregivers, and Finn Gardiner for his views on the intersection of racism, ableism, and anti-LGBTQ bias in police violence. I am grateful to Henny Kupferstein and Antonia Min Berenbaum for helping me understand the detrimental effects Applied Behavior Analysis can have on autistic children. Although we never actually managed to connect, I want to thank Lydia X. Z. Brown for their willingness to talk to me about their indefatigable work against the Judge Rotenberg Center. I also owe a debt of gratitude to the countless autistic individuals whose words I plucked from their blogs and podcasts and posts on Reddit, Twitter, and various autism forums to include in this book. I made the assumption that anything not explicitly marked "private" or "do not reproduce" was fair game. My apologies if I have cited anyone against their will.

So many debts. Thanks are due to the various groups who have read parts of the book or listened to me present some of my findings and provided valuable feedback. Most important here is my magnificent sister Lissa, poet and editor extraordinaire, without whose help this thing would have been even more densely academic than it already is. If parts are still unreadable, it is certainly not her fault. I am also grateful to my husband Howard for his professional advice and his patient copy-editing. Of course, any remaining errors are entirely my own.

Finally, I am grateful to my friends and above all to my family who have been so patient with me and so unfailingly supportive during hard times.

Contents

A Note on Terminology

I refer to autism as a "disability" in this book. This is not because I consider the condition inherently disabling, but rather because our society makes it almost impossible for autistic people to succeed. According to polls, roughly 80-85% of those who have been or could be diagnosed with autism prefer "identity first" language. I will therefore be using identity first language ("autistic people," "autistic person," "autistics"), rather than "person first" ("person with autism") language most of the time in this book. (I very occasionally use person first language, just to ensure that those who prefer such language feel included.)

I have tried to use the terms most widely accepted by members of racial and ethnic minorities: Black (and White), Latino/a, Native American, and so forth. I have also done my best to use people's preferred pronouns throughout. If I have made a mistake with anyone's identity, please forgive me.

Introduction

To be considered eligible for human rights,
one must first and foremost be considered
a part of the human population . . .[1]

By current estimates, about 2-3% of all Americans have been, or could be, diagnosed with autism.[2] The federal Centers for Disease Control and Prevention reckons that there are more than 5 million autistic adults in our country—if we add in children, the number becomes considerably higher.[3] To put this in perspective: there are more autistic people in our country than there are all lawyers and doctors combined. The number of American tourists who visited the Grand Canyon last year is significantly smaller than the population of American autistics.[4] Autistics, then, make up a significant portion of our citizenry. But often they are not treated like other Americans.

Most of the world today recognizes that everyone is entitled, simply by virtue of being human, to enjoy certain rights. The right not to be killed or tortured by the state. The right to get an education and to get married. The right to work and earn a living. Yet America often—not occasionally, but <u>often</u>—fails to recognize the humanity of autistic people, thus enabling abuses of power.

Jesse was a lonely 17-year-old, long the target of bullies at school because of his peculiar behaviors. This all changed when he made a new friend—"Dan"—who was willing to hang out with him regularly and treat him with kindness. One day, though, Dan asked Jesse to find him some "weed." Now, Jesse had once smoked a marijuana cigarette, but he was not a regular drug user and he had no idea where to find what Dan wanted. Nevertheless, he was so desperate to keep his friend that he made a special effort. He took the $20 Dan offered him, located and bought a small package of marijuana, and handed it over. He was then arrested and charged with two felony counts of selling drugs. It turns out "Dan" was actually an undercover police officer, conducting a sting operation.[5] "Dan" insisted that Jesse was a dealer, when he was not even a real drug user. This police officer took advantage of an autistic teen's loneliness and naivety to improve his own arrest record.

Judges in some states have the right to use their own personal assumptions about autistic people's intelligence to cut them off from participation in our democracy. With the best of intentions, a mother petitioned a judge to make her the legal conservator of her 18-year-old autistic son, Gregory. Since Gregory struggled to communicate, despite his innate intelligence, his mother thought a conservatorship might help her manage his finances and health care. The judge, however, decided that her petition actually meant that Gregory was "mentally incapacitated," and on that basis took away his right to vote. Gregory is not and never has been mentally incapacitated." He is quite capable of making informed choices between candidates for office. But now he can't act on those choices.[6] Thousands of autistic (and other) adults have been disenfranchised in this way.

Lorena had successfully raised one child to adulthood. But then she fell on hard times, and she and her two younger daughters became homeless. When she applied to Social Services for help, they convinced her to place the children in foster care temporarily until she got on her feet again. But the two children were separated in foster care. One child, autistic like Lorena herself, was placed in a special needs foster care setting, where her physical and emotional condition deteriorated rapidly. Lorena wanted to get her kids back, but Social Services insisted that she submit to two psychological examinations before they would allow this. Lorena failed the exams, and when she brought a case against So-cial Services, her attorney was unable or unwilling to provide her with an adequate defense. She lost her case, and with it her parental rights, including the right to visit her own kids.[7] Like other disabled adults, autistics have a hard time building and keeping a family. They struggle to obtain fertility services and to be approved for adoption. They are much more likely than other people to lose custody of their children to non-disabled partners in divorce proceedings, to have children taken from them temporarily by social service agencies, even to have paren-tal rights completely terminated.

Historically the U.S. has played an important role in establishing the concept of human rights. After all, our Declaration of Independence proudly declared: "We hold these truths to be self-evident, that all men are created equal, that they are endowed by their Creator with certain inalienable rights . . ." Ideas drawn from the Declaration, from the Bill of Rights, and from other American documents, as well as from else-where in the world, helped shape the Universal Declaration of Human Rights, adopted by the General Assembly of the United Nations in 1948.[8] An aspirational document, the Universal Declaration spelled out principles, but provided no enforcement mechanism. After 1948, though, the United Nations gradually developed a series of inter-national "covenants," or treaties on human liberties. Countries that signed on to these treaties agreed to abide by their provisions.

The United States is a signatory to the Universal Declaration of Human Rights. But our country has not been eager to join/abide by international human rights covenants, or to enforce human rights at home. In 1966, for example, the General Assembly of the United Nations unanimously adopted the International Covenant on Civil and Political Rights, protecting such familiar liberties as freedom of conscience and religion, freedom of association, and the rights to life, liberty and security of person. The Covenant required signatory governments to outlaw practices such as torture, slavery, and cruel, inhuman or degrading punishment within their borders.

Only twenty-six years later, in 1992, did the United States Senate finally ratify the International Covenant on Civil and Political Rights. But in doing so, it made an unprecedented number of changes, which left the document essentially "powerless under domestic law."[9] In 1994, the Senate ratified the Convention on the Elimination of All Forms of Racial Discrimination, but again with so many "reservations, declarations, and understandings" that it had little effect. Even today, racial discrimination is widespread and largely unpunished in our society.[10] Also in 1994, the Senate ratified the International Convention Against Torture, and Other Cruel, Inhuman or Degrading Treatment or Punishment. But after 9/11, the Senate, the House, and many ordinary Americans supported the government's use of torture against prisoners at various "black sites" and at Guantanamo Bay.[11] Nor has the U.S. Senate ever ratified international conventions on economic, social, and cultural rights, on the elimination of discrimination against women, on the rights of persons with disabilities, or the rights of children.[12]

Such organizations as the American Civil Liberties Union, Human Rights Watch and Amnesty International have catalogued an alarming number of human rights abuses in the United States in recent years. According to the ACLU, "in many areas — including national security, criminal justice, social and economic rights, and immigration policy — the U.S. has an abysmal record compared to other liberal democracies."[13] Having once proclaimed that "all men are created equal," the United States still fails to treat all men (let alone women and children) equitably. Groups at particularly high risk of illegal and abusive treatment include women, racial and ethnic minorities, the poor, LGBTQ+ people, immigrants, the young, and people with disabilities. Americans living at the intersections of such groups (for example, women of color, poor disabled people, child immigrants) remain especially vulnerable.

Most Americans know nothing about the abuses people with autism suffer. Others excuse mistreatment on the grounds that people with autism are somehow less than human— "deficient," "backward," "aggressive." Similar claims were made in the past about other stigmatized populations—for example, Native and African Americans. They, too, "had to be controlled" for the good of society and "protected" from the consequences of their own "defects" by their white superiors. While members of these groups still struggle for their rights, only the lunatic fringe questions their essential humanity today. This book is an attempt to move the status of people with autism in the same direction—to assert their humanity, dispel some of the myths about them, and create an empathetic awareness and acceptance of autistic people and their struggles. To this end, I feature autistic people themselves describing their experiences and asserting their rights. I also incorporate the findings of researchers (some autistic themselves) on neurodiversity and its implications for our understanding of human nature.

Part One is devoted to the core issue: autistic people's humanity. Chapter One examines some widely disseminated but inaccurate beliefs about autism—myths typically used to justify the bad practices described above and in later chapters. And this first chapter also looks at the manifold ways in which autistics are just like all the rest of us. Chapter Two focuses on the characteristics that distinguish autistics from other Americans—very human differences that leave them no less deserving of human rights.

Part Two focuses on autistic children. Chapter Three demonstrates how officially recommended interventions often result in the abuse of young autistic children, frequently leading to lasting psychological damage. Chapters Four and Five explore the traumatic experiences of older autistic children in the American educational system. Our schools offer them an inadequate education, based on low expectations and excessive use of discipline, which often prepares them poorly for adult life.

Part Three looks at adult autistics and how they manage to support themselves. Chapter Six focuses on the discrimination and abuse adults with autism face in the workplace. Chapter Seven looks at how they survive (or sometimes fail to survive) when they cannot find employment.

Part Four examines the deeply troubling relations between autistic people and our health care system. Problems with access to physical health care, poor quality care, and denial of care—all of which resonate with the experiences of other "medically underserved" groups— are the subject of Chapter Eight. Chapter Nine looks at the many ways autistic people are ill-served by America's mental health system.

Part Five might disturb readers the most. It reveals realities well known within the autistic community, but unrecognized by the general public. Chapter Ten is devoted to the torture and killing of autistic people by police officers. Chapter Eleven looks at the hideous "treatments" practiced in one infamous institution still operating today. Chapter Twelve examines the murder of autistic children and adults by their own family members. While the incidents described in these three chapters are horrific, they have provoked a powerful and growing reaction from the autistic community. As the Conclusion shows, autistic people are fighting back. They are organizing, forming alliances, advocating, protesting, and voting to attain and protect their rights our society owes them—just because they are human. There is hope for tomorrow.

I wrote this book because I am the mother of an autistic adult of remarkable intelligence, talent, and compassion. I have never been labelled autistic myself (despite the fact that I share my daughter's dislike of bright lights, loud noises and crowds). And precisely because I am "neurotypical," I have made a concerted effort to foreground autistic voices and autistic viewpoints in these pages. For as Eric Garcia has said, it is "essential for autistic people to be included in all parts of the conversation" about them.[14] So I want to emphasize here that the pioneering work on all the subjects discussed below has been accomplished largely by autistic people. Gifted writers like Donna Williams, Temple Grandin, Dawn Prince-Hughes and John Elder Robison produced the autobiographical works that first made autism visible to Americans. As scientists, Michelle Dawson, James Cusack, and others helped design the experiments that made autistic neurology and behavior more accessible to their fellow scientists and to the general public. Therapists and educators like Liane Holliday Willey and Judy Endow empowered autistic (and other) students to flourish in school and in life generally.

Most importantly for the purposes of this book, autistic activists have shaped the agendas of government panels, organized protests against human rights abuses, developed projects to educate the general public about neurodiversity, and helped young autistic people accept and celebrate their identities. These activists include the many members of the Autism National Committee, the Autism Network International, the Autism Acceptance Project, the Autistic Women and Non-Binary Network, and the Autistic Self-Advocacy Network. Many other organizations and a huge number of individual bloggers, Facebookers, Redditors, Tweeters, podcasters, and authors continue to fight the good fight. Their views on many of the subjects discussed below differ as much as their neurologies do. (As Dr. Stephen Shore famously said: "If you have met one person with autism, you have met one person with autism."[15]) Nevertheless, all passionately assert their human dignity.

PART I

On Autistic Humanity

YES, AUTISTICS ARE HUMAN BEINGS. Even when we do things differently based on our different neurology WE ARE FULL-FLEDGED HUMAN BEINGS. We do NOT need to first be made to act neurotypical before you grant us the status of HUMAN BEING because WE ALREADY ARE HUMAN BEINGS.[1]

CHAPTER ONE

We Already Are Human Beings

A utism is not a single thing. It is a blanket term we use, as a convenience, to describe a huge "spectrum" of conditions. It involves a variety of neurological characteristics, most related to communication, social interaction, and responses to physical sensations. Autistic characteristics are caused by "irregularities" in at least one hundred genes and many other parts of the human genome, interacting with one another as well as with a myriad of environmental factors.[2] This is one reason why efforts to "cure" autism are so fruitless—there is, quite simply, no single autism to "cure." (Whether a cure is even desirable is another question. Many autistic people would say it is not.)

"Autistic" characteristics also extend well into what we call the "normal"—what autistic people may call the "neurotypical"—population.[3] Almost everyone who is considered neurologically normal also has some qualities which, in their more severe form, define autism. By this I do not mean what people often mean when they say, "Everyone is just a little bit autistic."[4] My intention is not to downplay the difficulties that autism causes or, for that matter, the advantages it confers. I simply want to show that autistic Americans are not as distinct from the rest of the population as is often assumed. We all struggle with communication ("I just didn't know what to say. . . ") under certain circumstances. Many people lack social skills, although to very different degrees (think of your crude uncle, your shy cousin, your embarrassing, "motormouth" friend). Repetitive, self-soothing behaviors (finger-tapping, fingernail biting, twirling hair around a finger, etc.) are very widespread. Although many people can tolerate loud noises and bright lights—unless they're hungover—most of us still have some sensory sensitivities. My completely neurotypical husband, for example, cannot stand the itchiness of a wool sweater. In this sense, autism is a matter of degree.

Conversely, every individual our society labels "autistic"—even the most severely affected—is also, to a very large extent, perfectly normal neurologically. The differences that define autistics are far less significant than their similarities to the rest of us. Non-speaking and "low-functioning" (an unscientific and misleading term) autistics still think, dream, imagine, plan. Indeed, autistics have the same range of intelligence as the rest of the U.S. population. They feel the whole gamut of human emotions, including (despite the stale stereotype) empathy for others. Unless they have additional problems unrelated to autism, they can see, hear, smell, touch, and taste the world around them. Most are eager to communicate, though their efforts may not always be successful. And many (perhaps most) long desperately for friends and lovers. In such important ways, they are just like everybody else.

The dividing line between what is neurotypical and what is autistic is inherently nebulous. In fact, individuals may move back and forth between "normality" and "disability" throughout their lifetimes. Many Americans are rated "normal" for decades before finally being diagnosed as autistic. In addition, those professionals charged by our society with diagnosis (psychologists, psychiatrists, other physicians, social workers) sometimes disagree with one another about who is and who is not autistic. This is precisely because "autistic" characteristics can be found, in milder form, among so many members of the general population.[5] Moreover, these characteristics may manifest themselves more or less powerfully at different times, even in the same person.

This chapter is necessary because far too many Americans (including some who really should know better) continue to imagine that "normal" and "autistic" are completely distinct categories. Far too many associate being human with being "normal," denying that autistic people are as human as the rest of us, or even human at all. Believing that autism somehow makes you weird, robotic, aggressive, animalistic, potentially dangerous, Americans far too often accept discrimination, isolation, and the infliction of pain on autistic people as justifiable and necessary for the good of society—even "beneficial" to the people targeted. Some even condone the murder of autistics, out of sympathy for their "suffering" families.

Deficit and Difference

In America, autism is usually defined as a disorder characterized by abnormalities and deficiencies. (It is worth noting that in some other countries autism is increasingly referred to not as a "disorder," but as a "condition"—a far less stigmatizing term.) In the United States, psychologists, psychiatrists, and physicians use the American Psychiatric Association's *Diagnostic and Statistical Manual of Mental Disorders*, 5th edition (*DSM-5* for short) to diagnose autism.[6] Its diagnostic criteria consist almost entirely of deficits: "deficits in social-emotional reciprocity," "deficits in nonverbal communicative behavior," "deficits in developing, maintaining, and understanding relationships."[7] In other words, a diagnosis is reached by making assumptions about what humans "should" have, then scanning for what an autistic person supposedly lacks. The major scientific journals that inform the work of physicians, scientists, educators, and public policy makers use similar language. The deficits studied are many and varied: "Facial Emotion

Recognition Deficits," "Postural Control Deficits," "Motor Memory Deficits," "Joint Attention Deficits," "Executive Function Deficits," etc., etc., *ad nauseam*. A relentless focus on what is lacking in people with autism already makes them seem less human.

Deficit language has also been used by researchers to explicitly deny autistics their humanity. A case in point is "mind blindness." Since the 1990s, researchers have frequently asserted that autistic people are mind blind—that is, they lack "theory of mind," the ability to discern mental states (emotions, beliefs, knowledge, desires, intentions, etc.) in others, and even in themselves. Well-known Cambridge University researcher Simon Baron-Cohen famously argued that mind blindness is a core feature of autism.[8] He also asserted that theory of mind played a key role in human evolution, making possible the development of human societies. "A theory of mind," he claimed, "remains one of the quintessential abilities that makes us human."[9] Logically, then, people without it must not be really human.[10]

Was he right? Not really. Recent research indicates that autistic children do actually develop theory of mind, although at a slower pace than their "typically developing" peers. It turns out the structure, not the content, of a mind blindness test can determine how successfully an autistic person will complete it.[11] What's more, recent studies have revealed that some neurotypical people also lack theory of mind.[12] To be fair, Baron-Cohen himself modified his views in later work; he has even begun including autistic researchers as colleagues in his studies. But his early theories, published in the late 1990s and early 2000s, effectively dehumanized autistic people, by denying them one of the "quintessential abilities that make us human." And these theories haven't gone away, despite Baron-Cohen's change of heart. They remain hugely influential even today within the American scientific community.

Shortly after the publication of Baron-Cohen's book on mind blindness, Harvard psychologist Steven Pinker compared people with autism to robots and chimpanzees, creatures who remind us "that cultural learning is possible only because neurologically normal people have innate equipment to accomplish it."[13] In Pinker's view, too, autistics were sub-human. Other scientists concurred. Bryna Siegel, director of the Autism Clinic at the University of California, San Francisco, wrote, "It's as if [autistic people] do not understand or are missing a core aspect of what it is to be human; to be and do like others and absorb their values."[14] Such "expert opinions" have long set the tone for public discussions of autism in the United States.[15]

Professor Morton Ann Gernsbacher of the University of Wisconsin, a past president of the Association for Psychological Science, was among the first to counter the prevailing narrative. In a 2007 column entitled "On Not Being Human" in the Association's newsletter, Gernsbacher described past attempts to de-humanize stigmatized groups, linking these to contemporary research that de-humanizes autistic people. She attributed the distorted findings of this current research to researchers' "inability to accept human diversity."[16] Like a slowly growing number of scientists in the years after 2000, Gernsbacher had begun to view autism not as a collection of deficits, but as a form of human diversity, like sexual orientation.[17]

This understanding may have been new for scientists, but it was not new for everyone. Autism activists had already begun to conceptualize autism as a natural and positive variation in human neurology in the 1990s.[18] The term "neurodiversity" was coined by Judy Singer, an Australian social scientist, herself autistic.[19] It first appeared outside the context of academic work in a 1998 article in *The Atlantic* by Singer's (also autistic) friend, Harvey Blume. Focusing on the advantages of an autistic brain in the high-tech world of the late 20th century, Blume wrote: "Neurodiversity may be every bit as crucial for the human race as biodiversity is for life in general."[20]

Neurodiversity advocates celebrate the advantages of autistic ways of thinking—deep focus, attention to detail, the ability to discern patterns that are invisible to "normal" people, and intense creativity.[21] They criticize the social structures that turn these qualities into deficits, and autistics into marginalized victims. Proponents of neurodiversity generally view the existence of different neurological types as an evolutionary advantage for humans, rather than as a set of historical dead ends. And they call for accommodations to allow autistics to function not only successfully, but comfortably. Since the 1990s, the neurodiversity movement has grown dramatically among autistics and people with other neurological differences, like cerebral palsy and ADHD. It has generated international organizations, publications, and political action campaigns. It has also influenced, albeit slowly, the scientific community and the general population.

Inevitably, it faced a backlash. What have been called the "Autism Wars" pitted neurodiversity advocates against certain researchers, some parents and even a few autistic people, who criticized neurodiversity theory for whitewashing the harsh realities of life with autism. These critics were absolutely right to argue that autism can lead to serious problems, from physical pain, to anxiety and depression, to deep loneliness. (Of course, they might have been more convincing if their research and writings had focused more on the sufferings of autistic people themselves, and less on the sufferings of their caretakers.) Critics complained that only "high-functioning" autistics believe in neurodiversity, and that they don't speak for, and indeed misrepresent the situation of "lower-functioning" people. This argument loudly ignores the many supposedly "low-functioning" individuals with limited communication skills and high support needs who proudly identify themselves with the neurodiversity movement. Opponents of neurodiversity say what is really needed is a "cure" that will make what they consider a painful, disabling condition just go away.

The problem is that such a cure is literally impossible, even if it were desirable. We apply the term "autism" to multiple variations in neurological systems, the "hardwiring" of the brain. There is, then, no single "autism" to cure. It is, moreover, hard to see how one could "cure" someone's neurological system. But much more importantly, autistic proponents of neurodiversity say they don't want to be cured.

> Autism is part of my identity. It is not a disease, it is not an afflic-
> tion, it is part of who I am. A cure mindset exists as the violent
> opposite to this reality. It is based on the belief that I am not enti-
> tled to my own body, a neurotypical is. It is based on the belief
> that my mind is not legitimate, but a neurotypical's would be. It is
> based on the belief that my DNA is a bastard in my own body, a
> squatter to be kicked out so the proper tenant can take his place.
> And you know what? I like who I am.[22]

Perhaps it is obvious by now that I myself belong to the neurodiversity camp. To me, being autistic is a valuable way of being human. Our society could only improve if we found more and better ways to tap the potential of autistic minds and incorporate autistic citizens fully into our civic life. In the following pages I will do my best never to downplay the many physical, emotional, and intellectual struggles facing people with autism. At the same time, I will concentrate on how our society can help autistic people enjoy the same basic human rights as other citizens. First, however, we should review the many ways in which they are just like those citizens.

Intelligence

Less than a week into the 2015 school year, six-year-old Xavier Gresham faced suspension from his elementary school in rural Louisiana for "disrupting class" by "speaking out of turn." His doctor had diagnosed him with autism, Xavier's mother argued. Consequently, he needed a behavioral intervention plan from the school district to get his behavior under control. But this help could not be provided unless the district itself evaluated him. Xavier's mom claims that her request for a district evaluation was refused on the grounds that her son was "too smart" to be autistic.[23] Apparently, the school administration, and perhaps even the district's special education staff, associated autism with intellectual disability; they couldn't accept the possibility that someone like young Xavier—at the top of his class academically—might be autistic.

One of the greatest "deficits" traditionally attributed to autistic people is a lack of intelligence. Popular culture demonstrates this: even today "autistic" is still frequently used as an insult, indicating stupidity.[24] But the belief has long been popular within the scientific community, too. In 1996, a group of notable American scientists asserted that "most, if not all" people with autism suffered from some degree of (what they were then calling) "mental retardation."[25] Nine years later, in 2005, a Canadian researcher reviewed the existing literature on autism and intelligence and concluded that 55-70% of those with autism had an intellectual disability.[26] Another nine years later, in 2014, the U.S. Centers for Disease Control found that 31% of the autistic children studied in their most recent survey had an intellectual disability.[27]

How to explain these rapidly changing numbers? Why, over the course of twenty years, did the proportion of autistic people considered intellectually disabled drop from "most, if not all" to less than one-third? And why have scientists since 2014 continued to find more evidence that autistic people are intelligent? One significant factor is that the population being studied has changed. Recent research includes people who have what used to be called "Asperger's Syndrome." Earlier editions of the *Diagnostic and Statistical Manual* characterized people with Asperger's as having some of the "deficits" associated with autism, but also average or above-average intelligence, as measured by standard intelligence tests. The latest edition of the *DSM*, however, drops "Asperger's Syndrome" as a category, incorporating those formerly diagnosed with it into the general autism spectrum. Simply including these individuals in research populations automatically raised the average IQ found.

But an equally important part of the explanation has to do with the methods by which autistic intelligence is studied. From the 1960s to the 1990s, scientists regularly used intelligence tests designed for neurotypicals (Stanford-Binet, Wechsler, etc.) in their research, seldom questioning whether those tests were really appropriate for autistic subjects. Around the turn of the millenium, however, some researchers began to raise serious questions about these tests and their results.

One very basic issue is the use of language-based tests in studying a population that is defined by "communication deficits." A 2007 study conducted by a team of scientists based in Montreal—a team that included an autistic researcher, Michelle Dawson—elegantly demonstrated the unreliability of conventional tests in assessing the intelligence of those who think in non-conventional ways. The Montreal researchers looked at what happened when autistic children and adults, along with a group of neurotypical controls, took two different intelligence tests. The first was the widely used Wechsler test, which includes both verbal and non-verbal sections. The second test was Raven's Progressive Matrices (RPM), which assesses high-level analytical skills but is entirely non-verbal, requiring the completion of visual patterns. What they found was striking. As expected, the autistics did worse than the neurotypical controls on the Wechsler test—especially on the verbal sections. However, on the RPM test, autistic scores rose dramatically (in some cases by as much as 70 percentile points) into what would be considered the "normal" range for a neurotypical population, while the neurotypical scores remained basically unchanged. [28] The Montreal team concluded that supposedly low autistic intelligence was the product of inappropriate testing. This point is confirmed by the personal experiences of many autistics. A contributor to the *Wrong Planet* website writes: "When I was 8 years old, my standard IQ scored in the moderately mental retardation range, but I scored 135 on a nonverbal IQ test at that same time."[29]

Equally critical is the drastically varying ability of most autistic people to concentrate and communicate from day to day. This results from a wide variety of factors, including how much sleep they've had, the degree of powerful emotion they are processing, how tiring they find the test itself, and whether they are facing sensory overload. Neurotypical people also have changes in ability, but autistic people experience more extreme swings. A single intelligence test is always a snapshot of intellectual functioning at that particular time, rather than a reliable indicator of overall intelligence. A middle-aged autistic man who uses the moniker "Horus" online notes that

My own IQ scores have changed dramatically and I've taken seven professionally administered tests in my life. I scored 120 on the first one I took in 9th grade. I only scored 94 on the next one I took at 23. On the five tests I've taken since....I've scored as high as 143 and as low as 104.[30]

Consequently, autistic intelligence can only be accurately evaluated through a series of tests, given over the course of different days.

A further fundamental problem has to do with the "global" scores derived from intelligence tests—the single number that most of us think of as someone's "IQ." In our society, an IQ of 100 is typically defined as "average," one below 70 indicates intellectual disability, and one above 160 signifies "genius." But where do these global scores come from? They are calculated, using a variety of formulas (depending on the test being used) from the sub-scores on the different parts of the test, making the global score something like an "average" of all the sub-scores. Global scores are widely used in research, to make claims about the intelligence of different groups in society (including racial and ethnic minorities, as well as autistics), and in everyday practice, to make decisions about what classes to place children in, or what special services to offer them.

Calculation of a global IQ score is, however, based on the assumption that an "average" actually has some meaning—that the sub-scores on the different parts of the intelligence test will be at least roughly comparable with one another. And indeed, for most neurotypicals, sub-scores tend to be consistent overall. Some will be a bit higher, some a bit lower, but usually all fall within the same general range. Thus, the global score can give us some indication of how smart the individual actually is. It has been repeatedly shown, however, that autistics perform much better on the non-verbal than on the verbal sections of intelligence tests. It is also the case that they score much better on some of the subtests within these two large categories than on others, thus ending up with wildly different sub-scores. Looking at an autistic person's sub-scores across all the different sections of an intelligence test often reveals a wildly spikey pattern of highs and lows, with the highest highs being very much higher than the lowest lows. (It is not unusual for someone with autism to achieve a "genius" level score on one part of a test, and a "sub-normal" score on another.) How to factor such varied results into a global IQ score? How useful is an average, when the numbers being averaged are so dissimilar? Based on these discrepancies, a 2015 article in the *Journal of Autism and Developmental Disorders* declared global IQ scores for autistics essentially meaningless.[31]

The last decade has revealed that people with autism are much more intelligent than used to be thought. In fact, some scientists have concluded that there is no difference in intelligence at all between neurotypicals and autistics.[32] Like other people, some individuals with autism have limited intelligence; others are incredibly smart. What's more, we still don't know how to measure autistic intelligence accurately. How logical and just is it, then, to deny autistic people a proper education, jobs, or the opportunity to live independently, on the mistaken assumption that someone who is autistic cannot also be smart? Giving them the benefit of the doubt and assuming normal intelligence is surely more responsible.

Feelings

We feel joy—sometimes a joy so intense and
private and all-encompassing that it eclipses
anything the world might feel.[33]

The stereotype of the emotionless autistic is widespread in American society. In 2021, physician Melissa Stoppler wrote on a popular medical website: "... lack of emotion can be seen with different conditions including autism."[34] Similar claims appear in popular culture. "Someone with Asperger's feels no emotion and does not really care about a lot of anything," write two neurotypical students in a class presentation on Aspergers Syndrome.[35] An autistic person asks plaintively on the *Quora* website, "How should I deal with being called an emotionless robot?"[36] The "emotionless robot" stereotype is based largely on neurotypical misreadings of autistic facial expressions. And it is simply incorrect. Not only do autistics feel the same emotions as other people, but some evidence even suggests that they feel them more intensely than other people. Let's look at a few of the emotions autistics are often said not to have.

Love and Loneliness

The terms "autism" and "autistic" derive from the Greek word, *autos*, meaning "self." The scientists who first described people with these terms assumed that they were almost entirely self-centered: uninterested in engaging with others, unwilling to socialize, uncommunicative. These presumptions have had a long after-life, enduring in scientific literature until recently, and still alive in popular discourse.[37]

True, some people on the autism spectrum have little to no interest in other people (although they may have an intense interest in animals, astronomy, stones, traffic lights, etc.—which belies the claim that they are <u>self</u>-centered). Some may long to be hermits, free of complex and confusing social interactions.[38] And still others simply find other people too exhausting to be around for long (more on this below). But the opposite is also very true. Many, perhaps most, autistic people crave and actively seek out friendships and romantic relationships.[39]

> . . . (T)here are autistic people who desperately wish to fit in, but don't know how. No matter how carefully they study other people and try to imitate them, they stand out and are recognized as being odd and out of step. Also, this kind of constant desperate effort to fit in, and repeated failures to do so, lead to a lot of anxiety, emotional exhaustion, depression, and low self-esteem.[40]

Convincing evidence exists that the majority of autistic individuals seek out romantic relationships and are unhappy when those relationships fail. In a study conducted in Germany, for example, 44% of the autistics studied were involved in romantic relationships, while 72% of those not in a relationship were distressed by the fact.[41] Sites like *Wrong Planet* and *Autism Forums* buzz with questions about how to make friends and find romantic partners, and laments when these endeavors fail.

It is sometimes said that autistics only want people around who can help them, and that their interest in others is entirely self-centered. This is patently untrue. Those lucky enough to have special people in their lives often express warm feelings towards them:

> I adore my mum. I love her to the moon and back.[42]

> I love my wife more than my own life, but expressing that is

almost impossible for me.[43]

... the love I have for [my children] is the biggest, scariest, most beautiful feeling I've ever had.[44]

And it's not just talk. Autistic people will go far outside their comfort zone to help the people they love, if they know what is needed. Even though caregiving is difficult for them, they play the role of caregivers surprisingly often. Autistic parents, for example, pay tender attention to their kids, changing babies, feeding toddlers, arranging outings, dealing with schools or developing homeschool programs, etc., just like neurotypicals. Autistic people also serve as caretakers for older parents:

I am payed by the state of Texas to be [my father's] caregiver. its not a lot but it does help with the bills, plus its my old man and I love him, I love to stay home and take care of him.[45]

I am currently the primary caregiver for my 92-year-old mother ....At the moment, I'm having a particularly difficult time dealing with the stress and confinement of this job.[46]

And they care for their partners:

I'm ... caregiver ... for my disabled wife (cerebral palsy & bipolar disorder). While it certainly isn't easy by any means, it gives me a sense of purpose ...[47]

My fiance has been post-op from surgery 2 weeks out. It is getting easier and she is more independent but holy shit, this is stressful. I have to be able to do everything for me to stay sane, for her, for us and for our cats. I almost feel like I cannot handle it but I will continue, for her, for us.[48]

Though people with autism actively and consistently nurture social relationships, they often find them tremendously stressful. Maintaining conversations when words don't come easily, giving up comforting personal routines in the face of mounting anxiety, ignoring sensory issues so as to take care of someone else's needs or be a "good sport"—all these drain energy.

> As I've said before, it's not that I can't socialise – if I have my own agency in the situation, like having chosen who I'm socialising with or being free to leave when I hit my spoon barrier[49] – but that forced socialisation is something that just sends me spinning. It would happen as a kid at family or friend gatherings, surrounded by people I may not have chosen to hang out with myself and unable to leave without my parents. This would normally result in me getting into an argument, breaking down, or suddenly feeling sick and needing to be taken home.[50]

The main reason people let go of romantic relationships in the German study mentioned above was that they were simply too exhausting.[51] Or, as one American put it: "I have had relationships, but it always ends up with the same outcome. I always end up getting too drained by having another constantly near me."[52]

Autistics in relationships want to spend time with their family members, friends, or lovers. Most also need time alone to recover from those interactions.[53] It's a struggle to find a balance between time together and time alone. Sometimes finding the energy to maintain relationships they would otherwise like to keep is just too overwhelming.

Nevertheless, loneliness remains a common complaint. Even when they actively seek out friendships and romance, autistic people often experience rejection. The feeling of being alone and unwanted begins early in life. An autistic five-year-old told her mother, "school is the loneliest place on earth."[54] But this problem does not end with childhood:

Loneliness has been a constant companion in my life. I laugh when I read the news articles which try to say that people with Asperger's "have no desire for human companionship." I can't speak for all - it may be true of some, but it has certainly not been true for me. It can feel like a curse - having the acute desire for human interaction, togetherness, but constantly struggling to make it happen.[55]

The most widely disseminated public narratives about autism sensationalize the "tragedy" of the condition—the despair and misery it supposedly creates, especially for the parents of children with autism. These narratives were brought to special prominence in Autism Speaks' notorious 2009 ad campaign "I Am Autism," which featured overwhelmed parents, attendant divorces, financial stress, etc. Ironically, though, the real tragedy of autism is not any of these things. It is to be found, rather, in autistic people's desperate longing for human connection, which is either denied to them entirely, or which they discover they cannot tolerate.[56]

Fear

"The principal emotion experienced
by autistic people is fear."[57]

Most of us can't imagine how full of fear autistics' lives are. In up to 84% of all autistic individuals, anxiety impairs quality of life. Some 40% suffer from a clinically significant anxiety disorder—as compared to 18% of the American population overall.[58] As Max Sparrow puts it:

I have anxiety so bad and have had it for so long that I didn't even realize how anxious my baseline state is until the first time I smoked marijuana and experienced what it's like to feel peaceful. My anxiety makes every day a struggle. Even my good days are riddled with anxiety.[59]

Several research studies associate "greater severity of ASD symptoms" with higher levels of anxiety.[60] It remains unclear, however, whether anxiety is simply built into autistic neurology—in particular, into the unusual way the amygdala (the part of the brain that detects threats in the environment) can develop—or whether it arises from the unceasing stresses of the autistic life.[61] Regardless, many of the autistic behaviors that perplex neurotypicals arise out of fear. Deep anxiety often drives meltdowns (see below), self-harm, obsessive self-stimulatory behaviors, and even aggression against others. Even more unbearable—and even more baffling to neurotypical observers—is the sensation of dissolving into an abyss of chaos and unpredictability. As a child, Tito Mukhopadhyay became entranced by his own shadow, which he understood as part of himself. But at night, when his shadow disappeared, he panicked:

I remember my voice screaming when I could not see my shadow anywhere around me. I wondered whether it had left me here all alone. I was afraid that I would lose my existence because my shadow had left.[62]

The world is a wildly unpredictable, and therefore deeply threatening place to many autistics. Indeed, some scientists conceptualize autism as essentially a "disorder of prediction.[63] Difficulties in reading and responding appropriately to cues from other people make social situations next to impossible to predict, producing intense social anxiety.[64] Imagine how scary it would be if everyone you met wore a face mask and used a voice filter that deadened variations in tone. All the familiar clues that tell you whether the person you are dealing with is friendly or hostile, all the clues that indicate whether the words spoken to you are meant literally, ironically, or sarcastically would evaporate. Could you ever know whether you were being accepted or rejected, praised or ridiculed, told the truth or being lied to? This is the condition in which autistics must live every day.

But social anxiety represents only the tip of the iceberg. Even the experience of the physical world and one's own body are permeated by unpredictability. Sensory issues (on which more below) can be as terrifying as social interactions.[65] Someone with acute tactile sensitivities must constantly worry about unexpectedly touching something painful; another with sensitivity to sound may be so terrified by a sudden loud noise that she screams out loud. A thirsty child may find himself suddenly unable to drink a favorite soda, not expecting the soda to be so cold this time. A violent meltdown follows. Not just because the child remains thirsty. More importantly, what had been a predictable source of comfort has now inexplicably turned into something unexpected. Uncertainty about the future fills autistic people's lives with dread.

Psychologists do not always grasp the causes of high anxiety in autistics or see the link between their anxiety and particular behaviors. Ordinary citizens, including police officers and judges, are even less aware, sometimes reacting to "odd" behavior with violence. In 2012, for example, the city of Chicago paid half a million dollars in damages to the family of a young autistic man, Oscar Guzman. Back in 2009, Oscar was standing outside his family's restaurant, quietly watching pigeons, when a police car pulled over. The officers began questioning him. Oscar became upset and fearful when he couldn't answer their questions and ran back inside. The police followed and— despite family members shouting at them that Oscar was autistic— beat him on the head with a metal baton, injuring him so severely that his wound had to be closed with staples.[66] Oscar's case is by no means unique. Not trained to deal gently with people behaving in unusual ways, police are inclined to force compliance. But someone motivated by terror cannot comply. Serious injury, even death, can be the result.[67]

Empathy

I had a surprising moment interacting with a young man with autism who works at the Duke Center for Autism and Brain Development. I was feeling especially hurried and stressed that day, but none of my colleagues seemed to notice. The young man approached me to ask how my day was going. I described my back-to-back appointments to him. He looked at me with concern and said, "Dr. Dawson, I think you need a break." He was right, of course. Many people are unaware that people with autism are often very sensitive to others' emotions.[68]

Social media accounts often describe autistic children who don't respond to parents' smiles, teens who show no concern if other people get hurt, adults who seem indifferent to their peers' enthusiasms. A common assumption is that autistic people lack empathy, the ability to share and respond to other people's feelings.[69] Hence the stereotype of the cold, emotionless autistic. And indeed, for a long time this was the scientific consensus. In 1996, for example, Professor Geraldine Dawson (who speaks in the above quotation) wrote that peculiarities of the amygdala in autistic people might be linked to difficulties with empathy.[70] In 2004, Simon Baron-Cohen and Sally Wheelwright found that "adults with AS [Aspergers Syndrome]/HFA [High-Functioning Autism] scored significantly lower" on their Empathy Quotient questionnaire "than matched [neurotypical] controls."[71]

But people with autism don't agree. In their own writings, they lay full claim to empathy:

. . . the whole "autistic people lack empathy" designation does not apply to us all. Often I have to turn off the emotions I feel when I read the news, otherwise I feel terrible all day.[72]

There is no question that I feel empathy, but I cannot exhibit it intuitively like my partner can. . . . I can come across as cold, indifferent, robotic even, and yet I don't ever mean to nor desire to.[73]

In fact, excessive empathy may lead some autistics to avoid people or even change careers, to minimize emotional pain.[74]

I . . . was/am exceedingly emotionally empathetic, to the point of it being part of the reason I avoided people. I was told by professors that I'd make a fine therapist but my first few practicum were too much for me to bear & I had no way to manage or block it. So I ended up going into IT instead, because computers are emotionally blank & don't affect me that way (although I do project feelings onto them).[75]

Those who feel deeply for others may still struggle to find ways to help:

. . . I don't always know how to interact with a person emotionally. If I'm with someone, and they start crying, I'll be unsure what to do/say, debating actions in my head. "Do I put my hand on their back? Do I hug them? I want them to feel better, but I don't know what to say!!"[76]

By the early 2000s, autism researchers were beginning to draw a distinction (already developed by psychologists) between two kinds of empathy—cognitive empathy, in which someone can intellectually understand how another person feels, and affective empathy, in which someone really "feels your pain."[77] Most autistic people, it was recognized, had impaired cognitive empathy. It was hard for them to recognize or understand the reasons for other people's emotions. Yet for most autistics, affective empathy was largely intact.[78] This distinction made sense to many autistic folk:

> Cognitive Empathy is what I have difficulty with. I don't just "see" what someone is thinking (and I think it's creepy that other people do), I expect them to tell me. I would think that's what talking/speaking is for. If you have something to communicate, please just tell me, don't hint at me. . . . Affective Empathy, I have tons of, to the point of getting in the way lots of times. I pick up on a vibe in the room so to speak, and it can bring me up or down depending on what's going on. I have to make a concerted effort to NOT be affected by the people around me.[79]

Gradually researchers began to recognize what autistics had long asserted. When they saw someone was in distress, they would respond emotionally and try to help (even though their method might not necessarily feel helpful to the other person).[80] Within the last decade, scientists have begun to focus more closely on the specifics of empathy in autism.[81] A few have even begun to acknowledge the damage done to the autistic community by earlier claims about lack of empathy.[82]

Why is it so important to recognize that people with autism have empathy? Autistics have frequently and incorrectly been compared to psychopaths, deeply troubled people who are incapable of empathizing with others. The 2012 case of Adam Lanza, an autistic man who shot 20 children and 6 adults at Sandy Hook Elementary School in Connecticut, raised a popular outcry against autistics in general. A Facebook group called "Families Against Autistic Shooters" described "the soulless, dead eyes of autistic children," and characterized all autistic people as "cold, calculating killing machines with no regard for human life!"[83]

These misperceptions have real-life effects. An autistic teen with no history of violence was targeted as a potential "shooter" and forced to stay away from school for his own safety.[84] An autistic college student was brought to official attention as a "deranged stalker" because he had discussed a murder with another student who was uncomfortable with him. Again, he had no history of violence, and the college eventually determined that he posed no threat at all.[85] Indeed, no evidence exists that autism by itself increases the likelihood of violent behavior (with the exception of self-injury).[86] On the contrary, autistics are much more likely to be the victims than the perpetrators of violence.[87] When they do attack others, it is not because they are autistic, but because—like other violent offenders—they suffer from delusions brought on by mental illness, have been abused at home, or mercilessly bullied at school.[88]

Joy

The word "joy" is seldom associated with autistic people. So far as I can tell, the emotion itself has never been studied by those who do research on autism. But autistics themselves write frequently about the intense delight and deep pleasure they find in their special interests, in the sensory world around them, and especially in the practice of "stimming" (short for "self-stimulatory behaviors," also known as "repetitive behaviors"—one of the hallmarks of autism, according to the *DSM*-5). Here is Julia Bascom, in a blog post that has circulated widely within the neurodiversity community:

> One of the things about autism is that a lot of things can make you terribly unhappy while barely affecting others. A lot of things are harder.

> But some things? Some things are *so much easier*. Sometimes being autistic means that you get to be *incredibly happy*. And then you get to *flap*. You get to perseverate. You get to have just

about the coolest obsessions. . . . It's that the experience is so *rich*.
It's textured, vibrant, and layered. It exudes joy. . . .Being autistic,
to me, means a lot of different things, but one of the best things
is that I can be *so happy, so enraptured* about things no one else
understands and so wrapped up in my own joy that, not only
does it not matter that no one else shares it, but it can become
contagious.[89]

The very intensity of the autistic experience—the heightened sensory
experience (see Chapter Two below), the deep focus on special interests, the broad awareness of multiple stimuli—can hurt when beyond
the individual's control. Yet if a person can make use of that experience for his own ends, it can also give rise to astonishing experiences
of beauty, delight, sensual pleasure, and sheer joy.

Autistics achieve such moments of delight primarily through
"stimming"—what scientists often describe dismissively as "repetitive" behaviors: hand flapping, rocking, spinning, bouncing, etc. For
decades, therapists tried to eliminate such behaviors in their attempts
to normalize autistic people. The mantra "quiet hands" was regularly
chanted in special education classrooms.[90] More recently, though, scientists and autism professionals are realizing the importance of stimming as a calming response to stressful situations. So therapists have
backed off a bit from trying to eliminate these behaviors completely,
although they still encourage clients to self-soothe in more "socially
acceptable" ways, rather than in ways of their own choosing.[91]

But even today scientists and other "autism professionals" still fail
to recognize the value of self-stimulation as a source of deeply positive emotional experiences. Those who wish to understand autism
would do well to consult autistics themselves on the joys of stimming:

When I flap I get a feeling of overwhelming joy and creative
thoughts and images come from no where. My brain functioning

becomes super fast and I can create perfect images or beautiful sentences in my mind.[92]

In the past year I have rediscovered the joy of stimming. I have unearthed a playfulness within me that I thought was lost.[93]

Stimming is not just a response to distress. Rocking, hand-flapping, and spinning are also, and much more importantly, forms of play. They provide intense satisfaction, mental stimulation, and sensory delight.[94] Joy created by stimming is a wonderfully positive thing. It should be encouraged, not discouraged, in autistic children—and celebrated in autistic adults.[95]

Just Like the Rest of Us

As we have seen, autistics have basically the same range of intelligence and emotion as neurotypicals. They share these essential human characteristics with everyone else in our society. Why, then, the disturbing persistence of dehumanizing attitudes towards them?[96] While there can be no excuses for such attitudes, a partial explanation for them can be found in the areas where autistics differ most strongly from neurotypicals: in communication and in reactions to sensory stimuli. These are the subject of Chapter Two.

CHAPTER TWO

Different, Not Less

In the spring of 2016, a Philadelphia mother received an anonymous note aimed at her autistic son. The note begins:

> The weather is getting nicer and like normal people I open my windows for fresh air. NOT to hear some BRAT screaming his head off as he flaps his hands like a bird. I don't care if its the way you raised him or if he is retarded. the screaming and carrying on needs to stop. No one wants to hear him act like a wild animal, it's utterly nerve-wracking, not to mention, it's scaring my normal children.[1]

This is obviously not a nice person. But note the assumption that there is a sharp line between autistic and neurotypical. Whatever the child is, he is not only abnormal, but he should be prevented from doing things that disturb those who are normal. The writer also identifies the source of the abnormality: the child is acting like a bird or a wild animal, not like a human being.

It is sadly common for autistic people to be identified as "animals," a profoundly dehumanizing idea.[2] The "autistic as animal" trope is common in American culture, most closely connected with one of the core "deficits" of autism. By the *DSM-5*'s definition, someone diagnosed with autism must struggle to one extent or another with communication. The "animalistic" slur is most closely associated with individuals who have the most communication "deficits." In everyday speech, these people are typically labelled "low functioning." In *DSM-5* terms, they are "level 3" autistics, meaning they are completely or almost completely non-speaking, as well as struggling with other issues. Roughly 25% of the autistic population falls into this category.[3]

Communication

Such people do often make non-speech noises. They may repeat random syllables, hum, whistle, grunt, sigh—and yes, scream.[4] These noises are often understood as meaningless/ "animalistic." Yet this is clearly a mistake, as the wonderful video, "In My Language," by the late non-speaking activist Mel Baggs, illustrates.[5] The video begins with Baggs moving around their room touching, tasting, and smelling things, while they flap their hands and sing softly all alone. To most neurotypicals, they would appear deeply disturbed. But after a few minutes we begin to hear the computer voice generated by Baggs's typing. They explain they consider "normal" speech impoverished, because it is directed only at people, whereas they enjoy a much richer experience, communicating through taste, touch, sight, and sound with the non-human as well as the human world. This is their own, natural language, with which they are completely satisfied, even though they understand the need to type to make neurotypicals understand them.

"My personal experience is that I was born without the capability to talk due to apraxia," writes Diego Pena.[6] Indeed, most non-speaking autistics are kept from speaking not by low intelligence (as too often assumed), but by apraxia:

a neurological disorder characterized by the inability to perform learned (familiar) movements on command, even though the command is understood and there is a willingness to perform the movement. Both the desire and the capacity to move are present but the person simply cannot execute the act.[7]

Apraxia of speech (AOS) is perhaps the best known of the many forms of apraxia.

AOS . . . affects the brain pathways involved in planning the sequence of movements involved in producing speech. The brain knows what it wants to say, but cannot properly plan and sequence the required speech sound movements,

according to the National Institute on Deafness and Other Communication Disorders.[8] In other words, autistics with AOS understand what is being said to them, and know what they want to say in reply, but they cannot make their muscles produce the correct sounds. As you can imagine, this is painfully frustrating. Nor is apraxia limited to speech. It can also affect someone's ability to control both fine and gross body movements. Ido Kedar describes the intense frustration he felt in school when—knowing perfectly well the correct answer to a question—he just couldn't get his finger to point to the picture representing it.[9] A related, but less severe, neurological condition is dyspraxia, which refers to a limited ability to control movements. Dyspraxia, too, can affect speech.

Augmentative and alternative communication (AAC) devices can help non-speaking autistic people communicate. AAC ranges from simple picture or letter boards to complex computer programs that provide pictures of commonly used words, so users don't have to spell everything out laboriously, letter by letter. Some of these devices will even generate a computerized "voice," allowing the user to "talk" with someone else. Because they cannot control their hands well enough to point or type accurately, apraxia affects many autistics' ability to use letter boards or computer programs. However, through special physical therapy and long practice, they can often overcome this hurdle.

While the process is usually very slow, it is also sometimes possible for apraxic non-speakers to learn to type their own words on a computer. Often, they begin with someone supporting their arms as they type—a practice often condemned by "experts." Because autistics were supposedly far below average in intelligence, scientists and educators assumed for a long time that it was the people holding their arms who directed what was being written. And sometimes that was indeed the case. Several experiments showed that "facilitated communication" could be a scam.[10] But then some autistics who had begun to communicate via facilitated communication learned to type or point to letters independently. And at this point it became clear that their words really were the products of their own minds. Ido Kedar and Diego Pena, typing independently in public presentations and interviews with reporters, have clearly demonstrated how smart and articulate they are.[11] So while some cases of facilitated communication may indeed be scams, others show vigorous minds slowly finding their way towards independent communication. This is essential. For too many years the intelligence of non-speaking autistics has been underestimated simply because they couldn't communicate in "normal" ways.[12]

In the autism community (and the disability community more broadly), a common aphorism goes: "Just because I can't speak doesn't mean I have nothing to say." We are hugely mistaken to assume that non-speaking people are unable to understand speech. This is why it is better to describe them as "non-speaking" rather than "non-verbal," which implies an inability to understand words. This is also why autism activists so often warn parents and teachers to be careful when they talk in front of non-speaking kids. Sadly, people do often say cruel things about these kids—sometimes to their very faces. And when something hurtful is said, the kids will hear it and take it in. Being told you are stupid, incapable, "like an animal" is deeply traumatizing. False assumptions about non-speaking autistics can literally ruin their lives. Non-speakers are the ones most likely to be abandoned in institutions, the most likely to suffer from abuse, and the most likely to be murdered by their parents or caregivers. Yet all this is completely avoidable. Given a decent education, and the chance to show what they can do, people without speech can make valuable contributions to society.[13] One recent example is Hari Srinivasan, who graduated from the University of California at Berkeley and is now studying neuroscience at Vanderbilt University. He is already playing a role in making federal policy, on the Interagency Autism Coordinating Committee—despite his inability to speak.[14]

Most people with autism can speak, at least to some extent and at some times. Many repeat words and phrases they have heard, instead of producing their own. They can actually communicate quite effectively in this way, if the people around them can learn what such "echoes" signify. In *Life Animated*, Ron Suskind describes how his son Owen began to communicate using, as a kind of scaffolding, lines from his favorite animated Disney movies. Having watched the movies alongside his son, Ron picked up the implications of those lines and came to understand what Owen was trying to say. Eventually Owen moved on to speaking in a more "normal" manner.[15] Speech pathologist Barry Prizant has spent decades working with such "echolalic" children. He points out how much they are able to convey through their repeated phrases. While teachers and therapists often discourage "echolalia," Prizant says, this is really a mistake. Echolalia is often a first step towards more sophisticated communication.[16]

Other autistics can speak "normally," but only with exhausting effort. They may have begun their lives as non-speakers or as echolalics, and then slowly, laboriously learned to speak in the way other people expected. But at the end of a long, tiring day, they may begin to slur or mispronounce words, mix up sentences, and perhaps revert to echolalia or not speak at all: "It's like my mouth goes on strike and won't do what it's told."[17] Reversion to echolalia or even complete loss of speech can grow out of depression:

> When depression started at around the age of 13, I slowly regressed into a complete inability to speak in any setting that wasn't home. This was from about age 14-18. At school I didn't speak a word.[18]

This is "selective mutism"—the inability to speak in certain settings or with certain people.

The loss of speech is also related to anxiety. When overwhelmed by fear, some autistic people simply lose the ability to speak:

> When I'm experiencing any kind of extreme emotion, sensory overload, or too much anxiety or stress, I'm not able to force my vocal cords into action no matter how hard I try. This is especially challenging because sometimes I can speak just fine, so people who have heard me do so tend not to believe that I actually can't speak at other times.[19]

Morenike Giwa Onaiwu has described an encounter she had with a police officer that rapidly escalated due to her race and her autistic manner of speaking. When the officer approached her car, she remembered how her father once was beaten so badly by the police that he had to be hospitalized. And this frightened her so much that when the officer questioned her, she unwittingly reverted to her childhood practice of echolalia. She began repeating his own words back to him, which not surprisingly made him angry. In the end nothing too bad happened, but the episode did amplify her pre-existing fear of the police.[20]

In contrast to the non-speakers and echolaics, there are autistics who have large vocabularies and are fluent with words; indeed, some are talented writers and public speakers. Yet they, too, struggle with communication. Facial expressions, body language and tones of voice may be largely invisible to them, and so they miss some of the fine nuances of neurotypical communication. And those who can talk very well can be defeated by non-literal speech, such as irony, sarcasm, or figures of speech.[21] They may understand perfectly well what these forms of speech are, but, because they tend to be literal thinkers themselves, they just aren't prepared for non-literal language from others. Some can learn, with effort, to know when a speaker is being sarcastic, or lying, but this does not come naturally—another reason why communication "deficits" is one of the diagnostic criteria for autism.

Functioning Labels

Communication issues influence how people with autism are labelled—in schools, in therapy, in housing, in employment, in civic life, in everyday conversations and in scientific research. Non-speaking and echolaic people almost always receive more demeaning designations. DSM-5 has substituted various "levels" (from 1 to 3) for the traditional "high-functioning" and "low-functioning" terms, but even today, some scientists still employ "functioning labels" in their research. School assessments draw the same distinction, as do health, therapy, and other public services. Media accounts of autism are full of such labels.

But it turns out that "functioning labels," like global IQ scores, are essentially meaningless. Those who cannot speak or who speak only with echolalia are assumed to be intellectually disabled and are generally labelled "low-functioning;" those who can speak more or less "normally" are assumed to be intelligent and considered "high-functioning." But it is far from clear how closely intelligence is correlated with the ability to speak (as opposed to communicating in other ways). Indeed, intelligence—as measured by standard intelligence tests—is poorly correlated with autistic people's overall ability to function in society.[22]

Many people (both autistic and neurotypical) with excellent speaking abilities nevertheless have poor executive functioning skills (basically, the set of abilities people need to guide their behavior towards a goal). These people find it difficult to maintain employment and a household. They may be unable to feed themselves regularly, take necessary medicine, and keep themselves clean. Others with "normal" speech may have crippling anxiety, or extreme sensory sensitivities that trap them at home. On the other hand, some people with very little spoken language are nevertheless able to attend college, work, pay their bills, and live on their own, with only minimal assistance.

These labels attempt to create a clear distinction, where none exists. Any one autistic person may be "high-functioning" in some areas of life, and "low-functioning" in others. Consider this child:

> My "high functioning' child is not yet potty trained and still has to use diapers. . . Wait, does that make her 'low-functioning"? I get confused because she is also reading 'The Hobbit", which might make her "high-functioning." It's almost like I was right when I said that functioning labels are arbitrary, ableist and totally made up.[23]

Adults also vary in their ability to function, often depending on the situation:

> If the situation I face is needing to figure out how to get from point A to point B by public transit, I am in good shape. I'll function GREAT. If the situation is a crowded gathering where I need to politely interact with people, I might manage the length of the party (or I might not.) Then I go home and shut down. My functioning in that area is kind of cruddy.[24]

As with sensory issues and the ability to speak, the ability of a person to live autonomously can change over time.[25] "High-functioning" autistics with stressful jobs or difficult personal relationships may eventually suffer from "autistic burnout;" they lose, at least for a time (and sometimes permanently), the ability to live independently. They can no longer do their jobs, visit the grocery store, remember to feed themselves, perhaps even speak as they once did.[26] How closely, then, do functioning labels, usually attached to people in childhood, actually reflect their ability to function as adults?

Such meaningless labels may harm autistic people more than their real "deficits" do. Not only are they demeaning, but they also immediately attach expectations to individuals, simply because some expert, at some point, has relegated them to a particular category.[27] Children labelled "low-functioning" will almost automatically be shunted into special education classrooms, where they will be taught virtually no academic subjects, which in turn will limit their options later in life. The "high-functioning" label, in contrast, makes it harder for someone to get accommodations from schools, and later from workplaces— even though such accommodations are mandated by law and may be essential for that person's success. Functioning labels are how neurotypical people try to categorize autistic people; they do not describe the realities of autistic lives.

Faces

Another very important way in which autistic people differ from neurotypicals has to do with their ability to recognize faces and interpret facial expressions. A certain portion of the autistic population has prosopagnosia—a visual processing difference that makes it difficult or impossible to recognize faces. As Lydia Brown puts it:

> I'm capable of seeing people next to each other and realizing they do not look identical, even if they present their gender very

similarly, are close in age, have similarly sized/shaped bodies, and are from the same racial group. But I can't reliably tell people apart in sequence, or out of context from when/where/how I usually encounter them, or after a few days or weeks or months since regular contact.[28]

Some degree of congenital (genetically caused) prosopagnosia occurs in about 2.5% of the general population.[29] It is said to occur more frequently in people with autism, although I have not been able to locate any research that shows how much more frequently. In any case, the failure to recognize faces is obviously socially debilitating. And it can be dangerous. For example, autistic children may be subjected to more intense bullying if they cannot recognize and then report their tormentors to school authorities.[30]

Even when autistics recognize people's faces, it may still be difficult for them to "read" those faces accurately. Beginning in the late 1960s, psychologist Paul Ekman began arguing that certain facial expressions were universal. In cross-cultural experiments, he and his colleagues showed how people in very different cultures around the world both used their own faces and read other people's faces in similar ways. No matter what their background, the people he studied expressed a small number of basic emotions (happiness, sadness, surprise, etc.) using the same facial muscles. When they saw those muscles come into play on someone else's face, they were generally able to interpret correctly the emotion the other person was feeling.[31]

From there, Ekman and his colleagues developed and refined FACS, a system for systematically coding the movements of facial muscles, and then EMFACS, a system for interpreting spontaneous displays of emotion by analyzing the movement of facial muscles.[32] Psychological research on emotion widely deploys both FACS and EMFACS. In addition, other researchers have developed their own coding systems, based on their own theories of emotion and its physical expression.[33]

One of these was used at Cambridge University in the development of Mindreading™, a computer program intended to help children with autism learn to read neurotypical faces in the same way neurotypicals do.[34]

There is a market for this and other, similar products because most autistic people (even those who can recognize faces) cannot instinctively read emotions in faces. It is true that many autistics have learned—through study and practice—to interpret facial expressions quite well. In fact, South African author Estelle Ryan has based a fascinating series of mystery novels on this learned ability. Her autistic protagonist, Genevieve Lenard, studied psychology (and presumably something like the EMFACS system), eventually becoming so adept at reading the fine details of facial movement and body language that an art insurance company employs her to detect people lying in videotaped conversations.[35] Lenard is the fictional exception, however. While many autistics will eventually learn to detect basic emotions in people's faces, more complex expressions—such as those of embarrassment or veiled hostility—generally elude them.[36] An important challenge to communication is their difficulty interpreting the facial cues that accompany and modify spoken words.

This struggle has attracted a great deal of attention from psychologists, neurologists and other researchers. A large body of scientific literature exists on autistic problems with reading emotions and their neurological causes.[37] However, a closely related problem has received almost no scientific attention. How well do neurotypicals read autistic faces? Autistic facial expressions often look very different than neurotypical ones.[38] The *DSM*-5 lists "a total lack of facial expressions" as one of the possible characteristics of autism. "Flat affect" (or the less severe "restricted affect") is fairly common among autistic people. Their faces just move less than those of neurotypicals. They may talk with stiff lips, not using any other part of the face—in other words, without facial expressions easily recognizable to neurotypicals. This can be intensely frustrating for an autistic person who really wants to communicate his or her feelings: "Imagine your face staying flat and bland when inside you are furious, sad, or wanting to smile in greeting."[39] It can also lead to serious misunderstandings.[40] Neurotypicals have a predisposition to expect particular facial expressions during certain kinds of social interactions. This is true across cultures, at least for some basic emotions, as noted above. Neurotypicals experience someone who does not produce the "right" expression at the right time, or whose face simply remains immobile, as somehow "off." Consider, for example, this interaction between autistic blogger Cynthia Kim and a little boy visiting her house. The two played together enjoyably in the morning, and the boy wanted to sit next to her at lunch. But after lunch he told Kim: "You scare me." Kim eventually concluded that it was the lack of expression on her face the child had found so frightening."[41]

Not all autistics have "flat affect," however. Some autistic people "make faces"—that is, they produce facial expressions commonly considered inappropriate (unless produced by young children, playing with other children). They may purse their lips, scrunch up their noses, frown deeply, stick out their tongues, etc.—often while making non-speech noises of one kind or another. Sometimes, adults do this on purpose, to express anger or disgust (autistic children, of course, sometimes do it just to be annoying). However, inappropriate "faces" may also be unplanned and even unnoticed by the person making them. One little boy got into trouble for "making faces" at his caregiver. His mother asked what he was doing, and he replied,

Mommy, sometimes I just make faces for no reason. I didn't know I was making faces at Miss X. I was just making them. Sometimes it just happens and I don't know why it's happening. I don't make them for any reason.[42]

"Making faces" is not necessarily intentional or expressive of any particular emotion. It does, nevertheless, often cause offense.

Neurotypical parents often try to correct their face-making autistic children. Sometimes this is simply a matter of making them aware of what they're doing. The mother mentioned above would stop her son if he moved his face in potentially problematic ways and ask him whether he was trying to tell her something with his face. She tried to explain to him gently why people might "think he is trying to tell them something" even though he didn't mean to.[43] Self-awareness of "making faces" seems like a useful skill for a parent to teach his or her child. Many other neurotypical parents (and some teachers), though, reject teaching for policing—criticizing and even punishing kids for "smirking" or "scowling" at the wrong times.[44] Autistic children are often subjected to "social skills training," which generally includes instruction on using "appropriate" facial expressions.[45] A computer program, developed by a professor at Virginia Tech, teaches children with autism not only how to recognize other people's facial expressions, but also to imitate them. Children are corrected if they make the "wrong" face.[46] But imagine how damaging it is for a child to be consistently told that her face looks "wrong." What is it like to have your face constantly corrected? In the next chapter, I will have more to say about such attempts to "normalize" autistic children.

Many autistic people clearly display sad, angry, fearful, concerned, or delighted faces—but in ways that are not typical. From a neurotypical point of view, they may show too much or too little expression for a given context, or their expressions may appear a little too early or too late. Autistic facial expressions are often viewed as "awkward," "mechanical," or just plain "odd"—by scientists as well as ordinary people.[47] In addition, neurotypicals regularly interpret these expressions incorrectly.[48] A particular expression may be taken as evidence of anger, lack of interest, disgust, or mischievous intent, when the autistic person actually experiences nothing of the sort. "Normal" people often see "flat affect" as evidence that an autistic person feels no emotion at all. In short, neurotypicals appear to have just as much trouble reading autistic faces, as autistics do reading neurotypical faces. Compared to the extensive studies that have been conducted on autistic "face-blindness," very few have been devoted to neurotypical "face-blindness."[49] As a result, we do not know whether the failure of neurotypicals to read autistic faces is simply because autistic people express emotion using different facial muscles (in which case, Ekman's claims for "universality" fall apart), or because neurotypicals actually have a deficit of some sort in the ability to read faces different from their own.

One study does, however, reveal the negative effects this inability has on people with autism living in a neurotypical world. A group of researchers showed videos of autistic children to their typically developing peers. The viewers had no other interactions with the kids they were watching and did not know that they were autistic. Nevertheless, they gave low ratings on attractiveness, kindness, helpfulness, and trustworthiness to the autistic children, and were disinclined to want to play with them, even when those children were otherwise physically attractive. [50] Unable to properly interpret autistic facial expressions, young children were already rejecting autistic peers without even having contact with them. Prejudice against people with autism sets in at an early age.

Sensory Issues

Autistic people share the same physical senses as other people, but they may experience and process sensory input in unusual ways. It is not yet widely recognized in our society that the greatest challenges many autistics face are sensory ones.[51] In the latest edition of the *DSM*, sensory differences have finally been added to the diagnostic criteria for autism, making scientists, physicians, and psychologists more aware of them. But few members of the general public understand the nature of these differences or realize their profound impact on autistic people's experience of the world.

Autistic individuals vary tremendously in their reactions to particular sensory stimuli. Some are extremely sensitive, while others are the opposite (or somewhere in between). One person delights in touching a range of different textures, while another can tolerate only very smooth surfaces. Some people seek out loud noises, while others find them excruciatingly painful. To make things even more confusing, the sensory experience of any given individual frequently shifts over time. The same person may be able to ignore farmyard smells one day, and gag at them the next. An autistic child may be able to tolerate eye contact on Tuesday and find it unbearable the rest of the week. The technical terms for these differences are "hyposensitivity" and "hypersensitivity." Hyposensitive people not only tolerate but actually seek out intense sensory experiences. Hypersensitive ones may be most comfortable in a dark, quiet room, with soft furniture. But the situation for any one autistic person will be distinctly individual, and the same person may move back and forth between hypo- and hypersensitivity over the course of time. Such fluidity is not caprice, but something rooted in the person's neurology.

"Sensory processing" refers to the unconscious mental processes of organizing and making sense out of sensory input: turning signals from the eyes into recognizable sights, signals from the ears into comprehensible sounds, signals from the skin into such known categories as hot, cold, smooth, sticky, and so forth. While it is relatively easy for neurotypicals to understand hypersensitivity and hyposensitivity, it is much harder for those of us with "normal" neurology to wrap our minds around differences in sensory processing. Autistic people may find unusual patterns in sensory information, they may not receive certain kinds of information at all, or they may be overwhelmed by too much of it.

Most scientists agree, for example, that a typically rare condition called "synesthesia" is more common among people with autism. [52] In synesthesia, information from one sensory system finds its way into the mental processing for another system. Music may appear visually as colors, while moving shapes on a screen may make specific sounds. My own daughter has a history of "tasting" voices, while one professional chef actually experiences tastes as shapes on his hand. [53] Beyond such differences, people with autism may also process information from their senses more slowly or more quickly than neurotypicals. Many autistic children, for example, struggle in school because their minds are turning the sounds coming out of their teacher's mouth into words just a tiny bit slower than the other children, leaving them constantly scrambling to catch up with the class.

Our society usually identifies five senses: sight, hearing, smell, taste and touch. But we all have other senses as well, seldom discussed because for most of us they don't cause problems. But they may be a source of serious trouble for people with autism. For example, our vestibular sense helps us maintain our balance. Vestibular difficulties in people with autism may lead to lightheadedness, a loss of balance, poor depth perception, difficulties with posture, gait and fine motor skills, trouble focusing eyes, confusion, disorientation, and difficulty maintaining attention. Not surprisingly, such vestibular problems create anxiety. They also exacerbate autistic people's social and emotional struggles. [54]

Proprioception is awareness of the body's location in space, in relation to other objects. Some scientists have viewed proprioception as a strength in autism and assert that the clumsiness of many autistic people arises from too much reliance on proprioception, while ignoring visual cues. Many autistics, on the other hand, describe themselves as having relatively weak proprioception.[55] They report living with constant worries about bumping into things or falling because they have misjudged distances: "I have to watch my feet when I walk because I don't get enough feedback as to where they are. I trip a lot and stumble on uneven ground."[56] Worse, they may sometimes not be able to feel their bodies at all.

My perception of where my body starts and ends is muted too. I recently cleared out my wardrobe and found a coat that I had bought. It was way too big. In fact, it had always been too big and my husband recounted how I have always bought clothes of the wrong size.[57]

Eerie experiences of floating, of being ungrounded can be very frightening, and quickly become intolerable. Children with proprioception differences may jump up and down or purposely bang into walls, frantically seeking deep pressure, trying to locate their bodies in space. Teachers and other adults may interpret these behaviors as willfully "bad," when they are really just attempts to keep terror at bay.

Interoception is awareness of the body's internal processes and states--the ability to feel one's breathing, tell whether one is cold enough to need a coat, identify a physical sensation such as hunger or pain.[58]

Many autistic people have dampened or muted interoception. We just don't seem to notice what's going on in our bodies until it reaches a level that other people would find intolerable. And often when we do notice it, it goes from 'oh that's happening' to intolerable really darn fast.[59]

Poor awareness of bodily states can have unfortunate, even dangerous consequences in the real world. It is, for example, extremely difficult to toilet train young children with poor interoception, because they genuinely have no idea whether they "need to go" or not. Adults who lack the ability to detect physical states may forget to eat or sleep or obtain needed medical care. If they do seek medical care, it may be denied because even though they know something is wrong, they can't identify and therefore can't explain what is bothering them. It is not surprising, then, that mysterious bodily sensations—or the lack of any bodily sensation at all—may cause increased anxiety. But interoception is also closely tied to self-awareness and emotion. The inability to sense how one's own body feels right now or to predict how it will react in the future creates a fearful sense of one's very self as insubstantial and fragile, easily disrupted or destroyed.

Eye Contact

Autistic writers and speakers have long struggled to explain the impact that these sensory differences have on their functioning in the world, but with only limited success. A case in point is eye contact. Many, if not most, autistic people would prefer to avoid eye contact. Yet neurotypicals continue to be puzzled and offended when such a person won't "look them in the eye."[60] They may interpret this as rudeness, even dishonesty. The truth is, for many autistic people eye contact is literally painful:

It's like biting into a really sour lemon or licking the end of a battery. The feeling of tiny creepy crawlies shimmering under your skin making you cringe. Butterflies in your tummy trying to escape out through your head.[61]

When I make eye contact, the world around me blocks out. I can only process the immense pain and discomfort that comes to my brain.[62]

Eye contact is hard. It hurts. It feels like car headlights are flooding your brain and you can no longer think.[63]

The last two quotations emphasize how difficult it is to think or engage with others while making eye contact. In her excellent *Ask an Autistic* video series, Amethyst Schaber identifies two main factors that make this so difficult: the sensory discomfort of experiencing the other person's complex facial expressions, and the difficulty of processing visual cues from the eyes at the same time as auditory cues from the voice.[64] Some autistics claim it is simply impossible for them to do both at the same time:

> Whenever I actually have [a job] interview, I can't seem to talk and look the interviewer in the eye at the same time. I either have to talk while looking away, making occasional eye contact, or if it's full on eye contact then I'm not talking because my mind goes blank. On top of that, I can't listen to the interviewer and try processing their facial expressions and body language. It's like I can only do one thing at a time. I either listen or try to watch but not both.[65]

Despite multiple efforts to explain this issue to neurotypicals, the eye contact problem continues to have real-life consequences. Many American schools, for example, emphasize "active listening," which typically includes something like "eyes on the speaker" or "make eye contact." The problem is that having "eyes on the teacher" may make it harder for an autistic student to understand what the teacher is saying.[66] And if students fail to keep eyes on their teachers, in an effort to follow what they're saying, they usually get reprimanded for not listening properly.

Adults unable to maintain eye contact face other kinds of problems. They may be denied jobs for which they are otherwise qualified, because interviewers see them as "shifty" or "weird."

I was once told (after not getting a "sure thing" job) that the person I would be working under didn't want me. Why not? Because he felt I was unreliable! I don't know how you are suppose to know this after a 5 minute informal meeting but I guess I didn't make enough eye contact to satisfy him. I just wish my impeccable work history would speak for itself.[67]

Justifiably, autistic job-seekers view this as unfair: "Why is the eye contact thing allowed to interfere with us getting a job that we're qualified for?"[68]

People with autism trying to live in American society face sensory challenges that others may not even recognize. Visual and auditory processing differences make work at school and at jobs harder; heightened sensitivity to lights, noises and tastes creates regular sources of physical discomfort; vestibular disturbances, as well as issues with proprioception and interoception intensify both fatigue and anxiety. Even more troubling, such sensory differences contribute to the popular perception that people with autism are weird, crazy, unreliable, "not like us." In other words, not fully human.

Proud to Be Autistic

I would never change being Autistic. I would never hide my Autism. I am proud to be Autistic.[69]

People with autism are not angels. They share with the rest of us the full panoply of human faults and virtues, as well as intelligence, feelings, and senses. Some neurotypicals are rude, lazy, self-centered, or just plain mean. So, too, are some autistics. The goal of this book is not to demonstrate how wonderful autistic people are (although many are indeed wonderful). It is rather to demonstrate that, despite how different they may seem, they are, in the end, only different—never less than human.[70]

Back in the 1970s, a congresswoman from New York City, was famous for being loud and abrasive, for wearing huge hats, and for energetically supporting Black people, the elderly, women, gays, and the disabled. Bella Abzug was also known for her catchy phrases, one of which has stuck with me through many decades. While working for women's rights, she once remarked, "We don't so much want to see a female Einstein become an assistant professor. We want a woman *schlemiel* [Yiddish for an "awkward" or "clumsy" person] to get promoted as quickly as a male *schlemiel*." I don't think Bella would mind me using her language for my own purposes. Autistic advocates and their neurotypical supporters aren't interested in seeing an autistic Einstein recognized for her or his accomplishments. We want an autistic *schlemiel* to enjoy the same rights as a neurotypical one.

In other words, the goal of autism activism is not just for "high-functioning" autistics to get jobs or have homes and families. We want all people with autism, whether brilliant or intellectually disabled, emotionally expressive or flat, self-harming or safe, speaking or non-speaking, to be treated like human beings—entitled to a basic education, a chance to contribute to society, a decent place to live, adequate health care, and freedom from abuse and stigma. Because, as Julia Bascom, president of the Autistic Self-Advocacy Network, puts it:

> *We are fine. We are complete, complex, human*
> *beings leading rich and meaningful existences and*
> *deserving dignity, respect, human rights, and the*
> *primary voice in the conversation about us.*[71]

PART II

Children

Would you treat a neurotypical like child this?[1]

CHAPTER THREE

Intensive Early Intervention

Don't assume autism is the primary obstacle to the individual's happiness. Figure out what that really is, and act on it. Teach self-acceptance when you find yourself interacting with Autistics, especially young ones.[2]

M ost parents, after their child is diagnosed with autism, begin a frantic search for advice and resources. They may turn to their pediatrician, or to a developmental specialist, or to websites such as those maintained by the National Institutes of Health. No matter where they turn, they will almost certainly be told that their child needs "intensive early intervention." The Autism Society of American says "early educational intervention is key to improving the lives of people with ASD."[3] The National Institute of Mental Health says that "treatment for ASD should begin as soon as possible after diagnosis."[4] A training module for physicians developed by the Centers for Disease Control and Prevention declares: "The earlier intervention can begin, the better for long-term outcomes."[5]

Let's unpack this a bit. Does every autistic child really need intervention? Perhaps not. Many have grown to adulthood—often quite happily—without it. Does every autistic child need "early" intervention? Again, perhaps not. Even more autistics have received therapy

— 59 —

only later, in their adolescence or adulthood, with no ill effects. Why intensive early intervention? What is the goal here? The experts usually say they want to "optimize long-term outcomes." [6] But what does this mean? Of course, each child is different, and each will have different needs, so it is difficult for experts to be very specific. Perhaps a good start would be "in order for the child to become a self-confident, productive autistic adult"? Yet this is seldom suggested. What's more, the specific methods to be used for early intervention are often left rather vague—although it is agreed that they should be "evidence-based." Early intervention programs may be completely benign, even useful for some children. But, as we will see, they may also be harmful. So why this insistence that every autistic child have them? Perhaps it is for reasons that have nothing to do with the children themselves.

Autism Meets Capitalism

We have a lot of really bad behavior analysis that's going on while the people doing it are getting rich. [7]

Autism diagnoses began to increase in the 1990s. What had once been considered a very rare phenomenon became, if not exactly common, at least not entirely unexpected. Shifts in diagnostic criteria were a major factor in this change. In the first two editions of the *DSM*, autism had been treated as an unusual form of schizophrenia, with its onset in childhood. *DSM*-3 (1980) re-defined it as a type of developmental disorder. In 1994, *DSM*-4 recognized autism as a spectrum disorder, with "mild" as well as "severe" cases. It also recognized "Asperger's Syndrome"—characterized by less obvious behavioral differences than in other forms of autism and by excellent verbal skills, although whether this was truly a form of autism remained under debate. [8] (Today, Asperger's has disappeared again, folded into the general category of autism spectrum disorders in *DSM*-5). Because of these changes, children who might once have been considered mentally ill or intellectually disabled were diagnosed in the 1990s with autism. Others, who might once have been considered normal, but just a bit "quirky," were now diagnosed with Asperger's.

With changes in diagnostic criteria, along with growing public awareness of autism, the number of children considered autistic rapidly increased in the 1990s. [9] Diagnoses exploded in the 2000s, with estimates of autism's prevalence in the population rising from 6.7 out of 1,000 children in the year 2000, to 1 out of 36 in 2022.[10] Fears of an "autism epidemic" emerged, with various causes (mostly environmental—including the now totally debunked theory that the condition is caused by vaccination) proposed.[11] This panic ultimately proved unjustified. Autism was not actually becoming more common. It was simply being diagnosed far more often.[12]

But as diagnoses rose, so did interest in "curing" or at least "treating" autism. The traditional method of dealing with it had been institutionalization—locking autistic people out of sight in psychiatric hospitals. These were basically warehouses for the unwanted, which provided food and shelter, but little actual help. In the 1960s, psychiatric institutions came under fire, as the horrid conditions inside them were exposed. But even as institutions were drained of most psychiatric patients, autistic people stayed behind, still living with squalor and abuse. Only as diagnoses increased in the 1990s and 2000s did parents make greater efforts to keep their autistic children at home, and have them "treated" or even "cured." Such established organizations as the Autism Research Institute began developing new programs like "Defeat Autism Now!" (DAN!—established in 1995, closed down in 2011). These programs aimed at "curing" autism through heavy metal chelation or special diets. Autism Speaks, founded in 2005, was also originally devoted to finding a "cure for autism;" it only removed "cure" from its mission statement in 2016.[13]

Autism families represented a big business opportunity. Thirty years ago, parents didn't want to see their children locked up in institutions, but they really had no other choice. Now entrepreneurs realized there was money to be made from desperate parents. A whole range of quacks began peddling supposed "cures" for autism—hyperbaric oxygen chambers, camel's milk, "detoxifying" clay baths, nicotine patches, and a huge variety of dietary supplements.[14] Some of these were, and still are, extremely dangerous. Jim Humble, a former scientologist who founded the "Genesis II Church of Health and Healing," began touting "Miracle Mineral Solution" (MMS) in 2006, as a cure for a variety of conditions. Despite repeated denunciation by scientists, and even the jailing of some of its marketers,[15] MMS (also sold under other names) is still available and still in use. Its proponents claim it "treats" cancer, AIDs, the common cold, Covid-19, and various other diseases, as well as autism.[16] But its biggest market was and still is the parents of autistic kids. What is MMS? Nothing more than industrial-strength bleach. When given to autistic children (and other people) orally, in baths, or even as enemas, it causes horrific physical and psychological damage.

Meanwhile, a growing number of people began marketing various autism "treatments," some just as far-out as camel's milk. "Dolphin-assisted therapy" may have been fun for some kids, but it left autistic characteristics untouched. "Forced holding," which claimed to establish attachment bonds between children and parents, was in vogue for some time in the early 2000s, despite being pointless (autism is not an attachment disorder) and potentially traumatic.[17] The LearningRx company boasted that its very expensive "brain-training" techniques improved the cognitive functioning of children with autism. Forced to pay the Federal Trade Commission a $200,000 fine in 2016, LearningRx agreed "to stop making a range of false and unsubstantiated claims."[18] Despite this setback, it remains in business and continues to market its training for autistic children, although there is no reliable evidence that it accomplishes anything at all.[19]

By far the best-known early intervention program for autism is Applied Behavior Analysis (ABA). The program has been around for the longest time and claims the most scientific evidence for its success—although it is important to note that this evidence is not nearly as strong as proponents of ABA claim, and that its definition of "success" is highly questionable.[20] Nevertheless, ABA is still the program most often recommended by government agencies and by autism organizations (at least those run by non-autistics). It is one of the few treatments for autism that insurance companies will (sometimes) cover.

So what exactly is ABA?

Applied Behavior Analysis

Psychologists often study thoughts and emotions, but the behaviorist school of psychology focuses on behaviors and how to manage them. "Applied behavior analysis" (ABA) makes use of the principles of behaviorism to shape behavior in real life situations, by finding ways to encourage what the analyst considers desirable behaviors, and discourage undesirable ones. Over the past half century, considerable research has been devoted to understanding why particular behaviors occur and to devising the most effective techniques for shaping them. Today, fields ranging from marketing to organizational management to political consulting use ABA techniques to meet their own goals. ABA has become the most widely used early intervention for autistic children. It is also used in animal training.[21]

In and of itself, applied behavior analysis is a fairly neutral technique. It can be extremely helpful in a variety of difficult situations—for re-training aggressive dogs who might otherwise be euthanized, for example, or for teaching young children with severe oral sensitivities to eat. Yet by its very nature, it contains the potential for misuse, a potential greatly increased when the practice is commercialized.[22]

Behavior analysts must walk a careful line to avoid using their interventions in damaging ways. Unfortunately, many fail at this.

The ethics of ABA remain hotly debated—and nowhere more so than in the application of the technique to autistic people. Let's start by examining the potential ethical pitfalls. The first issue is the relationship between a discipline designed specifically to shape behavior, and the dignity and autonomy of the individual whose behavior is being shaped. Certainly, in order to function in society, individuals must be "socialized," at least to some extent. They must be taught to behave in ways that will allow them to get along with others, complete essential tasks, and, ideally, live a meaningful life. Our society expects parents to socialize their children in an appropriate manner—indeed, those who don't are considered neglectful. But how should this socialization be accomplished? And at what point should the views of those being socialized be taken into account?

While children are very young, most parents instinctively use techniques closely, if informally, related to ABA: "Look! You sat on the potty for five minutes! Here's a cookie;" "If you bite your brother, you won't go to the zoo!" ABA would call these examples of "positive reinforcement" (offering something pleasant, like a cookie, to change behavior) and "negative punishment" ("negative," because something the subject wants, such as a trip to the zoo, is removed). But as children grow older, parents generally move away from ABA-style manipulation of environment and consequences. They begin to rely instead on moral and practical reasoning: "Shop-lifting is a form of theft— you should return what you stole and apologize to the store owner;" "If you go to the party tonight, you won't have time to study for your exam tomorrow. Do you really want to fail that exam?" This gradual move towards reasoning recognizes the older child or the teenager as someone with a claim to rationality and autonomy, as someone who is already making personal decisions for herself. While some parents continue to "bribe" their older children in subtle ways, most adolescents would see being offered a cookie for washing their hands as an insult.

Many adults would also be angered if they realized the extent to which ABA techniques are used on them to shape their employment, purchasing, and political behaviors.[23] This is just as much an affront to our dignity and autonomy, as the cookie offer is to the adolescent. One of the most significant ethical critiques of ABA, then, is that it is designed to ensure compliance with the behavior analyst's/marketer's demands. It doesn't encourage subjects to decide what the right thing to do is on their own.[24] Encouraging compliance may be ethical when working with animals and very young children, but it quickly becomes problematic as children grow older. And unthinking compliance in adult humans can be extremely dangerous.

A second problem: ABA involves real differences in power. Behavior analysts are always adult humans, while their subjects are generally animals, children, or adults who, for a variety of reasons, are vulnerable.[25] Regardless of the specifics, it is always the behaviorist who gets to determine which behaviors are desirable and to be encouraged, while the subject's views are ignored. In the case of young children and animals, this is in keeping with our society's ethical standards. We generally allow adults to make decisions about how children should behave and humans to make decisions about how animals should behave, because we assume that adults/humans are wiser than children/animals, and therefore better equipped to determine what is best for them. But the wisdom of adult humans in general, and behavior analysts in particular, certainly cannot be taken for granted. They may be well-meaning. But even if they are, they may still make significant mistakes in deciding which behaviors to encourage and which to discourage. Under these circumstances, behavior may end up being shaped in ways that are not really in the subject's best interests.

A final, but very important, ethical issue also results from the power differential. Because of their position, ABA practitioners have the power to abuse their subjects. If they are good practitioners, they will not use that power. However, among poorly trained or indifferent practitioners, the temptation may be too great. Sometimes abuse may be imposed for the subject's "own good"—because the poorly trained therapist misunderstands what is "good" for a particular child or animal, or imagines the benefits outweigh the costs. But this neither excuses the abuse, nor alleviates its impact. As Bob Christianson puts it:

> The result of this mindset is that Autistic kids are repeatedly forced to do things that are unnatural, uninteresting, and sometimes painful or dangerous. It's all done in the name of "therapy" – and all with smiles and upbeat attitudes from the therapists. The kids might cry. They might try to escape. They may refuse to take part. But they have to do it, because it has been decided that it is good for them – that they're being helped. They just may not be able to see it or understand it at the time.[26]

Tragically, abuse may also result from a therapy company's thirst for increased profits, or from the therapist's own impatience. Occasionally, it may even stem from sadism.

A Bit of History

In 1943, Leo Kanner of the Johns Hopkins University was the first in the U.S. to recognize autism as a distinct condition (although it now looks as though Kanner "lifted" some of his data and ideas from the Austrian psychiatrist Hans Asperger).[27] Examining only a few children from relatively well-to-do families, Kanner concluded that autism was an extremely rare form of mental illness.[28] For the next three decades, most American psychologists followed his lead, assuming autism to be a psychological disturbance, and trying to address the problems their autistic clients presented through psychotherapy of one kind or another.[29] Over the course of the 1960s and 1970s, however, scientific views slowly began to shift. Autism was still considered a very rare condition, and few scientists had any contacts with people recognized as autistic. But those who did were beginning to see autism not as a mental illness, but as a developmental disorder, the expression of unusual wiring in the brain. That view has been confirmed over recent decades. CAT scans and MRIs have revealed some differences in structure,[30] connectivity,[31] and levels of neurotransmitters[32] in the brains of autistic people. (Even though no clear-cut line separates autistic from "normal" brains.)

The shift from a psychological to a biological explanation for autism in the 1960s had several interesting corollaries. First, estimates of autistic intellectual capabilities changed with startling rapidity. Before the late 1960s, the received wisdom was that autistic people had normal, perhaps even superior intelligence.[33] This is what Kanner had claimed in his original study. But the developmental disorder theory led to the assumption that autistics were what was then called "mentally retarded."[34] Scientists were wrong about this, as we have already seen. But their investment in the developmental disorder theory contributed to the conceptualization of autistic people as not just neurologically different, but inherently defective. Such unexpected mental wiring "must" be profoundly dysfunctional, and little could be done about that. So, from the late 1960s through the 1980s, most doctors counselled parents of children diagnosed with autism to send them into institutions, then try to forget about them.

Ivar Lovaas

An exception to this rule was Ivar Lovaas of UCLA. Like his fellow researchers, Lovaas viewed autism as a severe developmental disorder. But he concluded that he could use behaviorist principles to improve the way young autistics acted. As an intervention for autistic children, today's Applied Behavior Analysis remains rooted in the methods Lovaas first used at UCLA in the 1960s, although many variations on his techniques have been developed over the years. Not surprisingly, when Lovaas died in 2010, he was lauded by other psychologists as the compassionate champion of children with autism.

Many autistic people reject this appraisal. For one thing, Lovaas's methods were very nasty indeed. They involved not just the use of aversives (unpleasant stimuli), but of extreme aversives (screaming, face-slapping, electric shocks, food deprivation, prolonged isolation, etc.) to extinguish what he considered problematic behaviors in young children.[35] (A few years later, he began using similar techniques on gay men, in order to "train" them to be heterosexual.) Lovaas's expressed attitude towards the subjects of his experiments was in some ways even more appalling. Here is what he said in a 1974 interview with *Psychology Today*:

> You see, you start pretty much from scratch when you work with an autistic child. You have a person in the physical sense — they have hair, a nose and a mouth — but they are not people in the psychological sense. One way to look at the job of helping autistic kids is to see it as a matter of constructing a person. You have the raw materials, but you have to build the person.[36]

In other words, Lovaas's autistic subjects only became human to him when he had molded them into the shape he wanted. To note these facts is not to undermine Lovaas's scientific achievements. But it is important to recognize that his attitude, as well as his methods, has been bequeathed to modern ABA practitioners.

Any knowledgeable and well-to-do parent seeking help for an autistic child in the late 1960s and 1970s usually ended up at UCLA, where Lovaas and his assistants honed ABA techniques specifically for use with this population. Eventually, other university centers arose, employing the same techniques (including, at first, the same extreme aversives) to treat the children that they, too, did not recognize as "real people."[37] But autism diagnoses began to increase in the 1990s. More and more parents were being told that their newly-diagnosed children needed early intervention, and that ABA was the most effective treatment. At this point, university centers could no longer meet the demand for services, so for-profit treatment centers emerged to fill the gap. Applied behavior analysis mutated from an academic specialty into a profession, with an Association for Behavior Analysis accrediting programs that granted degrees in the subject, and an affiliated Behavior Analyst Certification Board offering certification to graduates of those programs who passed the required exams.[38] Today ABA is an industry. Large ABA corporations offer franchising opportunities to local operators, the ones who actually treat clients. In 2021, the industry generated over $4 billion in profits. Just thirteen of the largest franchising corporations grossed $946 million in that year.[39] As one franchising company put it: "ABA centers are an extraordinary growth opportunity for franchisees. A growing patient pool and increasing demand for treatment assures a profitable industry."[40] People looking to ensure profits are not those we would ordinarily trust with our children.

The Positives of ABA

Modern ABA companies claim to have helped many children with autism. And some autistic people say they have indeed benefited from the treatment. One writes:

When people say it's evil, horrible, and conversion therapy for autistics. That's where I disagree. I was never abused in any way shape or form. I had no self control and my behaviors were over the top and I had horrible attempts to articulate feelings until I had therapy. Had it not been for therapy I would never live on my own, function in society, hold a job, and other stuff that is important.[41]

Another says:

I've had ABA therapy on and off over the years. I have found it very beneficial. That said, I've had some bad therapists who mistreated me so I wouldn't want to work with them again. However, I don't condemn the therapy itself since it has helped me a lot.[42]

And a third: "Overall, ABA has had a positive effect on me . . . . When used correctly, it is a very good method to improve communication skills and independence."[43]

When properly practiced, ABA (like other forms of therapy) can help young autistic children. Unfortunately, it is all too often practiced improperly and unethically.

"Today's ABA"

Asked about the problematic techniques associated with their field, many ABA companies will respond, "We don't do that anymore." "Today's ABA," they say, is not like what Lovaas and his students did in the 1960s. But this is not entirely true. The "new ABA" remains, in many ways, very much like the old. To begin with, most ABA companies still insist autistic children receive therapy for 40 hours a week—the same amount Lovaas called for. In practice, insurance companies are generally unwilling to pay for 40 hours. The norm is actually somewhere between 20 and 30 hours per week, although some clients still get the full 40.[44] Therapy is hard work, though. Even 20 hours a week may be simply too much for young children:

Think for a moment how exhausted you, a grown adult, are after 40 hours of work in a week and you will begin to understand why we get so concerned about putting a three-year-old child through such a grueling schedule. Being Autistic doesn't give a three-year-old child superpowers of endurance. Forty hours a week of ABA is not just expensive, it is painfully exhausting.[45]

Working so hard and so long, autistic children do not get to be children, playing and exploring on their own as children need to do:

> Children start ABA as young as 2 years old. That's 25-40 hours in which they cannot make a free choice. They're not playing as they want to. They are having to conform to hours of operant conditioning while their non-Autistic peers are playing in sandboxes, having naps, and scribbling with crayons. They're being robbed of their childhood . . . .[46]

And not just childhood fun. ABA robs children of the independent learning kids gain naturally in unstructured environments.

Many ABA practitioners also maintain Lovaas' other expectations—that children must comply with therapist's demands, that they must be attentive in ways that make sense to the therapist (not necessarily to the child), that the therapist's goals are the "right" goals, and that making young children's lives unpleasant (if not actively painful) is acceptable, if it's "for their own good." What makes maintaining these attitudes easier is the remarkable ignorance about autism displayed by many—if not most—of those using ABA techniques with autistic children.

Autism and the ABA Practitioner

ABA treatment centers are usually supervised by Board Certified Behavior Analysts (BCBAs), who typically have a masters or sometimes a doctoral degree in ABA. BCBAs generally have had extensive training in a range of behavioral techniques. But few know much about the autistic children who make up most of their client base.[47] In order to get an M.A., students usually must take at most one course about applying the concepts of ABA to children on the spectrum. (Such courses focus on techniques, not the condition itself.) Some programs don't require even that much. The main professional organization in the field, the Association for Behavior Analysis International, has a "verified course sequence" for graduate programs. Not a single course on autism is included.[48]

This is why we see such basic mistakes in the ways BCBAs deal with autistic children.[49] For example, today's BCBAs see "tantrumming" as a problem for their clientele, just as Lovaas did. Eliminating "temper tantrums" may be a major goal in a child's treatment plan. Yet practitioners often conflate "tantrums," which are voluntary behaviors, with "meltdowns," which other scientists have long since recognized as completely involuntary, triggered by overwhelming sensory or emotional stress.[50] You cannot get rid of meltdowns through any behavioral technique—because the child has no control over them. Despite the observable differences between tantrums and meltdowns, many BCBAs remain oblivious to this crucial fact.[51]

"Behavior technicians" (BTs) perform most of the work at ABA companies. BTs work directly with children undergoing therapy; they are the ones actually implementing the plans laid out by their BCBA supervisors. Most BTs are well meaning—they get into ABA because they want to "help kids"—but they are seldom paid very much, nor are they very well trained. Most newly hired BTs have no knowledge of autism or ABA. Most of their training comes on the job, and it focuses on ABA techniques.[52] And so, it is with people who don't really know anything about them, people who merely follow the rigid rules established by higher authority, that autistic children actually spend most of their early intervention time.

You see the inherent problem? Ideally, BTs would be taught early in their careers that their own sensory experiences, their own social expectations and goals, their own capacity for verbal communication and expression of emotion are not reliable guides to appropriate therapy for this client population. Since this is not something they typically learn, they may decide (with the encouragement of a supervisor) that a child is running away to escape an unwanted task, when the child is actually fleeing because the fluorescent lights in the ceiling are making him or her feel sick. BTs may try to "extinguish" self-stimulatory behaviors such as hand-flapping, which they imagine distracts the child from the task at hand. They don't realize that the flapping actually helps the child concentrate.

Even the physical spaces in which therapy is administered can be disruptive to learning, and not only because of the lighting. One older client describes his experience during therapy:

> I can't handle hearing young children screaming, and it's happening all the time. Sometimes, they have very young kids in the room with me, as young as three years old. This is not just because of autism and noise sensitivity. I never see anyone comfort the kids who are screaming. The sound is constant, like a horror movie soundtrack. They tell me that I'll "have to get used to it" every time I ask what the children are screaming about behind the gates.[53]

Let's set aside for a minute the question of why an ABA company is failing to provide comfort for young children in distress. The instruction to "get used to it" displays a profound ignorance of autism. Autistic people do not <u>ever</u> "get used to" sensory or emotional overload—they just grow more deeply distressed.

Dr. Gregory Hanley is an ABA reformer with long experience working with autistic clients. Now a trainer for other practitioners, he teaches that both the BCBA and the BT preparing to work with autistic clients should find out as much as possible about them, and then prepare a setting for therapy "in which the autistic person will be happy, relaxed, and engaged, one in which they will feel safe and in control."[54] Notice Hanley's focus on handing control to the child, not the therapist. Sadly, this runs counter to what BTs typically do and what their BCBA supervisors are telling them to do. Other certified behavior analysts have begun to acknowledge the ethical problems in their profession—and are finding ways to work not only more effectively but also more compassionately with vulnerable clients.[55] Yet for many commercial treatment centers, Lovaas's 1960s have never really gone away.

Compliance

When my non-autistic younger daughter was about four years old, she wanted to take violin lessons. We had heard that the Suzuki method was the most effective way of teaching violin, so we found a highly recommended Suzuki teacher. She was from Korea and had herself been taught the method in a very traditional way. So she bowed to her students when they entered the room, and she expected them to bow back. My strong-willed daughter was having no truck with that, though. She refused to bow. The teacher insisted. At the end of the first lesson, my daughter had not yet touched her tiny violin. The same thing happened at the second lesson, and the third . . . After a few weeks, she had yet to touch her violin because she still refused to bow. We would come in at the end of the lesson and she would be lying on the floor, completely ignoring her instructor. It was time to find a new teacher.

Many ABA providers resemble this Suzuki teacher. Before they even try to teach anything substantive, they insist that children be "table-ready" or "ready to learn"—sitting calmly at a desk, with hands on the table or in their lap, and with eyes on the therapist.[56] Too bad if this requires shoving their hands into place over and over again. Too bad if it requires forcing eye contact, despite the distress this causes (and the loss of focus that usually results). Too bad if it requires pushing a two-year old repeatedly back into a chair. The expectation is compliance with the therapist's demands, regardless of the consequences.

Compliance is high on the list of things ABA centers teach. One disenchanted former practitioner writes:

> The rule is, once you give a command as an ABA Therapist, you must follow through with it no matter what. If a child tries to cry or escape or engage in any other 'behaviors,' you can't give in, because then you are only reinforcing their bad behaviors and making it more likely that they'll use them in the future.[57]

Proud practitioners actually agree with such critics. An ABA consultant describes best practice: "from the first meeting with an early learner, we begin working on compliance."[58] A treatment center prides itself on the fact that "Compliance Teaching is used 100% of the day with every demand placed in our classrooms."[59] A child's failure to comply is not simply a choice—it is "maladaptive," "problematic," or "disruptive."

Some ABA practitioners link non-compliance in early childhood with more serious problems later: "Addressing noncompliant behavior at an early age is crucial. If problem behaviors are not attended to they can escalate into aggression or other problem behaviors."[60] Behavior analysts assure parents that they teach compliance because it is something the child will need in life. They will need to comply with teachers in school, with bosses on the job, with police on the streets.[61] And to a degree, this is true. But it is true of all children, not only autistic ones. Everyone needs to learn to do what authorities tell them. But most two-year-olds aren't forced to comply at all times. And their compliance seldom looks like "table-readiness." Would parents treat a neurotypical child this way?

Autistic advocates have long been concerned about ABA's focus on compliance, especially when physical force (even gentle force) is used to ensure that a child obeys. They argue that denying children the right to control their own bodies sets them up to be victimized later in life.[62] As one autistic adult wrote:

> In my personal experience and in talking to many other autistic adults, I've found that the experience of defaulting to compliance scripts – yes, okay, whatever you want is fine – is incredibly common for autistic people no matter what our ages, cognitive abilities, communication abilities, education levels, or work experiences may be. Everyone I have talked to about this, including myself, has had the experience of agreeing to something – or being too afraid to refuse something – that caused us direct harm. Not just once or a few times, but repeatedly throughout our lives.[63]

Neurotypical researchers have begun to recognize what autistic advocates have long known. One study found that the compliance taught by ABA practitioners in childhood results in lower self-esteem and "prompt dependency" (the need to be told what to do) in adults.[64] Another, considering ABA from an ethical perspective, concludes that its demands for compliance infringe on children's autonomy, by closing off options during a crucial period of identity formation.[65]

Dr. Greg Hanley recommends that therapists show signs of submission in their interactions with clients. And while teaching a skill,

> if the autistic person shows any explicit sign of distress, discomfort, or protest in the form of either minor or severe problem behavior while transitioning from essentially their way to your way, acknowledge it immediately and relent. Let the autistic person return to their way and resume following their lead until

he/she/they gets back to their version of happy, relaxed, and engaged for a short period.[66]

Such flexibility leads to clients' success.

"Touch Nose, Gummi Bear"[67]

Many years of my life were spent in ABA school. I was made to do my drills over and over until I was so bored and frustrated with my teachers. I would melt down. I am telling you ABA is not the solution. ABA is long hours meeting pointless goals like pointing to flashcards and pointing to my nose.[68]

The insistence on repetition in today's ABA reflects a basic concept in behaviorist psychology. The idea is that if you repeatedly reward or "reinforce" a particular behavior, it is more likely to occur in the future. A child who gets a cookie for sitting on the toilet is more likely to sit on the toilet in the future. By the same token, consistently "punish" a behavior and it is less likely to occur in the future. A child who loses screen time for skipping homework is less likely to skip homework in the future. The first problem with this is that autistic children have different neurological and emotional responses to stimuli than neurotypical children—and of course, autistic children differ amongst themselves in their reponses.[69] Therapists with little expertise in autism are often baffled by why autistic children respond to stimuli as they do. But what they consider reinforcement may not, in fact, be rewarding for an autistic client; what they consider punishment may not discourage a behavior at all. It is counterproductive to repeat something that gets the wrong result.

The second problem with repetition is boredom. Typically, whatever the practitioner considers "socially desirable" skills are broken down into small, more manageable tasks. Each smaller task will then be practiced over and over, with each successful attempt (or each genuine effort to do what is desired) rewarded in some small way. At first the technician prompts the client to perform the task, but gradually these prompts are "faded," until the client can perform the task independently. Such "Discrete Trial Training" (DTT), while somewhat less common than it once was, remains a core feature of most ABA programs.

So—imagine you are asked to "touch your nose." Over and over and over. Even if you get a gummi bear for each successful attempt, how many times can you stand to touch your nose on command? Endless repetition is inherently boring for any child. Moreover, some research shows that autistic people do not learn well from repetition.[70] Still, that has not stopped ABA companies from relying on it. To be fair, other forms of ABA try to avoid repetition. Pivotal Response Training (PRT), for example, was designed specifically to address the needs of children with autism. It allows children to choose from a variety of tasks, rather than constantly repeating the same task, thus increasing a child's motivation to learn. But Discrete Trial Training is still at the heart of most ABA, and it poses problems beyond boredom.

Being asked to repeat a behavior you already know very well is demeaning, because it suggests the therapist thinks you're stupid. It can also be deeply frustrating for children with apraxia, or difficulties with motor control, because even though they know perfectly well what they are supposed to do, they are physically incapable of complying. Here is Ido Kedar:

When I was a small child [in the 1990s] I had ABA (Applied Behavior Analysis) therapy forty hours a week. I sat at a table and I was asked to demonstrate my understanding of basic concepts by pointing to flashcards arrayed in front of me during drills. My instructors took data regarding whether I pointed to the right card or not. They thought they were collecting data on my receptive understanding of language. They were not. I understood everything, as any other child my age would. The data they were collecting, though they did not know it, actually measured my poor ability at that time to get my hand to touch with accuracy the card I wanted, and did not reflect an accurate measure of how much I understood. My mind might be screaming, "Touch tree! Don't touch house!" and I would watch, like a spectator, as my hand went to the card my hand, not my brain, wanted. And down in the data book it would be marked that I had not yet mastered the concept of tree.[71]

ABA prides itself on its scientific rigor. This requires massive data collection, to track student progress. Yet how the data is interpreted may not reflect what is actually happening in the therapy session at all.

"Nice Lady Therapists"

Once ABA practitioners decide what task they want a child to perform, they find ways to get him to do it. They may begin by "prompting" him to perform that task, and then gradually "fade" the prompts until the child is acting on her or his own. There are a variety of techniques for prompting. BTs may simply tell the child what to do or hint at what the right answer is. They may gesture towards an object, or nod or shake their head to indicate a right or wrong answer. They may use pictures to get the correct response. But they may also use physical prompting to obtain the desired result, and this is where their methods become questionable, to say the least.

When I was a little girl, they held my hands down in tacky glue while I cried.... When I was six years old, people who were much bigger than me with loud echoing voices held my hands down in textures that hurt worse than my broken wrist while I cried and begged and pleaded and screamed.... When I was a little girl, I was autistic. And when you're autistic, it's not abuse. It's therapy.[72]

Julia Bascom, now president of the Autistic Self-Advocacy Network wrote this justly famous passage. When autistic advocates quote Bascom to today's ABA practitioners, the response is almost always: "We don't do that anymore." But this is inaccurate.

Watch an instructional video on Discrete Trial Training (easily available online), and you will see how often a child's hands are grabbed and placed in her or his lap.[73] Even when she is crying and trying to cover her face, her hands will be pulled away. A Behavior Technician trying to enforce eye contact might hold a child's head in position until a pre-determined number of seconds have passed. A child trying to leave an unpleasant situation may be pushed back into a chair, or even dragged where the BT wants him to be. This is form of prompting teaches children that their bodies can be controlled by someone else legitimately, "for their own good."[74]

Even more shocking, though, is how some practitioners rationalize this practice:

. . . in adult services, doing full-physical prompting would be a human rights violation. However, you're not working with adults in the instance you described. When you're working with children, sometimes you do need to engage in those physical prompts to be able to teach them.[75]

It is apparently acceptable to violate children's human rights.

Some ABA practitioners, like Mary Barbera, do recognize that full physical prompting can be unethical:

. . . in my two decades in the autism world, I've seen a lot of physical prompting that would definitely be considered physical restraint and a few instances where some would consider it even abusive. . . . if you're using physical prompting that's crossing over to restraint on a daily or weekly basis, you need to really evaluate what to do instead . . ..[76]

Unfortunately, this seem to be a minority concern within the ABA community.

In addition to prompting, ABA therapists can also use a client's likes and dislikes to encourage compliance with a demand. In fact, much of the preparatory work done before an autistic child begins therapy involves discovering her preferences. These can then be used in interventions—sometimes in perfectly reasonable, and sometimes in completely inappropriate ways. The most common way of shaping behavior in ABA is through positive reinforcement—giving the child something he or she likes as a reward for doing something the therapist wants. She might be given a small treat or allowed to watch a short video of her choice. Negative reinforcement, on the other hand, means that a child faces something unpleasant, which then goes away if he or she does what the therapist wants.

But where does the unpleasant stimulus come from? It might be something natural—hunger, fatigue, etc. When a child gets hungry, for example, a BT may legitimately keep a favorite snack out of reach, until a child uses a picture board to show which food he wants—as long as the child is allowed to have a less favored snack without using the board. Red flags arise when the BT deliberately creates or fosters a client's discomfort, and then prolongs it until there is compliance. It is simply wrong for the BT to keep ALL snacks out of reach, letting a child get hungrier and hungrier until he uses the picture board. It is wrong for a BT to open a window, letting winter air blow on a child until she "uses her words" to say she is cold. Such practices are not particularly unusual in today's ABA. But they are frankly unethical and represent infringements on the child's human rights.

The same is true of positive punishment, which has long been used in ABA. This is where something unpleasant—often deeply unpleasant—is added to the situation when a child fails to comply. Lovaas used loud shouting, face slaps, and even electric shocks to punish autistic children for what he considered undesirable behaviors. Over time practitioners moved towards methods less likely to cause open controversy, but still painful. Here is what a former behavior technician has to say about her work at an ABA center around 2010:

> When children consistently failed to perform or acted out, they might be punished. The idea was that this only happened as a "last resort"... Though in some classrooms that meant nothing. Punishments, or "aversive consequences" as they are called in the industry, could get creative. At this treatment center, we screamed "NO!" at children, sprayed water in their face, made them stand up and sit down repeatedly, put them in time outs, and used what are euphemistically called "taste aversions." . . . Vinegar was the most common, though we also used wasabi, cayenne pepper, and whatever else was found to be effective. I was told this was the only evidence based intervention available, and without it children would suffer more. I was told the brutality was necessary.[77]

Typically, ABA company advertising will say that the company never uses punishment. But it is simply a fact that aversives are still being used to punish autistic children today. I heard a story in the spring of 2020, directly from the behavior technician involved. A child was in therapy to help with toilet training, but since he was only three years old, he still had accidents fairly often. Whenever he had an accident, the supervisor said, the BT should make him walk ten times back and forth between the place he had the accident and the toilet, touching both soiled surfaces (which he very much disliked), while still wearing his wet pants. The company called this "negative reinforcement," which doesn't sound too bad. But "negative reinforcement" actually means the removal of an unpleasant stimulus as a reward for doing what is wanted. In reality, what they were doing was "positive punishment," that is, the imposition of an aversive (touching soiled surfaces) in order to reduce an unwanted behavior (toileting accidents). This is unethical—and it also doesn't work. A child will indeed learn from punishment, but not usually what the therapist wants. Punishment engenders fear and anger, not eagerness to do the expected task. Only a few weeks into therapy, the three-year-old described above had become terrified of the toilet and was even less willing to use it than before.

Adding an aversive to the situation is called "positive punishment." In contrast, "negative punishment" involves removing something a child likes. This is sometimes a perfectly reasonable intervention. For example, a child who purposely kicks a therapist should probably have to give up her favorite doll for a while. However, at the very beginning of therapy, some ABA companies will pre-emptively take something highly valued away from a child, in order to use it later as a reinforcer. "The child should not have free access to highly reinforcing items. If they do, what is their motivation to complete tasks or comply?" [78] In companies that act in this way, access to things children want, even things children really <u>need</u>, becomes contingent on their compliance with demands. I call this technique "kidnapping and holding for ransom." ABA literature does not recognize this as an acceptable procedure, yet it is sadly common in practice.

Some children have had their communication tools—their IPads or letter boards—withheld until they complied with directions. Youngsters have been denied access to their teddy bears at bedtime, until they have completed a mandated task a specified number of times.[79] This is not only cruel, but ineffective. It teaches children that (1) no one cares about their feelings; (2) therapists and even parents are their enemies; and (3) unthinking obedience is the only way to recover the things they love. To take something away from a child when they have done nothing wrong is clearly unethical.

The experience of "kidnapping and holding for ransom" can be incredibly traumatic to the child involved. One British teenager, for example, adored poetry. He was studying it voraciously in preparation for his university applications, just as he began to receive ABA therapy:

They then set up the reinforcers they would use. They took from me my phone. They instructed mum to bring to the next session every single one of my poetry books and not buy me any more. . . . When they said that I wouldn't be allowed to read poetry, I freaked the fuck out. I said I have to for uni applications, and they said "well you better behave then" and sent my mum out of the room so they could work with me. At this point, two other therapists came in, so there were 4 of them and 1 of me. They took from me the books mum had made me bring, the ones I had at my dads house for the holidays. This included my collection of Auden's poetry, which is my heart and soul, my Larkin, and my Ginsberg. My favourite poets. At this point I panicked. I started stimming like mad, rubbing my hands on the sides of my head to try to calm down and stop the buzzing in my mind that was coming from the panic of being separated from my sense of self. Mistake number 1. They told me to stop, and I didn't acknowledge them. Mistake no 2. They then took my hands, physically. This hurt, because I do not like physical contact with people I'm not comfortable with at the best of times so when I was having a meltdown, it felt like electric shocks. I screamed and started crying and shouting to not touch me, desperately trying to get my hands out of their grip. Mistake no 3. At this point, two of them had hold of me, one on each arm. When I tried to get away, the other two essentially wrestled me to the ground, forcing me to kneel then lie on my back. They restrained me like this, while I was crying and screaming and trying to get away.[80]

These therapists did not just take away this teenager's poetry books. They deprived him of his very "sense of self." No wonder he panicked.

Many autistic people feel traumatized by ABA while they are undergoing it. Some even claim to suffer from Post Traumatic Stress Disorder (PTSD) as a result of it. Ruti Regan describes her own childhood encounter with ABA in a blog post sarcastically entitled "Nice Lady Therapists":

Nice Lady Therapists tell us that, whatever they do to us is by definition nice, and good for us. And that we like it, and that they love us, and that they are rescuing us, and that we are grateful. . . . And every interaction with them is degrading in a way that's hard to pinpoint, and hard to recover from. They do all kinds of things to kids with disabilities that typically developing kids would never be expected to tolerate. And they do it with a smile, and expect the kids they're doing it to to smile back.[81]

Some autistic children find ABA so intolerable they will do anything to get away from it. This young man was in therapy in 2020:

The most recent ABA drop off was the most difficult, because not only was I dealing with school, I was dealing with other stressors. Mostly, I could not bear the idea that I would have to do this [ABA] until I was 18. I had a panic attack after my mom dropped me off, and I ran before entering the door to the clinic. The therapists who always wanted to "help" me chased after me, and I felt like I had no choice but to run into the middle of moving traffic. I could not work anymore for ABA, and that was what I kept repeating to myself in my aching head as I ran into evening traffic. I tried to run back to the sidewalk, but it was too late. I was hit by a car. The two behavior therapists who had been chasing me slowly backed away, and I watched them leave me there. That was definitely helpful. I went to the emergency room in an ambulance, feeling traumatized. After all, I got slammed on my side by a car and watched people who said they only want to "help" walk away.[82]

Autistics, already prone to anxiety disorders, appear to have a much stronger likelihood of developing PTSD than neurotypicals.[83] A recent study, based on data from 460 autistic respondents, found a link specifically between experience with ABA and subsequent PTSD. Among the conclusions of the study: "Respondents of all ages who were exposed to ABA were 86 percent more likely to meet the PTSD criteria than respondents who were not exposed to ABA."[84] And yet the "authorities" still recommend this as the best early intervention for young, vulnerable autistic children.

Recently, practitioners like BCBA Jo Ram have acknowledged that their practices do harm:

If we were to truly care about our field, our clients, and ourselves, we would work to address and end bad practices we KNOW exist in ABA, the exact practices our many clients and critics repeatedly bring to light.[85]

The Normalization Agenda

Imagine being told every day of your life that who you are is bad, shameful, and broken. Imagine that the people who love you the most and who are supposed to support you, your family, insist that you have to pretend to be someone else every day for the rest of your life.[86]

What, exactly, is ABA intended to accomplish? To be fair, most ABA companies target communication, which is indeed an essential skill. They often teach the names of colors, the sounds that farm animals make, and other things most toddlers learn. But in most programs, major goals include such things as toilet training and other hygiene issues, "mealtime related skills" (table manners), "greeting others," "following directions," "sharing," "time management" (i.e., meeting other people's scheduling expectations), etc.[87] These goals are aimed at making autistic children more socially acceptable to others, not necessarily more self-confident and productive in themselves. In short, most ABA practitioners still focus on making a child look more "normal."

At UCLA in the 1960s, where ABA for autistic children got its start, this was an explicit goal. Lovaas wanted the autistic children he worked with to look and act just like other children, and he punished their naturally autistic behaviors savagely. In a 1987 article still frequently cited today by ABA practitioners, Lovaas claimed that out of a group of autistic children who had been subjected to 40 hours/week of intensive behavioral interventions beginning at age 3 and continuing for years, 47% eventually became "indistinguishable from their normal friends."[88] (Notice that 53% did not become "indistinguishable"—we'll come back to them.) Since then, researchers have repeatedly failed to replicate Lovaas's findings. Recent research has shown that intensive intervention leads to only 25%, or even fewer, passing as normal.[89]

Lovaas's phrase was "indistinguishable from their normal friends." Today the more common formulation is "indistinguishable from their peers"—a phrase that still appears frequently in advertising for companies that offer ABA treatment.[90] But the key word has remained "indistinguishable." This is what practitioners and ABA researchers call the "optimal outcome"—and what I call the "normalization agenda." The goal is still to make autistic children look "normal," or at least "more normal than before," regardless of the cost to the child.[91]

Is being "indistinguishable" even an achievable goal? Bear in mind that in Lovaas's 1987 article, 53% of the children who had had intensive intervention for years still remained obviously autistic. Today, researchers would say the number is more like 75%, or even more. Only a minority of autistic people can ever learn to "pass" as normal. Most don't achieve this outcome, no matter how hard they try. Many, for example, never learn to speak—not out of stubbornness, or because they are stupid, but because their motor difficulties make it impossible for them to produce the necessary sounds. They can usually learn to communicate using word boards, or, increasingly, iPads. But they never manage to "speak normally." Others never learn to toilet in the ways our society expects—again, not because they are stupid or contrary or "dirty," but because their differences in interoception prevent them from feeling the "urge to go" until it is too late.[92] They may always need to wear adult diapers, which will always distinguish them from most neurotypicals, although it hardly prevents them from leading full and satisfying lives.

A young autistic man of my acquaintance has clearly been trained in how to greet people. Whenever he came into the room where our choir was practicing, he would go up to each person, grin broadly, shake hands, and say (a little more loudly than expected) "Hi! How are you?" Everyone else in the choir, on the other hand, just said "Hi" quietly as they arrived. His behavior was endearing. But it scarcely obscured his differences. He was one of the majority of autistic people who won't ever look "normal," even if they undergo therapy until the day they die. And there is nothing wrong with that. Why shouldn't my friend look autistic? Whose fault is it if someone so obviously well-meaning is not accepted by society? Clearly, the fault lies with society—not him.

The ABA normalization agenda raises a human rights issue that the legal profession has never addressed, to my knowledge. Do autistic people have the right simply to be autistic? If the answer is "yes," then further questions arise. Is it ethical to subject autistic children to many hours a week of exhausting therapy, over the course of years, with the explicit or implicit aim of making them appear "indistinguishable from their peers"? Is this ethical when it is actually impossible for most to achieve this goal, and when the experience can inflict deep, enduring, and incapacitating trauma even on those who can?

Here the ABA community will step in and say that I just don't understand. I'm talking about things that don't happen anymore, they no longer try to make children "indistinguishable from their peers," they are just teaching useful skills that everyone needs to learn. They say that they accept autistic children as who they are, that they would never try to suppress stimming, that they understand sensory issues, and so forth. And this may be true for some ABA companies. But even these enlightened companies still target behaviors that annoy, frustrate, or disgust neurotypical people, and sometimes at the expense of ignoring other, more important behaviors. Whose rights, invariably, come first?

"Recovery"

Through ABA or exhausting personal effort, some autistic people do manage to achieve a "normal" outward appearance. And this has sometimes been equated with "recovery" from autism.[93] In 2014, the *New York Times* published a story on "The Kids Who Beat Autism."[94] "Recovery" language is ubiquitous in the books and websites that tout "treatments." Current ABA industry advertising makes similar claims. One company asks potential clients: "Did you know that up to half of children diagnosed with autism can recover if they are treated very aggressively with ABA therapy when they are very young?"[95] Claims for recovery also occur in scientific papers focused on the small number of "recovered" autistic children. These are children who appear to have achieved the "optimal outcome," by becoming "indistinguishable from their peers." They can speak more or less as other people do and can engage in ordinary conversations. They are successful in mainstream classrooms. They have "typically develop-ing" friends. But the question remains: have they really "recovered"? Does their new behavior actually reflect a change in their experience of the world? Has ABA therapy, or any other form of intervention, af-fected the underlying neurology behind the observable symptoms of autism?[96]

The answer is: no one knows. Surprisingly few people have even tried to find out. [97] Given the plasticity of the human brain, especially early in life, it is quite possible that some interventions might alter autistic neurology, moving the young autistic brain towards a more typical structure and function. However, we just don't know whether today's interventions have that effect. Scientists have not performed the necessary studies. And teachers, therapists and parents are not in a position to report reliably on this subject. While they can observe normalized behaviors, they can't say what's going on in the heads of people whose behavior has been normalized. Only those whose behavior was not originally "normal" can speak to this.

Absent reliable tests based on extensive before-and-after-inter-vention brain scans, I went to the web for personal testimony from "normalized" autistic people. Do any of them say they are no longer autistic? In fact, very few do. After extensive searching, I have found only three first-hand accounts of "recovery" on the web. This suggests their relative rarity. In one video, a young man who went through the Lovaas program, as still practiced at UCLA, proudly declares that he has recovered from autism.[98] In another, a young woman also claims to have recovered—not because of intensive early intervention, but because of a "sensory enrichment program" she participated in during elementary school.[99] A third account makes no mention of therapy at all, but attributes recovery to prayer.[100] It may be that most sup-posedly recovered individuals are more interested in getting on with their lives than in recording their transformation. But it is also quite possible that what looks like "recovery" to parents, therapists, teachers and scientists represents only a shift in behavior—and no significant change in experience at all.

"Indistinguishable" But Still Autistic

No amount of torture disguised as therapy will make a neurodivergent child neurotypical.[101]

In contrast, it is extremely easy to find first-hand accounts written by adults who say they have learned to act normally or "neurotypically," even though their neurology has remained autistic. They identify themselves as autistic and engage with the online autism community. What they report is not "recovery." On the contrary, they say that ABA taught them to stop doing what comes naturally to them. After extensive intervention, they now engage in behaviors they find unnatural or even unpleasant. They have managed to suppress their stereotypic or self-stimulatory behaviors (what the autistic community calls "stims"—hand-flapping, rocking, stroking particular textures, etc.), even though they still want and need to use them. (Usually these people stim in private, when no one is watching.) They have learned to endure the painful process of looking people in the eye. They know how to "use their words," even though words fail to adequately express what exists in their imagination. They have memorized a large number of scripts that they can rapidly scroll through and then employ in casual conversation. In other words, while still neurologically autistic, they can "pass" or "mask" as normal. And many of them see intensive early intervention, and specifically ABA, as their introduction to such "masking."[102] Some autistics distinguish between "camouflaging" (simply remaining inconspicuous or invisible) and "masking" (hiding autism traits when camouflaging is not possible).[103] In the writings of autistic adults, both activists and non-activists, "passing," "masking," or "camouflaging" are all shorthand for "still autistic, but sometimes able to appear indistinguishable." Or, to put it slightly differently, "Masking is what we do to keep us safe."[104]

But masking never becomes natural to autistics. Even after many years of practice, starting in childhood, it takes a lot of skill and effort for an autistic person to pass as neurotypical. It requires

> enormous self control. Focus on identifiable social signals (like a deaf person can learn to read lips if they look at someone speaking). High efficiency in processing information. . . . And great motivation to put all the effort into it and to suffer in silence.[105]

An educational consultant and well-known speaker on autism, Judy Endow, writes a blog called *Aspects of Autism Translated*. An older woman, she did not have early intervention available to her when she was young—instead her family committed her to a psychiatric institution. Judy taught herself social skills to escape institutionalization, to escape poverty and homelessness in her early adulthood, to learn to raise her own autistic kids, to obtain college and graduate degrees, and finally to establish a satisfying career. She learned to "pass" as normal because she had to, and she points out in her blog the many ways passing has been useful to her and others. But like most other autistic writers—and unlike most scientists and professionals—she also recognizes that passing has a high cost for those whose neurology remains autistic:

> *I know in the field of autism we have made it our goal to get autistics to look neurotypical . . . Many people congratulate themselves when it happens. I am here to tell you . . . that this may NOT wind up to be a good thing for autistic people.*[106]

The Costs of Normalization

But why not? What's wrong with learning to act "normal"? What happens when very young children (as young as 2 or 3) spend many hours a week being taught to act in socially acceptable ways? They learn that their natural instincts and behaviors are all wrong. Why else would adults spend so much time trying to fix them?

> . . . intensive ABA therapy will . . . teach a child that there is something fundamentally wrong and unacceptable about who they are. Not only is that child trained to look normal, they are trained to hate who they are inside. They are trained to hate who they are and hide who they are. . . . All those years of ABA therapy will have taught them that they are fundamentally wrong and broken.[107]

One autistic participant in a reseach study was asked why they still strove to appear normal in adulthood. "A lifetime of conditioning," they responded. They went on to say, "not being normal was bad as a child and now it seems impossible to turn [masking] off."[108] This is the unspoken message of the intervention itself, which the autistic child will learn alongside eye contact, the names of colors, and the value of sharing, unless the therapist and the parents involved take great care to counteract it. Sadly, however, far too many parents, desperate for their child to be "normal," actually reinforce the message. Here is Larkin Taylor-Parker, now a young adult, describing their fairly recent experiences:

> Learning to pass took me years of practice with a special method: every time my family went out in public when I was a child, the ride home was a lecture on my failings. I was upbraided for gait, demeanor, eye contact, manner and content of speech. The reward for perfect success was a moment of rare parental affection.[109]

Even after early intervention comes to an end, American society constantly tells autistic people they have a shameful defect. At school, the vast majority of autistic children are mocked and bullied for being "weird." Adults continually absorb negative public messages. The infamous Autism Speaks campaign from 2009, called "I am Autism", made it clear to older autistics that they were to blame for publicly humiliating their relatives, bankrupting their families, and breaking up their parents' marriages. Autism Speaks has removed that video from its website, but similar messages still circulate widely even today. Advertising depicts autistic people as "burdens" to their families and to society. Publicity campaigns and public events focus on "preventing" and "curing" autism—that is, at making autistic people disappear from our society—rather than on helping people with autism live successful and happy lives.

As Jocelyn Eastman, who writes the *Art of Autism* blog, puts it:

> We are portrayed as broken and as needing to be cured. We have had people tell us to our faces that they would rather have a child die of a preventable disease than to have their child become autistic. We have had people tell us that they can't wait for prenatal testing so that people like us can be aborted, and that we won't have to be burdens anymore. All the while, we are expected to accept that others feelings about autistic people are acceptable and understandable. . . "[110]

Internalized shame—born of such messages and usually accompanied by fear of exposure—burdens even adults who have learned to behave "normally." Such fear sets in at a very early age: "Being aware of the dissimilarities between me and my peers didn't make things any easier," writes Nicole Wildhood. "The awareness made me hyper-vigilant about appearing 'normal,' and so all the more anxious. By age 5, I had begun a high-level construction project, creating a new outward-facing version of myself to fit with the social norms I perceived."[111]

For a variety of reasons, people with autism suffer significantly from anxiety. For those who can sometimes "pass" as normal, pressure to "maintain the act" becomes a major source of anxiety.[112] Can you ever tell anyone who you really are? Disclosure may lead to greater understanding and acceptance. It may lead to greater accommodations at school or work. But it is equally likely to lead to rejection. Autistic adults who can sometimes appear neurotypical constantly agonize about whether they should reveal their autism to those around them.[113] The very prospect of disclosure heightens existing feelings of shame. And this, in turn, skews the decision-making process: "I never tell anybody. I'm too ashamed of it."[114]

Improving Early Intervention

Challenging the autism-ABA industry's ethics requires that autistics are seen as human beings with human rights. We do not live in a society that acknowledges this. We are in a society in which autistics have rights only if and when we resemble non-autistics.[115]

We could be doing things to prevent the outcomes described above. First, and most importantly, we need not autism awareness, but autism <u>acceptance</u>. And for acceptance to find a home in America, autistic children must be allowed to be both autistic and children. Their own idiosyncratic ways of doing things, such as playing or dressing themselves, must be respected and encouraged. Their sensory issues must be recognized and accommodated. Their ways of learning (which will vary from one autistic child to another) must be consulted in designing interventions for them. They should never, ever, be punished for stimming, for reacting to sensory or emotional stimuli, or for appearing autistic— "indistinguishability" is not an acceptable goal. Like other children, autistic children must be given plenty of time to play and learn independently. And like other children, they must be given the right to say "no" when faced with something harmful to them.

My goal in this chapter is not to reject the skills, knowledge, and dedication of well-meaning BCBAs and BTs. It is to argue that ABA (and other early interventions) must be put to much better uses, in more ethical ways, than it is in the vast majority of practices today. What might a skilled and ethical ABA have to offer? It could encourage children's natural behaviors, while teaching additional ones, so that the child is reassured that the way she naturally behaves is good—that she herself is inherently good—strengthening her against the damaging narrative she will hear for the rest of her life that she is defective and bad. It would avoid forcing eye contact on young children. Yet when they are old enough to understand, it could also help them learn what a social convention is, that eye contact is a social convention in our society, and then teach them some effective ways to fake eye contact, in ways that won't cause them pain. A better ABA might target self-harming behaviors by identifying, and then helping a child identify for himself the "antecedents" or triggers, for his behaviors. It would then teach him how to avoid these triggers, and if the triggers do occur, how to react in a more benign manner. It might even honor the reality of meltdowns (as opposed to tantrums), help a child learn to recognize the warning signs and teach calming techniques to help head them off.

Although many autistics will disagree with me, I believe ABA is redeemable.[116] In the future, I hope more ABA practitioners will learn to use their powers for good, and not just for profit. In the meantime, parents of young children with autism must be made aware that ABA is not essential. Other scientifically validated treatments are also available. Occupational therapy can help address sensory challenges. Autistic children can learn to communicate through speech therapy.

And if communication remains an issue, assistive technology can be tremendously helpful. The idea that 40 hours a week of ABA is the only way an autistic child can ever be successful has simply cost too many lives.

CHAPTER FOUR

Education?

*"What I saw in those classrooms, that's what really
radicalized me."*[1]

T oday, more autistic children than ever are being served by the American public school system. They are entitled, by the Individuals with Disabilities Education Act (IDEA) of 1990, to a "free, appropriate, public education" (FAPE) provided in the "least restrictive environment" (LRE) possible.[2] By law, their teachers should be "highly qualified," and should use scientifically validated instructional methods in the classroom. If needed, autistic students are entitled by law to privileges like preferred seating, written instructions for assignments, and extended time on exams. These accommodations can sometimes be provided informally through a 504 process,[3] or more formally through the Individualized Educational Program (IEP) process.[4] However, in education as in other areas of life, a significant gap always exists between what the law requires and what actually happens.

The Challenge of Low Expectations

Suppose an autistic child has been appropriately diagnosed and has been offered special services at school, whether through an IEP or a 504 process. The next problem is the faulty assumptions educators make about such children. By far the most damaging is the belief that autism equals low intelligence. We have already seen that autistic intelligence cannot reliably be assessed through standard IQ tests. We also know that the ability to speak (expressive language) tells us nothing about intelligence; usually it only reflects levels of motor control. Nevertheless, schools continue to assign meaningless labels to autistic students, based on IQ testing, speaking ability, and "life skills." Those labelled "low-functioning" are assumed to be intellectually disabled. Even those identified as "high-functioning" are often perceived as stupid.

Like most Americans, educators tend to assume that someone not toilet trained or able to conduct a "normal" conversation cannot possibly succeed in a challenging academic environment. Hence the ridiculously low academic goals written into many IEPs (see below). Functioning labels are completely unreliable predictors of academic success, though. An autistic middle school student may be perfectly capable of reading and enjoying *The Hobbit,* and yet still need diapers.[5] An autistic high school student may ace a test on *Macbeth*, yet need help tying his shoes.[6] Baffled by autistic deviation from "normal" developmental patterns, teachers struggle to judge what level of instruction is suitable for their pupils. Sadly, the tendency is still almost always to underestimate.

Unless they can effectively mask as "normal," autistic students are usually seen as "dumb." Well into the 2000s, educational research on autistic students continued to focus almost exclusively on ways to teach them functional life skills.[7] An influential book published by the National Research Council in 2001 devoted a grand total of two pages (out of 229) to teaching academics.[8] Even the most recent books on teaching autistic kids still tend to dismiss their academic learning needs.

The fate of "low-functioning" children is to be shunted off into special education classrooms. These provide very little in the way of academics.[9] Emma Zurcher writes:

> In New York City kids like me are not attending mainstream schools because we are believed to be unable to learn complex subject matter. I was sent to both public and private special education schools, specifically created for speaking and non-speaking autistic students and those believed to have emotional issues. Because I cannot voice my thoughts and so rely on favorite scripts, my spoken language causes people to assume my thinking is simple, I am unable to pay attention and cannot comprehend most of what is said to me. As a result, none of these schools presumed that I, or the other students, were competent and their curricula reflected this.[10]

Now in high school, Philip Reyes reports that his teachers "were well meaning but believed I could not understand much of anything because I could not talk or write to communicate that I was smart and understood everything going on around me." Instead, Philip says, he was trained like an animal in school, "as everyone tried to make me act normally with candy rewards."[11] In other words, his teachers focused primarily on his behavior. Eventually Philip learned to communicate through typing, developed his own blog, and in 2020 began learning to hand-write, even though he still struggles with poor motor control.[12]

Children end up in special education for many reasons, often behavioral reasons that have nothing to do with their ability to learn. Bright children may spend years in these classes hearing basic arithmetic facts or the names of colors repeated over and over, learning nothing substantial that might help them later as either workers or citizens. Ido Kedar, another non-speaking autistic, endured this kind of non-teaching in his early years. He fiercely criticizes the thinking behind these practices:

> The assumption that people with severe autism all have impaired thinking has resulted in the underestimating of the true abilities of thousands of individuals, lack of adequate educational opportunities, isolation, loneliness, boredom, frustration, hopelessness, and a life of entrapment within one's own body. This price is too high.[13]

Perhaps there are good reasons why a child should be in a special education classroom, but that doesn't mean it cannot challenge him intellectually. Certainly, one focus should be teaching functional skills, but students should also have access to a range of books (including audiobooks), videos, apps, and other educational materials. This would give them a chance to learn some academic material as well, perhaps with the help of aides.

The problem of low expectations extends to the "high-functioning" kids who sit side by side with neurotypical children in mainstream classrooms. Under IDEA, every student identified as having special needs must be provided an IEP (Individual Education Plan), which spells out her or his yearly goals. For kids in most other disability groups, academic goals are a regular part of IEPs. However, in a 2010 study, academic goals (learning to read certain kinds of text, learning to solve certain types of math problems, learning to understand certain scientific facts) made up only a small fraction—at most, about 11%--of the goals in autistic students' IEPs.[14] Another study, from 2014, found that only 56% of the IEPs for autistic students in mainstream classes contained any academic skills at all. And when they did, the academic goals were often significantly below the student's grade level.[15]

A decision reached by the U.S. Supreme Court in 2017 may eventually help autistic kids receive a better education. In *Endrew F. v Douglas*

County School District, the issue was what constitutes FAPE—the "free, appropriate, public education" guaranteed to disabled kids since the passage of the Education for All Handicapped Children Act in 1975. Did a school merely have to provide a program with "some educational benefits" for the child? Or was it legally required to offer something with "meaningful" educational benefits? A child's "educational program must be appropriately ambitious in light of his circumstances," the Supreme Court ruled. "An IEP for a child fully integrated in a 'regular' classroom should aim to enable the child to make progress, 'to achieve passing grades and advance from grade to grade.'" The IEP need not aim for grade-level advancement "if that is not a reasonable prospect." Nevertheless, it must be "appropriately ambitious" for the child involved and must "provide the chance to meet challenging objectives."[16] Regardless of their individual abilities, the opportunity to meet such challenges is surely something all autistic kids deserve.

Individual Differences and Shifting Abilities over Time

Only very recently have education researchers begun to explore approaches to academic instruction for autistic students. And only very slowly are undergraduates in colleges of education being exposed to the results. The now widely used *"You're Going to Love This Kid!" Teaching Students with Autism in the Inclusive Classroom*, by Paula Kluth, offers thoughtful advice to aspiring teachers, including ways to respect their students' sensitivities, provide them with support for transitions, and encourage peer relationships. It even includes a separate chapter on teaching literacy (although nothing on teaching mathematics, science or history). Statements by "really autistic" students are included to support her points, and Kluth encourages readers to always "presume competence." Kluth recognizes the intelligence of the students her audience will be working with.[17] Yet even this excellent book occasionally misses the mark.

First of all, it does not sufficiently emphasize the fact that <u>every single autistic student is different</u>. As we have already seen, a huge range of "autisms" exists. Autistic children differ among themselves, perhaps even more than neurotypical children do. Some are highly vocal and may have strong academic skills in reading, but struggle in math.[18] Others may have limited speech, but still be capable of average or above average work in science. Some non-speaking autistic children may experience only limited academic success, while others have the potential to complete AP courses and move on to college. Successful teachers of autistic children must therefore be willing to devote time, energy, and creativity to discovering the best way to reach each individual student.

Teachers must also realize that any one autistic student's intellectual and emotional abilities can vary tremendously from day to day and from year to year, depending on stressors of which instructors may not even be aware. A student who welcomes and successfully deals with difficult math problems on a good day, may reject engaging with similar problems on a day when her schedule has unexpectedly changed (a source of great anxiety). Abilities and sensitivities can shift dramatically when a child is going through puberty, or transitioning from middle school to high school. Teachers who fail to recognize these variations—not in inherent ability, but in adaptation to changing circumstances—may lower their expectations out of sheer frustration. This hurts students. Teaching autistic children well requires recognition of shifting abilities, tremendous personal flexibility, and imagination. Those who can do so enthusiastically should be honored for their efforts.

Sensory Issues

A kaleidoscope of shape and blinding lighting, with vague outlines which are probably other students. Deafening noise. The stench of different smells. The confusion of many voices, including some heard through walls from neighbouring halls and classes. School uniform that feels like barbed wire on my skin.[19]

In an excellent chapter, Paula Kluth talks about the sensory challenges autistic students face, not only in the classroom, but in school hallways, lunchrooms, gyms, and playgrounds. Those who are hypersensitive may find fluorescent lights overly bright and disorienting, the sound of clanging lockers and trampling feet during class change painfully overwhelming, and the smells of cafeteria and gym gag-inducing.[20] These kids may scream out loud, clap their hands over their eyes or ears, vomit, or resort to rocking or head-banging to distract themselves from the pain. Sometimes neurotypical adults expect kids to "just get used to" sensory stressors. This isn't going to happen. If you don't believe me, imagine this. Someone hitting you hard on the forehead with a hammer demands that you "just get used to it." Would that work for you? So why demand this of young children facing sensory onslaughts in school?

By the same token, some autistic students suffer because they don't get enough sensory stimulation in school. Hyposensitive children often get into trouble for "inappropriate behavior" directly related to their sensory needs. In the absence of vestibular stimulation, some feel dizzy and disoriented—these are the kids you'll find swinging furiously or twirling around and around in place during recess. Sometimes they may also be attacked by dizziness in the classroom. Then they must choose between just falling out of their seats or standing up and twirling, despite the teacher's objections. Others, lacking sufficient proprioceptive feedback, experience the terrifying sensation of losing the location of their body in space. An exceptionally gifted autistic educational consultant, Judy Endow, describes a child she once worked with who would "pitch a fit," as his teachers put it, whenever he left the classroom with the other students. He'd throw himself to the floor, yelling "No, no, no!" But if a teacher helped him get up, he would immediately settle down and move on quietly. To his teachers, this looked like willful, manipulative behavior. But after Judy worked with him for a while, she discovered his unreliable proprioceptive sense left him panicked when he lost track of where his body was in space. Leaving the classroom, moving from one space to another, with other students simultaneously moving all around him, and lighting shifting between rooms made him feel disembodied and floating. During transitions, he fell down in order to get some reassuring physical pressure from the floor. A teacher who held his hand and pulled him to his feet, however, provided enough proprioceptive input to calm him down. This was not a troublemaker, but a child trying to cope with insufficient sensory input.[21] Those who work with autistic students must be very conscious of their sensory issues. Overload can be removed and needed input provided without disrupting the class. But of course this takes awareness, foresight, and considerable flexibility.

Perceptual Issues

Countless autistic students struggle with perceptual issues that directly affect learning, yet very few teachers are aware of this.[22] If students can't make sense of what they hear or see in the classroom, they will inevitably fail in school, regardless of how bright they are. Many autistic students have difficulties with auditory processing, for example.[23] It may take them a fraction of a second longer than neurotypical students to turn spoken sounds into intelligible speech. Constantly playing "catch-up" with the rest of the class, they may fall far behind. They may also have trouble distinguishing significant sounds from background noise. Such students struggle to follow a lecture or video, or comply with their teacher's spoken demands. Group work is especially hard. It may feel impossible to focus on what people in the group are saying, while ignoring other sounds and conversations filling the classroom. (Viewed as a form of "active learning," group work has become central to U.S. education; unfortunately many autistic students find it massively frustrating.)

Work-arounds exist for auditory processing issues. Special seating near the front of the classroom, close-captioning for videos, the provision of both spoken and written instructions, exemption from group work, can all help. But the instructor has to be aware of the problem first. Many a well-meaning teacher has insisted on a phonics-based approach to reading for a child with poor auditory processing skills, only to provoke frustration, even a meltdown. For such a student, a "whole-word" approach might work much better. [24]

Other autistic kids have trouble with visual processing.[25] They may be able to see clearly only with peripheral vision, forcing them to look at their teachers with their heads turned sideways.[26] The teacher's insistence that the student "look at me"—meaning "turn your face towards me"—actually ensures that the student won't see the teacher. Also common among autistic kids is "Meares-Irlen," "Scotopic Sensitivity," or "Visual Stress" syndrome. In this syndrome, letters, words and numbers appear to float around on the pages of a book or on a classroom whiteboard, making reading almost impossible.[27] Tests using scantron sheets ("fill in the circle" answer sheets) can present a total disaster. Even if she can read the test itself, she may go to the wrong column or row of the answer sheet when filling in circles.

Thanks to this syndrome, my daughter on the spectrum got stuck in math limbo while she was a university undergraduate. Even though she is good at math (not a prodigy, but way better than average), it took her years to fulfil the statistics requirement for her college major. She had already taken (and gotten an "A" in) statistics at our local community college while still in high school. She moved on to college, and the university gave her credit for that course. But her major department wouldn't accept it. She had to take their own statistics course to fulfill the major's requirements. But before she could take that course, she needed to either get a high enough score on the math portion of the ACT or pass the university's own placement exam, to show she understood the fundamentals of math. Her visual processing issues made both options impossible.

It takes my daughter forever to do math problems using her unique color-coding system (see below); plus, she can't really see scantron sheets well enough to complete them accurately. So her math score on the ACT was too low. Now she faced the university's placement exam. But the exam was available only on the university's computer, which meant she had no way to compensate for her visual problems. After three unsuccessful tries on the computer, she eventually took a remedial math course, which allowed her to take the fundamentals course, which then allowed her to take the department's statistics course. Basically the same one she had already passed in community college two years earlier. Autistic students in public schools face the same kind of roadblocks to progress all the time. They shouldn't have to.

Colored overlays or tinted glasses can sometimes help students affected by this syndrome.[28] Other workarounds are also available. For example, an Ipad with a font size large enough to display only a single line of text on the screen can make reading much easier. Some kids find their own ways of dealing with visual problems. In high school, my daughter developed her own (admittedly, very time-consuming) system of writing out math problems using different colored pencils for different rows or columns. The colors helped her keep numbers in their proper places, eventually leading—yes—to her completing the statistics requirement for her college major.

Teachers have to recognize what the problem is before they can help their pupils effectively. Every school district's plan for working with autistic children should include screening for auditory and visual processing. Having accurate information on these impairments is essential for student and teacher success.

Placement: Where Do Autistic Students Learn Best?

By law, students with autism are entitled to a free, appropriate, public education in the "least restrictive environment" that is "appropriate" for them. But what, exactly, is "appropriate"? What works for one will not necessarily work for other autistic students. Unfortunately, other factors—entirely irrelevant from an educational standpoint—can also determine where students are placed. Individual state policies and finances, for instance, may make as much difference in determining placement as a student's abilities and potential.[29] For that matter, so do the policies of individual school districts. In 2020, I was involved in negotiating the placement of a four-year-old disabled child. Over the course of the negotiations, it became clear that his school district automatically placed any student with an IEP for any disability in a separate special education classroom. This is flagrantly illegal under IDEA, yet they did it without hesitation. How many other districts do the same?

Theoretically, the gold standard, the "least restrictive" of all educational environments, is the full-day, mainstream classroom. However, the "mainstreaming" of autistic students continues to inspire explosive debates at school board meetings and legislative sessions, in newspapers and law courts, on Twitter feeds, and even at family gatherings. At the core of these debates is the issue of autistic behaviors. Should autistic students be included, or will they inevitably be disruptive to other students? More and more parents, teachers and school administrators are championing inclusion whenever possible. But others remain vehemently opposed. They claim the presence of autistic students, in particular, prevents other students from getting an education. Sometimes these complaints are justified. More often, I would argue, they are not.

A 1994 memorandum from the federal Office of Special Education rationalizes the removal of disruptive children from inclusive educational settings:

> If a student with a disability has behavioral problems that are so disruptive in a regular classroom that the education of other students is significantly impaired, the needs of the disabled student cannot be met in that environment. However, before making such a determination, school districts must ensure that consideration has been given to the full range of supplementary aids and services that could be provided to the student in the regular educational environment to accommodate the unique needs of the disabled student. If the placement team determines that even with the provision of supplementary aids and services, that student's IEP could not be implemented satisfactorily in the regular educational environment, that placement would not be the LRE placement for that student at the particular time, because her or his unique educational needs could not be met in that setting. [30]

An amended IDEA strengthened school districts' rights to discipline children with disabilities in 1997--especially if they behaved threateningly or used drugs, but also just for being disruptive. At the same time, it provided for interventions directed at lessening or entirely preventing disruptive behaviors, so that a child could remain in the general education classroom.[31]

During the late 1990s, public debates and in-school struggles over classroom management placed the behavior of children with disabilities under special scrutiny. In 2000, newly elected Senator Jeff Sessions of Alabama (later Attorney General of the United States) attributed the decline of "civility" in public schools to the disruptions caused by disabled children. In a speech on the senate floor, he cited a letter from an Alabama educator:

> There is no telling how many instructional hours are lost by teachers in dealing with behavior problems. In times of an increasingly competitive global society it is no wonder American students fall short. Certain children are allowed to remain in the classroom robbing the other children of hours that can never be replaced.

Sessions added his own comment:

> I think these teachers make a point. It is a matter we need to give careful consideration to, not overreact, not undermine the great principles of the Disabilities Act Program. But at the same time, we need to say that a child is not allowed to commit crimes, to disrupt classroom, to curse teachers, principals and students, and abuse them and do so with impunity. [32]

The fight over full inclusion continues today. Clearly mainstreaming offers autistic children their best chance to achieve independence and success as adults. In every other setting (except, under some circumstances, homeschooling), exposure to information is much more limited and future options restricted. Even when they excel at teaching functional living and social skills, few segregated special education classes or separate "autism schools" offer any real academics. That's why parents who believe their autistic kids capable of academic achievement will fight like grizzly bears to keep them in mainstream classrooms.[33] And many of these mainstreamed kids do successfully move on towards graduation.

The End Game

The Individuals with Disabilities Education Act assumed that students with disabilities would probably not finish school on the same timetable as other students. So, kids with disabilities can keep their place in school and their accommodations through age 21. But what happens to them at the end of that time? The National Center for Education Statistics looked at students aged 14 through 21 who were being provided with services through IDEA in academic years 2019-21 (the last years for which we have full data.) The Center found that 2-3% of students with autism stayed in school until they "aged out" of the system at 21. They didn't graduate at that point: they just left.

Others got the "cheap pass" out. In 2019-2021, roughly 20% of autistics—those who had spent their time in segregated special education classrooms or separate schools—left with "certificates of completion" or "certificates of attendance."[34] Such certificates provide proof that a student has spent twelve (sometimes more) years at school but say nothing at all about what was learned in those years. They have no benefits in the real world. Most employers will only hire someone with a real high school diploma or a GED. Some community colleges, in some parts of the country, will admit someone with a special certificate; the vast majority of colleges and universities will not.[35] Even the armed forces require a diploma or a GED before they admit someone to their ranks—a certificate of completion doesn't count.

American schools issued 8,076 certificates of completion to students with autism in 2021. In my view, this is an admission of failure, an admission that 8,076 kids were cheated out of a real education. Of course, a few students genuinely cannot do the required work—they have a very severe intellectual disability or medical problems that get in their way.[36] But in many cases autistic students don't graduate with regular diplomas because for years their schools have assumed that they can't succeed and treated them accordingly.

There was a period of time five or six years ago when the narrative was that I would never graduate from high school. In fact, school counselors and therapists (supposedly people who were supposed to be on my side) explicitly said this several times.[37]

According to one special education teacher,

> I had a former administrator tell me a student didn't matter because his family would take care of him after graduation and to focus all my attention and resources on another student who, she said, actually had a chance of being fully independent. I basically ignored her. They are now both working in the community with support.[38]

The kids who "don't matter," the kids who were "never expected to graduate" deserve better from our schools. In Washington, DC, Tyrone C.'s high school placed him in a track that would have led to a "special certificate," but Tyrone's mother "turned grizzly" on the school, got him back on the regular track, and he finally graduated alongside the rest of his class with a regular diploma.[39]

In 2019-2021, about 6% of autistic students dropped out.[40] This is higher than the percentage of dropouts among all high school students (4-5%), but lower than the percentage of all students with disabilities who drop out (13%).[41] Students in general drop out of school for a complex set of reasons. Socio-economic status (SES) plays a huge role—not only are lower-income students more likely to drop out of school, but lower-income students in areas with more income inequality and little social mobility are especially likely to drop out— presumably because they see such limited opportunities available to them that they believe a high school diploma will be of little use.[42] Race certainly plays a role, although some researchers have concluded that if SES is accounted for, most of the racial differences in dropout rates disappear.[43] Sex also plays a role, with more males dropping out than females.[44] Family status, peer bullying or gang membership, homelessness, physical and mental health issues: all affect dropout rates. All of these factors probably play a role for autistic students, but no one has really studied why they leave school without their diplomas.

One recent study has found that school engagement and environment play an outsized role in adolescents' ultimate decision to abandon high school. This study distinguishes between overall stressors that would predispose a kid to drop out, and the "turning point" when he or she finally makes the decision to go. Students often give up when they no longer see school as relevant to their lives, when they are bored for too long, when they are failing too many classes or being held back repeatedly, or—importantly—when they don't think anybody cares whether they attend or not.[45] As we shall see, the belief that someone cares has helped many autistic students overcome obstacles and make it through.

And finally, there are the 72% of autistic students who, after years of struggle and against all odds, manage to graduate with a regular high school diploma.[46] In America, having that diploma is an important first step towards getting into college, finding a better job, and earning higher wages. Without a diploma, the chances of being unemployed,[47] homeless,[48] and involved in the criminal justice system increase.[49] While the interactions between education, health, and overall quality of life are complex, people without high school diplomas are more likely to lack health insurance, and generally face poorer health outcomes, ranging from increased problems with alcoholism and drug abuse, to heart disease, cancer, and suicidality.[50] A handful of autistic people with special talents, such as John Elder Robison or Dawn Prince-Hughes, have managed to succeed in life without a diploma. But the outlook for most non-graduates is grim. So, getting that diploma has important, concrete, long-term benefits. Whether it benefits autistic as much as neurotypical graduates remains to be seen.[51]

Does Anybody Care?

My history teacher told me she knew l could do better. My art teacher told me he would expect me to be a commercial artist out of the entire class. And my drama teacher was very support-ive. If it wasn't for these great teachers, l am not sure what would have happened. That's why it's important to encourage younger kids and to be supportive because it's something a lot don't get from parents, teachers, peers. [52]

Educators' low expectations of their autistic students are very often unjustified.

When I was four years old, my parents were told that I would never make it to high school and that I would always require special needs. I managed to struggle through high school, grad-uate and get accepted into college.[53]

A group of researchers recently interviewed almost 250 autistic high school students about their experiences at school. The study reveals that most of these students found school harrowing, dark with bully-ing, feelings of isolation and loneliness, trouble with self-regulation, and—especially for female students—the constant stress of masking. These students said they had received what they considered inade-quate support in their academic struggles:

When asked about how teachers could have offered better dis-ability-related support, responses included providing more help, showing more care about students' welfare, providing more tar-geted instructional strategies and learning accommodations, providing personal attention, and by relying on valid knowledge

about ASD in their work with students, as opposed to reliance
on stereotypes.

Surprisingly, most of the students found teachers a positive force in
their high school experiences. But they also stressed that many teachers were not doing enough, that teachers needed to show them "empathy, kindness, and respect." What they really wanted, they said, were
teachers who cared about them. [54]

Teacher concern is especially important to autistic students. Even a
tiny dose of kindness, a smidgen of respect, or a smile goes a long way
for those going through hell at school. Autistic students may not always
be able to communicate their appreciation in the moment. But long
afterwards they remember how good teachers touched their lives:

> Just the nicest guy, and the sort that you could talk to about any-
> thing. A lot of other teachers would just sort of ignore whenever
> I was having some screwy sensory issue . . . but he'd hear me out
> and try to help.[55]

> Mrs R, in high school who encouraged me in every class. You
> were a great teacher![56]

Aware of what a difference teachers can make, a small but growing number of autistic young people have entered teaching themselves. Cassandra Crosman is currently a graduate student in Special
Education:

> I want to be someone who empowers neurodiverse and disabled
> people. I want to help students reach their goals and teach them
> how to advocate for themselves. Students do not need to fear
> going to school. Students do not need strict compliance or to
> be secluded from their peers or restrained when teachers don't

know how to handle meltdowns. Students need a teacher that will understand and accept them, and I want to be that teacher for neurodiverse and disabled students.[57]

The educational establishment can learn so much from students like Cassandra.

CHAPTER FIVE

School Discipline

Please, please, please open the door. Please, I'll be good.
Open the door and I'll be quiet.[1]

I n November 2018, Alex Campbell, 13 years old and autistic, travelled from his home state of Virginia to Washington, D.C. There he spoke to congressional staffers and disability activists about being physically restrained and secluded in his elementary school. A seasoned advocate, Alex started talking to Virginia legislators about these abusive practices at the ripe old age of ten. The trip to Washington in 2018 was his second visit with federal legislators and staffers. Alex plans to be a civil rights lawyer when he grows up.

But back when he was only seven, Alex attended a private elementary school for children with disabilities. What he remembers is being repeatedly dragged from his classroom to the school's "crisis room," a converted storage closet with black-painted walls and a tiny window. The teacher or administrator who took him there would shove a heavy desk against the door so it couldn't open, and then leave him alone, confused and terrified. "When I asked for help or asked if anyone was still there, nobody would answer," Alex said. "I felt alone. I felt scared."[2] At that time, Virginia didn't require private schools to inform parents if their children were restrained or secluded. And in fact, Alex's principal threatened to shut him in the "crisis room" for the rest of the year if he said anything to his parents. But his mother and father noticed their son's unexplained bruises and his growing anxiety. Eventually, he broke down and told them what was going on.

Sadly, stories like this are far from unusual. Every year thousands and thousands of autistic children are manhandled, dragged around, handcuffed, and locked up. Thousands more are suspended from their classrooms and even expelled from their schools. Why does this happen? Because teachers and administrators don't understand autistic "behaviors." Because they find such behaviors alarming and too often use inappropriate methods to try to stop them. Here's what they are so worried about.

Making Noise

I have what's called "cough-variant" asthma—instead of wheezing when I have an asthma attack, I cough. When I was a child, my asthma went undiagnosed and untreated, I lived with two chain-smoking parents, and as a result, I did a LOT of coughing. Sometimes it was just intermittent mild barking. But when I got sick, my cough became an almost constant, deep-chested, disgustingly gooey hacking that went on for weeks. I might cough all day at school, seldom stopping except to gasp for breath. In retrospect, I am sure my coughing regularly distracted and annoyed other classmates. Indeed, "Suzie" once indignantly informed me that my coughing had made her do badly on a test. But no one ever complained to the teacher or the school administration, and no teacher ever even mentioned it to me. I never got in trouble for all the noise I was making. I was a White, middle-class, neurotypical child, so no one questioned my motives. If they thought about it at all, they probably assumed—quite correctly—that the coughing was beyond my control.

A significant proportion of autistic students engage in

vocalizations—making random sounds or repeating words or phrases to themselves. Others may tap on their desks with pencils or their fingers, as a form of stimming. Typically, these activities are beyond their conscious control, just as my coughing was. Yet these students seldom enjoy the tolerance I did. Autistic noisemaking tends to be seen as deliberately "disruptive." Students, teachers, and administrators get angry, insisting these kids are doing it "on purpose," and could "stop if they wanted to." Most of the time, though, these students don't even realize they're making noise. Once confronted, they may obediently stop for a while, and then unconsciously start up again. Or they may become agitated and do whatever they have been told to stop doing even more. Now they are labelled "defiant."

In real life, classrooms are almost never quiet, peaceful places. Teaching is constantly being "disrupted" by noises outside the school (garbage trucks, distant sirens, kids laughing and yelling on the playground), inside (squeaky shoes in the hallway, announcements on the overhead), and in the classroom itself (kids dropping books, tapping pencils, coughing, sneezing, and whispering to each other). Could the milder noises made by autistic students be explained to other students as just one of many distractions? Could strategic seating, perhaps the use of closed cubicles, reduce the problem? Could other forms of self-soothing be provided to autistic students as needed? If teachers and students could learn to treat autistic students as I was treated, back in the day, classrooms would be happier and safer for everyone.

Persistent screaming is, of course, a more serious problem. Usually today the screaming child is simply removed from the classroom. But isn't it worth pondering why the child is yelling in the first place and what can be done to lessen her distress? Teachers often fail to realize, for example, that subtle bullying may be making a child scream with anger and frustration. Dealing with the bullies will reduce the problem. Some students with auditory processing issues, or who feel they are being ignored in class, may scream in a desperate attempt to communicate. Social stories can be used to help kids learn about "inside voices" and understand why they scream in the first place. Caring teachers can usually find positive ways to deal with this problem, without taking the child out of class.

Moving Around

I could not understand what was happening. Instead of praise, I was constantly getting reprimanded. Nothing made sense. Even [the school principal] no longer meant what he said. He said I could come and see him whenever I wanted, but he lied. When I rose from my seat, walked out of my classroom, and went down the stairs to the main office to see him, I was in trouble. "Youngs lady, you cannot just walk out of [the teacher's] class and come down here." Tears welled up in my eyes as I tried to make sense of it.[3]

Autistic students generally need to move their bodies a lot, and they often move differently than neurotypical students. They may flap their hands, bounce up and down in their seats, twirl in the aisles, hide under their desks, get up and wander around the classroom, or try to leave the room, even the school. These "movement behaviors," even more than vocalizations, are viewed by some schools as barriers to inclusive education for autistic students. Unexpected movement makes teachers uneasy because it breaks the visual pattern of an orderly classroom and appears to undermine discipline. Disturbing motivations are sometimes attributed to autistic students who move "too much." Because they look a lot like "acting out," "movement behaviors" are often viewed as acts of willful disruption. But few kids who flap and rock and hide under their seats want to be disruptive. (I will describe the rare exceptions below).

Especially in their early years at school, many autistic kids simply assume they can move their bodies any way they want. If they bounce or twirl at home, why not at school? Failing to pick up on their peers' social cues, they may view demands to stop as nonsensical. What's more, sensory issues can make it impossible to stop. Researchers and teachers are only now beginning to realize how movement is often necessary for autistic children.[4] Rocking may help a dizzy student feel less likely to fall out of his seat. Bouncing may help diminish the terrifying feeling of being "disembodied," lost in space. The only choice for some children may be to run away from an intolerably painful fire alarm. Movement helps kids distract or protect themselves from sensory overload, or—and this is extremely important—gives them the sensory stimulation they need, helping them stay focused on their schoolwork.

More teachers are beginning to understand the connection between movement behaviors and sensory needs. Most still do not realize that autistic students also move around out of an eagerness to learn. Children with auditory or visual differences may rove through the classroom, looking for the best spot to hear or see the information being presented. Others discover that they can hear and understand their lessons better from a desk in the hallway, where they will be less overwhelmed by classroom sensory overload. They learn they can get to the hallway by breaking the rules about movement.[5] Still others, bored with their own "dumbed-down" curriculum, may wander through the classroom to catch a glimpse of the more interesting things other students are doing.[6] Engaging in "undesirable" movements can be key to learning for these kids.

And emotional issues may play a role. Jeanne Davide-Rivera was quoted at the beginning of this section. Her restlessness came from a desire for emotional support and human connection—something autistic students are often assumed, incorrectly, not to want. That's why she left her classroom to visit the nice principal she had met the first day of class—the one who had actually told her she could visit him any time she wanted! More often, though, movement is a response to anxiety. Heavy academic, social, or sensory pressure can intensify rocking, bouncing, or hiding. Real or perceived academic "failures," or cruelty from teachers and classmates can drive a student to bolt out of a classroom or the school itself.[7]

Intentional Aggression and Self-Injurious Behavior

When autistic students become agitated, they have been known to break their teacher's arms, knock out their teeth, and even give them concussions. They have banged their own heads against walls, scratched their arms until they bled, and bitten their fingers. And they've injured their classmates. Schools are rightly on the alert for such potentially dangerous behaviors. It is true that some students on the autism spectrum intentionally harm themselves and others. But schools cannot treat every autistic child as a ticking time-bomb, ready to explode. Unfortunately, relatively little research has been done on the prevalence of aggression in this population. But the limited findings indicate that "the violent autistic child" is much rarer than commonly assumed.

For example, estimates of "self-injurious behavior" (SIB) have been skewed by the populations sampled. A 2012 study looked at 250 children and teens with autism who were enrolled in genetic studies at the Hospital for Sick Children in Toronto, Canada. They found that 52% had engaged in SIB at some point in their lives.[8] This influential study led many scientists and educators to believe that more than half of autistic kids were likely to injure themselves. In 2016, however, a different group of scholars pointed out that, simply because it was conducted in a hospital, the 2012 study had "over-sampled" kids with challenging behaviors and major impairments. The 2016 study, looking at a broader sample of 8,000 children within the general population, calculated the percentage of all autistic kids who self-injured to be 28%. This is still a significant number, but only about half that of the 2012 study.[9]

What about aggression against other people? The issue has been complicated by the failure of some scientists to distinguish clearly between the prevalence and persistence of different forms of aggression. One study concluded that 68% of the children studied had at one time or another demonstrated aggression against their caregivers, and 49% had at one time or another been aggressive towards non-caregivers.[10] But these figures covered the children's entire lifetime, including when they were toddlers, a period when all kids are prone to hit, kick, and bite. Focusing on behavior at the precise time of the study, they concluded that 56% of the autistic children sampled were aggressive towards their caregivers, while 32% were aggressive towards non-caregivers (a drop of nearly 20% in each case).

These authors still found the prevalence of aggression among autistic children "high." However, something interesting happened when they left out the toddlers, and then broke down "aggression" into different types of behavior. It turns out, only 35% of the kids in the study engaged in what the researchers called "definite aggression"—hitting, kicking, punching, etc. Another 25% were "mildly" aggressive—they played rough, verbally threatened other people, or lashed out after being provoked. Most importantly, 40% of the sample showed no aggressive behavior at all. In other words, the majority (65%) of the kids in this study displayed no "definite aggression."

According to scientists, kids who exhibit aggressive behaviors tend to be younger, irritable and hyperactive. They include those who experienced early regression, those who suffer from gastrointestinal problems and sleep poorly, those unable to communicate in other ways, and those whose sensory processing problems make the world unpredictable and often painful.[11] Teachers and administrators would do well to attempt mitigating these factors before they condemn autistic children as "aggressive." They might also consider something else.

Reactive Aggression: What Autistic People Have to Say

Teachers and school administrators, as well as scientists tend to assume that the aggression they see is intentional. But many autistic children's violent behavior is not something they choose to do; it is, instead, "reactive." Here's a personal example of "reactive aggression." I have an instinctive fear of snakes. It's not a phobia. If I have time to think about it, I can talk about and look at snakes. I even petted a snake once, to show my kids reptiles aren't dangerous. But if I'm out walking and a harmless little garter snake wiggles across the sidewalk in front of me, I'm likely to jump a foot in the air and run away. And if—God forbid—a snake were to fall out of a tree onto my shoulder, the poor thing would get whacked off me. Really, I'd have no conscious intention of hurting it: my reaction would be purely instinctive.

Many autistic adults report a similar instinctive response to being touched by other people. With advance warning, they can avoid lashing out. But taken by surprise, they panic, just as I would if a snake suddenly landed on me:

> i have often hit people who have touched me without warning, particularly if they touch me from behind, a sharp elbow flies backwards. . . . it is a reflex reaction for me, i have no concious control over it.[12]

> I would punch them in a panic. Turns out they were just trying to be friendly.[13]

These are reactive, self-defensive behaviors, but schools typically interpret them as aggressive and punish the "perpetrator." Autistic adults remember how out of control they felt at times like these:

Did any of you have a problem as a kid where if a kid hurt you (even unintentionally), you would hit them without thinking? I used to get suspended multiple times year for punching other kids because they pinched me between a desk or bumped me while playing soccer. It was a reflex I was unable to control until I was older.[14]

Some children do eventually learn to control their reactions. However, many adults still struggle with them:

if someone touches my face, my cheek especially, i can barely control myself from hitting that person. being stuck in a slow moving crowd, i feel trapped and want to scream my lungs out. i feel like pushing people aside violently, i don't do it because it's wrong, but i slam my fist in an open palm and growl like an animal. i go crazy and no one notices.[15]

And, of course, children in general—whether autistic or neurotypical—have much less control over their reflexes.

Childhood "aggressors" often feel ashamed after the fact. They know perfectly well that hitting others is wrong and they don't plan to hurt anyone. But they have no control over their reactions:

When I was a kid-I was at a friends house when a friend of his . . . came up from behind and grabbed me-now I do not like to be touched or grabbed from behind-now I know its because of AS-I did not know it was him and I turned around and punched who ever it was in the mouth and it was him-he ran crying and I felt so bad that I hurt this boy who was just playing and meant no harm but I thought I was being attacked and hit this poor kid-I felt really bad,so bad I pledged I would never hurt anyone for any reason ever again and I still live up to that to this day.

It still upsets me to think about the incident and the thought of hurting an innocent,harmless person.[16]

Should such unplanned behavior even be considered "aggressive"? Certainly, these kids need help becoming desensitized, as much as possible, to unexpected touch. But meting out punishment for an instinctive reaction just seems inappropriate.

The Dreaded Meltdown

Autistic meltdowns may be frightening to observers, but at their most intense, they are nothing less than pure psychological torture for the person experiencing them. I feel as if I am caught in a war zone, terrified for my very life. My senses are on fire and I have very little control over myself.[17]

Schools are overwhelming places for autistic children—full of blinding lights, unexpected loud noises, determined bullies, and endless social, physical, and intellectual demands. It is hardly surprising, then, that these children sometimes melt down in school settings. A meltdown may be a relatively quiet affair, in which the child rocks back and forth, covering her face or ears to shut out a flood of sensory stimuli—some autistic people call this a "shutdown," to distinguish it from a "meltdown" proper. The latter is usually much more dramatic. Screaming or uncontrollable crying may be involved, as well as kicking, scratching, hair-pulling, biting, punching, throwing various items, or self-harming. Other autistic people call both types of reaction a "meltdown," because the internal experience is roughly the same for both types of reaction.

Meltdowns are the behavior most feared by teachers and other school staff. They don't understand them and they don't know how to deal with them. The most common error is to equate a meltdown with a temper tantrum.[18] This mistaken conflation leads educators to characterize autistic children who melt down as "cunning" or "manipulative." This, in turn, leads to punishment. Now it is true that meltdowns and tantrums look somewhat similar. However, the two phenomena arise from different causes and run very different courses. What's more, they can be distinguished through careful observation.

Temper tantrums really are manipulative behaviors, designed to gain attention, avoid unwanted demands, or obtain material rewards. Neurotypical children who tantrum will—even as they scream or kick—keep an eye on the people around them to see whether the desired outcome is forthcoming. They may even adjust their behavior if one strategy is not effective. They are careful not to hurt themselves as they flail around. Once they get what they want, the tantrum stops. Autistic children do occasionally have genuine temper tantrums. But this is not very common, for the simple reason that they usually lack the social skills needed to analyze and manipulate those around them.[19]

In contrast, meltdowns are an expression of terror. They are an instinctive "fight or flight" reaction to an overwhelming situation. Unlike tantrums, meltdowns are unplanned and have no goal. As Geoff Colvin and Martin Sheehan have noted in their excellent book on preventing meltdowns in schools, "One of the defining characteristics of a meltdown is that the student is basically oblivious of anyone and anything in the environment."[20] The child suffering a meltdown never keeps an eye on the people around them to see how they react, cannot adjust his or her behavior to achieve a particular purpose, and cannot bring the meltdown to an end until it has run its course. Older children and adults may eventually learn to recognize the signs of impending meltdowns in themselves, and—if they are lucky—can sometimes manage to head them off.[21] Most schoolkids, however, do not have this level of self-perception. They are generally unable to either recognize the signs or take action to prevent a meltdown from happening.

It is extremely important for educators to remember that autistic children (and their adult counterparts) do not enjoy having meltdowns:

When I was a kid my meltdowns were very violent, I would scream and hit things, crying and all sorts, scratch myself, hit my head against the wall, if anyone touched me it got worse. I would blank out and not remember anything, then finally fall asleep after crying so much I got a headache.[22]

I couldn't stop the headache that built until my eyes wouldn't focus properly; The thudding pressure between my eyes and at my temples. My thoughts started swirling like a Jackson Pollock, and I kept finding myself stuck in loops of fragments of sentences. I started unconsciously tapping my forehead with the knuckles of my right hand, whilst my left firmly held the back of my neck. I felt overwhelmed, and ashamed by that feeling. I felt lost and embarrassed. Thoughts were reduced to feelings (despite feelings being thoughts) I found it hard to do anything beyond feel pain. . . .[23]

Autistic children experience meltdowns as a complete loss of control over their minds and bodies. And when it is over, they often have no memory of what happened. If they do, they usually feel deeply embarrassed.

The reason why I feel so disappointed with myself after meltdowns is firstly because of the misery I cause others, and secondly because I can hardly believe how little control I have over my emotions...[24]

It gets to the point that when I know [a meltdown] is coming, I start to feel ashamed preemptively. I've been told off for constantly apologizing, partly because I can't figure out what to say (communication is conking out) and partly because I'm so ashamed.[25]

Some kids may choose to engage in temper tantrums. But why would anyone seek the terrifying, physically painful, shame-inducing experience of a meltdown? Autistic children who melt down in school need help—not criticism nor punishment, least of all the restraint and seclusion that are still the primary reactions to their terror in many schools today.

Dealing with Meltdowns in School

It is perfectly possible for teachers to reduce both the frequency and violence of student meltdowns.[26] But this requires that they understand autistic children not as willfully naughty or manipulative, but as overwhelmed and frightened. Staff need to be willing to observe these kids' behavior carefully and to make "meltdown plans" well in advance. Given the already heavy burden carried by educators today, this may seem a lot to ask. In the long run, though, managing meltdowns humanely will greatly reduce educators' stress. Several excellent and readily available books can help teachers deal with meltdowns.[27] All these books clearly distinguish meltdowns from temper tantrums. All see melting down as a process, one that can be interrupted by an observant and skilled teacher. And all offer practical advice for teachers on preventing (or at least minimizing) meltdowns in their classrooms.

Geoff Colvin and Martin Sheehan propose a six-phase model of the "meltdown cycle," in which a student who had been in a state of calm is subject to one or more triggering events, which then lead to increasing agitation until he or she reaches the point of no return and melts down. Once the meltdown has played itself out, a period of re-grouping follows, when the student is beginning to recover but may easily melt down again if pushed too hard. Finally, the student becomes calm enough to start over, despite some lingering anxiety, uncertainty, and irritation.[28]

All the experts agree that "avoiding it in the first place is the most effective way of preventing a meltdown."[29] In other words, the teacher needs to find ways to help the autistic student remain in the calm phase. This essentially comes down to consistently using what are already recognized as best practices for teachers of autistic students: providing individualized sensory interventions as needed, using visual supports, having clear rules (systematically taught to the whole class), planning ahead, adjusting the curriculum as needed, and heading off bullies. Most experts also encourage teachers and aides to identify and limit triggers that may disrupt a student's calm participation in class—whether these be sensory issues, unexpected breaks in routine, or something else.[30] The unrealistic expectation that autistic children "learn to deal with" such triggers simply ensures that meltdowns will continue.

Teachers must then learn how to recognize the signs of increasing agitation, and how to intervene gently to de-escalate the situation. This is the key moment for intervention. According to Colvin and Sheehan, agitation is "normally an observable manifestation that something is wrong with the student."[31] While some students move very quickly through the agitation phase to a full-blown meltdown, offering little time for intervention, more frequently an observant teacher will notice increased stimming, wriggling, bouncing and noise-making, or decreased interaction with others, including partial or total loss of the ability to communicate, non-compliance with directions, covering eyes and ears, staring into space, hiding hands or even seeking isolation.[32] Teachers who spot signs of agitation can step in to provide reassurance and empathy to an agitated student, offer opportunities for breaks or movement to quiet spaces, and encourage self-management (if the student already has some skills in this area).

But one thing is essential: school personnel must not become agitated themselves during this phase. This will simply hasten the onset of a meltdown.[33]

If a teacher misses or ignores the signs, agitation will grow until a meltdown is going to occur, no matter what.[34] This is the "point of no return." Once the meltdown begins, nothing can be done to stop it. Teachers, aides, and school police officers must recognize that the student <u>cannot</u> control her or his behavior at this point—and neither can they. Shouting commands or grabbing a terrified child in the middle of an instinctual fight-or-flight reaction only makes it more likely that someone will be injured.

If a child is having meltdowns in school, she <u>must</u> have an IEP, and that IEP should include a meltdown action plan. Staff should be trained ahead of time in ways of providing support for the student in meltdown—by limiting additional sensory input (turning out bright lights, limiting noise if possible), remaining calm, staying nearby (but not too close), and saying encouraging things in a slow, low-pitched voice.[35] According to Deborah Lipsky, the quiet, sympathetic use of the student's name during a meltdown can be especially helpful.[36] The meltdown plan should indicate how to calmly and gently guide the student to a safe place; it must also ensure that someone observes the child while he or she is there. Sometimes clearing the classroom of other students, until the meltdown is over, may prove easier.[37] If the student or those nearby face an immediate threat of injury, strategies should be in place for using (and later reporting to parents) safe forms of restraint—but only as a very last resort. Police involvement is unlikely to be helpful and may cause a lot of harm.

It is cruel and counterproductive to criticize a student after their meltdown has ended.[38] The child is already physically and emotionally exhausted, and probably deeply embarrassed. Neither is it useful to interrogate the student about why it happened. (This discussion can occur later—preferably the following day.) Autistic children are still on precarious emotional ground during the "regrouping" phase; they may escalate into a second meltdown if pushed too hard. Rather, as a way of bringing them back from the fight for survival into the ordinary world, the teacher or an aide should continue to offer quiet support and can encourage the student to use a stim toy or pursue a special interest.[39]

Eventually, the student will return to a relatively normal, non-agitated state (the "starting over" phase). If he left during the meltdown, now he can return to the classroom. Nevertheless, he is likely to still feel anxious, irritable, and uncertain, and should not be pushed too quickly to engage in classroom activities. The best activities for this period are concrete learning tasks which the student has already shown he or she can perform; engaging in such tasks restores confidence and helps the student return to his original state of calm.[40] Anything that can be done to assuage anxiety is helpful at this stage. Good teachers in some parts of the United States have already learned how to manage meltdowns successfully, using these and similar techniques. It is long past time for such practices to become standard in all schools.

Only rarely, then, is autistic "acting up"—whether it involves noise, movement, aggression, self-harm, or meltdowns—intended to disrupt the class. And even if the intention is disruption, it is not always for the reasons teachers or administrators imagine. Autistic students seldom enjoy school. Very few educators understand just how hellish the school experience can be for these kids.[41] Day after day they endure sensory bombardment by glaring lights and noise, the pain of (failed) social interactions, and—worst of all—the attentions of sadistic bullies. After suffering for months or even years, some kids consciously decide to just be "bad," hoping to be suspended and allowed to stay home.

After I had been suspended the first time and got to stay home from school, I CONSTANTLY was trying to get in trouble in order to get suspended again. My parents never let me watch TV or anything like that on the day I was suspended, but it didn't matter I was happy to be home, away from bullies.[42]

Wrong Planet, an online forum for autistic people, has had several discussion threads over the years focused on seeking suspension from school as a way to avoid bullying.[43] Many posters stated that they tried as hard as they could to be "good" in school, until the moment came when they just couldn't anymore. Misbehavior was their last, desperate resort. It's time for teachers and administrators to appreciate all the other possible motives, beyond disrespect, for autistic behaviors. Then they might be better equipped to help autistic students cope with distressing problems, rather than writing them off as unfit for inclusive classrooms.

Functional Behavioral Assessment and Behavior Intervention Plans

Teachers often want to move "disruptive" autistic students—those who make noises, move around too much, or have meltdowns—out of their own classrooms and into separate special education classrooms or even a completely different school. But separate is far from equal. These segregated environments offer smaller class size and more adult supervision. But they almost never provide the same academic opportunities as mainstream ones. Instructional time is more limited in these settings and the curriculum is simplified. This is precisely why the Individuals with Disabilities Education Act (IDEA) stipulates that students with autism be taught in the least restrictive environment possible for them. IDEA also requires teachers and administrators to take certain specific steps before shifting a student from a less to a more restrictive environment.

The 1997 and 2004 re-authorizations of IDEA require schools to make an effort to resolve behavior problems before this happens.

First, they must conduct a Functional Behavioral Assessment (FBA) of the student, to get a better understanding of why unwanted behaviors occur.[44] In an FBA, interviews are conducted, and data is systematically collected on when and where the unwanted behavior occurs, what its "antecedents" (what happened just before) and what its "consequences" (aftereffects) are. A behavior analyst then analyzes this data to determine what function the behavior serves for the student. Does it help to attract attention? Provide sensory stimulation? Let the student escape from difficult tasks?[45]

IDEA also requires that the school team develop a Behavior Intervention Plan (BIP) based on the FBA. The BIP describes steps that can be taken to reduce unwanted behavior. For example: if a student screams every time the bells ring for class change or for a fire alarm, then nearby alarm bells might be covered up to dampen the sound. If a student runs away while transitioning from one classroom to another, she can be taught the steps for making a safer transition: stop and wait by the classroom door, hold the teacher's hand in the hall, etc.[46] According to IDEA, the student cannot be moved to a more restrictive environment if there has been no FBA, if there is no BIP, or if the BIP has not been properly implemented.

The best means we currently have for helping autistic students remain in mainstream classes is the FBA/BIP combination. But it is far from a perfect solution. Ideally, a trained school psychologist or other experienced specialist oversees the FBA/BIP process. But in impoverished rural or inner-city school districts the burden often falls on teachers with no training at all in this kind of analysis.[47] However well meaning, their analysis and their attempts to modify complex student behavior often miss the mark. The result may be the unnecessary removal of a student to a more restrictive environment. By law, FBA/BIP is required only if a disruptive behavior is considered a "manifestation of the student's disability"—which is open to interpretation.[48] In practice, many students are removed from mainstream classrooms and even yanked from regular public schools with no attempt to improve their behavior. If teachers decide behavior is simply "willful" or "manipulative," a student may disappear to a more restrictive environment with no FBA or BIP.

A final issue is the very nature of FBA/BIP. The FBA/BIP process, like ABA, has its roots in the behaviorist school of psychology. The focus is on observable behaviors, not on the mental processes that produce them. Observing a behavior and its antecedents and consequences can provide some clues as to its function. But the reasons for many behaviors elude even the most skilled analysts. Behaviorists tend to forget that the mental processes of all children are complicated. Memory and reasoning, as well as simple reactions to the environment, all play a role in determining behavior.

No instrument used for tracking behavior was ever meant to capture the internal experience of an autistic student. And as a result, invisible stressors go unnoticed. The analyst may not understand that a student is sleep deprived or suffers from chronic stomach pain. He may not realize that a student systematically bullied for many years now experiences apparently innocuous remarks by teachers and other students as insulting and infuriating. Or that a particular smell arouses overwhelming memories of a traumatic experience long past. The focus on observable behavior is especially likely to be problematic if the student was never interviewed during the FBA process.

When earlier stressors go unnoticed, behavior analysts often miss the cumulative impact of multiple events. What if a student keeps getting up and using the pencil sharpener in a math class immediately after lunch? Quite reasonably, the behavior team may try to modify the student's lunchtime experience, perhaps by letting him or her eat in a quieter setting. But what if the demands of the math class actually represent the breaking point in a day that began with (unobserved) teasing from a sibling during breakfast, (unobserved) bullying on the bus, (unobserved) failure to understand a reading in English class, (unobserved) feelings of humiliation in gym class and only then the chaos of the lunchroom? Going to the pencil sharpener repeatedly during math, even after lunch in a quiet room, may represent a desperate effort to avoid a complete meltdown, not an attempt to "escape task demands." Under the circumstances, this student deserves a response more humane than being ejected from math class altogether.

Many Behavior Intervention Plans do work, and unwanted behaviors are diminished or eliminated. I am not suggesting that the FBA/BIP process is useless—far from it. At least some schools are employing it successfully to keep autistic students in regular classrooms. But when behaviors continue or intensify, teachers, aides and administrators might want to think more broadly and more creatively. The disruptive behaviors disturbing to teachers and school administrators often stem from perfectly normal human efforts to belong and thrive in school. Educators can help these efforts blossom. Those who choose to punish these behaviors, on the other hand, may unwittingly be rendering autistic kids "dangerous," when they are not naturally so. The most ineffective and dangerous punishments of all are restraint and seclusion.

Restraint and Seclusion

Despite lobbying by parents and students like Alex Campbell, no federal law currently exists regulating the use of restraint and seclusion in schools. According to the U.S. Department of Education's Civil Rights Data Collection for 2017-2018 (the latest period for which full data is available) 70,833 disabled students were physically restrained, 27,538 were secluded, and 3,619 were subjected to mechanical restraints across the country during that school year.[49] But this is certainly an undercount, perhaps a serious one. Many school districts don't collect the relevant data, or they fail to deliver it to the Department of Education as required. Even when they do, the information provided may not be accurate. For example, the internal records of Cedar Rapids Community School District in Iowa showed that 1,400 restraint/seclusion incidents occurred between 2012 and 2014. But not one was reported to the U.S. Department of Education, prompting Iowa's two senators to launch an investigation.[50] Likewise, Fairfax County Public Schools in Virginia reported zero cases of restraint or seclusion during the 2015-16 school year. Then, following a journalist's investigation of the records, the number of cases suddenly rose to 1,700 during the 2017-2018 school year.[51] According to a 2019 study of schools in Illinois, a special education cooperative covering two counties in northwestern Illinois reported 441 cases of restraint and seclusion in the preceding school year; investigative reporters discovered the real number to be more than two times higher.[52] In the Department of Education's CRDC survey for 2015-2016, roughly 70% of all school districts nationwide reported zero cases of restraint and seclusion.[53] If their reports were anything similar to those from Cedar Rapids, Fairfax County, or the Illinois school districts, countless children are being restrained and secluded out of public sight.

Children with disabilities (primarily autism and ADHD) are much more likely to face physical restraint and seclusion at school than their peers.[54] The U.S. Department of Education Civil Rights Data Collection for the 2017-18 school year makes this starkly clear. While children with disabilities represented only 13% of students nationally, they represented 80% of those physical restrained, 77% of those secluded, and 41% of those mechanically restrained.[55] In a 2023 report from Washington state, students with disabilities made up only 15% of enrolled students, but 96% of those restrained and 94% of those isolated.[56] Disabled children of color are especially likely to face violent retaliation, sometimes for very minor offenses. In 2014, 11-year-old Kayleb Moon-Robinson kicked a trash can during a meltdown. His school's resource (police) officer filed charges of disorderly conduct in juvenile court against the Black autistic child. As punishment,

Kayleb was allowed to leave the classroom only after all his classmates were gone. A few weeks later he broke this rule by leaving when the other kids did. The principal called the same officer, who grabbed Kayleb and tried to take him to the office. When Kayleb resisted, he was slammed down, handcuffed, taken to juvenile court, and charged not only with a second count of disorderly conduct (a misdemeanor) but also with "assault on a police officer" (a felony). A judge later found him guilty on all charges. He faced time in a juvenile detention facility, but due to public pressure, the case was eventually dropped.[57] Remember, this all began with a kicked trash can.

Against these practices children have few legal protections. A 2012 resource document from the U.S. Department of Education explicitly warns against using restraint "except in situations where the child's behavior poses imminent danger of serious physical harm to self or others."[58] Yet as of 2019, only 26 states required such limits.[59] Elsewhere, students can still be restrained and shut into "crisis rooms," storage closets—even bathrooms—sometimes for hours at a time. They are often handcuffed by school police officers. Ten-year old Thomas Brown of Denton, Texas, couldn't get his shoes on and had a meltdown. During this meltdown he swung a computer mouse around, poked one of his fellow students and pinched another. Later, school security footage shows Thomas hiding in his classroom cubby and refusing to come out. At that point he posed no threat to anyone, but his teacher and the resource officer dragged him out of the cubby, down the hall, and into the seclusion room, where he was manhandled over the course of two hours and twice handcuffed by the officer.[60]

Even where laws banning non-emergency seclusion exist, they are often flouted. A 2019 study of Illinois schools found that, in roughly a third of all the cases examined, children were restrained and secluded when no danger existed—because they had spilled milk, not completed classwork, or swore at a teacher. One special education center in southern Illinois served only 65 students in total. Reporters found

1,288 instances of seclusion there over the course of 15 months. 72% of these incidents involved no safety concerns.[61]

The U.S. Department of Education says that mechanical restraints such as handcuffs or leather straps should never be used.[62] Yet as of 2019, only 25 states forbade the use of such restraints.[63] Many others continue to let children be tied to their seats with handcuffs, straps, duct tape, and other materials—a significant safety hazard in case of emergency. In 2018, it was discovered that an 8-year-old Indiana girl regularly spent all day strapped into a homemade restraint chair. The child's parents had never been informed.[64] As of 2019, only 21 states forbade the use of "chemical restraints"; the other 30 still allowed children to be heavily sedated to keep them under control. 16 states still allow the use of physical restraints that impede breathing, include potentially deadly prone restraints.[65]

These practices are dangerous, both for the children subjected to them and for the staff imposing them. They expose everyone involved to physical dangers: bruises, bloody noses, broken limbs—even death. "Prone restraint," in which a child is held face down on a surface, is particularly dangerous. In 2018, Max Benson died after the staff of his California school subjected him to a prolonged period in prone restraint.[66] In 2021, a school in Texas used prone restraints on Xavier Hernandez until he went into cardiac arrest.[67] The use of such restraints in schools is against the law in both states.

Photos of "quiet rooms" in Illinois show scratches from desperate efforts to escape, and marks where kids banged their heads or threw their bodies against the walls.[68] Many children in this situation self-harm out of anxiety.[69] Isaiah Knipe was repeatedly sent to the seclusion room in his elementary school. The school nurse documented dizziness, tinnitus, and possible concussions from his frantic head banging while confined, but the school didn't stop locking him up.[70] Other kids become suicidal; some even succeed in killing themselves in seclusion.[71] Failure to observe the child in seclusion can lead to injury or death, but, as of 2016, only 32 states required that secluded kids remain under observation.

Even more disturbing are the psychological effects of restraint and seclusion. As we've seen, autistic children can't stop themselves from having meltdowns under intense emotional or sensory stress. Neither can they control themselves while a meltdown is going on. Even before they are punished by an exasperated teacher or an untrained police officer, the meltdown itself usually terrifies them. The added stress of being manhandled and locked up makes them panic and fight back even harder. An autistic blogger remembers being secluded in school for hours, just for crying in class. She remembers it as "torture."[72] Hannah Grieco's son needed a year of "intensive therapy" to recover from the restraint he suffered at school.[73] Kids who have been subjected to restraint and seclusion may scream or hide when next they see their school; they may beg their parents not to leave them there.[74] Children have killed themselves during seclusion (when a school has failed in its duty to keep them under watch). Other kids have committed suicide at home, after being repeatedly punished in this way.

Though widely used, restraint and seclusion are completely useless forms of discipline. As former Secretary of Education Arne Duncan put it: "There continues to be no evidence that using restraint or seclusion is effective in reducing the occurrence of the problem behaviors that frequently precipitate the use of such techniques."[75] While these practices teach children to fear their teachers, aides, or school resource officers, they teach them nothing at all about managing their own behavior—which is, in the case of meltdowns, out of their conscious control anyway. Autistic students become more anxious, more stressed, and therefore more likely to suffer meltdowns after these experiences, creating a vicious cycle of stress, classroom disturbance, punishment, escalating stress, and further eruptions. Restraint and seclusion will not help kids learn to control their behaviors.

Suspension And Expulsion: The Experience

Sometimes schools don't even try to help. In addition to restraint and seclusion, U.S. schools often use suspension from class as punishment for all kinds of minor infractions of the rules, not only for serious offences. Crying at school may lead to "unofficial" suspensions, in which parents are told to pick up their children and take them home. "Official" suspensions are based on codes of student conduct that may be vaguely worded, leading teachers to interpret subjectively terms like "insubordination" or "willful defiance." Students can still be suspended in many places for eye-rolling, walking away from a teacher without being dismissed, failing to complete homework, or even tapping their feet on the floor.[76] Students may be suspended for not meeting the school dress code (even very young children, whose parents pick out their clothes), for having the "wrong" hairstyle, or even for carrying a backpack with the "wrong" picture on it.[77]

Students of all neurotypes can experience unfair discipline. Autistic children, though, face special challenges, as do children from minority groups. In December 2018, an 11-year-old Black autistic child asked to use the bathroom in his elementary school. The principal of the school—who was escorting him and another student back to their special education classroom—refused to let him go. This is already disturbing, but what happened next is worse. The child couldn't get around the principal to reach the nearby bathroom, so he went out the back door of the building to find another restroom. The principal ordered school staff to lock all the doors and not let the student back in. The child spent 15 minutes circling the school, as adults ignored his appeals for help. Those inside pulled down window blinds in his face. Those outside walked past him without speaking. Finally, another student took pity and opened a door for him. The school sent his parents an incident report, never mentioning the dangerous and illegal lock-out. Instead, for leaving the school building without permission, the child received a two-day suspension. Only after the school's security tapes were reviewed did the truth come out.[78]

Many teachers don't acknowledge their own role in triggering such outcomes. In New Mexico, for example, a second-grader had a meltdown because his teacher yelled directly into his face, and then took away his Ipad—a critical comfort object for him. During the meltdown that followed, she got too close and was punched in the nose. Functional Behavior Analysis would call the teacher's actions the immediate antecedents to the meltdown—in other words, the whole incident was her own fault. Yet not only was this 8-year-old Black child suspended from school, but his teacher actually pressed battery charges against him.[79]

In Florida, Seraph, an autistic fourth-grader, endured a long, stressful day of testing. Bothered by the noise when his teacher put on a movie (presumably as a reward for the other students), he put on headphones and sat at a computer to distract himself. But the movie was still too loud, so he started tapping the keys hard to drown it out. Immediately the teacher called in the dean, the assistant principal, and the school police officer to remove him from his classroom. Seraph was willing to leave. He entered the school media room, seeking a quiet place to recover from the day's stresses. Then another teacher began reading a book to him. More noise! His hands covering his ears, Seraph knocked at the book with his elbow. He never touched the teacher, but suddenly the school police officer tackled him to the ground with so much force that Seraph ended up with carpet burns on his face. Then he was suspended for several days.[80] For tapping computer keys too loudly.

I received three suspensions from my school during my time there, two for leaving the room to seek sanctuary in the library when the entire class (teachers included) united in mocking me, and one for deliberate non attendance over a period of days (truanting).[81]

Autistic students are disproportionately bullied at school.[82] And staff rarely intervene. They may not witness what happened (and bullies are very adept at flying under the radar). They may believe the bullies—because a highly verbal neurotypical bully can be much more convincing than an autistic victim. Or because there are multiple bullies whose united testimony outweighs hers (something my own daughter experienced). School staffers may not care: "People beat me up and they'd go free and I'd be in detention."[83] Or the teacher may be hostile, even joining in the mockery. One autistic student explained why she hated school: "Being bullied and being told it was my fault. Being my teacher's punching bag.[84]

As someone psychologically brutalized, "Aristophanes" describes his lousy options:

Attempting to avoid a fight, getting flat out sucker punched instead, and going to the principal who gave me as much detention as the aggressor, reasoning "you're going to be an adult soon, you need to learn to solve your own problems, that's the lesson here." Going back literally a week later, getting punched again, and retaliating by stomping my heel on the kid's ankle, fracturing his tibia and earning me a suspension that go around.[85]

Former students remember being punished for fighting back:

Once [a privileged person] tried to stab me and he got off without a punishment simply because [his] family was rich. I got a suspension and was threatened with expulsion because i kicked him in the stomach and dropped him to the ground.[86]

A growing number of parents are filing lawsuits against school districts that enable such injustice. On Staten Island a teenager was suspended for three days because he allegedly knocked down bullies who had been physically assaulting him for years—even breaking his arm at one point. His parents sued the school district, "claiming he was wrongfully punished for something his school should've done — and that's stop his bullying."[87] A lawsuit is also pending in Cinncinati, Ohio, against a local school district. It alleges that a young autistic young man was suspended over and over when he fought back or just shouted at the students bullying him.[88]

The tragedy is that many autistic students view suspension and expulsion as rewards, not punishments. Despite the serious long-term consequences of missing an education, they can't wait to be removed from an academic environment they find unbearable. Sebastian, a student in New Mexico

relished being sent to in-school suspension, which he came to see as a haven from the stress of the classroom. Once, his mom says, he randomly punched a classmate in the parking lot in an effort to get sent back to the peace and quiet of in-school suspension.[89]

Similarly, "deog" was delighted to be expelled:

My misery and depression was profound. I got expelled by my sophmore year. i was ditching certain classes almost every single day... I was so happy when I got expelled and I have no regrets about that because I was just done ..."[90]

Suspension and Expulsion: The Law

So are schools really allowed to just push "disruptive" students out? Not according to the law. Under the current, amended version of

IDEA, children with autism and other disabilities are entitled to FAPE (a free, appropriate, public education), in the least restrictive environment possible. School actions that might remove them from the classroom, thus denying them FAPE, are subject to legal limitations.[91] A school must avoid removing a child temporarily (suspension) or permanently (expulsion), if the child's behavior is a "manifestation" of her or his disability—that is, if the behavior is caused either by the disability itself, or by the school's failure to carry out the child's IEP plan. Suppose, for example, that a child has an auditory processing disorder which makes it difficult or impossible to hear the teacher. If the accommodations for auditory processing disorder written into his IEP have not been fully implemented, he cannot legally be suspended or expelled for not sitting down immediately when a teacher tells him to do so.

To decide whether the child's unwanted behavior is a "manifestation" of her disability, the law requires that the school hold a "manifestation determination review." If it is a "manifestation," additional efforts must be made to modify her behavior. The school must review the child's Individualized Education Program (IEP) to ensure that it is being fully implemented. In most cases, it must conduct a first or a new Functional Behavior Analysis (FBA) to determine why the child is "misbehaving." And then it must find ways (i.e., a first or new BIP) to teach her "better" behaviors. Say a school wants to permanently move a child to a special school just for autistic students (a more restrictive environment). It must first demonstrate that it has offered the student all reasonable accommodations and training in "better" behaviors, without success. Since a more restrictive environment almost without exception means a poorer education, parents can and should appeal a school's decision to move their child.

Suspensions cannot be used in ways that turn them into unofficial "changes of placement" to more restrictive environments. Following a particular incident, federal regulations say a disabled child cannot be suspended either in-school or at home for more than ten consecutive school days. To extend the suspension, the school must provide appropriate educational and other services specified in the child's IEP, either at school or at home. The child's education must continue. Now even for students whose behavior is linked to their disability, exceptions to the "ten-day" rule exist. If guns, drugs, or serious violence against another person is involved, a student may be pulled from school for up to 45 days, so long as educational services in an "interim alternative educational setting" are provided. The law does not specify the setting—it simply stipulates that the child should continue to receive educational services. Under some circumstances, in some places, children may be sent to special programs run by the school district but located away from the school itself. Under other circumstances, children may be sent to juvenile detention centers, residential treatment centers, even psychiatric hospitals. Needless to say, educational opportunities at these places are minimal.

Even when guns, drugs or violence aren't involved, autistic students can be legally suspended more than once a year, so long as educational services continue to be provided. But once a disabled child is repeatedly suspended for the same or similar behaviors, the school is moving into dangerous legal territory. A "pattern" of repeated suspensions can begin to look like an unofficial change of placement (a denial of FAPE). So federal regulations actually dictate that disabled students not be suspended for more than 10 days total, over the course of a single school year.[92] The school district decides, on a case-by-case basis, whether such repeated suspensions constitute a change of placement, while a parent retains the right to appeal to the courts on the grounds that her child is not receiving FAPE. What if a school decides to expel an autistic child? The IEP team must hold a manifestation determination review within 10 days after the decision is made.[93] If the child's behavior is found to be a manifestation of autism, then the child cannot be expelled. But what if the behavior is found, rightly or wrongly, to be unrelated to disability? Parents have the right to call for a due process hearing, in which the IEP team's decision will be reviewed by a hearing officer from the district or the state. Parents dissatisfied with the results can bring a civil law case against the school district.

This is the law as laid out in the amended text of IDEA and in federal regulations. Disabled students' rights to a free, appropriate, public education must be protected. Yet many school districts still find ways to remove "troublesome" students, in clear contravention of federal (and sometimes state) law. And few parents know they have the right to resist.

Suspension and Expulsion: The Data

Schools often manage to evade the limits set on suspensions by law by doing things "unofficially." A school can, for example, suspend a child "unofficially," by saying he or she is having a "bad day" and would be better off at home. Administrators call the parents to pick the child up, but don't register this event as a suspension—which means it's not covered by law.[94] This occurs with stunning frequency. A report on the suspension and expulsion of disabled students in Washington state featured two extreme cases. One autistic young man, Austin, was suspended for more than 100 days during middle school (far beyond the 10 days annually allowed under IDEA and federal regulations). Another was officially suspended for 24 days, and unofficially for 45 days during a single school year. He missed classes for a total of 69 days that year.[95]

Students with disabilities, as a group, are much more likely to be suspended from school than students without disabilities. A 2018 report from the Center for American Progress finds that pre-school children diagnosed with autism are ten times more likely to be suspended or expelled than their "typically developing" peers.[96] As they grow older, disabled kids are still suspended and expelled at roughly twice the rate of other students.[97] Students of color, especially African Americans, face even higher rates of disciplinary removal from school. One study found that among students with identified disabilities, roughly 9% of Whites and Latinos/Latinas were suspended in any given year, compared to 21% of Native Americans and 23% of Black students.[98] Bear in mind, too, that many minority students (and girls) have not yet been formally diagnosed with autism. This means that unless they have another, recognized, disability, they enjoy no protection from suspension or expulsion under IDEA.[99]

Repeated removals from school hobble children's educational opportunities, leading them to fall farther and farther behind their peers academically. But beyond that, being removed over and over again can have devastating emotional effects on children. As Austin (the one suspended for 100 days in middle school) put it: "I felt like I was one of the worst kids that ever was because they were just constantly sending me home."[100] Disciplinary removal may alienate children from schools they see as simply not wanting them. Children repeatedly suspended and expelled are much more likely to drop out altogether.[101] "As a teen, I was expelled from the entire county school system and my parents had to find a private school willing to take me. At sixteen, I dropped out of school altogether," recalls one autistic adult.[102]

Finally, repeated removals promote entry into the "school-to-prison pipeline," especially, but not exclusively, for young Black or Latino males.[103] Armed police officers all too often intervene in school disturbances in inappropriate ways. A vicious cycle may ensue. Once handcuffed or jailed, a student may view all authorities as the enemy and act out accordingly. Too many suspended or expelled students spend their days unsupervised at home or on the streets, sometimes engaging in criminal activities that ensure eventual arrest and imprisonment.

Research has repeatedly shown that disciplinary removal from school has no positive impact at all on student behavior. On the contrary, it is more likely to worsen it.[104] As a result, the policy guidelines in many school districts state that suspension and expulsion should only be used when necessary to protect other students and staff, or when guns or drugs are involved. As we have seen, however, these disciplinary techniques too often "punish" students for merely skipping classes, failing to complete their homework, or talking back to their teachers. Autistic students lose faith in teachers and schools doling out such senseless, even malicious, punishments.

PART III

Getting By

" . . .even as a 27-year-old adult, I'm still struggling to get by in the world." [1]

CHAPTER SIX

Employment

E rin McKinney works as a basketball operations assistant for a professional basketball team. She travels with the team, providing video breakdowns and statistical analysis for the coaching staff. A few years ago, McKinney contributed an article to *The Mighty*, outlining why work is important to her, as an autistic person. McKinney says:

> One of the first things that working means to me is an increased level of independence. This is multifaceted. With any type of employment, individuals gain some level of financial independence. Autistics are no different here. Beyond financial independence, I have also gained more independence in my daily life. It is up to me to get myself ready for the day and to get to work on time while managing other household responsibilities. Perhaps the most important facet of independence, to me at least, has been the independence I have found at my job itself. . . . Through my job, I have proven to myself I am capable of more than what many people said I would be. . . . As a result of my newfound independence, working means an increased level of confidence.[2]

All of us, neurotypical or neurodivergent, are dependent on other people.[3] Not just for our emotional needs, which tie our well-being to other people's. A common web of social structures attaches us to other people and to societal supports for all sorts of things, all the time.[4] The most powerful politician still relies on staffers to keep her informed, arrange meetings with other politicians, do fund-raising and so forth, while other people do her laundry, clean her house, etc. The truck driver depends on dispatchers and forklift operators, while the small business owner needs employees, an accountant to keep the books, perhaps a web-designer to maintain the business's online presence. All of us, neurotypical or neurodivergent, need doctors and the medical system to keep us healthy. And we can't do without society's infrastructure: roads for our cars to drive on, snow plows to keep them clear, street lights, sewers, and so forth. The only truly independent humans are hermits living alone in the woods, hunting and fishing using tools they make themselves, growing all their own food, constructing their own clothing, cut off from communication with the outside world. Americans like to draw distinctions between those who are "independent" (good) and those who are dependent (bad), but this exercise is ultimately futile. Our lives are all, inevitably, interdependent.

Yet American society continues to prize "independence" as one of our greatest values. So what does it take to be considered independent? Usually, it requires having enough money to make your own choices and to hire others to do things that you can't or won't do for yourself. Absent an income, even a healthy neurotypical must turn to family, food banks, homeless shelters, and other forms of aid in order to survive. We tend to dismiss such people as "dependent."[5] Now consider someone who is so severely disabled he needs help getting into and out of the bath, getting dressed, doing laundry, and preparing food. But what if he's a billionaire? What if he can easily hire people to provide the help he needs? Elon Musk has described himself as autistic, but with all his billions, he will never be labelled dependent.

Money paves the way for autonomy and choice in our society. Even leaving aside the outliers like Musk, some autistic adults do manage to achieve enough financial success to become more or less "independent" in this sense. Perhaps they can hire aides to help them navigate airports and shopping centers, or to keep them from getting so lost in special interests that they don't eat. Perhaps they own an expensive computer system to communicate with others when they struggle with speech. Autistics with enough money are no more dependent than anyone else. But most never achieve financial autonomy. (The reasons are discussed below.) Most autistic adults will never be able to afford helpers or expensive labor-saving devices. And as a result, they are seen as a drag on society. Researchers have even calculated the economic "costs" of autism to American society—as though a group of human beings were nothing more than a troublesome economic problem.[6]

The difficulties autistics face in obtaining and maintaining employment, and in achieving workplace promotion are a direct product of our insistence on infantilizing them. Many Americans still believe that autism is a "disorder" of childhood, one that somehow miraculously disappears later in life. But the more than five million autistic adults in the U.S. today can testify that this is not the case. They are grown people with adult minds, but they are not treated as such. And this keeps most of them from achieving that financial independence our society idealizes. The problem begins even before they enter the job market.

Transitions

It used to be that shortly after people left high school or college, they found a first job and began saving to move into their own apartment or house. In the first decades of the 21ˢᵗ century, this transition period has lengthened for everyone. Upheavals in the economy, the growing burden of student loans, delayed marriages, the high cost of housing, and many other factors have played a role. It is now the case that a large minority of all Americans aged 18-34 still live with their parents (the number grew during the pandemic, when so many lost jobs). But the traditional transition to adult life has always been much more difficult for autistics. Viewed as eternal "children" (regardless of their age), we never expect very much from them. To make matters worse, we pull away the services that might help them find and keep a job the very moment they leave high school.

Falling Off the Cliff

The image is common among psychologists, educators, and social service providers: when young adults with autism leave high school, they "fall off a cliff." They not only lose access to the various services provided by schools (speech therapy, occupational therapy, social skills classes, etc.), they seem to also become invisible. In the media, the face of autism is still, almost always, the face of a child. We never notice that autistic children grow into autistic adults. Philanthropy is seldom directed at grown-ups; federal, state, and local funding for adult services is negligible. This sudden cut-off of support has huge implications for an autistic child's ability to grow into an autonomous adult.

Systems intended to support autistic young adults do exist. Schools form their core. The original Individuals with Disabilities Education Act (IDEA) of 1990 endorsed the idea that schools should provide students with disabilities "transition services," meant to facilitate movement into higher education or employment.[7] The 2004 reauthorization of IDEA fleshed out the process, and, importantly, required that older students be active participants in the process. While young children are usually not personally involved in IEP meetings, IDEA 2004 requires that disabled teens be present for transition planning meetings, or—if this is not possible—that their preferences and interests be considered.[8] Transition planning is supposed to set goals for the student's future (with their input), create pathways towards fulfilling those goals (for example, by linking students to work experiences), and help introduce students to whatever adult services they can access after they graduate. Once a student reaches age 16, the law requires that all schools develop Individual Education Programs (IEPs) that cover not only programming for the last years of school, but also specific programming to help the student transition into higher education and employment.

Some young adults do get excellent help from this process:

> When I was in k through 12 I was lucky to be in a town that had amazing resources. I had a lot of support. . . . They gave me one on one support academically for the last few years which meant I didn't really fall behind it that area. And they found a grad student from a local college to teach more more advanced subjects like linear algebra, electronics, and someone else for English literature. . . . The teacher in the special ed classroom also helped me get services after school as well. I spent a lot of time with OT and other services getting better at getting dressed and other similar things.[9]

But this case seems to be an exception. Studies show that parents of autistic students find transition services less helpful for their child than do the parents of children with other disabilities. Often, they report that they only learned about transition services from other parents—not from the school system. The reality of transition planning is revealed by interviews with students, parents, teachers, school administrators and service providers, who complain about "inappropriate goal-setting, ineffective communication between stakeholders, and inadequate involvement of all decision-makers needed to inform planning."[10] Such poor quality planning fails to align with either IDEA's legal mandates or theoretical best practices. Worse, it tends to exclude the very students whose future is in question. By law, both students and parents are supposed to participate in the transition planning process. However, autistic students are generally less well-informed about and less likely to participate than students with other disabilities. About 62% of autistic students either never attend transition meetings at all, or take no active part when they do attend.[11] Many report not being allowed to speak, or being ignored when they spoke. As one put it: "I feel like I have to just sit down and listen to somebody." [12]

Other young adults and their parents report that they never received any transition services at all. One teen was asked whether his IEP included transition planning. His response: "It [the IEP] doesn't really say a whole lot."[13] Transition planning is especially ineffective with the poor and with members of ethnic and racial minority groups.[14] One study of 25 Chinese and Vietnamese families with autistic children found that the families urgently wanted to be part of transition planning. But they faced formidable obstacles. Schools seldom provided translation services, so non-English-speaking parents couldn't actively participate. School professionals were sometimes impatient, and often ignored their questions or requests. Shockingly, schools failed to inform these families about training in work skills and functional independent living skills available through school, about how schools could help finding voluntary or paid jobs, or about the availability of essential services locally. In fact, some parents were clearly surprised when told by researchers that schools could help with these things. They had assumed that families were completely on their own. In one extreme case, a Vietnamese mother only learned that transition planning even existed when her daughter had turned 21, ageing out of all IDEA-related services.[15] In 2017, the Government Accountability Office urged federal agencies to take additional actions to support transition-aged youth. While school districts usually provided some career counselling, the GAO noted, they less often offered work experience or job coaching. The GAO also pointed out the difficulties facing autistic young adults and their families in accessing adult services offered by other government agencies.[16]

For schools are not the only places designated by law to provide services for young adults with disabilities. The 2014 Workforce Investment and Opportunity Act (WIOA) requires individual states to develop plans to help adults find jobs. All adults are eligible for employment and training services through the state; additionally, disabled adults, including military veterans, can access Vocational Rehabilitation (VR) services to help them prepare for and enter the workforce. According to WIOA, disabled high school students must receive job and college counselling while still in school, along with opportunities for work experience and training in workplace readiness and self-advocacy.[17] This is the law. In practice, WIOA support seldom suffices to get transition-age autistics the jobs they want and need. According to one study:

After school, [autistic] youth struggled to access the services stipulated in their transition plans due to inadequate planning, overburdened services, and insufficient accountability for adult service providers. Finally, a failure to include appropriate skill-building and insufficient interagency and community relationships limited efforts to gain and maintain employment.[18]

Lack of funding is one important factor. Far more potential clients need help than most service providers can possibly cope with. Typically, too, providers have little training or experience in working with autistics, so identifying and meeting their clients' needs is difficult for them.[19] But an element of disinterest is also at play. Many VR professionals are too burned out to be effective. Or they simply believe autistics can't be successful. One client reports:

Voc Rehab did NOTHING to help me find a job. My counselor threw out a couple idea for places I could apply & after that she did nothing to help me find a job except have meetings with me where she kept telling me to assert myself which I already was doing.[20]

Few states recognize that autistics are an underserved population in many of their VR programs. Only 50-60% of adult autistics who have received VR services across the nation ever get a job. Among those who do, most work part-time for low wages, earning less than their peers with other disabilities.[21] Research suggests some best practices for autistic VR clients: customized, unpaid, but long-term internships to introduce potential employees to workplaces that might interest them; job coaching, using evidence-based teaching techniques known to work for autistics; and individually designed accommodations. Technology, like virtual reality job interview simulations and personal digital assistants, can help young adults transition from internship to paid work. Up to 90% of clients who receive this kind of support later obtain competitive paid work in an integrated setting (i.e., in ordinary workplaces).[22] But only a handful of VR centers actually follow these best practices. The results are entirely unpredictable when the typical young autistic graduate tries to enter the workplace with no real transition plan in place during school, without adequate experience or training, and with only minimal services, at best, from Vocational Rehabilitation.

Autism and Employment

*"It cannot be right that so many more
aspies end up in poverty."*[23]

In general, people with disabilities have lower employment rates than non-disabled people do.[24] But the situation is absolutely dismal for those with autism. A 2015 study focused on people in their early 20s, found that over 90% of those with learning disabilities, speech/language impairments, and emotional disturbances, as well as 74% of those with intellectual disabilities had been employed at some point. But only 58% of those with autism had ever held a paying job.[25] An even more discouraging report from 2017, based on a huge sample of more than 47,000 autistic adults, found that only 14% held paying jobs in integrated settings (that is, regular jobs in ordinary workplaces) at the time data was collected. Another 15% worked in sheltered workshops or similar settings, where they were typically paid less than the national minimum wage (see below). 22% did unpaid volunteer work, and the rest either spent their time in programs at adult day-care centers or simply stayed home. [26] Non-speaking autistics were especially likely to be unemployed: only 3% of those dependent on non-verbal forms of communication had a paid job in an integrated setting at the time the data was collected.[27] Employment also tends to elude autistic women and members of minority groups. While autistic women enter the workforce at roughly the same rate as autistic men, more of them drop out over time.[28] And young Black and Latino/a autistics are employed at only half the rate of their White peers. [29]

A growing number of employers have learned the value of "hiring autistic." By and large autistics are honest and loyal, show patience and persistence in getting the job done, and habitually treat others fairly (at least as they perceive fairness). There are some kinds of work in which they outshine neurotypicals. Finding patterns and deviations from patterns is a particular strength. Some software companies have found that their autistic consultants consistently identify 10% more bugs than do its neurotypical ones. Autistics also tend to be faster and more accurate in finding specific targets hidden among other elements.[30] Not all autistics are "pattern thinkers," of course. Many are "visual thinkers" who may excel at graphic design or photography. Others have special auditory skills, enabling them to identify and remember sounds better than neurotypicals, helping them perform well with security agencies or in music.[31] These are not just theoretical claims. People on the autism spectrum are currently working successfully in almost any field you can name. Still, for multiple reasons, they constitute only a small minority among all autistic adults.

Standard hiring processes tend to eliminate autistics right out of the gate. Overwhelming workplace stressors often drive them to burn out and quit. Their perceived "weirdness," rather than any inability to perform the job, keeps them from being promoted and may lead to them being fired.[32] None of this makes autistic underemployment right.

Getting Hired

For most of the past century, more people have been applying for jobs than could possibly be hired. This has put most of the power in the hiring process in the hands of employers. In such a labor market, employers use the hiring process—resume review, contacting references, job interviews—to weed out applicants as fast as possible. Yet this process discriminates powerfully against autistic people. In the first place, employers value experience and proven ability, so neurotypical as well as autistic young adults struggle to land a first job. But only 24% of autistic high school students have had any kind of paid work experience during high school—far fewer than neurotypicals or students with other disabilities.[33] As a result, autistics tend to enter the adult job market utterly untested, and to their intense frustration:

> I have no job experience and I need a job. I need to start building for my future. I cannot get any work experience if I don't have a job. Its like a catch 22, no experience, no job, but no job no experience.[34]

. . . since I don't have any experience, I can't get a job unless someone is willing to give me a job without experience. And they'd only do that if they knew me or we had a mutual friend aka networking. I wish I had known how crucial experience was in college. Employers won't even consider me if I don't have experience. I know this because I have called up and asked and they said I need "x amount of experience."[35]

While many are able to put together resumes, locate job openings, and fill out applications, all on their own, or with the help of friends, family, or vocational counsellors, young autistics without experience struggle to reach the interview stage.

The Job Interview

I went on 60 interviews for business jobs in
my senior year of college and didn't reach the
second round of a single interview.[36]

Despite what employers and human resource managers sometimes say, formal job interviews aren't intended to identify the best qualified candidates for a job. Reviewing resumes and calling references verify qualifications before interviews are even scheduled. The interview's real function is to help employers identify which qualified candidates have "potential for growth in the job," or—more simply—who they want to work with. Now the focus is less on technical qualifications (degrees, certificates, previous work, etc.), than on "soft skills" and "personality."[37] Interviewers want "good communicators," people who can "think on their feet," those with "people skills," and "team players." So they include open-ended questions and unpredictable elements in interviews, and look for the ability to make fluent conversation. Usually, extended social interaction is required. All this is disastrous for most autistic job applicants, who, by definition, have difficulty communicating and engaging in social interactions.[38] As Chris Bonnello points out, "There's a difference between being good at a job, and being able to talk about being good at a job."[39]

Autistics thrive on the predictable. They're flooded with anxiety when things don't go as planned.[40] Individual companies shape their interview formats according to the idiosyncrasies of individual interviewers or groups of interviewers, as well as traditional business practices and the latest management theories. While some elements are commonly included, there is no standard format from business to business, making surprises inevitable. Very few interviewers understand the degree of terror this inspires in these applicants. Faced with a change in venue, the presence of an unexpected interviewer, a question out of left field—even one they know the answer to—their minds may go blank:

> If an interviewer puts me on the spot to demonstrate my knowledge I freeze up even if I have the skills. My last interview was a disaster. It was a phone interview and the interviewer expected me to tell him SQL code over the phone. This caught me off guard and I was like a deer in headlights. I told him I wouldn't be able to do that over the phone and he insisted. It was painful and definitely killed any chance I had at getting the job even though I probably would have done good at the actual job had I gotten it.[41]

People with autism may actually be quite good at "thinking on their feet" in a concrete job situation. But in an interview, where they are already highly stressed, this strength disappears. Even those with excellent job skills may come off as ignorant or incompetent:

> I have a BS degree, graduated Summa Cum Laude, but can't interview for shit. I have a huge vocabulary, am a very eloquent

speaker, but get me in front of strangers and I turn into a bumbling idiot! I stutter, repeat myself continuously, saying the same thing but in several different ways. I have trouble holding eye contact, so I dart a glance here and there at the interviewers. I always feel like I look shifty and wonder what they think. I can tell you I have never gotten a professional job in my field.[42]

Autistic people are concrete thinkers. The kind of open-ended questions interviewers love tend to baffle them. "Tell me a bit about yourself"—a common inquiry in job interviews—leaves the autistic candidate desperately searching for the right answer. Should she talk about what is most important to her—for example, a special interest? If not, what should she talk about? And how much information is "a bit"? Autistic candidates are often dismissed simply because they responded with too few or too many details. The ever-popular "tell me about your greatest strengths and weaknesses" can throw even neurotypicals for a loop.

Companies who genuinely want to hire autistic people would do well to modify their interview process. According to one study, when asked more structured and concrete questions autistic job candidates answer more confidently, significantly improving interviewers' perceptions of them.[43] Some businesses have already begun to ditch the formal interview altogether. Instead, they ask the candidate to "hang out" and show what they can do alongside other employees for a few days.[44] This works very well for many autistic jobseekers.

"Likeability"

Perhaps the biggest obstacle faced by autistics in job interviews is the issue of perceived "fit" and, by association, "likeability." Hiring decisions often hinge on this. As one jobseeker noted, "the problem is the fixation on 'fit.'"[45] But it turns out interviewers may dislike, and thus find "unfit," job candidates for all sorts of reasons that have nothing to do with ability and much to do with individual or institutional prejudice. [46] Extensive research has shown the degree to which bias has excluded from jobs women, sexual minorities, those considered physically unattractive, foreign language speakers, older workers, members of racial and ethnic minorities, and the disabled. [47] "Likeability" is entirely in the eye of the beholder.

Autistic individuals are especially helpless against this barrier to employment. All autistics lack some social skills, by definition. Unless they are exceptionally good at masking, they will rapidly be identified as "unpleasant," "not one of us," "weird," and then shunted to the side. [48] Let's consider how this works. Self-presentation or "impression management" involves such intangibles as wearing the "right" clothes, giving "proper" handshakes, having the "correct" level of eye contact, speaking at the "appropriate" speed, making the "right" kind of small talk, and looking "comfortable" during the interview. All these skills confound autistics. [49]

> I had a job interview, and I had a friend on the inside who told me that I had secured the position. Then a couple days later I called him and he apologized, informing me that I had not secured the position – the very last person who I met before I had gone home the day of the interview, was a VP and he shot me down because he did not like my hand shake. [50]

> Before I accepted my current job seven years ago, I interviewed for another higher paying position that I was well qualified for. I had to sit through three interviews in succession. . . I heard I did not get the position because I appeared nervous or stressed to the hiring manager. [51]

Post-interview, many autistic people have been told that they "talked too much" or "not enough," that someone thought they were "devious" because they failed to make eye contact, or that they were "creepy" because they stared at the interviewer (typically, trying too hard to make the eye contact they detested). It's all too easy for an autistic person to come across as "unlikeable."

Disclosure

The ultimate stressor in interviews is the emotion-laden question of whether to "disclose" your diagnosis to a potential employer. Autism itself is an "invisible" disability—not necessarily obvious to the casual observer. Of course, other conditions (like dyspraxia) can make it visible. So can the inability to communicate "normally." Such candidates have no choice but to disclose. Those who have successfully learned to "mask," however, face a choice during the hiring process. Should they share their autistic identity? Or try to hide it? Each choice presents its own pros and cons. [52]

On the one hand, disclosure may mitigate some of the candidate's "likeability" issues. Informed employers may actually recognize social awkwardness and signs of anxiety as a manifestation of autistic neurology, not some failing of the applicant. [53] They may also recognize the strengths that autistics can bring to the workplace, and make a job offer. Such employers may be open to offering accommodations to help the new hire "fit in." [54]

On the other hand, disclosure to an uninformed employer, who thinks all autistics are "freaks" or "morons," may result in automatic rejection. [55]

I worked for a company that tried to get people with ASD into jobs with local employers. Tried. If anyone gave us the time of day, no amount of explaining why someone with ASD could do as good or better of a job would get past the stigma of "Autism?!!" [56]

I have just been fired from my new job. I worked there a total of two weeks and two days. My managers told me, specifically, that I was being fired because I had Asperger's Syndrome. Their exact words were, "You should have told us during the job interview that you had Asperger's, because we would never have hired you."[57]

Some hard evidence backs up the claim that ableism interferes with hiring. A group of researchers submitted identical resumes to employers. Some of these said nothing about disabilities. Others mentioned disabilities, including Asperger's Syndrome (a form of autism). The resumes that mentioned disabilities of any kind received 26% fewer expressions of employer interest.[58]

Some employers are hesitant to hire autistics because they dread the potential cost of accommodations and the legal repercussions of firing someone theoretically protected under the Americans with Disabilities Act.[59] Sadly, their fears are misplaced. As one economist points out, "while hiring discrimination is illegal under the ADA, it is difficult to detect, prove, or enforce, which could cause the hiring disincentives to dominate."[60]

Despite lack of experience, the misery of the interview process, and overt discrimination, some autistics do eventually manage to get a job or start an enterprise. And some have remarkable success. When James Cusack was a child, his parents were told that he would probably have to be institutionalized for the rest of his life. Now he is the CEO of Autistica, England's largest autism charity.[61] Well-known lawyer, Lydia X.Z. Brown, specializes in disability rights. They have held positions as policy analyst at the Autistic Self-Advocacy Network, and as a fellow at the Judge David Bazelon Center for Mental Health Law, while lecturing at major universities. They are currently Chair of the American Bar Association's Disability Rights Committee, Director of Policy, Advocacy, and External Affairs at the Autistic Women and

Non-Binary Network, and Policy Counsel for Disability Rights and Algorithmic Fairness for the Privacy & Data Project of the Center for Democracy & Technology.[62] In Norway, Greta Thunberg kick-started a global movement of climate activism.[63] The careers of other autistics have been less spectacular, but equally successful. They include realtors,[64] train engineers,[65] psychologists,[66] teachers,[67] faith leaders,[68] bank tellers,[69] technology specialists,[70] stage managers,[71] sound engineers,[72] elected officials,[73] and on and on. Autistic people can successfully fill many roles—if given the chance.

Keeping the Job

Overt discrimination keeps autistics from playing the role they should in the workforce. Founder and editor of online magazine NOS Sarah Luterman, writes:

Disclosing an autism diagnosis at work can hinder advancement. People's low expectations of me were noticeable. I felt stuck. After asking for a promotion after some major achievements, I was denied. Then, after further achievements, I was given a title change but no pay raise, despite the existence of pay bands. I made $5,000 less than the low end of the pay band for my new job title.[74]

Discrimination like this keeps autistic workers stuck in low-level jobs. So does their inability to engage effectively in the office politics that lead to promotion:

I can't brown-nose or kiss butt worth a damn either. I believe the corporate world calls that relationship building. To me it's an astronomical waste of time and productivity.[75]

Would a chance at promotion without having to schmooze represent a "reasonable accommodation" for autistics? Some say absolutely:

> I guess, if a person has ASD, and by extension, is not inherently good at playing politics, then a reasonable adjustment in the workplace must take that into account. It is certainly NOT the case that a person on the spectrum is missing critical information or knowledge or expertise, or insight, or creative ideas. Organisations, in the interests of equity, yes, but also for their own sake, need to hear the voice. Distill what is said and they will almost always discover that a person of substance, care and detail have just spoken.[76]

Such an accommodation is seldom provided. Instead, autistic employees are routinely silenced and passed over for promotion.

What's more, many autistics have trouble even keeping their jobs. They experience repeated cycles of getting hired, working for a relatively short time, and then either quitting or being fired.[77]

> In my 25 years of employment I have never been fired but I've also never stayed in one job for longer than 2 years.[78]

> I used to work, a long while ago. Had one job after another, never stayed in any one of them very long. Always ended up fired. Too absentminded; I have enough trouble remembering things that happened yesterday, let alone keeping track of really amazingly boring things in a job that's about as mentally engaging as a brick and just as slow. Now though, I'm 34, and I aven't [haven't] worked in.... er... some baffling amount of time. Gotta be at least 9 years now. It's unlikely that I'll ever have a job again.[79]

Many jobs are ill suited to someone who is "absentminded." But a job may not be a good fit for many other reasons. Few autistics do well in jobs such as sales that require lots of nuanced interaction with customers. Success at telephone call centers will elude the subset of autistics with auditory processing disorders.

Yet plenty of jobs exist whose requirements may be perfectly suitable and which the new hire can perform with ease. So why do autistics still fail at these jobs? The most important reason is workplace stress.

I have moved through a series of jobs across the private, public, charitable and educational sectors in the hope of finding somewhere I could just fit in and work without the accompanying stress. I left each job on good terms with every employer seemingly unaware of the personal stress that I was under (I really am that good at disguising it), but the challenge of hiding it was taking a real toll on my mental health.[80]

Most neurotypicals can't imagine how much stress their autistic co-workers experience. Beyond the ordinary demands of the job, they must also contend with sensory bombardment, sudden and stressful changes in setting or routine, an absence of reasonable accommodations, social exclusion, hostility and outright bullying by bosses and co-workers, failure to be promoted despite excellent performance reviews, and persistent fear of being fired. Over all this looms the constant terror about being "outed" as autistic (unless they has already disclosed their neurotype). The relentless strain of "passing" is a high price to pay for a job.

The Physical Environment

The physical environment in many workplaces is painful for autistic employees.

The workplace can be a sensory nightmare and it can be diffi-cult for some people to an access reasonable adjustments at work for sensory reasons. That being said sensory accessibility in the workplace is the same as any other accessibility need such as ramps and lifts for wheelchair users. Employers are required to provide accessible workplaces and if that means sensory accessi-bility that so be it.[81]

The Americans with Disabilities Act (1990) requires employers to make

reasonable accommodations to the known physical or mental limitations of an otherwise qualified individual with a disability who is an applicant or employee, unless such covered entity can demonstrate that the accommodation would impose an undue hardship on the operation of the business.[82]

Expensive or overly inconvenient accommodations can legally be refused under the ADA. Ironically, though, many sensory problems can easily be mitigated with minimal cost, or even with a saving for the employer. What's lacking is not the resources, but the willingness to make small changes to the environment. Take lighting, for exam-ple. The fluorescent lights ubiquitous in American workplaces can be overly bright, while their constant buzzing grates on autistic nerves.

When I physically had to work in an office under fluores-cent lighting, I was having regular sensory overloads, regular migraines, actually, a lot more meltdowns too. I had more anx-iety. The lighting in the office just really amped me up and I was on edge all the time because I was always so uncomfortable. It's the same kind of lighting, actually, that there was in school when I was younger.[83]

Switching to energy-efficient LED lights or providing a workspace full of natural light seems a simple solution. It could alleviate the torment of fluorescents while also providing savings to the employer. Why is it not more common?

Autistics with temperature sensitivities can't concentrate if their environment is too hot or too cold. Permission to bring in a personal space heater or fan can make all the difference.[84] Yet some employers resist this. They may also frown on clothes that aren't "business attire" or a uniform: "Professional wear has always made me feel all stuffy and claustrophobic. Not to mention overheating issues and fabric texture issues."[85] One answer might be finding a compromise on work attire (different fabrics, an alternative to the collared shirt) acceptable to both sides.

Big open spaces in stores, warehouses and offices echo with loud noises. "I work in an open plan office," writes one employee, "and I just get overwhelmed with all the noise and different conversations going on, so I'm really quiet most of the time or I have headphones on.[86] Permission to wear noise-cancelling headphones costs the employer nothing and can help the employee greatly. Why are these free or low-cost concessions still so rare?

A regular schedule can be an essential, but simple, accommodation for autistic workers:

Have a predictable schedule. Everyone is different but a schedule all over the place can be overwhelming. Esepcally [Especially] unexpectedly calling them in on off days. We need the off-days to recharge. Autism burnout.[87]

Sometimes, of course, businesses must make changes without sufficient warning. The start of the Covid pandemic, for example, threw many autistic people for a loop. One woman loved her job at a bank, where things were pretty much the same every day. But due to infection concerns, the bank suddenly had to change its practices:

> Things were different when I went into work yesterday. The open-
> ing routines were the same, but everything changed after that.
> The lobby was closed. We could only help people in the drive-
> through. I could handle that, but then more changes came. Our
> cash machine was not working, and they asked us to wear gloves
> the whole shift. I started to feel anxious. The longer I wore the
> gloves, the more anxious I became. And customers kept com-
> ing, so I did not have time to process all the changes and adjust
> to them. After an hour, I took an early lunch to get away from
> everything. I broke down in the break room and could not stop
> crying.[88]

Luckily, this woman had a sympathetic manager. She sent her home
to deal with her emotions and the next day she was able to return to
work.

Another person also had a good job with a wonderful, understanding boss. But then she faced wholesale, ongoing changes that were
simply too disruptive for her:

> Then came the inevitable round of "re-structuring" and soon
> everything was changing very quickly into a world of chaos for
> me — new manager, bigger team, new tasks and a large open
> plan office. I simply couldn't cope and knew I had to start over
> again somewhere different.[89]

Sometimes expectations or procedures do need to be revamped at a
business, and the disruption may force an autistic worker to quit. This
would be less likely to happen if managers announced such changes in advance, and then found ways to limit their impact on autistic employees. Wouldn't providing more predictability be easier than

having to open a new job search because you've just driven away an experienced worker?

The Social Environment

Most existing research on autistic success in the work environment focuses on changing employee behavior—improving social skills, using video prompting to teach workplace practices, etc.[90] Some scholars recognize, however, that if autistic employment and retention rates are to improve, bosses and co-workers also need to learn about autism, accept autistic difference, and simply behave better.[91]

> I have changed jobs close on 23 times to get away from various forms of bullying. The key predisposing factors are that they seem to target those who are quiet, and get on with the job. The louder and more outgoing you are in a company, the more likely it is that you will be able to join the clique and become untouchable.[92]

Workplace rules can be a source of stress if they are unevenly applied. Autistic workers are typically reassured to learn that their workplace has rules; it means they know what they should be doing. They generally try hard to follow them. But when other employees treat the rules inconsistently, it can be deeply unsettling:

> When it suits them; they don't stick to the rules; when it suits them; they do stick to the rules, but fail to realise that they are so contradictory and I actually admit, I have walked out on a few jobs, because I can't cope with that attitude.[93]

Co-workers who flout the rules confuse autistic workers. Should they too be ignoring rules or following them? These scofflaws make the job unpredictable, exasperating, and anxiety-provoking.

Just as autistic children are bullied at school, so adults are bullied in the workplace. Co-workers, supervisors, human resource managers, even the job coaches hired to "help" them can be involved. Bullying can critically undermine job success, leading to the autistic employee being fired or deciding to quit.[94] It is thus an important factor in the autistic unemployment problem. Yet it gets almost no attention from companies that insist they are trying to hire and retain autistics.

Autistics too often run afoul of incompetent and unsympathetic bosses. These people may bully by withholding pay, refusing to report injuries so that the sufferer can receive workers compensation, engaging in or permitting sexual harassment, or humiliating an employee. One of the worst incidents led to the death of an autistic employee. Graham Gentles worked as a cashier at a Target store in California. Arriving for work one morning, he was met by his managers, store security, and the police. He was then handcuffed and paraded through the store in a ritual that Target workers call the "walk of shame," usually reserved for those who have stolen from the company. But Gentles had stolen nothing; no charges were ever filed against him. It remains unclear why he was humiliated. What is clear is that three days later he jumped to his death from the roof of a local hotel. His mother sued the Target corporation. She blamed them for her son's suicide.[95]

Co-workers may take credit for autistic employees' work, badmouth them to superiors, hide their equipment, steal money from their desks, pour coffee over their computer keyboard, key their cars in the parking lot and break their eyeglasses. They may even try to boss around the autistic worker, without the authority to do so:

I have a steady job now, for the first time in many years. I work as a fry cook at a restaurant, where, through great perseverance, and no small amount of patience on my manager's part, I've actually managed to learn my job fairly well. . . . [Then the restaurant hired a teenager, much younger and less experienced than the cook, to work at the drive through] . . . Yesterday when I took a quick break to grab a drink, she stopped serving the customer at the drive through, and whirled around and said, "Hey you need to get back there right now." I thought she was being playful so I tried to joke with her by saying, "You're not the boss of me!" Like kids do, you know? Then she yelled - loudly and clearly NOT joking, pointing to the back, "You get your ass back in there right NOW!"[96]

This attack was overtly aggressive. Sometimes, though, more subtle, repeated harassment occurs: "Mine is not so much blatant bullying as it is microaggressions and discrimination. Death by 1,000 paper cuts."[97]

"Masking" at Work

Autistic adults are keenly aware the stigma associated with their neurological difference.[98] Those who can manage it often see "looking normal" as the key to getting hired and keeping a job.[99] Of course, the majority of autistics, regardless of intelligence, ability, or determination, lack the ability to pass as neurotypical. This means they must disclose their autism to employers and co-workers. Disclosing makes it much harder to find a job, but sometimes easier to keep it. If you disclose, no one expects you to look or act "normal" at work. You may still be bullied, but you are somewhat less likely to be fired for being "weird." But there are excellent reason for those who are able to mask to do so:

In an academic or workplace environment, autistic people may not disclose their autism due to a fear of others believing they are incompetent due to being autistic. . . . In the workplace or during a job interview, autistic people may not disclose being autistic due to a fear of misconceptions about autism that could lead to not being promoted or being accepted for the job, such as the misconceptions that autistic people lack empathy, that they will not be a good communicator, or would not be an effective "team player." This hurts autistic people not only because of the assumption of incompetence, but also because when they feel that they cannot disclose their autism in an academic or work environment, they also tend not to ask for accommodations that they may need to help them better perform in a classroom or at their job, and may feel ashamed for even having to ask for them.[100]

Yet masking is highly stressful.[101] You must mimic the behavior of people around you and memorize "scripts" to use in social situations.[102] "I am exhausted at the end of a work day," writes Judy Endow,

> because it takes a great deal of effort for me to continually stifle my reactions to sounds, sights, smells and movements that others do not typically notice. I have to particularly pay attention to conventional social mannerisms such as remembering to look at people during conversation, track which words are 'work words' and which words are 'social fluff words' and respond accordingly. I work at this because I like to be able to fit in and in many respects my continued employment depends on it.[103]

Michael Scott Monje (the pen name of Athena Michaels-Dillon) describes what it's like to "artificially hold" their face, for hours, to hide the fact that their eyes are not symmetrical and that their mouth naturally twists so that one side is open.[104] They also have trouble speaking "normally," as fatigue sets in:

> I can talk for extended periods, but the more tired I get, the more

my speech impediment slips out. It starts as a stutter, then I go tonally flat, and eventually I lose control over my enunciation and start to sound like the stereotypical autistic. Usually I also get frustrated and have a hard time keeping myself from shouting when this happens, because I stop being able to say the words I intend to say, and instead I insert similar-sounding but incorrect words, like saying "speak" when I mean "steep". When it gets really bad, I will be able to see the word in my mind's eye, as if I was silently reading, but I will not know how to say it out loud. [105]

Finally, there are the social expectations. Imagine submitting to the pressure to go out for a drink with co-workers, to "relax and have fun" after work—even though being in a crowded, noisy bar after a stressful day at the job feels like being in hell.[106] All of this extra labor is piled on top of doing your official work.

And it is hugely exhausting. Passing takes:

constant anxiety, calculation, cognition, because remember, those of us who pass are trying to be a person we aren't, a member of a species that, should it know our true identity, expels us. The trick to passing, to passing well, is to make it look natural. Passing means repressing, memorizing rules, sublimating, jumping through hoops, and turning tricks so we can get the human treatment. It means making it so that when you reveal your diagnosis to someone they "never would have guessed it".[107]

When I'm in public, I am painfully aware of how I am standing, what I'm doing with my hands, how I'm positioning my face. I'm terrified to cross one of society's invisible lines, so I make myself as small as possible. I wait until the conversation hits a lull before speaking up. I fold my arms in tight. I try not to fidget, try not to even breathe too loudly. I don't know what normal is, but I know

I sure as hell am not it, so I try to be as unlike myself as possible. Even when I want to open up to people, it's a real struggle. Controlling my every word and movement is so instinctive that I can't let it go.[108]

"I try to be as unlike myself as possible." What a horrible burden.

Trying to "pass" as neurotypical at work, autistics can't use their best coping mechanisms to reduce the strain—they can't stim to release tension, they can't hide in a dark, quiet room, they can't even have a meltdown, because any of these will break through the neurotypical disguise and expose the autistic beneath. (The meltdown may even lead to a police call and involuntary hospitalization.) All you can do is suck it up:

> What [the people around me] don't see is my suffering. They don't know that sometimes I am panicking on the inside or going through sensory overload right in front of them. How could they? . . . I learned to hide these things years ago. Nobody sees me freaking out, knows when I am having stomach issues, or my head is pounding from the florescent lighting of the office I work in two to three days a week. I don't complain. I smile, push forward, pull up my big girl panties and do what I have to do to make sure that I am able to provide the best possible life for myself.[109]

The Physical Costs of Passing

"I identify as tired."[110]

In the absence of a "typical" neurology, it takes enormous mental and physical energy to maintain the façade of normalcy. Ironically, this makes employees much less productive at work. By the end of the day, maskers desperately need to recharge their batteries by sitting in a dark space at home, petting their animals, or stimming.

For every hour that we manage to pass, we spend two or three or five recovering. We pull off a great passing act at work and pay for it by needing the whole weekend to recharge.[111]

Being something that I neurologically am not is exhausting. Wearing the mask of neurotypicality drains my batteries and melts my spoons.[112]

Sometimes even this is too much for an overworked nervous system. Many autistics come home only to immediately fall asleep.

I get through the door and drop my bag. I crawl and stumble up the stairs and make it to the bedroom, collapsing on the bed without even the energy to remove my shoes, my eyes are heavy, exhaustion pulling my lids shut.[113]

People worn out from the stress of passing at work may be too tired to buy groceries, prepare meals, take showers, or otherwise look after themselves. Camouflaging leads to additional physical symptoms of stress: headaches, muscle tension, upset stomachs, high blood pressure, and so forth.

The amount of energy I have to expend to hide my autism prevents me from having enough left over to enjoy the fruits thereof, like a regular job, or extracurricular activities, or going out with friends. How many of us are like me, having perfected the mask, but at such a great cost?[114]

The Psychological Costs of Passing

If you have to hide who you are, musn't there be something terribly wrong with you? The primary psychological cost of camouflaging autism is internalized shame. One employee writes, "After trying so hard and making so many mistakes, eventually I can't help but think of myself as intrinsically broken."[115] Another says, "passing is not good for your mental health. It teaches us to have shame in who we are. It gives a message that we are not good enough."[116]

This feeling of being inherently defective is a poisonous mental state, inviting constant self-criticism, negative comparisons between oneself and others, anxiety, depression, and suicidality.[117] Masking is very strongly associated with anxiety. A participant in one study actually confessed that she was "more worried about making a [social] mistake than dying."[118] Such anxiety can be paralyzing, reducing the ability to perform professionally, decreasing the capacity to function outside of work. Hiding autistic identity on the job is closely associated with depression and suicidal thoughts.[119] Letting the mask slip feels like failure. What's wrong with me? Why can't I just act like everyone else?

What's more, creating a false neurotypical identity in the workplace ultimately means that any success you achieve is not really yours at all. The ultimate cost of passing is self-betrayal.

> . . . in passing I have still felt the pain of lying to myself, forcing myself into a predetermined mold - the one who I refer to as my 'impostor'. I was not accepted as 'normal', was still regarded as the odd one out, different, could not be accepted into the inner circles of the university in which I worked, regarded as cold, awkward, abrupt, standoffish, eccentric. Even though I became head of my department, I felt the constant pressure from those

who ostracized me. It affected my health, my mental state, as well as my own sense of self. . . . After my 'successful' career, I find that I have not been successful at all – I feel that I have given too much to someone who I am not. I betrayed myself, and feel the intense pain of that, and suffer the consequences at this stage, too intense to detail.[120]

Burnout

Academic psychology databases are full of articles about "burnout" as a problem for autism parents, special education teachers, even ABA therapists. But, as the author of a 2020 article noted, "the concept [of autistic burnout] is almost completely absent from the academic and clinical literature."[121] Only very recently have psychologists begun to consider that in the face of job stress and the relentless struggle to appear normal, autistic adults themselves might burn out.[122]

To the autistic community, "burnout" is what happens when someone no longer has the energy to maintain the "normal act."[123] Exhaustion forces the burned-out person to abandon work, or school, or whatever else she was engaged in—sometimes for a few weeks or months. Sometimes forever.[124]

There goes my job and my relationship. I had to move back in with a friend. Now, a year and a half later, I have no other friends aside from the two I've limited to online-only contact, barely speak to my family, and panic at the thought of leaving my house. I stim openly in public, wear headphones wherever I go, don't force myself to do anything that is too overwhelmingly stressful, and... overall just feel "more autistic" than ever.[125]

The neurotypical camouflage, carefully constructed over many years, now simply disappears: "The Mask coming off is exactly what happens during the Autistic Burnout period, your Autistic traits become more obvious as your brain goes into Safe Mode."[126]

Amethyst Schaber describes burnout and recovery from her own experience, defining it as

> something that happens to autistic people who have been in a sustained state of anxiety or exhaustion, or to autistic people who have been passing as non-autistic without enough time to be themselves and recover. It is awful. It's like a mental break-down, with skill loss and what professionals call 'regression' thrown in there too. Many autistics in burnout are depressed and many experience suicidal ideation.[127]

Sometimes autistic people refer to burnout as "regression," because the burned-out person loses the ability to mask and reverts to their authentic autistic self. Others find the term "regression" offensive, because it suggests that the authentic autistic identity is somehow inferior to neurotypical identity.

Regardless, burnout can be psychologically devastating. Max Jones writes that when autistics

> finally crumble from years of hiding their sensory pain and years of performing their social scripts and blaming themselves every time a script doesn't carry them successfully through a social situation, they will be angry at themselves and blame themselves for their nervous breakdown and autistic burn-out.[128]

Here the dangers of the normalization agenda discussed in Chapter Three come home to roost, its consequences dangerous, if not deadly: self-blame, anger directed inward, depression, suicidal thoughts and sometimes actions.[129]

And this bears directly on job turnover among autistics. Repeated cycles of burnout— periods of inability to work, followed by a return to work—is a common experience.[130] Some stay at one job until the mask fails, and then move on to another:

> a pattern throughout my life is that I would keep changing workplaces so I could have new groups of people I was working with so I could re-start the masking because I found that though I hate change and I like to get into a nice work routine, at the same time, when the masking starts breaking down, life starts to collapse around me in the workplace which results in burnout and me handing in my notice even though I do not have any-where else I can go to, and I would not be able to do much until I recover from the burnout . . .[131]

To avoid this cycle, many autistic adults try to work remotely. Or they attempt to set up their own businesses:

> After several bouts with suicide due to mental exhaustion, lack of support, beating myself up for not being able to conform to the rest of society, and not understanding why it was so hard for me, I decided that fully-remote work or self-employment was it for me.[132]

Some, however, are just too damaged by years of hiding themselves. Work becomes an impossibility: "I'm 35 years old and have been masking my entire life. It's exhausted me, and I can't do it anymore."[133]

CHAPTER SEVEN

No Reliable Source of Income

About 14% of autistic people work alongside neurotypicals in "integrated" or "community" workplaces—your standard "9-to-5" job. (Although many of these folks work less than 40 hours a week.) But autistics work in other places as well. A family business, where you are understood and valued by those who know you well, may be a great opportunity. Some families even start new businesses specifically for this purpose. In 2013, a Florida businessman founded a carwash for his son Andrew; the business has since expanded into three locations, all of which hire autistics.[1] The bakery Jacob Wittman's mother established for him not only provides meaningful work for her son, but also hires others on the spectrum. There they gain experience and job skills they can then use elsewhere.[2] But only a small minority of families have a business into which autistic relatives can be integrated, friends willing to hire their children, or the financial wherewithal to start a new business. So where do workers go who can't find "integrated" jobs? They may quit the regular job market entirely, as many do, hoping to subsist on government benefits (see below). A "sheltered workshop" or "work center" is pretty much their only other option.

Sheltered Workshops

Some 1,500 of these workshops exist nationwide today, employing somewhere between 100,00 and 400,000 workers with all disabilities.[3] (How many of these are autistic isn't clear.) Sheltered workshops are segregated facilities which hire exclusively (or almost exclusively) people with disabilities. Some are run by non-profit or charitable agencies like Goodwill. Others, affiliated with government programs for the disabled—Ability One is an example—are usually run by local community rehabilitation programs. These enterprises generally contract with businesses or government agencies to provide such services as stuffing envelopes, shredding papers, preparing goods for recycling, all for a low price. The ostensible goal of sheltered workshops is teaching workers job skills which will help them move into the integrated job market.[4] Frustratingly, they seldom meet this goal.

Very few "sheltered" workers ever move into non-segregated employment. Between 2017 and 2022, only 2.3% of such workers in Missouri managed to "graduate" into such employment.[5] And those who did make the transition, a 2012 study found, generally fared worse than people with disabilities entering the labor market on their own—requiring more expensive support services to maintain integrated employment and earning lower wages.[6] Far from preparing autistic and other disabled people for the ordinary world of work, sheltered workshops are static, segregated environments. Workers often languish there for decades.[7]

The most controversial aspect of the sheltered workshop model is its wage structure. Thanks to section 14(c) of the Fair Labor Standards Act, passed back in 1938, the disabled can be paid much less than the federal minimum wage. The original intention, in 1938, was to encourage the hiring of those with disabilities, who then very seldom had jobs at all. Attitudes towards the disabled have changed since then. But the wages have not. In the Missouri study cited above, some workers are still making less than $1 per hour. A 2020 report by the U.S. Commission on Civil Rights declared:

> Although Congress enacted the [sub-minimum wage] program with good intentions, the Department of Labor's enforcement data as well as several key civil rights cases and testimony from experts show that with regard to wage disparities, the program is rife with abuse and difficult to administer without harming employees with disabilities.[8]

Over the last decade, investigators have found that many workshops violate even the rules about sub-minimum wages, paying workers less than they are entitled to. Although wages of between $2 and $4 are common, some workers earn as little as 4 cents/hour. So, the Commission on Human Rights recommended that sheltered workshops be gradually phased out and replaced by programs that actually move disabled workers to integrated employment settings.[9]

This is a controversial finding. Sheltered workshops still have their supporters. The National Council on Severe Autism (NCSA), a parent- and professional-run organization, claims that shelter workers enjoy many benefits beyond wages:

> Workshop compensation typically represents just a small fraction of the benefits conferred on the disabled individual: the full support package may include Social Security Income (which can be reduced as wages increase), Medicaid-funded supports, in-home assistance, residential care, behavioral support, respite, recreation, and other therapeutic services.[10]

Of course, "respite" is actually a benefit for parents, not their autistic children. And people are generally entitled to Social Security Income and Medicaid services without participating in any workshop. The NCSA also argues that when workshops close, its employees often remain idle at home. This is true. But it's also clear proof that workshops are failing in their duty to prepare participants for integrated settings.

In 2012, workers with intellectual and developmental disabilities filed a lawsuit against the state of Oregon, arguing that under the Americans with Disabilities Act they had the right to work for no less than the federal minimum wage in an integrated workplace. In 2015, a federal judge found in their favor.[11] Autistic self-advocates generally support the Commission on Civil Rights' position, that even people with severe autism, some of whom have worked in sheltered work centers, deserve better. Today it seems the opponents of sheltered workshops are winning. The U.S. Department of Labor's Office of Disability Employment Policy has begun supporting a new national movement, Employment First, "centered on the premise that all citizens, including individuals with significant disabilities, are capable of full participation in integrated employment and community life."[12]

Under Employment First, state-run mentoring programs help shift disabled people out of sheltered workshops into competitive employment. In the spring of 2021, Cathy McMorris Rodgers and Bobby Scott introduced in Congress a bill designed to encourage transition to competitive integrated employment for people with disabilities.[13] The Transformation to Competitive Integrated Employment Act freezes any new certificates allowing employers to pay less than the minimum wage, offers grants to state governments to help them change how they support disabled workers, and to employers to "transition their business models," as well as increasing federal contributions to state funds that provide employment supports. As the fact sheet accompanying the bill states: "when individuals with disabilities transition to competitive employment, they are better able to achieve financial independence."[14] It remains to be seen whether the bill will actually pass. But it represents a big step forward for disabled people, including autistics.

Government "Benefits"

*. . . a fundamental belief of the United States is
that if you don't work, then you don't deserve
to live about [above] the poverty level.*[15]

A large minority of autistic adults simply can't work. They may be in agonizing physical pain from an illness. They may suffer from profound visual/auditory processing issues, extreme anxiety, or severe dyspraxia. Maybe they can't communicate with others or keep track of a schedule. Any number of other problems may prevent them from working. And so many rely on their families for support. But if their families can't or won't support them, they must fall back on government programs to survive. And frankly, the American system of disability "benefits" is a disgrace. Today's government benefits are designed to keep those who must depend on them in dire poverty. They provide few options for improving their situation. And they leave participants terrified about losing even the meager support the government provides.

The federal Social Security Administration manages two aid programs for the disabled. Supplemental Security Income (SSI) is supposed to help those who have never worked or have worked for only a short period of time, and who have few other financial assets. In contrast, Social Security Disability Insurance (SSDI) provides for those who were able to work and pay into the Social Security system for a certain number of years, accumulating a certain number of "credits" based on their earnings, before becoming too disabled for employment.

As one autistic recipient informs his peers, applying to these programs is complicated and onerous: "Sad to say, but you'll have to find a lawyer; it's almost impossible to get [SSI] on one's own. I think I was rejected twice before I found an attorney."[16] Applicants must prove they have a disability as defined by the Social Security Administration, whose definitions don't always correspond exactly with people's conditions. This is "medical eligibility." They must also demonstrate that they have very few financial resources. Both SSI and SSDI require extensive documentation. An almost obsessive attention to the application process is needed.

Most SSI recipients enter the program as children. Payments go to their families. But once they turn 18, they must re-apply on their own. Unfortunately, as one study found, two-thirds of disabled young adults who apply at ages 17 and 19 are turned down. Those who apply at exactly age 18 are twice as successful, but many of the 33% rejected at this point never try again.[17] Evidence exists that people who are dyspraxic or unable to speak (that is to say, more "obviously" autistic) do better at acquiring adult SSI benefits. Still, autistics who qualified as children are too often rejected at age 18.[18] "I've tried to get on government assistance, but they have hung up on me every or just flat out said 'No.' Not my fault they don't do the calculations right and refuse to listen."[19] As for SSDI (the program for those who once worked), only about 30% of disabled applicants are successful the first time they apply. The number who eventually receive SSDI payments increases as people reapply and appeal negative decisions.[20] Yet many abandon the process in frustration. It is just too demeaning to pursue.

Why is the application process so insulting? In the first place, public attitudes towards these programs are deeply negative. Despite being based on actual work history, SSDI is frequently viewed as a form of "welfare," rather than as a "right," like Social Security retirement payments.[21] The public perceive SSI recipients—especially those with invisible disabilities (like autism)—as "scammers" or "lazy" people, who "could really work if they wanted to".[22]

I've been on ssi since I was 19 and recently got off of it. After a while it gets boring not working and people treat you like a piece of s**t loser. You only get $700 a month [this was in 2017] which is barely enough to survive on, so it's not like you can buy nice things. You will not be "living the life" and people will hate you for living off their taxes especially with an invisible disability. Trust me, you WILL be thought of as a loser, especially as you age.[23]

It's easy to internalize such views, and refuse even to apply for payments the law entitles you to:

I had an uncle who had a developmental disability. It was very difficult for him to work. And he refused [to go on Disability]. He called it 'welfare' and he kept working even though it was very hard for him to work . . . [h]e had a real stigma attached to [welfare] . . .[24]

It's demeaning just to prove you're disabled. Even neurotypical people, who may once have taken pride in their strength or skill, must now prove that they no longer have those prized qualities. "Applying for disability is a demeaning, humiliating, invasive process," writes one such person.[25] But autistics must sink even lower. The price of benefits is conforming to the dehumanizing stereotypes defining autism in the SSA's infamous "Blue Book." Applicants must declare and provide evidence from a medical practitioner that they have a "mental disorder," involving both "qualitative deficits in verbal communication, nonverbal communication, and social interaction" and "significantly restricted, repetitive patterns of behavior, interests, or activities." In addition, they must provide medical evidence that they suffer from "extreme limitation of one, or marked limitation of two, of the following areas of mental functioning: understand, remember, or apply information;

interact with others; concentrate, persist, or maintain pace; adapt or manage oneself."[26]

These deficits may not be the real reasons an autistic person can't work. Overwhelming sensory sensitivities or extreme anxiety may be what disables them. But as neither is mentioned in the Blue Book, you may have to claim that you are "unable to interact with others" or "manage" yourself—even if this is a lie. Some applicants—especially women—may not present "restricted, repetitive patterns of behavior, interests, or activities." But since having such patterns is central to the Social Security Administration's definition of autism, telling the truth will result in denied benefits.

Even qualifying won't really do you much good. The Social Security Administration's "benefits" are meager, to put it mildly. In 2023, the maximum amount an individual could receive from the SSI program was $914/month; this comes to $10,968/year.[27] The federal poverty line for a single individual was $14,580/year in 2023. Even worse, if the recipient earns more than a nominal amount of money, receives too much support from family or friends or has more than $2,000 worth of personal possessions, benefits are reduced proportionally. SSI payments will be suspended altogether if earnings are more than $1,470 in any given month (although if earnings drop the next month they may be reinstated).[28] SSDI payments, in contrast, vary by how long someone worked before applying to the program. On average, in 2023, recipients received $1,483 a month, which comes to $17,796/year—above the poverty line but still not much to live on.[29] Again, benefits shrink if the recipient is still earning a "significant" amount of money or has saved too much. A spouse's income or benefits paid to children can also reduce the payments the autistic recipient receives in either SSI or SSDI.

Both programs provide access to the federal SNAP program, reducing food costs. Importantly, basic health care is also provided. SSDI recipients qualify for Medicare, and SSI recipients for Medicaid.

Autistic people would often rather work, at least part time. But for the sake of the health care benefits, they stay on SSI/SSDI:

> The thing is that I am afraid of losing the Medicare (the only medical insurance I have, and really that is all I can afford) if I decide to try my hand at re-entering the competitive job market. The thought of having hallucinations again because I have limited access to mental health care is not a good one. Especially in my state, which is notorious for warehousing mental health patients without treatment for indefinite periods of time. I want to be my own man again, but I do not want to lose the only security I have and be left with nothing if things do not work out alright.[30]

Where in the United States can you actually survive on SSI or SSDI alone?

> I actually get SSI for my Asperger Syndrome, and take it from me you may think you can live on that much money but it becomes very hard to make that money last I almost always run out a week before the next pay.[31]

> I am on SSDI and PUA [pandemic unemployment assistance] and can barely cover my rent and food . I can't afford Medicare copayment . I can't afford basic things like dental care either.[32]

Most SSI recipients devote their entire benefit check to housing costs, with nothing left for other expenses. Interviewed during the first wave of the Covid pandemic in New York City, one autistic woman told the reporter that she "receives monthly Social Security Disability Insurance (SSDI) payments, but they don't come close to covering rent and other basic expenses, particularly given the high cost of living in NYC."[33] She did dogwalking on the side, but still struggled to make ends meet.

Many SSI/SSDI recipients depend on getting paid under the table. They join the informal economy to avoid reporting their earnings to the government. Otherwise, their benefits would be reduced or eliminated, and they couldn't make rent. They run errands, clean houses, mow lawns, care for people's children, do a little data entry. Not because they are lawless scammers. They have learned (often painfully) that trying to survive on disability payments alone will kill you.

Acceptance

... it seems like independent living is way easier for most NT [neurotypical] people. Even NT people with substantial problems.[34]

There will always be some autistic people (and some neurotypicals) who simply cannot work, due to physical problems or psychological problems, or both. There will always be some autistic people (and neurotypicals) who earn very little, regardless of how hard they try. Far too many Americans view such people as a drag on their families, their neighbors, and society as a whole. True, some require expensive medical care. And some may be self-destructive or even threatening to others, requiring constant supervision. Unable to support themselves and in need of substantial support from others, they are not "independent" as this term is popularly understood. We cannot forget, though, that even the most "burdensome" are still human. They remain independent as unique human beings, even if not in other ways. The American regard for human dignity demands that they, too, be accepted. A society that simply throws them away has thrown away its own moral compass.

And we should never forget our own role in creating their dependence. Most autistic people today cannot earn enough to live on, and are therefore compelled to rely on the government or others. Lack of social support, discrimination, and hostility towards those who are "different" all contribute to this situation. Not that unemployed autistics are inherently doomed to dependence. Despite the ineffectiveness of Vocational Rehabilitation programs, autism job clubs[35], programs run by disability organizations such as The Arc[36], and various corporate initiatives[37] are helping autistics get hired. As to businesses: some simple shifts in hiring practices, the creation of more sensory-friendly workspaces, and a willingness to make minor accommodations, could put countless autistics on their own two feet. The changes needed are relatively inexpensive, but they do require employers and co-workers to tolerate employees "of difference" just as they are, without demanding they camouflage as something else. Lack of acceptance is the real barrier. A concerted effort to increase not just autism awareness but active appreciation of autistics could result in enormous savings for government programs, for families, and for communities. Wouldn't this be a prudent investment in our future?

PART IV

Health Care

"It's like Satan designed an autistic hell." [1]

CHAPTER EIGHT

Physical Health

M el Baggs, influential blogger and autism activist, suffered from a variety of medical problems that worsened over time. On March 28, 2020, she posted the following on one of her blogs. It is not written in her usual, carefully honed style—she was too desperate:

> I am going to run out of crucial meds. This is me shamelessly begging for money. . . . It needs to be real money, not a gift card, because we have to use it at the pharmacy. If the pharmacy is open. And it needs to be a whole lot of money because meds are expensive and we are running out of ones that will keep me alive. . . . something is massively messed up with my benefits I have no access to them. Please help please someone help ideally lots of people help.[2]

Mel died less than two weeks after she put up this post. She was 39 years old.[3]

Citizens of developed countries with national health services may be shocked at how commonly people beg for money to pay for medications and medical treatments in the U.S., where we supposedly have "the greatest health system in the world." The idea of health care as a human right actually arose in America.[4] In 1944, President Franklin

Delano Roosevelt proposed to Congress what he called a "Second Bill of Rights," which would include "the right to adequate medical care and the opportunity to achieve and enjoy good health."[5] But this never became law in the U.S. Currently the idea of universal health coverage is being debated, but we are very far from agreement on the subject.[6] But in the absence of such coverage, how do Americans manage to obtain health care? The answer: they find a way to pay for it, they beg for help, or they go without it.

The one exception is emergency room care. Thanks to the Emergency Medical Treatment and Labor Act (1986), hospitals who receive federal funds for their services are obliged to offer anyone who comes in, regardless of ability to pay, certain medical services. If someone comes in with an "emergency medical condition" (the exact meaning of this phrase remains under debate, but it includes things like being in labor, having a broken leg, suffering a heart attack, etc.), they are entitled by law to receive an adequate medical screening exam, performed by a qualified professional and using whatever hospital facilities (X-Ray machines, MRIs, lab tests) are necessary. Once the cause of the problem is known, the hospital then must either stabilize the patient (get them to the point where their condition is no longer an "emergency") or transfer them to another facility that can achieve stabilization. And that facility is then required to accept the patient and work to stabilize them. But any non-emergency care (and follow-up care for emergencies) has a price tag.

Americans struggle to make such payments. Indeed, unexpected medical expenses are the most common cause of bankruptcies for middle-class families in the United States.[7] They, too, sometimes must beg for help.

Paying for Health Care

According to the U.S. Census Bureau, in 2020 about 54% of the

American population as a whole relied on private, employment-related health insurance to pay for health care. Another 10% paid for their own private insurance. 18% relied on Medicare (a government program for the elderly and the disabled), and another 18% on Medicaid (primarily a program for the poor). A much smaller group got their insurance based on their association with the military. And almost 9% of the population was uninsured and thus completely unprotected from medical calamity.[8]

Private insurance offers the best chance of receiving excellent medical treatment, but it is far from perfect. Many privately insured Americans still struggle to deal not only with the costs of the initial premiums, but also with the co-pays demanded for most services, plus any unexpected medical bills incurred (often unknowingly) while using a medical provider or ambulance service that is "out of network." According to the Kaiser Family Foundation, more Americans worry about unexpected medical bills than about the cost of rent, groceries, or heat and light for their homes.[9] 12% of families with private insurance struggled to pay these bills in 2018.[10]

Autistic individuals are much less likely to be covered by private insurance than the rest of the population. According to the latest data, only 39% of autistic children are covered entirely—as compared to 50% of children with other special health care needs, and 60% of children without such needs. And autistic children of color have even less protection than White children: only 21% of Latino/Latina kids, and 37% of Black kids are covered by private insurance, compared to 49% of White kids.[11] We have no reliable statistics on the number of autistic adults who enjoy private coverage, so all we can do is make educated guesses.[12] Remember, though, that only a minority work at all. Those who do seldom put in enough hours per week to meet the requirements for coverage under their employer's insurance plan (assuming they even offer one). Nor do they usually earn enough to pay their share of private insurance premiums. Some adults may be covered by a spouse's or other family member's plan. But relatively few autistic adults enjoy the benefits of private insurance based on their own employment.

While about 36% of the American public as a whole depend on public medical plans offered by the federal government, the percentage of autistics who use such plans is higher. 45% of autistic children rely on government plans exclusively; another 11% use a combination of private and public ones.[13] While data is lacking, there's no doubt that a larger percentage of autistic than neurotypical adults depend on government medical plans like Medicaid and Medicare.[14] Yet evidence also suggests autistic Americans are frequently unable to enroll and benefit from these programs, even when they are eligible for them. This is especially true of those belonging to racial or ethnic minorities.[15] Autistics who can't obtain Medicare or Medicaid coverage are generally left with no health insurance at all.

Medicare

Dealing with Medicare's complicated rules and bureaucracy can be tough for anyone. Even deciding what plan to enroll in can be overwhelming. This is what one magazine article, directed at the general public, had to say: "Using one word, how would you describe the Medicare health insurance landscape in the U.S.? Dizzying? Maybe. Overwhelming? Probably. Confusing? Definitely."[16]

Medicare, established in 1965, was originally designed for retirees who had paid into the Social Security system over the course of their working lives; coverage was added in 1973 for adults with disabilities who had worked for a specified number of years. If you're disabled and haven't paid into Social Security for long enough, Medicare will only cover you if you first qualify for Social Security Disability Insurance, which—as we already saw in Chapter Four—is not easy to do. Once approved, you must wait five months for SSDI benefits to actually kick in, then another 24 months before you're eligible for Medicare. So even after demonstrating your disability, you have to wait another 2.5 years before you are covered.[17] In the meantime, good luck paying for the medical care you need.

Threading the Medicare maze is especially hard for autistics. They tend to resist making the unavoidable phone calls, and they're wary of relying for advice on agents whom they don't know. And so, more often than neurotypicals, they get into problems by trying to "go it alone":

I decided to find a medicare advantage plan. I guess normally you'd talk to a sales rep to find the best plan and so on, but I strongly resist having to talk to anyone, so decided to look through the plans, find the one most appealing to me and put in an application myself. No problem there. But there are things I didn't know, like...... I already had a prescription drug plan and figured I'd just keep it so found an advantage plan that didn't include the drug plan. How was I supposed to know that by going with a new plan would cancel my current drug plan, even if it didn't include a drug plan. I get a letter that my application was accepted - AFTER open enrollment has ended so can't make changes. And I get a letter from social security with what my payment and deductions will be starting January with a higher amount ($60 higher) for the prescription drug plan, so with my increase I'd be getting less.[18]

What's more, Medicare doesn't cover important medications and services: dental care and dentures, hearing exams and hearing aids, eye exams and glasses. These gaps pose major problems for the very population it's intended to serve, the elderly and the disabled. Other programs like "Medigap" and Medicare Part F do cover these services, and help with the deductibles and co-payments for services in the

PHYSICAL HEALTH

other parts of Medicare.[19] But it costs money to add these programs. Many Americans—notably autistics—simply can't afford them.

For an older person, or a disabled person with complex needs, Medicare can be a much cheaper alternative to private insurance. But it is far from free, even if you've "paid into the system" your whole working life. Premiums, deductibles, and co-pays all cost money.[20] As one autistic adult put it:

> Am I the only one that thinks it is kind of messed up that you pay into Medicare all your life, and then, when you finally get coverage (either through age or proven disability), you still have to pay monthly plan premiums, deductibles, and don't receive even basic care like prescription coverage without buying additional plans?[21]

Medicaid

Unlike Medicare, Medicaid was expressly created as a medical safety net for the disabled and the poor. Medicare is run by the federal government. Individual states run and pay for Medicaid, with the help of funds from the federal government. What the eligibility qualifications for Medicaid are, what kinds of services it will pay for, how much it will pay for these services, how it will finance its part of the program's cost, and how long a waiting list for enrollment in the basic plan and for specific programs it will tolerate: all these depend on which state you live in. Plus, it only offers emergency services, family planning, pregnancy-related services, and preventative medicine for children for free. Adults have to pay for their own preventative care. For indigent autistic adults this is very difficult. And, just like Medicare, Medicaid charges co-pays for other services.

If you belong to a "mandatory eligibility group"—which includes the disabled—a federal mandate that overrides state choices assures you Medicaid coverage. But you must first enroll in the Supplemental Security Income (SSI) program, which, as we have seen, is tough to get into and still fails to provide support adequate for a decent life. Many autistics seek employment, hoping to lose their dependence on SSI. Yet if they do find a job, the Medicaid coverage they so desperately need abruptly disappears.

> I can't afford to go OFF disability right now because if disability wasn't covering my meds, the Abilify alone would cost hundreds of dollars a month. I feel kind of stuck in that regard, because unless I can find a job that I can work that has great insurance, I'll have to go off of it [Abilify] if I go off of disability.[22]

If you don't belong to one of the mandatory eligibility groups (or if you're disabled but can't qualify for SSI), you can only obtain medical assistance on the basis of poverty. But this itself requires a delicate balancing act. As of 2023, some 1.9 million Americans, both autistic and neurotypical, disabled and not, fell into the "Medicaid gap"— meaning they were too poor to afford private health insurance, but not quite poor enough to qualify for Medicaid based on their own state's definition of poverty.[23] Three quarters of these people lived in just four states: Florida, Texas, Georgia and North Carolina.[24] By refusing to adapt their definition of poverty to include the working poor (as encouraged by the Affordable Care Act of 2010[25]), these four states left thousands of their citizens completely uncovered for medical care. In Texas, for example, a single parent with two children must earn no more than $3,733/year (17% of the federal poverty threshold) in order to be eligible.[26] A parent earning that little may qualify for Medicaid, but she and her children will starve to death in the process. Autistic adults who work are especially vulnerable to the Medicaid gap. There are also racial and ethnic disparities in the Medicaid system. Whites are more likely to receive aid than people of color.[27]

Finding a Doctor

Many doctors and hospitals hesitate to accept patients whose only health coverage comes from Medicare or Medicaid. Government-funded health insurance pays much less than private plans for office visits, hospital stays, and prescription drugs. One study found that Medicare payments were only half as much as those from private insurers.[28] Medicaid reimbursements to doctors and hospital may be more or less than Medicare's, but they're still always lower than those from private insurers.[29] This is why some doctors and hospitals simply refuse to take patients covered by government programs. And under U.S. law, this is perfectly legal. According to research done by the Kaiser Family Foundation, about 1% of U.S. non-pediatric doctors "opt out" of all Medicare cases; about 7% of psychiatrists do.[30] More doctors continue to see old patients after they move to Medicare, but won't accept any new Medicare patients.[31] Medicaid recipients are even more likely to be refused. In 2017, only 74% of physicians were willing to accept new patients covered by Medicaid, while 96% welcomed those with private insurance.

For parents, even those with public insurance, it is relatively easy to find pediatricians for their autistic children. (They may never, though, have a single designated pediatrician, which has a negative effect on "continuity of care.") It's when the child reaches age 18 that problems abound. Overscheduled pediatricians are often unwilling or unable to prepare young patients for the transition to adult medicine.[32] And as we have seen, the social services they knew as children also drop away, leaving them with little or no support as they search for a new physician. As they have no advance contact with adult medicine providers, the new medical relationship may have to start from scratch. It doesn't help that this is the same moment they are cut off from children's Medicaid services, and left searching for coverage. This makes providers less willing to take them on as new patients.[33]

Disturbingly, many doctors simply refuse to see adult autistic patients. Doctors rejected autistic patients three times more often than patients with other disabilities, according to one study.[34] Often the concern is financial.[35] Autistic office visits typically take longer than neurotypical visits, placing a financial burden on both doctors and the health care systems they work for. As one physician put it:

> They [autistics] take more time and the more time you're spending with a patient, the less money you're making. Especially someone with severe autism and who may be non-verbal and may have a guardian, you can't do a 10-15 minute visit. You need a half-hour visit. And that's lost revenue.[36]

Unfortunately, health systems continue to pressure doctors to limit their time with patients, despite studies suggesting that this lowers the quality of care, while increasing the likelihood of medical errors and the need for follow-up visits.[37] (This also works against those who have suffered trauma, the elderly, and those who do not speak English.) All of these patients need more time, and time, of course, is money. So systems either rush them through, providing only second-rate care, or refuse to see them at all.

Braving the Medical System

The aim of American medical systems is to provide care at the lowest possible cost and with the least likelihood of financial or other risk to the institutions and medical personnel involved. These administrative systems frustrate even the neurotypicals for whom they were designed. Consider the dreaded phone call needed to get an appointment: long wait times and hang-ups can stymie anyone. Autistics with innate communication and social differences must navigate the same phone system to access care. [38] In one recent study, 38% of them reported that simply trying to set up a medical appointment could trigger a shutdown; 15% said it could lead to a full meltdown. [39] Of course, if you're a non-speaking autistic, someone else must make the phone call— unless a user-friendly computer system for making appointments is in place, and you have access to a computer.

Let us suppose, though, that you've managed to make an appointment. The day has arrived. For low-income people, regardless of neurotype, transportation to medical facilities can be a problem. But let's again assume that you've somehow managed to reach the medical office building. Now you must brave the check-in system. You try to calmly meet all its demands for information, in person or on the computer, while standing in a loud, brightly-lit, usually overcrowded lobby. Next comes the waiting room—also crowded, over-lit, noisy, smelly, frightening, uncomfortable. Waiting times are unpredictable, but typically long. A growing number of medical systems have begun providing "sensory packs," meant primarily to help autistic children. These represent a well-intentioned but somewhat misguided effort to reduce the stress of waiting. When I requested one of these packs from my own medical center, I was dismayed by its contents. Some of the toys might provide a bit of distraction, but there were no ear plugs, masks, or other means of reducing sensory distress.

Finally, you reach the doctor's office. The crowds, the smells, and the noise of the waiting room abruptly disappear. But bright fluorescent lights still assault your eyes, the scent of antiseptics sickens you, and crinkly examination gowns are a torment. Eventually (again, after an unpredictable waiting time) the doctor arrives. Few physicians, though, realize how to make things easier for their autistic patients. [40] One doctor learned that where she sat in the examination room made a real difference: "Sometimes I sit beside the patient, so I am not looking directly at them, I'm not facing them . . . And then, I focus on what brought them in today." [41] Good strategy, since many autistic adults are more comfortable talking when not being looked at. Some physicians also provide extra-large monitors for their computers, so their patients can see the same thing they are seeing. Some take extra time to explain the medical problem. Other possible accommodations might include lowered lights, stim toys for stress relief, updates on how late the doctor is really running, and warnings about how long the blood pressure cuff is going to be really tight. Still, accommodating medical staff are rare. I had to argue vigorously and repeatedly just to get the lights dimmed while my autistic daughter—who had migraines and acute light sensitivity—waited to see her doctor. Of course, they were immediately turned back up once the doctor arrived, but at least when the staff actually listened to me, she didn't have to be in pain so long.

As Eric Garcia notes: "It can be challenging for autistic people to communicate with their doctors successfully in a system that's built with neurotypical patients in mind."[42] The demand for speech, from people who find verbalizing difficult, adds undue pressure to an already traumatic situation. As one patient put it:

I'm autistic and the combination of my diseases and being autistic means that verbal communication is very hard for me. Most of the time I only get parts of what I want to communicate out of my mouth, but in healthcare the verbal communication norm is so strong that my requests for written communication have been denied.[43]

Because of their interoception differences, even those who speak fluently can have trouble describing their physical condition in ways that make sense to the physician, or identifying the location of pain. They may not be able to "rate your pain on a scale from 1 to 10": scales like this are almost always meaningless to them.

Few doctors realize how disturbing the physical contact required for a standard physical exam can be for autistics. "Stick out your tongue and say 'ahh'" is a nauseating demand for someone with a powerful gag reflex. Having your stomach palpated, lights pointed directly into your eyes, a cold stethoscope pressed against your chest may be just enough, after everything else that has gone on, to provoke a meltdown. Getting a shot may lead to disaster:

I have a crippling needle phobia which I'm pretty much at an impasse with. The overwhelming fear and anxiety always leads to a meltdown, which means that it has been physically impossible for me to get any needle procedure since I was 8 yo unless I'm put under a general anesthetic with gas.[44]

Exams must take place and shots must be given, of course. But until trust is established and clear explanations given for all procedures, many autistic patients will continue to avoid essential medical care.

In one recent study, 65% of autistic adults said they would wait until they had an emergency before seeking out a medical practitioner. This compares to 52% of non-autistic adults.[45] Doctors and nurses behaving badly explains only some of this delay. Autistic individuals sometimes fail to even recognize they have a medical or dental problem thanks to their difficulties with interoception. Parents may miss signs of ill-health in their autistic children, who may not recognize or verbalize them. And even if parents do seek help, physicians may still miss important medical issues, because autistics often don't "present" in the same ways neurotypicals do. So needs go unmet and health problems fester, sometimes until they become life-threatening.

What Do Doctors Know?

The quality of medical care is shaped primarily by practitioners' knowledge of their patients' physical and emotional needs. When it comes to autistics, that knowledge is often abysmal. Most American doctors, however competent, have never been trained to treat autistic patients.[46] Some admit to flying by the seat of their pants:

> I mean certainly we knew about autism, and we may have learned about it in some of our classes, but from a training standpoint in managing patients or understanding it, I think [we were taught] very, very, little. I don't recall any directed training in autism; you know, outside of the pathophysiology.[47]

Pediatricians tend to do better, since our society still believes (inaccurately) that autism is a disorder of childhood. Physicians who treat adults do far worse. In one study of a large medical system, 77% of the doctors sampled (including specialists) considered their own knowledge of and skill in treating autistic adults to be only poor or fair; for doctors in adult medicine departments, the number was 79%. None reported having received any formal training in screening or diagnosing autism in patients.[48]

We know autistic patients struggle to communicate with their doctors. But doctors are also at fault.[49] Indeed, a frequent complaint autistics make about doctors is that they seem to speak an alien language.[50]

> One problem I have encountered is communicating symptoms and answering questions in the way they [the doctors] want.. For example, ambiguity of questions like "is the pain sharp?" (What is their meaning of sharp? What does sharp mean applied to pain? Does it mean stabbing? Or do they mean is it the opposite of dull pain? And what is dull pain?) There has been so much miscommunication and misdiagnosis in the past that I now tend to say, "I'm sorry, I don't really understand what you are getting at". Though honest, this just seems to exasperate them - it's like an exam and I am refusing to come up with the answer they want."[51]

Because they can't understand, assess the importance of, or even believe what their autistic patients say, physicians too often dismiss their concerns. Many autistic adults have given up expecting their doctors to listen:

> Doctors? Might as well just sit there and have a staring contest with each other because they are going to ignore every word I say verbally and in writing anyway.[52]

> . . . in terms of communicating with my GP, I'm okay with the reality that he probably won't really understand the complexity of my issues, or my needs. I'm fine with him just taking my blood pressure, and screening me for the usual health problems, but if he decides that my vitals are okay, well then fair enough. I'll thank him, and go back home, and keep resorting to my trusty home remedies to deal with the myriad of disabling symptoms his exam failed to detect. Because I've learned over the years that complaining to doctors about my impossible-to-prove symptoms gets me nowhere, and generally just causes them to think I'm making it all up for attention.[53]

Not surprisingly, doctors have the hardest time communicating with non-speaking or echolaic patients; they tend to fall back on what a caregiver tells them, rather than finding a way to communicate directly with the patient. This works if the caregiver really understands the person being cared for. Too often, though, doctor, patient, and caregiver may all have competing ideas about what is going on and how to deal with it. Or the doctor and caretaker may agree while the patient doesn't. Unable to argue verbally, he or she may resist the prescribed treatment (possibly inappropriate anyway). Reliance on caregivers is most problematic when intimate matters such as sexuality or drug/alcohol use are under consideration.[54] Simply because they don't want it to be true or don't believe that it's possible, some care-givers may insist that their clients aren't sexually active. But they may be wrong. This is why too many autistic patients never receive contra-ceptives, screenings for sexually-transmitted diseases, pap smears, or any sex education at all. On the other hand, some gynecologists are glad to recommend sterilization at the care-giver's, not the patient's, request.[55]

Autistics often have more complex medical needs than other Americans. This leaves primary care physicians, already uncertain about their own competence, reluctant to offer comprehensive med-ical services. They concentrate on annual check-ups and treatments for acute illness; every other issue is referred to specialists, even when this is medically unnecessary. So patients wander from one physician to another, with no doctor understanding them very well, let alone advocating for them.[56] Potentially serious problems may arise when care coordination is hobbled. This is particularly evident when med-ication is involved.

Medicating Autism

Prescribing medicine effectively for autistic people requires knowl-edge, experience, and careful thought. Many physicians are too pressed for time to give their complex needs careful consideration, and most lack the necessary knowledge and experience to choose ap-propriate medications and dosages. For example, few doctors realize how frequently autistics have "paradoxical reactions," where a medi-cation has the opposite effect to the one intended. Tranquilizers like Valium and Ativan, for instance, may agitate rather than calm some autistics.

I had [an EEG], and it was supposed to include a sleep time, but that was a BIG mistake! That was how I discovered that anesthetics and sedatives work opposite on me from other people. They gave me a sedative (Medazolam, I think), and it made my heart race, and I began to hallucinate, got violent, began racing around the hospital and tried to break into an elevator shaft by mistake because I thought Hitler was there, and trying to kill me. I was only 8 years old. It took about a week before I could sleep after that, and normally I have no issues falling asleep easily. To this day, any kind of pain pill or sedative, sends me into manic orbit, but Adderall and coffee put me sound-asleep.[57]

Allergy medicines actually increase allergy symptoms of some patients.

Even fewer doctors appreciate how exquisitely sensitive autistics can be to drugs. A "standard" dose may actually be dangerous, while a much lower dose would be effective. And drugs that work for other people may simply not work for this population:

> I've been on a lot of psych meds, because I have the dubious honor of having anxiety and bipolar disorder besides Aspergers, and I've found that most of the meds I tried don't really work as intended. Either that, or the side effects are rare, severe or both.[58]

Physician ignorance and failure to monitor drug effects can seriously endanger autistic people, who take, on average, more medications than neurotypicals. Beyond prescriptions for common physical ailments like high blood pressure or diabetes, they may also take psychotropic drugs more often than neurotypicals. These are drugs that change brain chemistry, altering mood, thoughts, perceptions, and behaviors. Psychotropics include different classes of medications: anti-depressants, anti-psychotics, anxiolytics (for anxiety), ADHD drugs, mood stabilizers, etc. Some autistics (like some neurotypicals) actually need them to maintain mental health. But psychotropic drugs are not always prescribed correctly. Some doctors attempt to medicate what are really just symptoms of autism, exposing their patients to unneeded and potentially harmful substances. [59] As one autistic adult put it:

The propensity of psychiatrists to prescribe medication Is why I don't trust them. I was given a prescription the first day I ever saw a psychiatrist. Without having a firm diagnosis I was already being treated. Another psychiatrist I was seeing prescribed me medication without ever looking at my file. I had been transferred to her care and found out after a couple of visits that she didn't even have access to my file. She had no idea what my diagnosis was or any of my issues, but she was willing to offer me new medications, one of which made things much worse instead of better.[60]

Autistic kids are also overprescribed psychotropic drugs, which is particularly troubling since their brains are still developing.

Those Undesirable Behaviors

Despite ongoing, spurious claims to the contrary, medication can't "cure" autism. It is also a fact that no medicine exists to "treat" autism, in the sense of changing its core characteristics. What can sometimes be treated—by therapy, drugs, or both—are certain undesirable behaviors—behaviors that neither the autistic person nor those around him want—such as frequent meltdowns, aggression, and self-injury. The U.S. Food and Drug Administration has approved two drugs for the treatment of "irritability" and undesirable behaviors, and in each case only for children between the ages of 5 and 17. The two drugs are risperidone (Risperdal) and aripiprazole (Abilify)— two "atypical" or "second-generation" anti-psychotics. Originally developed to deal with severe schizophrenia, anti-psychotics achieve their effects largely by sedating the patient. So kids stop engaging in unwanted behaviors because they've essentially been knocked out.

About half of autistic patients receive little or no benefits from these drugs. The other half (typically those with the most serious problems) find irritability and aggression reduced by Risperdal and Abilify. And even then, their effects are only short-term. That is, their effectiveness wanes over time.[61] Not that anti-psychotics aren't worth trying, but they are dangerous medications, with potentially health-damaging and even life-threatening side-effects.[62] They should be only cautiously prescribed and quickly discontinued if ineffective.

Their sedating effects can themselves harm patients. Research on a large population of autistic and/or intellectually disabled children in Wales found that the same child was more likely to be injured when taking anti-psychotics than when not.[63] But increased risk of injury is far from the only problem. Anti-psychotics can cause significant weight gain: an average of eleven pounds during the first year they are prescribed, according to one study.[64] Obesity can have devastating effects on an autistic child's already fraught social life, and lead to the development of type 2 diabetes and/or heart disease. In children with co-occurring epilepsy, some studies have concluded that anti-psychotics may heighten the risk of seizures. Those who take these drugs long-term may suffer irreversible neurological damage, like tardive dyskinesia.[65] Terrifying emotional reactions may also arise, increasing the risk of suicide attempts. Finally, one study found that children taking anti-psychotics are significantly more likely to die unexpectedly than those not taking the drugs.[66]

The FDA has approved risperidone and aripiprazole only for the treatment of undesirable autistic behaviors, and only for use in children aged 5 to 17. But doctors have been quick to use these drugs "off-label" on adults[67] and even occasionally on pre-schoolers.[68] Other anti-psychotics, with similar dangerous side-effect profiles, are often used off-label these days for treating autistic "irritability." These include quetiapine (Seroquel), ziprazadone (Geodon), and clozapine (Clozaril). According to recent estimates, about 20% of autistic children and more than 40% of adults are taking (or at least have been prescribed) atypical anti-psychotics.[69]

If we look at what autistic people themselves have to say about anti-psychotics, the picture is mixed. Some are very happy with the trade-off between benefits and dangers:

Seroquel has been a godsend for me. It is the only thing that lets me sleep and does wonders for my anxiety. However, I have to take it with Klonopin because, in my case, it causes restless leg.[70]

I've been on two anti-psychotics, risperidone and aripiprazole, I'm still on the latter at 10 mg, a third of the maximum dose. To me it I haven't felt like I'm drugged, sedated or "chemically restrained", I just feel like me just without the anxiety and with more energy for everyday things.[71]

Others, however, find the effects much worse than the behaviors they are supposed to treat. In some, the drugs result in excitement rather than sedation (one of those paradoxical reactions): "I have personal experience with risperdol/risperidone. It made me feel constantly on edge, like I would lose it any minute."[72] Others were sedated, but found the state intolerable:

I took [risperidone] for months and months and months. Other people (people who didn't have to see me struggling to remember how to make ramen, dragging myself to the bathroom, and being unable to find the grocery store half a mile away) thought it helped because I could no longer verbalize depression or anxiety (or much of anything). I felt just as bad, if not worse, on the inside. I HAVE heard of people being helped by it. I just am not one of those people, nor do I know any of those people.[73]

In still others, anti-psychotics like Seroquel caused acute emotional distress:

It is beyond words, just the most terrible feeling of impending doom and unhappiness. I feel like my life is just terrible, and I will never feel happy again. I have had suicidal depression, anxiety, and panic attacks all my life, but this feeling is worse than all of those put together.[74]

Far too many physicians fail to adequately monitor the effects these powerful drugs have on their autistic patients.[75] As one researcher put it: "clinicians have little engagement with drug adverse effects (AE) monitoring programs due to their overwork, lack of education, and awareness provided by healthcare systems."[76] They may never notice that a drug is not working, or is causing dangerous side effects. If a problem is brought to their notice, some doctors simply increase the dose of an already problematic drug or switch the patient to another medication in the same class, again without monitoring the results. Lack of monitoring seriously compromises the medication of autistic behaviors. And the problems grow when multiple drugs are involved.

Polypharmacy

Of more than 700 children seen at a Seattle autism clinic in 2019, 75% were prescribed 2 or more psychotropic drugs, and 28% were prescribed more than four. 68% of these children had two or more drugs prescribed during a single visit to the clinic, and 15% were prescribed more than four during a single visit. Imagine all that powerful, mind-altering medication entering kids' still-developing brains.

Sometimes more than one class of psychotropic—anti-psychotics plus anti-depressants, for instance—were prescribed. [77] The children seen at the Seattle clinic may have been more heavily medicated because they showed particularly disturbing behaviors. But researchers have found that of all those diagnosed with autism and covered by commercial insurance in 2014, a little over 1% of 3-4-year-olds, 24% of 5-11-year-olds, and 45% of 12-17-year-olds were taking two or more psychotropic drugs. Adult numbers were similar to those of the 12-17-year-olds. Among autistic Medicaid recipiants in the same year, the numbers were even higher.[78]

"Polypharmacy" refers to the use of multiple drugs by a single patient for one or more conditions. Polypharmacy (the use of multiple drugs) is especially prevalent among autistics, but also very common within the U.S. population as a whole.[79] And this presents a major problem for all concerned: that of dangerous drug interactions. When the anti-depressant Lexapro is prescribed at the same time as the anti-psychotic Risperidone, for example, irregular heartbeat, sometimes leading to death, can result. Taking the ADHD drug Adderall with another anti-depressant, Bupropion, can intensify the side effects of Adderall, producing agitation, even seizures. Psychotropic drugs can also interact with many non-psychotropics. Risperidone, for example, interacts with a whopping 649 other medications.

Most medical systems have programs in place to prevent doctors from prescribing problematic drug combinations, and to prevent pharmacists from filling them. But such programs are only as good as the medical personnel who enter data into the computer. What's more, doctors can and sometimes do override these programs, based on their personal assessments of what's needed. Autistic patients may see multiple doctors, sometimes from different medical systems; one simply may not know what the other is prescribing. What's more, the drugs prescribed to autistics shift frequently—one drug may be discarded, either because it is deemed ineffective, or it has too many side effects, or because insurance will no longer pay for it—and another of the same type substituted. The consequences may potentially be lethal.[80] When doctors fail to monitor their autistic (and neurotypical) patients' medications properly, the results can be death, severe illness, or simple misery:

> I try to seek mental health care, and the end result is more drugs with devastating side effects (I'm already on a cocktail of psychotropic medications and struggle daily with the debilitating side effects. It is a vicious cycle...[81]

It should be clear, from what has been said so far, that the majority of American physicians know little about autism. They communicate ineffectively with autistic patients, and as a result make faulty diagnoses and offer inappropriate treatments. In short, the American medical system, as it now exists, endangers the lives of autistic people. But to make matters worse, "ableism" (bias against disabled people) sometimes leads to autistic people being entirely denied essential care.

Denial of Care: Transplanting Organs

In 2012, Paul Corby, a Pennsylvania adult with autism and anxiety, was suffering from increasingly severe heart issues. But he couldn't get a referral from his own doctor to a transplant center due to his "psychiatric issues" and his autism. The doctor couldn't get past the fact that Paul carried a doll with him as a source of comfort. He was also unable to name all nineteen medications he was currently taking. (Neither could his neurotypical mother, who had to rely on a list to keep track of them—something the doctor ignored). Despite multiple trips to the Cardiac Intensive Care Unit, Paul is still waiting for his heart transplant.[82] In 2020, the Pennsylvania legislature finally outlawed discrimination in transplants on the basis of physical or mental disability.[83] It remains to be seen how much good this change will do.

The United States, like other countries, has a severe shortage of organs for transplantation into people whose own organs are failing. About twenty-one Americans die every day waiting for an organ to become available. And waiting lists are very long—at the time I'm writing this 106,000 Americans are still on various lists.[84] But how do you get on a waiting list? And how are you eventually selected from the list to receive the heart, kidney, or liver you need to survive? To begin with, your own doctor must refer you to a transplant center—a hospital with specialists in organ transplant surgery. This was what stopped Paul Corby—his personal physician refused to refer him. Once the referral is received, the specialists at the center must judge whether you meet their criteria to be a transplant candidate. Only if your own doctor and the transplant specialists agree will you join the waiting list for organs. And even then, if your condition changes, you may move from the "active" list (eligible for organs as they become available) to the "inactive" list (not eligible until your condition improves). Lilly Parra was moved from the "active" to the "inactive" list at the age of four months. Why? She had a small amount of fluid in her brain. At some future date it might lead to an intellectual disability. Note: she didn't actually have a disability, simply a chance of developing one. And that possibility was enough to end her parents' hopes for the heart transplant Lilly needed to survive.[85]

Bias can creep into the decision-making process at any decision point in the transplant process. Until very recently, many transplant centers had explicit policies excluding patients with intellectual or developmental disorders from waiting lists.[86] In 2012, Lief O'Neill, a non-speaking, autistic nine-year-old, needed a new heart. Two transplant centers turned him down, openly admitting that it was because he had autism. They also failed to inform his family about potential "bridge therapies"—technologies to keep him alive while he waited for a new heart. In the end, Lief was accepted by Stanford University's Children's Hospital, where he was stabilized and eventually received his heart.[87] Today he is a bright young man, who recently graduated from high school.

Doctors actually admitted that Lief was being refused a transplant due to his autism. At transplant centers today, policies about disabilities are usually less formal and explicit, but they may still be "understood" and applied by the physicians who work there. Though a growing number of states with legislation forbid discrimination in transplants, and despite the promises made in earlier legislation such as the Americans with Disabilities Act, implicit bias against people with disabilities remains a serious problem. In 2021, bills were introduced in both houses of Congress, explicitly prohibiting the denial of transplants on the basis of physical or mental disability, testifying that bias is still in play. The American Academy of Pediatrics has recently warned its members against denying transplants on the basis of disability—another indicator that ableism is alive and well in medicine.[88] Autistic (and other) people are still dying because they are denied the transplants they need.

Insofar as it is articulated at all, discrimination against autistics (and against the intellectually disabled) is based on entirely faulty assumptions. One has to do with survival rates and the ability of such patients to maintain the gruelling post-transplant protocols. Doctors often assume that autistics and the intellectually disabled are less likely to survive (even if they have no additional medical problems) and will neglect the complex regimen of medication and avoiding infection that transplant recipients must follow. However, studies indicate that there is no real difference between how people with Intellectual/ Developmental Disabilities and other people survive and follow the prescribed post-operative regimen.[89] Autistics with no or comparable medical problems are no more likely to die than neurotypicals. The population group most likely to ignore post-transplant protocols is actually teen-agers.[90] But no transplant center has yet to suggest that teen-agers, as a group, be denied organs.

Discrimination by physicians and transplant centers also rests on faulty beliefs about "quality of life." As defined by the World Health Organization this is "an individual's perception of their position in life in the context of the culture and value systems in which they live and in relation to their goals, expectations, standards and concerns."[91] In other words, determination of quality of life must be based on an individual's own perceptions. It is not to be defined by other people. Yet American physicians too often believe that they have the right to assess other people's quality of life. Their own personal experience "shows them" that disabled people must have "less to live for" than those without disabilities.[92] But studies have consistently shown a disconnect between how disabled people, including autistics, assess their own quality of life and assessments made by those with power over them.[93]

In reality, disabled people often describe themselves as having an excellent quality of life, full of rich and pleasurable experiences. Autistics enjoy deeply satisfying hobbies and (in some cases) jobs, they have fascinating special interests, they take delight in stimming. Some, indeed, view themselves as enjoying better lives than neurotypicals. This is why, as the Autistic Self-Advocacy Network pointed out in its recent guidance for physicians on organ transplants, "there is increasing consensus among lawyers and bio-ethicists that health care providers should not deny treatment to people with disabilities based on the assumption that they have a lower 'quality of life.'"[94] The implicit bias against the disabled at work in organ transplants was even more evident in the rapid-fire, seat-of-the-pants decision making that characterized the worst stages of the Covid-19 pandemic.

Denial of Care: The Covid Pandemic

At the height of the pandemic, the sound of ambulance sirens filled the air of American cities. Vehicles jostled at the doors of emergency rooms, waiting to discharge their passengers, while the ERs themselves were in chaos. There was too little of everything—personnel, rooms, beds in regular units, beds in Intensive Care Units, medication, ventilators, and, above all, reliable information about this terrifying new disease that spread and killed so quickly. Nurses and doctors worked shift after shift, without sleep, and without adequate protective wear. They too became sick and died. The sound of people thanking health workers for their heroism by banging on pots and pans only added to the noise in the streets. Morgues filled up and refrigerator trucks had to be brought in to store the bodies of the dead.

Covid was one of the worst emergencies ever to confront the American medical system. Faced with severe staff and supply shortages, medical facilities were forced to "triage" their patients—separating them into different priority groups, based on who was most likely to benefit from treatment. Traditionally, triage involves doctors dividing patients into three groups: those who will never survive, those who can probably recover without care, and those who can probably get better if treated. The last group gets medical priority. This is formal triage. But we must also recognize the informal and unthinking kind of triage wrought by our country's systematic unwillingness to respect and care for people at the margins—the impoverished, the homeless, the uninsured. Countless autistic people fall into these categories.

During the worst days of the pandemic, the U.S. Centers for Disease Control and Prevention had a recommendation: if you thought you might have covid, stay home and do not go out in public. Fine if you had a home. But what if you had no money? What if you were living in your car? Or in a tent under a highway overpass? How could you ever get better if you were hungry and thirsty and sleeping in the cold? The CDC also recommended that, if your symptoms worsened, you call 911 or your local emergency facility. But what if you had no phone? Or you were an autistic who didn't speak? What if you didn't have a car or anyone to give you a lift to the hospital? Or you lived on a reservation a hundred miles from the nearest medical center? Under such circumstances you could never reach the care you needed to survive. The way our society is structured, then, ensured that some sick people died of Covid before they even got to the place where formal triage took place.

But let's assume that you do have access to our medical system. In a health emergency, formal triage is a multi-step process and can involve multiple decision-makers at more than one stage of treatment. For example, when many people need transportation, EMTs must decide who gets delivered to the hospital first; in the emergency room, triage nurses determine who gets examined first; in the Intensive Care Unit, the ICU Director says who gets one of the few available beds and who gets one of the rare available ventilators. This process of prioritizing and allocating scarce resources is always an ethical minefield. In theory, a medical practitioner's primary obligation should always be towards her or his individual patient. In contrast, a health system in crisis will be thinking not in terms of individuals, but of public health.

When individual and public health interests were in conflict, many hospitals, local governments, and states developed or revised existing "Crisis Standards of Care" (CSCs), a set of priorities to be used during triage to determine who should receive scarce medical resources. These were intended to help guide nurses, physicians and others in their decision-making, so as to maximize the public health benefits of the limited resources available.[95] But determining what was best for public health became itself a tangle of ethical conundrums.[96] Several of the CSCs developed during the early stages of the Covid pandemic overtly discriminated against people with disabilities. A notorious example is the state of Alabama's 2020 CSC. It specified that people with intellectual disabilities or dementia should not be allowed access to ventilators.[97] For a while, Utah actually reallocated to other patients ventilators that disabled people owned and had brought into hospitals for their own use.[98] An early draft of Pennsylvania's CSC allowed physicians to take into account personal assumptions about disabled patients' "quality of life" in allotting resources.[99] Guidelines like these were so obviously illegal under the Americans with Disabilities Act, and so obviously dismissive of the American Medical Association's own Code of Ethics, that they were eventually revised. But the fact that they ever emerged illustrates the animus that some (perhaps many) practitioners feel towards disability, as well as toward age or racial difference. In February 2021 a coalition of disability rights organizations, including the Autistic Self-Advocacy Network, pointed out the threat of "intersectional discrimination" in CSCs. Their report notes that "while crisis standards of care typically prioritize patients who are more likely to survive hospitalization, many have included provisions that discriminate based on disability, age, and race in violation of civil rights laws."[100]

Such activism ensured that most CSCs now overtly ban "categorical exclusions"—denying care to whole categories of people (the elderly, the disabled, members of racial or ethnic minorities or the LGBTQ+ community). Yet even when the Standards themselves are free of explicitly discriminatory language, the circumstances of treatment promote the quiet denial of care to certain groups of people. When the line is out the door, and hundreds of people are clamoring for help in the emergency room, what becomes of the autistic man who—overwhelmed by the ER's sensory pressures—has a meltdown? Who will find him a quiet place to recover enough to describe his symptoms? Will a nurse hold his place on the priority list while he calms down? Maybe. But maybe not. Or imagine the director of an ICU, exhausted and overwhelmed by the number of patients clamoring for help, having to decide who gets a ventilator. Will she decide that an autistic person's inability to speak indicates brain damage, and so the ventilator should go to someone else?[101]

What is clear is that Covid has had a disproportionate impact on the autistic community. One study found that autistics were nine times more likely to be hospitalized with Covid than other Americans; six times more likely to have a prolonged stay once hospitalized; and eighteen times more likely to die.[102] It's true that autistic people, on average, have a high rate of medical co-morbidities. They're more vulnerable to infection and more likely to die than other Americans. Living conditions also contributed to autistics' high infection rate. Many resided in "congregate care" settings such as group homes and psychiatric hospitals, where social distancing was impossible and Covid spread like wildfire.[103] Even those who lived independently or with friends or family struggled to get the care they needed. Medical institutions, never very welcoming to autistics, became even more difficult to access under emergency conditions.

As Dr. Martin Luther King once declared, "of all the forms of inequality, injustice in health care is the most shocking and inhumane."[104] Many American citizens are denied medical care, most often because they are poor. Still more troubling, though, are the biases—implicit and explicit—still rife within our medical systems.[105] These appear in many guises. Doctors are less like to prescribe pain medication for women than for men even when they have the same problems.[106] Black women die much more often in childbirth than White women, even with financial resources accounted for.[107] In 2009, nearly 27% of transgender people reported having been denied treatment, even when the care was unrelated to their gender status; in 2018, nearly 36% of autistic LGBTQ+ people reported being denied care.[108] The impact of discrimination increases, of course, in situations when supplies or personnel are limited. When health care must be rationed, for whatever reason, bias almost always plays a role in determining who receives scarce resources and who does not.

Mortality

I'll be 68 on June 4, 2021. Trust me. That's a
long time to be autistic. Average lifespan of
a male autistic estimated at 53...[109]

Autistic people die early--distressingly early. Their mortality rates (deaths over a given period of time) far exceed those of neurotypicals.[110] In one Danish study, autistics died at twice the rate of the general population.[111] Adults with autism die more often than others in American hospitals; women with autism do even worse off than men.[112] Overall life expectancy is much, much lower for autistic than for neurotypical people. One group of American researchers found that 39 years was the average life expectancy in the autistic population they studied— almost 38 years less than that of Americans as a whole.[113] A Swedish study based on a huge sample of autistic subjects found roughly the same life expectancy for what they termed "low-functioning" autistics, but a higher one (about 58 years) for "high functioning" people. But even their life span was about 12 years shorter than that of the general population.[114] Other studies have found similar results.

Scientists and physicians usually assume that their neurology leaves autistics more vulnerable to certain medical conditions. They are not wrong. But this is far from the full explanation. Autism results from the interaction of one or more of many possible genes with a myriad of environmental factors. Some of the genes associated with autism are also associated with other bodily functions, such as insulin production (hence higher than normal rates of diabetes among autistics), cardiac activity (hence the increased rates of heart disease), brain activity (related to epilepsy and schizophrenia), and the immune system (resulting in asthma and allergies).

But not all "autism genes" have these associations, and the ways in which these genes are expressed is extremely complicated.[115] One person may have genes broadly associated with epilepsy and diabetes, but never develop those conditions. Another, less fortunate, may end up with these and perhaps additional medical problems. So while it is true that, on average, autistic people have more co-existing conditions ("comorbidities," physicians call them) than neurotypical people, and that many of these conditions are genetically related to autism, no single co-morbidity in any one individual is simply "caused by autism." Instead, their genes interact with environmental conditions that differ widely from one person to another, to cause medical problems. People, autistic or not, who live in particularly harsh environments may develop these problems. Asthma, for example, is more prevalent in communities exposed to high levels of air pollution, such as exist in most American inner cities.[116] That being said, certain medical conditions occur more frequently in company with autism. Among these are neurological problems such as epilepsy and sleep disorders; gastrointestinal problems that can cause extreme pain, constipation/ diarrhea, or Irritable Bowel Syndrome (IBS); and psychiatric problems like anxiety and schizophrenia. In addition, more autistics than neurotypicals suffer from asthma, diabetes, and certain heart conditions.[117] But even high levels of "comorbidities" do not alone fully explain the high rate of mortality among autistic people.

Many other factors are at work. We know, for example, that autistic individuals are three times more likely than neurotypical people to die of accidental injury. One study found accidental injuries responsible for slightly more than one-quarter of all autistic deaths.[118] But we don't know why. Are epileptic seizures responsible? Or inattention, perhaps caused by overmedication? Or dangerous attacks by other people? Suicide is also much more likely among autistics. But does autism itself predispose people to suicidal thoughts? Or does constant bullying, an inability to find employment, the need to mask, and poverty reduce the desire to live?[119] To what extent is high mortality simply due to lack of access to medical care and medication? Why did Mel Baggs have to die at age 39?

A growing number of physicians now acknowledge that autistics represent one of our country's "medically underserved" populations, all of whom experience "significant health disparities, poorer health, and lack access to care."[120] A new group, the Autism Intervention Research Network on Physical Health, "seeks to establish and maintain a research network to enhance the physical health and well-being of autistic children, adolescents, and adults, particularly for underserved and vulnerable populations."[121] This group focuses on the health needs of autistics as defined by autistics themselves. Indeed, all research conducted by network members must be vetted by a group of autistic researchers, to ensure that autistic concerns are addressed. Already AIR-P members have published scholarly articles addressing many of the issues discussed in this chapter.[122] They hold out hope that the myopic American medical system can be changed.

Yet autistics today continue to face problems with poor quality medical care. Most doctors and other health practitioners still have only limited knowledge about autism and autistics. Even when well-meaning, they often make mistakes, sometimes serious mistakes, leading to misdiagnosis and improper treatment. At the same time, the structure of the American medical system, as well as physician bias, all too often prevent autistic people from accessing the health services they need. And the result is still unnecessary suffering, and, yes, even death.

CHAPTER NINE

Mental Health

*While it is understood autistic persons, just like their neu-
rotypical population counterparts, experience mental health
challenges, they seem to be particularly susceptible to quickly falling into a mental health machination that is both ill-
equipped to understand them, and one which– according to
autistic persons and their families– treats them quite badly.*[1]

A recent study found that young adults with autism were TEN
times more likely to end up in a psychiatric ward or hospital
than those without. The numbers are not much different for adolescents or for older adults. But why? True, anxiety disorders, depression,
and attention deficit problems burden a large percentage of autistics.
In addition, they are more commonly diagnosed with schizophrenia
and related conditions than neurotypicals. But does an autistic neurology naturally predispose people to mental illness? Perhaps. But
this propensity could also be related to the enormous pressures autistic people must endure in American society. Methodically taught to
"mask" their autism, dismissed by teachers, denied employment, ha-
rassed by classmates and co-workers, and stigmatized by doctors, is it
any wonder that they become anxious and depressed? Among those
with a genetic predisposition to the disorder, research suggests that

schizophrenia can be triggered by the kinds of trauma autistic people routinely endure.[2] Autistics themselves identify stigma and abuse as some of the main factors shaping their own mental health.[3]

Suicide

In 2016 the *British Journal of Psychiatry* published a Swedish study that contains a lot of food for thought. It looked at the life expectancy of more than 27,000 people with autism. The Swedish researchers found autistic life expectancy to be, on average, 16 years less than that of the general population. Most of this difference came from comorbidities (respiratory problems, heart disease, diabetes, epilepsy), conditions that kill autistic people at an early age. As we've seen, the autistics in this study were also more prone to fatal accidents. One finding, though, was particularly disturbing. It's well known that somewhere between 30 and 66% of all those on the autism spectrum have considered suicide. It's also known that autistic women are more likely than autistic men to attempt to kill themselves.[4] What the Swedish study showed, however, is that among those who could sometimes "pass" as neurotypical, the rate of completed suicide was NINE times higher than it is in the general population.[5] Autistics who can "mask" are killing themselves at appalling rates.[6]

Finding Therapy

Regardless of the cause, people with mental illnesses need help. Best practice for most of these is treatment with evidence-based therapies, accompanied by medication as needed. But autistics aren't getting therapy at the same rate as neurotypicals.[7] And only very rarely is it from someone familiar with autism—which is important because many forms of therapy must be adapted to be effective with autistics.[8]

The U.S. suffers from a severe shortage of mental health

professionals. Only one psychiatrist is available for every 11,000 people, and one psychologist for every 3,000.[9] In this country, most psychotherapy is actually offered by clinical social workers, licensed professional counsellors, behavioral health nurse practitioners, and similar professionals. But these, too, are in very short supply. If you live in a poor, segregated urban district, on a Native American reservation, or in a rural area the problem is even worse. Even in a major city, someone may have to wait months, even years to see anyone.[10] But if mental health professionals are scarce, the shortage of practitioners adequately informed about autistic mental health needs is nothing short of catastrophic. Many therapists simply refuse to accept autistic patients. Those who do often admit they know little about autism and even less about how to treat these patients.[11] So help, once obtained, will often be of poor quality. In one recent study, out of 22 autistic adults interviewed about psychotherapy received in adulthood, 20 reported negative experiences.[12] The most frequent complaint, in this and other studies, is that available therapists are not only unfamiliar with autism, but unable or unwilling to adapt their diagnostic or therapeutic practices to meet autistic needs.[13]

Practitioners who think of autism as a childhood disorder may fail to recognize that adults can even be autistic: "I saw a psychiatrist recently. I asked if he knew about autism his response was 'Of course I know about autism but I work with adults so I don't come across it.'"[14] Most mental health professionals have no idea what autism looks like in the adults they are supposed to treat. And so, too often, they mistake common autistic behaviors for indications of mental health conditions. A meltdown may be mistaken for psychosis or "excited delirium" (especially if the client happens to be Black).[15] A shutdown may be identified as "catatonia." Head-banging, self-biting or self-scratching may be assumed to indicate suicidality. Even simple stimming may look, to unfamiliar eyes, like Obsessive Compulsive Disorder. Stimming and OCD are very different conditions. Lining up favored items by size and spinning in circles are pleasurable activities, often serving as a source of joy for autistics. Compulsive behaviors, on the other hand, are more likely to be a response to fear. They typically stem from the desire to reduce anxiety or prevent some dreaded event. There may be some satisfaction in carrying them out, but certainly no joy.[16]

Mental health professionals are especially unfamiliar with autism in women—who, as a general rule, "present" their autism differently than men. Meltdowns, withdrawal, delayed processing, sensory sensitivities—typical female autistic behaviors—are often interpreted as "attention seeking," a "sure sign" of personality disorders: "…[The] health professionals who diagnosed BPD aren't familiar enough with the symptoms of a female with AS…Now it feels like I've got a BPD diagnosis and they refuse to look at anything else."[17] Researchers encounter significant numbers of adults who believe they have been misdiagnosed due to ignorance about autism.[18] As one person put it: "… If there was someone who both understood the condition [autism] and me, I feel progress would be made."[19]

Such ignorance of autism not only results in faulty diagnoses; it's also an obstacle to treatment. By definition, autistics struggle with communication and interpersonal relations. If the therapist fails to realize this, the whole therapeutic process may break down: "Every time I've had a therapist they couldn't relate to me on a personal level or misread what I was saying."[20] Therapists are trained to help people with their emotions. But they're likely to ignore or downplay serious distress, if they don't recognize what emotions look like in autistics:

> With hindsight a massive barrier was that I just don't show emotion the way other people do so . . . no one believed there was anything wrong with me or that I needed help. There are specific things depressed people are supposed to do, but I don't do them."[21]

Complicating this situation, significant numbers of autistic people have alexithymia, a condition which makes it hard to recognize, express, or describe your own emotions.[22] If the therapist does not realize this, the result may be poor therapeutic results. For example, Cognitive Behavioral Therapy (CBT), one of the most effective interventions for many mental health issues, requires patients to reflect on their own emotional states as well as their thoughts. But if you have no idea how you feel, you can't benefit from this kind of therapy. In adapting CBT for use with autistics, specialists encourage practitioners to add training in emotional recognition.[23] It is the rare therapist, though, who actually takes this critical step.

Unaware that autistic people may need extra processing time, therapists sometimes try to move the therapeutic process along too quickly. One told researchers she'd learned, "after [the] patient dropped out that I perhaps needed to take things slower."[24] Other therapists provide "treatment" that would be bad for anyone. They may, for example, blame a client's autism for any problems they may be experiencing, rather than offering help they can actually use:

The last therapist I saw was awful... He never believed how anxiety and discrimination affected my life and instead blamed almost everything on my "too technical/literal high-functioning autistic thinking" without any good advice.[25]

Still others focus on making their clients appear "less autistic," even if the client has requested help with depression, trauma, or self-harm. Such interventions—basically training in "how to mask"—only intensify anxiety and feelings of shame. And worst of all, some therapists treat the very people they are supposed to be helping with disdain.[26]

Heading for Hospitalization

I had a meltdown in front of a mental health worker today who called the ambulance on me... And sent me to the ER... But I recovered and ER ended up sending me home. Why do they insist when I have meltdowns I am having a mental health emergency instead... Grrrrrr[27]

It is not unusual for police, teachers, family members—even the mental health workers who should know better—to assume that someone who is simply acting "autistic" actually needs a psychological intervention.

I was in a shutdown in a public space and that's why I got picked up. I wasn't able to move or talk. The only thing I did was cry because I wanted to go home so badly, but I couldn't. Had to spend a week inside [a psychiatric ward] and it definitely shoved me back into depression. I still feel bad and this happened in april 2020.[28]

Autistics with no mental illness at all may end up in psychiatric wards or hospitals.[29] What have been dubbed "suicide attacks" often bring this on. Under extreme stress, an autistic person may say that he wants to die or is going to kill himself. Usually (not always) he has no real intention of killing himself and no suicide plan. Given time to recover—sometimes as little as ten or fifteen minutes—he will be fine again. But if someone mistakes such an attack for genuine suicidality, he ends up in an emergency room for evaluation. There he suffers from additional stress due to noise, crowding, blinding lights, and endless wait times. After a short visit with a mental health professional, during which (under stress) he may still talk about dying, he is assigned a mental health diagnosis and hospitalized. Not surprisingly, autistics taken to the emergency room in crisis are more likely than neurotypicals to be admitted to a psychiatric facility.[30] And often (not always) all they really needed was a little time and space to recover.

Psychiatric Hospitalization

Some willingly choose to enter such psychiatric institutions for help. And some say the experience really benefited them. But it is all too easy for autistics to be admitted by force.

Every time I had a meltdown, I was thrown in the psych hospital.[31]

I was involuntarily committed to a psychiatric hospital because of an autistic meltdown- which, if you are autistic yourself, you may recognize as truly the greatest fear that many of us have. I lost the ability to communicate, and despite my partner's best efforts to explain autism to the medical personnel at the hospital, I was strapped to a stretcher and escorted away by armed policemen.[32]

The odds of involuntary admission increase if you are non-White, regardless of your mental condition.[33] According to one study, people with communication problems are more likely to be involuntarily committed than those who can communicate "normally." Once inside, they are more likely to be subject to coercive treatment.[34] By definition, all autistics, but especially the non-speaking, fall into this category. It also includes people of any neurotype who must communicate in a non-native language.

Whether a ward in a general hospital or a separate institution, a psychiatric unit is not usually very therapeutic. Mental health issues are seldom actually resolved there. Such a unit functions, instead, as a holding ground. It is designed to prevent patients from "severe deterioration," or from committing "violence against self or others," while medical staff attempt to "stabilize" them. The expectation is that patients will have a relatively short stay (usually days or weeks), which means in-depth therapy is not even attempted. While some form of therapy is commonly offered, it is generally very limited, poorly executed, and almost never tailored to individual needs. The real goal is for the psychiatrist in charge to provide a diagnosis (which may or may not be correct) and then look for some drug or combination of drugs which make it possible for the patient to be released. In other words, the vast majority of psychiatric institutions are all about drugs.

Medication

As a young autistic adult, Michael Ancora held a part-time job and attended a part-time day program. He helped around his parents' house, taking out the trash and sometimes cooking dinner for the family. He was a sweet young man, although he did have occasional violent outbursts. This is why his parents had him hospitalized in 2017, in the hope he'd be stabilized on medication. But when Michael came home several months later, he was much, much worse than before. The frequency and violence of his outbursts were only increased by the powerful anti-psychotics the psychiatrist had prescribed. They also left him drooling, unable to sit in a chair without slumping over, unable to put on his shoes, bathe himself, or even pry the lid off a yogurt container. He could no longer work or attend his day program.[35]

For autistic patients who may be highly sensitive and/or have paradoxical reactions to medication, the psychiatrist's search for the right drug can be prolonged, painful, and dangerous.

By age 30 I had to be hospitalized due to severe panic attacks. Antidepressants of all types were tried and had no affect on the anxiety. Only made it worse.[36]

The longest stay [in a psychiatric hospital] was only about 2 weeks. It was only that long due to a manic episode induced by the meds. I have had other manic episodes though, it was just the combination of meds were wrong for people with bipolar disorder and is known to cause mania.[37]

Psychiatrists working in psychiatric units are typically in a rush to discharge patients, so they tend to cut corners. In general, patients should be carefully introduced to psychotropic medications, slowly increasing the dose over a period of weeks; if they must stop taking something, they should be weaned off the drug very gradually. This is because suddenly starting or stopping these drugs can endanger physical as well as mental health. But on the unit, the psychiatrist usually tries to find the "right" drug for the patient as fast as possible, to hasten discharge. She may ignore the guidelines for gradually increasing or decreasing doses, leading to bad patient reactions: ". . . after a really bad depressive episode, I received a huge-ass treatment with anti-depressants, anti-psychotics, mood stabilizers etc which would just make me faint in the morning."[38]

A study conducted at a well-known psychiatric hospital found multiple cases of wrong dosages, dangerous drug interactions, and omitted medications—and not just among autistics.[39]

Experiencing the Psychiatric Hospital

You are not allowed to be alone in your room in the daytime; you must be with all these other people. And every half an hour at night, another stranger comes into your room to check up on you.[40]

Psychiatric institutions tend to be unpleasant—often very unpleasant—places. Some people feel relatively comfortable there and believe they benefit from their stay. But countless others do not: "Some [psych units] are better, some are worse. I have been in some where I'd rather be in jail and I have been in some that are better then home."[41] Why are such facilities especially difficult for (most) autistic people? In the first place, any hospital environment disorients them. They typically rely on familiar places and familiar routines to cope with everyday life; hospitals, on the other hand, seem completely alien. Pulled out of their comfort zone, they remain terrifyingly uncertain about what will happen next. Theoretically the physical environment in such places is designed to be calming and comfortable. But this is seldom how autistics experience them.

To begin with, they are subject to an even greater number of sensory stressors than in their ordinary lives. And they can't escape. The noise, for example, is unceasing: "I am stuck in a psych ward after a recent ptsd self harm relapse attempt. And the noise of the other insane asylum patients screaming and hollering is driving me insane."[42] One of the foundations of good mental health, adequate sleep, is often impossible:

On the unit, I found it extremely difficult to sleep, the buzzer on the door of the unit really irritated me and sounded really loud, but it didn't seem to affect anybody else. The beeping noise of the fire alarms will keep me awake at night. I found myself in a situation where every night I spent in hospital my sleep was wrecked.[43]

(Even "normal" people begin to look mentally ill if constantly denied sleep.)

Food presents major problems, too. At the best of times, certain textures, tastes, or colors seem so nauseating that autistic people gag or simply can't get the food down. Those with food sensitivities may suffer from indigestion, cramps, and other physical distress.[44] Hospitals usually record and promise to honor such sensitivities. Too often, though, the meal service misses the message and sends up only food the patient can't eat. Going hungry, of course, intensifies psychological distress. Worse still, patients who refuse to eat (because the food is nauseating, or they are allergic to it) or those who vomit after indigestible meals may find themselves diagnosed with an eating disorder. "Therapy" for a non-existent "eating disorder" may be prescribed and they may be forced to eat a certain amount at each meal. (This is not to deny the reality of eating disorders in some autistics. But basing a diagnosis solely on eating behaviors observed in a hospital setting is nothing less than malpractice.)

Fellow patients can also present real problems for autistics: "If ordinary people in daily life seem frighteningly unpredictable to us, because we can't intuitively understand the unspoken rules by which they operate, imagine how much more terrifying the other patients in a mental hospital are."[45] Anyone who's spent time in a psychiatric unit will recall seeing or hearing other patients in great distress: screaming, struggling with security, and calling for help. And since many autistics are highly empathetic, the distress of others amplifies their own.[46] Yenn Purkis, an autistic activist with schizophrenia, has lots of experience living in psychiatric units:

My hyper empathy is pretty significant. Being around people in pain – psychical or psychological – and people who are angry and frustrated is just horrible. The psychiatric ward is often of the worst places in the world for negative hyper empathy. I used to say to my psychiatrist 'Please let me stay at home and be miserable with Mr Kitty than be with everyone's misery in the psych ward'[47]

And finally, privacy is non-existent in psychiatric facilities. To get their "spoons" back, autistic people almost always need some quiet time on their own, away from other people. Yet:

On the unit, finding a quiet area was impossible, even the areas which were called 'quiet areas' were always quite busy, and I can never find time just to be on my own. There were four beds in my dorm, even with the curtain around my bed I was never alone. I found this unbelievably difficult to deal with and consequently I spend my entire time on the unit on the edge of my nerves.[48]

This is especially problematic for patients who have suffered sexual abuse. Many a young autistic woman has been admitted to a psych ward with suicidal tendencies after being raped. She will be made to shower and toilet in front of staff members, some of them male. Because she is under suicide watch, her room will be frequently invaded at night: sometimes she will wake to find an unknown male staffer standing next to her bed. How can anyone recover under such conditions? Re-traumatization by hospital staff is frequently experienced by autistic (and other) people who have been sexually victimized.

Violence

Psych hospitals and wards are seldom gentle, healing places. In both "forensic" units (housing people who are both mentally ill and have committed crimes) and ordinary ones, violence is rife. Physical and psychological abuse is common, threats of abuse even more so. Some patients prey on other patients, forcibly demanding personal property or food. And too often, despite the unit's purported goal of preventing "violence against self and others," patients are attacked, injured, or raped. Precise data are very hard to come by. Staff responsible for patient safety may fail to observe what's going on, and never record such assaults. Many victims don't report them, sometimes because they're more scared of the staff than of the perpetrators. Moreover, few hospitals want to share with outsiders their failures to protect patients.[49] Attacks on staff safety are much better documented.[50] Anecdotally, though, we know that patients regularly hurt other patients. In one 2012 study, directors of state mental hospitals reported that 7% of their patients had been the victims of "major sexual misconduct" within the previous year.[51] If theft, extortion, verbal abuse, and physical assault were recorded, the percentage of patients victimized would be higher—perhaps much higher.

Nor are all hospital staff innocent bystanders. They too may harass or assault patients, ignoring the institution's rules for their own behavior. In 2014, four state hospital workers in Illinois held a 24-year-old autistic man on the floor and punched him repeatedly. Over a ten-year period, at least 26 staff members at the same institution, which served patients with developmental and intellectual disabilities, were arrested on felony charges for beating, whipping, choking, and raping patients.[52] Many autistic women are sexually victimized by staff members. And then there are the endless small cruelties. Someone on suicide watch, desperate for sensory relief, is denied a walk around the unit or outside in the hospital yard, not because it is forbidden, but because the staff member assigned to attend her "just doesn't feel like it." Personal possessions that would give patients comfort are withheld. Nurses sometimes ridicule patients for behaviors caused by their condition. As one autistic former patient put it, "My experience with psychiatric nurses has been terrible. I think they have their souls removed as part of their training."[53]

Compliance

The pain of not knowing what is going to happen next, or who is going to decide what is going to happen next, was far too much to bear. It forces you to go into yourself, to try and take yourself to a place where they can't get to. Control is everything to me, my life on the outside of hospital is very predictable, routines and structures without any surprises.

I control every aspect of my life. If this stops, my anxiety increases rapidly.[54]

Many of these places are like prisons—patients can't leave, and they're forced to obey the commands of those in authority.

. . . I hate having things decided for me. I hate being told to get up and eat when I'm exhausted and can't bear to look at food, especially hospital crap. I hate being told to sleep when I'm going to be up all night anyway. And I REALLY hate the lack of privacy, the constant personal space invasion.[55]

A few patients, who already feel out of control in their lives outside the institution, may relax when someone else is totally in charge.[56] But these are the exceptions. For the most part, patients—neurotypical or autistic—hate being controlled and will resist when they can.

We know unquestioning obedience is detrimental to good mental health. Yet immediate "compliance" with staff demands is set as a treatment goal in some institutions, just as it is in Applied Behavior Analysis. Even absent the pretense that compliance is "therapeutic," patients must obey staff without question. They must take their medications (even if those medications are not working or are making them sick). They must go to bed and eat their meals on the institutional schedule. They must attend therapy sessions, even if the therapy has no meaning for them. They must comply with demands to take showers, brush their teeth, wash their hair. They must wear the clothing they are told to wear. Minors must spend a little time doing "schoolwork" during the week, even if the work is too limited to teach them anything. Patients must pick up after themselves, stop activities they find enjoyable when told to, engage in other activities they don't find enjoyable when instructed. They are not to yell (even if they are overwhelmed) nor assume "inappropriate" positions (such as hiding under a chair or covering their ears). They must certainly not throw things, damage hospital property, or attack staff or others (unless the staff happens not to notice). These highly controlling aspects of institutional life—designed for the convenience of the institution and the safety of the staff—infuriate many patients. But for those who have already experienced traumatic experiences under coercion, this atmosphere can create greater trauma.

Even the practical repercussions of disobedience can devastate people already in distress. Failure to toe the line leads to punishment, beginning with "loss of privileges." One loses the right to wear one's own clothes or watch television. While it is illegal in many states for psychiatric units to withhold harmless personal property, deny patients contact with relatives, or forbid them to go outside in the hospital's fenced yard (if available), nevertheless, the non-compliant have their phone time and visitors limited. They may be forced to remain inside, deprived of natural light and fresh air, sometimes for months at a time. Perfectly safe and comforting personal possessions, such as small stuffed animals, may be confiscated until they "behave." Few patients actually know their rights in these matters. Institutional staff are unlikely to tell them when those rights are being violated.

Restraint and Seclusion

Trying to recover in this environment was awful. I was scared most of the time. I felt more like a prisoner than a patient. Restraint was used for the smallest infractions; it seemed more like a punishment than a method of protecting staff and patients.[57]

"Loss of privileges" is the least of the punishments imposed on non-compliant patients. Like too many American schools, most American psychiatric institutions regularly resort to restraint and seclusion.[58] It's common for burly security guards to violently force a patient into immobility. During this process patients (and indeed, guards) frequently sustain injuries. Some patients, like some school students, actually die from the improper use of dangerous "prone" restraints. Nevertheless, physical restraint is commonly employed, often followed by "pharmacological restraint." Patients who continue to struggle (perhaps because they are in meltdown and have no control over their actions) are forcibly injected with a sedative. Generally this is Haldol, a first-generation antipsychotic with particularly disturbing side effects. Devices can also be used for restraint. The classic one is the straitjacket, which forces the patient's folded arms across her chest and prevents her hands from moving. Though it is seldom used today, patients are still often strapped down in chairs or on their beds, unable to move. Critics view such mechanical restraints as nothing more than punishment, producing increased psychological and physical injury to patients without providing any treatment benefits at all.[59] Nonetheless, restraints are favored on many units.

Seclusion often follows—a patient deemed problematic is isolated in a locked room (in popular culture, a "padded cell," although the walls may really be made of bare concrete). The theory is that seclusion allows a brief "cooling off" period. In practice, patients may remain locked up for hours or even days. Regulations in almost every psychiatric ward and hospital prohibit the prolonged use of seclusion. Yet it happens anyway.

I remember I threw a can of soda five feet from my chair at a dust bin. The nurse told me to pick it up as per regulation. When I didn't, they told me to go to my room. I refused. They called security, and the security guards grabbed me and threw me to the ground. They punched me in the face several times. Then one of them bent my thumb back to the point that I exhibited pain. The nurses and the guards grabbed me and threw me into a concrete room and forgot about me. They often came to my room and teased me when I asked to be let out. I was in that room for nine days.[60]

Scientists have documented the damaging effects of physical restraint, forced medication, and seclusion for all involved. Simply witnessing other patients being restrained raises the observer's fear of being randomly attacked by staff. Those who have been restrained themselves develop feelings of powerlessness, dehumanization, and loss of dignity. "Criminalization" also occurs, whereby patients come to see themselves as "criminals," rather than as people seeking help. A review of recent literature found that somewhere between 25% and 47% of psychiatric patients developed post-traumatic stress disorder after being restrained.[61] Those who had already experienced trauma, such as childhood abuse or rape, were retraumatized—suffering nightmares and recurring thoughts about earlier events. While a few patients welcome restraint when they are feeling "out of control," the vast majority of patients do not. They regard restraint and seclusion as unfair "punishments," imposed by malicious staff. Not surprisingly, patients who have experienced restraint or seen others being restrained are less likely to trust staff.[62]

To make matters worse, these methods aren't used equitably in psychiatric units. Not only are patients with certain categories of mental illness (especially schizophrenia) more likely to be treated like this, but so are autistics who have meltdowns and engage in self-injurious behaviors, as well members of racial and ethnic minorities.[63] It is also worth noting that patients who assault a staff member are much more likely to be restrained and secluded than those who assault a fellow patient. Patients understand this to mean that their safety is of less concern to the institution than the welfare of staff.[64]

Recognizing the damage these practices can cause patients, the federal Substance Abuse and Mental Health Services Administration

(SAMHSA), which oversees psychiatric facilities in the United State is "committed to reducing and ultimately eliminating the use of seclusion and restraint practices in organizations and systems serving people with mental and/or substance use disorders."[65] Most institutions already have an official policy calling for de-escalation techniques to be employed, and for restraint to be introduced only when there is a real threat of self-injury or injury to others. Some institutional policies also explicitly prohibit the use of restraint and seclusion for the convenience of the staff or for punishment. But we have seen how often the same kind of policies in public schools are ignored. The same thing happens in psychiatric wards and hospitals.[66] While some individual hospitals have successfully implemented programs to reduce such practices, patients elsewhere are still frequently and unreasonably punished for minor failures of compliance.[67]

There is No Escape

Autistic patients spend more time in psychiatric wards and hospitals than neurotypical patients with the same conditions. The median stay for autistic patients in one unit was 52 days, while neurotypicals stayed about 25.[68] Similar differences have been found elsewhere. This can be explained in part by the poor-quality therapy practiced in these places, which is especially ineffective for autistics, and by the constant experimentation with medications that have adverse effects or don't work at all on them. Almost certainly, though, the main factor is the toxic hospital environment, which is particularly injurious to autistics:

Being bored and terrified of the others in care, then stuck with staff who have no sympathy and blame you for behaviors you cannot control, is a horror. Compliance to those who have no sympathy and very little patience, with no understanding of when you will ever leave this situation, is very difficult. Restraint (as in being tied up in 6 point restraints) exacerbates meltdowns... seems to drag them out on and on. Being group-tackled by staff during meltdowns was.... memorable. Lots of injections and restraints. Lights were too bright, sensory hell. Having no privacy as staff stands next to you when you use the toilet is beyond difficult. It seems to make you go more often, Likely from the anxiety of the situation. Being attacked by roommates is scary, and not being believed is hard.[69]

Another autistic writer remarked simply: "America's mental health system is barbaric."

As currently practiced, psychiatric hospitalization can render patients of all neurotypes more, rather than less, mentally disturbed.[70] But the evidence for such damage is especially strong for autistics:

When I was 17 I lived in a psychiatric hospital for 9 months and was diagnosed with all sorts sporadically, (BPD, bipolar, depression, anxiety). When I came out I struggled even more with low self - esteem, self-harm, communication and socialising and I had no idea what was "wrong with me" and what had always been "wrong with me"[71]

A few elite institutions are now aware of how bad such environments are for autistics; they have made changes to reduce length of stay and improve quality of care. Massachusetts General Hospital, for example, has a special "Autism Care" program. It focuses on dealing with the impact of patient distress on communication, lessening sensory overload, attempting to stabilize routine, and special training to help staff interpret symptoms.[72] One study found that fairly simple changes in the environment of children's wards—predictable schedules, use of visual cues, alternating preferred and less preferred activities—decreased autistic children's length of stay significantly.[73] But very few psychiatric facilities for adults make even these easy changes, let alone big ones like teaching staff how to react to meltdowns. As a result, patient stress in most units remains high. Stress pushes autistics to act in ways that lead to restraint, seclusion, and heavy medication. These further increase their distress, producing behaviors that invite more punishment. They become less and less likely to be cleared for release from the unit. Activist Yenn Purkis states:

Ignorance of autism is a huge issue in mental health settings. I had the parent of an autistic young man contact me a few years ago. The man was in a forensic mental health facility and was not allowed to leave. He had sensory issues in the institution and couldn't articulate this. Every time he got sensory overload he would have a meltdown. This was interpreted as wilful bad behaviour and his time in the facility would be extended.[74]

Self-injury in response to the stress of hospitalization, as well as meltdowns are treated as "acting out" or "seeking attention," resulting in longer and longer stays. One of the greatest fears many autistics with mental illnesses harbor is that once they enter a psychiatric hospital, they'll never escape. Hearing one person report they just got out of a psych ward, another wrote: "Glad you made it out alive, they tend to want to keep me and in fact would have last time had my mother and case manager not got me out."[75]

This is not some paranoid delusion. Recently Great Britain was scandalized by revelations about how many autistic people had been shut up (and often mistreated) in psychiatric institutions for many years.[76] But the problem is certainly not confined to Britain. Despite the Supreme Court's decision in the Olmstead case (1999), declaring it unconstitutional to keep disabled people segregated from the community in special hospitals, some Americans still become trapped in the psychiatric machine for weeks or months or years—sometimes until they die.

American psychiatric institutions are seriously deficient. They often create more psychological problems than they resolve. But I'll give a former autistic patient the last word on the subject: "

the moral of the story is that psych hospitals need to go or at the very least be retrained and be redone . . ." [77]

PART V

The Stuff of Nightmares

"We are worthy. We are valuable. We have the right to exist as we are without fear of violence."[1]

CHAPTER TEN

Police Violence

We look to a variety of social institutions for support and protection here in America. We have our families, whom we expect to nurture and stand by us. We have various institutions—schools, training centers, hospitals—designed to prepare us for the future and care for us if we develop serious problems. We have the state itself—federal, state, and local governments—whose most essential function is to protect citizens from external invaders and from the criminals among us. But what happens when these social institutions themselves turn against us? When those from whom we expect protection reveal themselves as enemies, it is a profound betrayal of our rights. The violence regularly perpetrated even today by state forces, by institutions, and by families against autistic people is the stuff of nightmares. Much of what I discuss in the following chapters is, quite frankly, sickening. Readers: beware. But it's also a story of fierce courage, activism, and hope.

"I'm Just Different"

On August 24, 2019, at 10:29 p.m., the police of Aurora, Colorado received a 911 call. A man was walking down the street who looked "sketchy," the caller reported. The caller couldn't tell whether he was "a good person or a bad person," but said that he was waving his hands around in the air, "making signals." The police dispatched a car to investigate. At 10:43 p.m., it pulled up at next to Elijah McClain, a young, slightly-built Black man, who was wearing a ski mask. He held a cell phone in one hand and a grocery bag in the other. Mr. McClain kept walking when the officer told him to "stop right there." Only later did the police realize he was listening to music on earbuds. When Mr. McClain did notice the officer, he said he had a right to walk where he was going (namely, to his home). According to the later investigation of the incident: "Officer Woodyard responded, 'I have a right to stop you because you're being suspicious' as he grabbed Mr. McClain's arms and began to try to turn him around. Mr. McClain said, 'Well okay' or "Whoa okay'."[2]

Other officers arrived. Another grabbed Mr. McClain's arm. The investigation noted that "None of Officers Woodyard, Rosenblatt, or Roedema asserted that they had reason to believe Mr. McClain had committed a crime at the time that he was stopped." Rather,

Officer Woodyard . . . told Major Crime investigators that he wanted to pat Mr. McClain down "based on him having a ski mask on Colfax in the middle of the night, and it was causing people to call in" and he "thought that he might have weapons on him." He did not explain why these circumstances led him to believe Mr. McClain may have been armed.

The police officers explained that they were suspicious because he didn't stop immediately when they asked him to and because he was "weird" and acting "crazy."

They began telling Mr. McClain to "relax" and "stop tensing up"—odd instructions to someone who is being physically restrained by multiple police officers. Meanwhile, Mr. McClain was protesting, "I am an introvert, please respect the boundaries that I am speaking" and "stop, stop, I'm going home." He kept asking them to leave him alone, but instead one of the officers snatched the grocery bag away from Mr. McClain, then the group pulled him over to a nearby patch of grass. As Mr. McClain continued to protest, he was pushed against a wall, his arms restrained. The body cam footage became blurred at this point, but one of the officers can be heard saying "He grabbed your gun, dude!" (In the absence of body cam footage, no evidence exists that Mr. McClain ever actually touched the gun.)

The officers reported that Mr. McClain wanted to get away from them, was not obeying their orders, and appeared "extremely freaked out." Taking him to the ground, they applied "carotid holds," a form of choke hold designed to render a suspect unconscious. There was a struggle. The police can be heard on camera saying "We've got his arms." Then one officer asks "Is he out?" and another replies "Not yet." Next, they made a call to the fire department for an EMT unit, while still restraining Mr. McClain. In an effort to handcuff him, they pulled his arm up behind his back so far that his shoulder "popped" several times. At this point, Mr. McClain began saying "I'm sorry" over and over, but the police didn't relent. One officer pulled out his taser and threatened to use it (although in the end he did not). Meanwhile, Mr. McClain's facemask had come off and they could see that he had vomited within it. He began saying again and again that he couldn't breathe, and that what they were doing was hurting him.

For the next thirteen minutes, the police stayed on top of the already handcuffed Mr. McClain, because he wasn't "calming down." One officer pushed his knee hard into Mr. McClain's upper arm to "enhance pain compliance." Mr. McClain, still vomiting, kept saying he couldn't breathe, apologizing and asking them to stop hurting him. He can be heard on the police audio stating,

I'm just different. I'm just different. That's all. That's all I was doing. I'm so sorry.

And later,

I will do anything I have to…Sacrifice my identity…I'll do it…I'll do it…

Then the emergency medical technicians showed up. They never touched Mc. McClain, never performed a physical evaluation. Based solely on what the police told them (the restrained man was "definitely on something") and what they were witnessing—Mr. McClain on the ground with officers on top of him—the EMTs immediately decided he must be in a state of "excited delirium." (I will have more to say on "excited delirium" below.) As they commonly do in such cases, the EMTs decided to administer the powerful anesthetic ketamine to Mr. McClain, at a very high dosage—500 mg. This was based on officers' claim of "excited delirium" and on the EMTs' guess that Mr. McClain's weight was 190 pounds. (In fact, he weighed only 140.)

At this point, Mr. McClain could no longer speak—and had largely stopped gagging, coughing, and moaning. He was unconscious, breathing deeply and rapidly, still vomiting occasionally. He was lifted into the ambulance at 11:03. At 11:07, less than 25 minutes after the first police officer stopped him walking down the street, he went into cardiac arrest. CPR was administered and once they reached the hospital he was put on life support. On August 27, he was declared brain dead and taken off the machines. He had committed no crime. Elijah McClain died because he did not immediately hear and comply with police demands, and because he struggled with the officers causing him physical pain. Mostly, though, he died because he was Black and autistic.

The Police Are Frightened

I have described the killing of this young man at such length not because it was unique, but because it is so commonplace. Much research has rightfully been devoted to the racist aspects of American police violence. But disabled people, including those with autism, are also disproportionately victimized by a government meant to protect them. Of course, many of them are also people of color. Does ableism or racism play the stronger role in these cases? It's hard to know. Nevertheless,

> Disabled individuals make up a third to half of all people killed by law enforcement officers. Disabled individuals make up the majority of those killed in use-of-force cases that attract widespread attention. This is true both for cases deemed illegal or against policy and for those in which officers are ultimately fully exonerated.[3]

Mr. McClain's story speaks to American police officers' fear of almost any behavior they perceive as unusual. In most American police academies, cadets are systematically taught to be afraid. Your communities are essentially battlefields, they are told. You are always under threat, and you must therefore remain hyper-vigilant. Police cadets get constant reminders that ruthless "bad guys," actively trying to kill police officers as well as commit other crimes, are everywhere. Actually, police deaths on duty are relatively rare. Yet, "officers' socialization into the police department encourages a view of police work in life-or-death terms and demands that every officer take the necessary steps to ensure that they and their fellow officers survive their shift."[4] In effect: police are methodically taught to suspect every person they encounter on the streets. So, in training, police cadets are instructed to be ready to respond aggressively to any perceived threat, no matter how minor, because it might potentially be life-threatening.

Frightened people are not fully rational people. Training in fear helps explain, but certainly does not excuse, some of the more bizarre police reactions to relatively harmless situations. In September 2020, a fourteen-year-old autistic boy from Topeka, Kansas, was stopped by the police. He was compliant, standing with his hands behind his back, waiting to be handcuffed, when the officer decided to tackle him, taking him to the ground and severely injuring his ankle. He pepper sprayed the boy's emotional support dog, Bella.[5] In January, 2021, a police officer in Rochester, New York decided to pepper spray a nine-year-old, suicidal, autistic girl who was already handcuffed and most of the way into the back seat of the police car.[6] In Wasilla, Alaska, in 2022, an eleven-year-old autistic child in meltdown was cornered by adults shouting at him and threatening him with restraints. Panicked, he threatened to stab them with his pen—the only weapon he had. A pen. Could anyone have been seriously injured? But a state trooper decided to pepper spray the boy anyway.[7] Such a response isn't rational. Who represents the real threat in these situations?

Fear makes people desperate for control. Their training inculcates in police officers an obsession with "control." They must be in charge of every situation, of every individual they come in contact with. As one of the officers involved in Mr. McClain's death explained to investigators, police in his department "tend to take control of an individual whether that be... a[n] escort position, a twist lock, whatever it may be, we tend to...control it before it needs to be controlled."[8] He saw this as a good thing. Certainly, the most important function of the police is to control criminals, especially violent ones. To those who do so under truly dangerous circumstances, we owe our thanks. But a fixation on control can result in unreasonable expectations. Problems arise when police expect the people they are addressing to obey them, no matter how unreasonable or incomprehensible their demands. They expect immediate compliance—even if the person they are giving orders to is deaf, doesn't speak English, can't understand what is being demanded. Failure to comply can have tragic effects. And even full compliance may not save you if you are a person of color.[9]

During training police cadets learn to see themselves as inherently different from the people they are supposed to serve. They are elite warriors. Everyone else is either a potential bad criminal or a weak victim needing protection. Cadets are also taught the "signs" that identify "bad guys": these may include ignoring a command, making unexpected hand movements, even just "walking strangely." Displaying any of these signs means you must be "controlled" for the officer's as well as society's safety. Police cadets are told not to racially profile. They are encouraged, though, to "criminally profile"—to look for the unusual.[10] If you are autistic, your normal body language, appearance and mannerisms can make you appear dangerous to the police. After all, why did Elijah McClain originally get into trouble? Not for any threat he posed. Just for making "weird" hand movements.

Autistics "Looking Criminal"

On November 12, 2014, Troy Canales was outside his own home, leaning against a car, when three police officers came by and asked him what he was doing. Avoiding eye contact (painful for many autistic people), Troy said he was just "chillin." The officers then threw him to the ground, punched him in the face, and restrained him. Troy's mother came running out of the house to explain her son was autistic. Ignoring her, they took the teenager into custody. He was held at the precinct for an hour before his mother obtained his release. No charges were ever pressed—because Troy had done nothing wrong. They assumed he was "up to no good," police told his mother, just because he was standing there.[11] One officer even claimed Troy made him "afraid for his life."[12] Apparently because he was leaning against a car.

If you are both a person of color and disabled, you are almost certain to have unpleasant, traumatic, even fatal encounters with the police over the course of your life.[13] As Tonya Milling, director of the Arc of Virginia noted, "the painful truth is that Black people with disabilities live at a dangerous intersection of racial injustice and disability discrimination."[14] Like Elijah McClain and Troy Canales, Stephon

Watts was a person of color. Stephon, aged 15, was usually a sweet and affectionate young man, but when he stopped taking his medicine, he could become angry and sometimes aggressive. His parents struggled in private with his behavior. His father, though, was always reluctant to call the police, fearing that they would kill his son. On the several occasions his wife did summon them, the dad drove Stephon away in his car to protect him. But on February 1, 2012, father and son got into a fight over Stephon's access to the family computer. Frustrated, the dad called the authorities, almost immediately regretted it, and tried to stop them. But it was already too late. Three officers arrived. They insisted on checking the house. Stephon's dad said his son had left, but hearing his voice from the basement, the police demanded to go down there. The father agreed to let one officer accompany him. Instead, all three followed him down the stairs. Just as they did, Stephon emerged carrying an ordinary butter-knife, with which he had been trying to pick the locked door to the computer room. No one was in danger. The knife wasn't especially sharp. But without even asking him to drop the knife, the officers fired their guns, killing Stephon instantly.[15]

Of course, even being White does not guarantee security from police violence. Thirteen-year-old Linden Cameron suffered from severe separation anxiety. When his mother tried to leave for work for the first time in nearly a year, Linden had a meltdown. His desperate parent called the Salt Lake City police. She explained that her son was autistic, unarmed, and "doesn't know how to regulate" himself. She was only asking for their help, she said. Shortly after the police arrived, though, she heard them screaming at the child to "get down on the ground," then the sound of several gunshots. Though he had no weapon and posed no threat to the officers, the slightly-built Linden was left with serious injuries to his shoulder, ankle, intestines and bladder. A local disability advocacy group pointed out that "officers from the SLPD expected a 13-year-old experiencing a mental health episode to act calmer and [more] collected than adult trained officers."[16]

Linden Cameron was shot because he had a meltdown under emotional stress. An autistic person in meltdown, even one who is White, but especially one who is Black or Latino/a, is automatically in big trouble with the authorities. This is true even when the police actually cause the meltdown. In 2010, at the age of 18, Neli Latson was sitting outside the Stafford, Virginia public library, waiting for it to open. Seeing him, someone called the police about a "suspicious" (i.e., young, Black, male) person. The caller claimed he had a gun. Mr. Latson didn't. He did, however, have powerful tactile sensitivities. He reacted badly to being grabbed by a sheriff's deputy. During his meltdown he ended up scratching the deputy and then breaking his ankle. He ran into nearby woods, where he was tracked down by police dogs, arrested and jailed.

His trial was a travesty of justice. The prosecution dismissed his mother's explanation that he was intellectually disabled, autistic, and liable to meltdowns if touched unexpectedly. They argued that Mr. Latson had "violent tendencies" and accused him of "racial hatred" (the deputy was White) and hatred of law enforcement in general. In the end, he was found guilty of two felonies and sentenced to ten and a half years in prison. His sentence was later reduced and Mr. Latson was released to a group home. Unfortunately, he threatened to harm himself there. The staff called police, he reacted badly again, and ended up back in jail, where he was tasered, restrained for long periods, and kept in solitary confinement for nearly a year. Following extensive investigations by news organizations and powerful advocacy from the disability community, the governor of Virginia finally granted Mr. Latson a full pardon in 2021. But the damage had been done. He now suffers from crippling anxiety: "I still have a lot of trauma to overcome. I am fearful and it's hard for me to do a lot of things."[17]

"Excited Delirium"

If an autistic individual goes into a meltdown during an encounter with the police, officers may jump to the conclusion that she or he suffers from "excited delirium." This is what happened to Elijah McClain. Police frequently use claims of "excited delirium" to justify the use of brutal restraints or to explain suspicious death in police custody. But what is excited delirium? Defined as a psychiatric condition involving extreme agitation, confusion, and aggression, it is said to be accompanied by such physiological effects as unexpected strength and stress on internal systems which can lead to strokes and heart attacks.[18] One physician described excited delirium as a "freight train to death," because, he claimed, the condition itself almost inevitably proves fatal.[19] Usually it is attributed to drug use. In the case of Elijah McClain, the police told the EMTs at the scene that Mr. McClain was "definitely on something," to bolster their later claim of excited delirium. Between 2010 and 2020, American medical examiners attributed the deaths of 166 people in police custody—43% of them Black—to this condition.

That Black people are disproportionately affected by these attributions is a serious problem. The biggest issue, though, is that excited delirium is an imaginary condition. It is not accepted by the American Psychiatric Association, nor does the APA include it in its *Diagnostic and Statistical Manual of Mental Disorders*.[20] Neither does the American Medical Association recognize excited delirium as a valid diagnosis.[21] A recent article in the prestigious medical journal *The Lancet* calls for it to be dropped entirely as an explanation of death in custody, noting its regular misuse by police departments in the U.S. and elsewhere.[22]

The term was coined by two physicians, Charles Wetli and David Fishbain, in the 1980s. While working as a medical examiner in Miami, investigating unexplained deaths, Wetli came up with it. He used the term primarily to explain the deaths in custody of Black people who had used cocaine, and his logic was explicitly racist: "Seventy percent of people dying of coke-induced delirium are black males, even though most users are white. Why? It may be genetic."[23] An

obvious alternative explanation is that Black people are more likely than Whites to suffer and die from brutality at the hands of the
police. After Wetli attributed the deaths of a number of Black women
to excited delirium, it turned out a serial killer had murdered them.[24]

Despite the skepticism of medical experts, excited delirium continues to be invoked by police departments trying to evade responsibili-
ty when a prisoner dies in custody. In two notorious cases, the police
claimed that George Floyd and Daniel Prude "died of excited delirium." People with acute mental health issues—extreme anxiety, para-
noia, or schizophrenia—seem especially vulnerable to harsh restraint,
unfair imprisonment, and even murder by state authorities. Yet excited delirium doesn't kill them. Police behavior does.

The Trauma of Police Encounters

Even though autistic adults appear to commit crimes at slightly lower
rates than other Americans, they are more likely to have had encounters with the police at some point.[25] Indeed, research indicates that
20% will have been stopped and questioned by the police by the time
they reach age 21.[26] In many cases, this is not because of anything they
have done, or even because they sought help as victims of crimes. They
were simply perceived as "threatening."[27]

Autistics are often traumatized by encounters with the police. In
Chapter One, I mentioned Morenike Giwa Onaiwu. When an officer
flagged her down and approached her car, she recalled that her father
had once being beaten so badly by the police that he had to be hospitalized. Growing more nervous, she began showing the outward signs of
autism she typically masks. She tried to make eye contact, but ended up
staring at the officer, possibly unnerving him. She also unwittingly reverted to her childhood echolalia as the officer questioned her. Hearing
her repeating his own words back to him, he assumed she was mocking
him and became angry. Then he noticed a metallic stim toy she had in

the front seat of her car—something she would normally have used to calm herself down. Interpreting it as a potential weapon, he ordered her out of the car. With her young, also autistic daughter watching from the back seat, Onaiwu got out, terrified. "It was frightening," she reports. "It could have ended so differently." Though she survived, the episode amplified her already paralyzing fear of the police. Finn Gardiner, Director of Policy and Advocacy at the Autistic People of Color Fund, feels much the same way: "I'm pretty scared when I'm walking down the street and see a bunch of police officers."[28]

Changing Police Training

To be fair to American police departments, the last decade has seen some efforts to teach cops more about people with autism. Unfortunately, the impact has been very limited. One 2019 study found that only 62% of officers surveyed had received any official training on autism at all.[29] In a more recent study, only 42% had received some.[30] And training may be too short (sometimes as short as 13 minutes) to adequately address such crucial skills as de-escalation techniques.[31] Plus, police may not be putting what they have learned to use in the field.[32] In another recent study, trained law enforcement officers were still resorting to highly controlling methods (restraint, arrest, involuntary hospitalization) in about 27% of their interactions with autistic people, when only about 13% of the time any criminal activity was involved.[33] Even today, the impulse of most police officers faced with a frightening situation is not to de-escalate, but to seek immediate, sometimes brutal, control.

Moving Towards Justice

I've got one thing to say to those who are taking baby steps to justice: MOVE IT! [34]

Autistic Americans, like other Americans, run the whole gamut of political affiliations. Some vigorously decry systemic racism while others deny it exists. Some may be strongly pro- or anti-police. Some may be suspicious of non-Whites—or of Whites. These divides are evident in, for example, an online discussion of the Neli Latson case on *Wrong Planet*.[35] But autistic people in general are painfully aware of their own vulnerability to police violence. And most refuse to take the *status quo* lying down.

What people of color, autistics, and other marginalized people need from you is to stop participating in a culture that excuses what needs to be fixed. It doesn't matter if #NotAllCops are bad. What matters is people are dying, and more will die, if we don't address the reality that police brutality happens and that Black and autistic lives are at higher risk.[36]

Outrage on social media and street protests over the murders of Eric Garner, Michael Brown, Daniel Prude and George Floyd, as well as Elijah McClain, have been joined by such autistic activists and organizations as the Autistic Women and Non-Binary Network and the Autistic Self-Advocacy Network.[37] Autistic intellectuals like Finn Gardiner and Lydia X.Z. Brown have played a role in public discussions of intersectionality—the issues that arise when someone is both Black and disabled, Latino/a and LGBTQ+, and so on.[38] Cooperating with other civil rights and disability rights organizations, autistic organizations continue to publicize the problem of police brutality and suggest solutions. In 2020, the murder of George Floyd brought a direct response from the Autistic Self-Advocacy Network, the American Association of People with Disabilities and the Green Mountain Self-Advocates. Together they published "*What is Police Violence?: A Plain Language Booklet about Anti-Black Racism, Police Violence, and What You Can Do to Stop It.*"[39] The booklet urges disabled people to join the

Black Lives Matter movement, interrogate how police work in local communities, and demand police accountability for the violence they commit. Autistic Americans are seeking common cause with other marginalized communities to advance a vision of justice that honors everyone.

CHAPTER ELEVEN

Institutional Violence

I think JRC has gotten away with what they did for so long for the same reason the Nazis' atrocities went unnoticed..... because people do not want to believe that well-educated supposedly caring professionals are capable of such evil. It shakes their view of what evil looks like. That it doesn't always come from obvious criminals on the low end of society but people just like themselves.[1]

Jennifer Msumba is an author, musician, and filmmaker.[2] She published an autobiography called *Shouting at Leaves*, which includes a description of the seven years (from 2002 to 2008) she endured at the notorious Judge Rotenberg Center (JRC), in Canton, Massachusetts. Jennifer was there for "treatment" for her "behavioral challenges." One day, for example, she didn't want to take her medication. Her assigned staff member picked up a clear plastic box with Jennifer's picture on it. Opening it, she pressed one of the buttons inside: "Fire ripped through my calf muscle . . . My entire left leg involuntarily shot out and lifted off the ground. I lost my breath and time stood still. After the eternity that was actually two seconds, the ripping, pulling, burning feeling subsided . . ."[3]

This was Jennifer's "treatment" for disobedience.

Jennifer's court-apppointed guardian had placed her at the Judge Rotenberg Center. There was no way her family could get her out. During those seven years, the only breaks she got were short home visits with her mother. Then one day, her JRC case manager announced Jennifer would no longer be allowed home visits, because she was "running wild" at home. ("Running wild"? All Jennifer remembers is her mom taking her out to a batting cage and for ice cream. Otherwise, they just stayed home.) Because the home visits were her only relief from what she endured at the center, she snapped and ran. The first of her two attempts at escape from the JRC.[4]

She told her story originally in an extended 2014 interview with Anna Werner on CBS News.[5] Jennifer is exceptional in that she is willing to talk about what she experienced. Most survivors don't give witness. But not because they didn't suffer. Some are non-speaking and can't communicate what happened to them. Some are simply broken—hollow husks of human beings, who "learned their lesson" at JRC. They no longer engage in "challenging behaviors"—they just sit and stare at the walls. And others just can't bear to remember. As one former staff member explained: "Most of the staff and students who were greatly disturbed by the violence and inhumanity at JRC are so traumatized that they are unwilling to speak out."[6]

Matthew Israel

The Judge Rotenberg Center was founded by Matthew Israel. A Ph.D. in psychology from Harvard University, Israel was trained by B.F. Skinner, the "father" of behaviorist psychology (the theory behind ABA). Israel took what he learned in new and disturbing directions, though. Skinner himself was generally opposed to the use of "aversives" (painful stimuli, like sudden loud noises, unpleasant scents, and physical injury)—not because he thought they were necessarily wrong, but because he saw them as ineffective or only temporarily effective in most cases. Israel disagreed. He made the use of aversives the centerpiece of his programs. He later claimed that in the institutions he ran aversives were used only exceptionally—only with parental consent, only when those he called "students" were a threat to themselves, and only after all positive reinforcement had failed.[7] But that is given the lie by the testimony of investigative reporters, former staff members, survivors and their parents. In many cases, pain was the first, not the last resort. His own graduate advisor, B.F. Skinner, expressed concern about Israel in 1978: "This is not the Matthew Israel I remember. I always regarded him as a very humane person with high ideals."[8]

To begin with, Matthew Israel was—and perhaps still is—extremely controlling. He explained that he set up his "treatment centers" with the goal of "having the whole environment under control."[9] He controlled his staff (mostly low-paid high school graduates) through constant surveillance and threats of job loss. He managed his "students" by frequently and severely punishing any behavior he considered undesirable. Terror reigned in the places he ran:

I was paralyzed with fear every day. No matter what I did I was doomed.[10]

I was terrified.[11]

I am scared and sometimes I feel like my life is in danger.[12]

Aversives

The propaganda issued by the various Israels' Behavior Research Institutes (BRIs) and by the JRC today always emphasize that good behavior is rewarded. But repeated inspections have found little evidence of rewards. Rather, the core of "treatment" at all of Israel's centers was the use of extreme aversives to punish "misbehavior." The menu of punishments offered was always extensive. In the 1970s and 80s, the preferred methods were spankings with a spatula, prolonged restraints, spraying with cold water, forcing the inhalation of ammonia, blocking access to bathrooms and then punishing soiling, and pinching hard enough to produce bruises and blisters. A Los Angeles couple discovered that their son had been spanked 174 times on a single day. The soles of another child's feet were pinched continuously for at least 30 minutes within 24 hours, until he couldn't walk. A 14-year-old was restrained face-down for a prolonged period.[13] He died.

A favorite technique was making residents "earn" their food by avoiding behaviors deemed undesirable. For each infraction, a portion was cut out of the daily diet, until there was not enough food to meet their dietary needs. Many lost significant amounts of weight and became malnourished. For the seriously recalcitrant, food was purposely made as unpalatable as possible, by mixing all the (ice cold) ingredients together and then sprinkling the mess with liver powder. Many ravenously hungry students could never bring themselves to eat the disgusting mess. After Jennifer Msumba finally got out of the Judge Rotenberg Center, she spent years hoarding food. She was constantly afraid of not having enough.[14]

Technology also played a role in Israel's program. A "sensory deprivation" helmet that blocked vision and used white noise to prevent hearing was used from the 1970s on. In 1985, 22-year-old Vincent Milletich died of asphyxiation after being strapped into a chair and helmeted with the device, although the exact cause of his oxygen deprivation was never determined.[15] It was in 1990, though, that Israel invented the device for which he is most notorious: the "graduated electronic decelerator" (GED).

The GED

"I still wake up with the smell of my own flesh burning in my nostrils some nights."[16]

When activated, the GED delivers a two-second electric shock to the wearer. The weakest of these devices, the GED-1, produces a shock of 30 milliamperes; the GED-4, used for more "recalcitrant" residents, produces at least 40 and up to 90 milliamperes.[17] In comparison, standard police tasers and "stun belts" produce about 3 to 5 milliamps for about a second.[18] Matthew Israel always insisted that the pain of a GED was no worse than a "bee sting," but he never let reporters experience it for themselves.[19] Former residents, on the other hand, described the pain as like "a million bee stings;" it was so intense they wanted to die.[20]

Even now, those assigned to shock treatment must wear the GED device all day and night, in a small knapsack or a fanny-pack, with wires carrying electrodes onto their chest and stomach, arms, and legs. They even have to wear the device in the shower, with one hand holding the device away from the running water. Reports indicate that it isn't just misbehavior that leads to a shock. Sometimes a staff member pushes the wrong button on the controller. Sometimes the device malfunctions. Sometimes a staffer just happens to dislike a particular resident. Most disturbing, though, are residents' descriptions of being restrained—spread-eagled and helpless—on the "four-point board," as repeated shocks are administered.

I would ask God to make my heart stop . . . And they won't be able to hurt me anymore.[21]

GED shocks cause muscle spasms; the resulting pain often lasts for days. Temporary neurological damage can follow: a person may no longer feel the body part that was shocked. Many survivors bear massive burn scars from the electrodes. The GED also leaves psychological scars: PTSD, anxiety, depression, suicidality.[22] The GED and other punishments have led multiple residents to desperate escape attempts. Jennifer Msumba tried twice to escape from the JRC.[23] At age 16, Silverio Gonzalez intentionally jumped from the transport bus taking him from the JRC to his residence center. He landed on Interstate 95, suffered massive head trauma and died.[24]

Israel always claimed his methods suppressed self-injurious and aggressive behaviors. That was the selling point for his school. What he didn't usually tell parents and inspectors from school boards and social service agencies was that his school punished all kinds of "undesirable behaviors"—even involuntary facial tics or loss of bladder control. Residents were sometimes given electric shocks while they slept for tensing up their muscles during sleep. Punishment might add up to hundreds or even thousands of incidents over the course of months or years. Brandon was a long-term resident of the Judge Rotenberg center. He was once shocked 5,000 times on a single day.[25]

As we have seen, "misbehavior" is often unintentional. Overpowering emotions or sensory distress may be the cause. Sometimes health issues are to blame. But Israel would have none of this. He consistently denied residents even psychotropic drugs that might have blunted their misery, insisting instead that punishment was the solution. In 1990, resident Linda Cornelison, age 19, began complaining about pain. The staff punished her more than 50 times for "complaining behavior" over the course of two days. Eventually, she was taken to a hospital, where she was diagnosed with peritonitis from a perforated stomach ulcer. Linda died. With earlier treatment, she might have lived.[26]

Israel set up his first "schools" for intellectually/developmentally disabled and mentally ill children in 1971 in Rhode Island and Massachusetts. Though he called them "Behavior Research Institutes," no serious research ever came out of them. Rather, they quickly aroused controversy. In 1976, Rhode Island pulled all children under state care out of Israel's program after investigators learned what was happening there. But private patients were still allowed. The mother of one such child wrote a letter to the Governor of Rhode Island in 1978. Her child had had to be hospitalized with blood poisoning, wrist lacerations from handcuffs, extensive bruising and evidence of food deprivation: "I think you have a snakepit in Providence, operating with impunity from the law," she wrote.[27] Despite repeated failures to meet state licensing criteria, the BRI in Rhode Island continued to operate at least into the 1990s.

In 1977 Israel tried to set up another Behavior Research Institute in California. At first his application was turned down by the state Department of Health. They cited his unnecessary use of painful aversives, and the scant evidence that he was "reputable and responsible."[28] It was allowed to go ahead after a group of parents re-organized the school as a co-op, and named Israel a "consultant" rather than director. Soon, though, Israel was in trouble for practicing psychology without a license in California.[29] In 1979, a staff member quit and went to the district attorney, asking for child abuse charges to be filed against the BRI.[30] Troubling stories continued to emerge. In 1990, after years of controversy, the state forbade the use of aversive practices on students with severe behavioral issues. Then Israel's wife, Judith Weber, took over the California center (now renamed Tobinworld, after her autistic son Tobin), while Israel refocused his attention on the BRI in Massachusetts.[31] He faced resistance there, too. In 1993, Massachusetts threatened to take away his certification due to failure to follow state regulations. When Judge Ernest Rotenberg ultimately ruled in Israel's favor, the Massachusetts BRI was re-named the "Judge Rotenberg Center." Lawsuits and attempts to close the center down multiplied in the following years. But none has succeeded so far.

In 2006, it was discovered that fourteen out of seventeen "psychologists" listed on the Judge Rotenberg Center website were not, in fact, licensed in the state of Massachusetts. Israel argued in court that psychologists are not required to have a license to practice at JRC. This was certainly news to the state licensing board.[32] It was becoming increasingly clear that Israel felt no compunction about concealing the truth about his programs from parents, state regulatory agencies, the press, or the courts. He had good reason for concealment.

"Treatment"

An inspection team from New York State visited the BRI in Rhode Island in 1979. They reported that the effect of Israel's program on his "students" was "the singular most depressing experience that team members have had in numerous visitations to human services programs."[33] They noted that the children they saw were constantly controlled by staff, "rather than in control of their [own] behaviors." They had no opportunities to grow, to make choices and decisions, or to enjoy any leisure time. Any transgression, no matter how small, was met with "swift and harsh" punishment. Even staffers admitted to the inspectors that residents weren't learning from this. Once the punishment stopped, they immediately reverted to their old ways.

Israel considered a huge number of behaviors undesirable: standing up without permission, humming, grinding teeth, putting hands to head, wrapping legs around chair legs, failing to maintain a neat appearance, not responding immediately to verbal instructions (even if deaf), stopping work for more than ten seconds, closing one's eyes for more than five seconds, refusing to complete a task, doing the task badly, complaining about being improperly punished (even if punishment was improperly imposed), and screaming and tensing up when punishment was applied.

Perhaps the most repellant aspect of Israel's programs were the "behavior rehearsal lessons." Such rehearsals can be an appropriate part of therapy, but not as practiced by Israel. A report in *The Guardian* newspaper in 2011 described how a resident would be placed in a chair, in restraints, and then ordered to engage in a forbidden behavior, such as slapping herself. Residents who refused (they weren't fools) would be punished for failing to obey; if they did as instructed, they were punished even more harshly for engaging in a forbidden behavior. Survivors describe rehearsals in which a staff member rushed at them wielding a knife—even flinching could earn you an electric shock. In such a situation, you suffer no matter what you do.

Over time residents tended to accumulate forbidden behaviors. In 2006, the New York State Education Department conducted a site visit at JRC. Among their findings:

One student's behavior chart documenting total inappropriate behaviors showed an increase from 800 per week during the first weeks after admission to JRC to average of 12,000 per week. Clinician notes only document the number of inappropriate behaviors. They did not denote any positive behaviors or academic progress. The data showing an increase in inappropriate behaviors is used to substantiate the need for Level III aversive behavioral interventions, and not for analysis to determine alternative forms of intervention.[34]

"A Bad Day"

By the end of the 1990s, disability rights advocates were already at work to stop these practices.[35] But in 2002, the appalling case of Andre McCollins generated such outrage it sped up organizing, among not only autistics, but the wider public. The video shown to the jury during the McCollins case was released to the media, making most of the American public aware for the first time of what was going on at the Judge Rotenberg Center.

On October 25, 2002, Cheryl McCollins received a phone call from the JRC, informing her that her son Andre had "had a bad day." When she got to there, she found Andre completely unresponsive—she described him as "catatonic." He had recently undergone several sudden changes, moving to a new residence, having a new case manager, and entering a new classroom. Any one of these was potentially overwhelming for an autistic young man. When he got to his new classroom on October 25, Andre refused to remove his jacket. This earned him his first shock of the day. Screaming, he tried to crawl under his desk. Staff rushed in and shackled him face down on the restraint board. As his muscles tensed up—an "undesirable behavior"—he earned another shock. "No. Don't do that!" he yelled. "I'm sorry. Sorry. Sorry." More shocks. "I won't do it again." "No, please." More shocks. "Help me. Help, help."[36] Each time he screamed, he got another shock. The staff eventually lost track of how many they had administered. It turned out to be 31 in all, over the course of seven hours. Finally, Israel himself walked in and told them to stop. Gradually Andre calmed a bit, but he wouldn't talk and he wouldn't eat. His mother found him like that. At a nearby hospital 3rd degree burns were found over much of his body and he was diagnosed with a stress disorder. Andre stayed hospitalized for 37 days before he finally went home. When Cheryl sued the JRC, the stunned jury had to watch the tapes of Andre's torture. She got enough money from the settlement to support her son in the future. But Andre has never been the same.

Both main-stream media and autistic organizations publicized Cheryl McCollins's case. In 2012, the Autistic Self-Advocacy Network ran a seven-part series on its website. Written by Shain Neumeier and called "The Judge Rotenberg Center on Trial," the series traced the course of Cheryl McCollins's medical malpractice suit—exposing the details of her allegations to a still wider public.[37] Campaigns gained momentum to stop the use of aversives and shut down the JRC. In 2004, soon after Andre's ordeal, the Alliance to Prevent Aversive Interventions, Restraint and Seclusion (APRAIS) was established. Today it includes nearly 30 national organizations.[38] Families of autistic and intellectually disabled people stopped applying to the Center. Many others began withdrawing their relatives. The "school" made up for the loss of its core population by taking in those involved with the criminal justice system or suffering from psychological problems.[39] Many came from America's deeply flawed foster care system, not only in Massachusetts, but also New York and other states. If they proved too much for foster parents to handle, the states shipped kids off to the JRC.

Prank Calls

Another scandal at the JRC set off further shock waves. On August 8, 2007, staff on the overnight shift at one of its group homes received a prank phone call. It instructed them to wake up two residents, aged 16 and 18, and punish them for behaviors they had supposedly committed during the day. Both young men were fastened to restraint boards. One was shocked 77 times, the other 29. Eventually it emerged that the calls were made by a former resident who had escaped from the JRC, and who apparently had a grudge against the two. He had been part of the new, more emotionally disturbed population there.

Heads rolled. Seven staff members were fired for obeying the phony phone call, although they pleaded inexperience, exhaustion from working extra shifts, and worries about being negatively evaluated if they didn't comply. Nevertheless, it turned out they'd never tried to check with the central office or even look at the treatment plans for the residents, to learn what level of punishment they could receive. In addition, they never notified nursing staff after the event, despite one victim's complaint that he felt like he was having a stroke. It wasn't just the staff members involved who lost their jobs, however. A state investigation was launched, which revealed that Matthew Israel had tried to have video of the event destroyed, even after being explicitly instructed to save it for examination. In 2011, indicted on charges of being an accessory after the fact and misleading investigators, Israel took a plea deal. He agreed to resign as executive director of the JRC, and to never work there or serve on its board of directors again.[40] Nevertheless, the events of 2011 were not the end for Matthew Israel. He continued to operate the "Tobinworld" centers in California until the state shut them down.[41] And neither did the events of 2011 spell the end of the Judge Rotenberg Center.

The Battle for the Ban

In 2013, Judge Isaac Borenstein, appointed to monitor the JRC on behalf of the courts, submitted a massive report to the Massachusetts Attorney General's office and the JRC's board of directors, outlining the many failings of the "school." It cited the Center's poor history of staff hiring, training and retention as contributing to the prank phone call debacle of 2007. It excoriated the Center's lack of a workable system for residents to voice complaints. (Never once had the so-called "Human Rights Committee" considered a resident's concern.) In addition, Borenstein pointed out that 99.9% of those approved for electric shock were autistic/developmentally delayed, though only 65% of the population at JRC still fit that category.[42]

In 2010, Mental Disability Rights International (MDRI—today Disability Rights International) sent a report called "Torture Not Treatment," about events at the JRC, to the United Nations Special Rapporteur on Torture, Manfred Nowak.[43] When the U.S. government failed to investigate MDRI's complaint, a new Rapporteur, Juan Mendez, took a further step. In a 2013 report on incidents of torture around the world, he explicitly condemned the JRC:

... the Special Rapporteur determines that the rights of the students of the JRC subjected to Level III Aversive Interventions by means of electric shock and physical means of restraints have been violated under the UN Convention against Torture and other international standards. The Special Rapporteur calls on the [United States] Government to ensure a prompt and impartial investigation into these continued practices.[44]

The appearance of these two reports—by Bornstein and Mendez—in 2013 set the debate about the JRC on a new course. Sites run by autistics exploded with outrage:

It is not treatment, it is torture. The United Nations say so. It cannot be done to prisoners, not even terrorists. It is called inhumane if done to animals. Yet, it has been done to the disabled with impunity.[45]

In 2013 APRAIS called for all federal organizations to stop funding the JRC.[46] Law student (now lawyer) Lydia X.Z. Brown launched a massive online archive documenting what happened at the "school." It is still being updated today.[47]

The American Civil Liberties Union and Human Rights Watch joined autistics in speaking out. From the ACLU:

The [GED] devices are clearly inhumane. But the fact that they are only used on people with disabilities is telling. In no other population would we treat people like cattle to be prodded or dogs to be trained not to bark.[48]

And from Human Rights Watch:

Few rights are as fundamental as the right to be free from

torture and cruel, inhuman, or degrading treatment. This right can be found in most major international human rights treaties, including the International Covenant on Civil and Political Rights and the Convention against Torture, both ratified by the US. . . . The practices at JRC amount to torture or cruel, inhuman, and degrading treatment, and they violate the inherent dignity of every person with a disability at JRC who receives the shocks. [49]

But the JRC still had powerful allies, including some important members of the Massachusetts legislature and judiciary. The Association for Behavior Analysis International (ABAI) and Autism Speaks were also on its side. What's more, government officials and members of various professions were generally unwilling to "rock the boat." In 2007, 154 disability professionals and advocates wrote to the American Psychological Association, asking the organization to take a stand on the use of extreme aversives such as electric shocks. The APA refused.[50]

Autistic and other disability activists continued speaking up. Already in 2009, the recently-founded Autistic Self-Advocacy Network (ASAN) joined other organizations in urging a list of government officials and influential individuals to stop the JRC's use of electric shocks and other extreme aversives.[51] In 2012, the national Centers for Medicare and Medicaid Services sent a letter to Massachusetts asking for assurance that no Medicaid waiver funds would be used in settings where aversives are used: "reasonable people will agree that electric shock and withholding of meals have no place in their homes or communities."[52]

Soon, though, advocacy efforts became focused on the Food and Drug Administration. The JRC claimed the FDA had officially approved its GED devices; the FDA itself questioned this.[53] In the spring of 2014, the "Neurological Devices Panel" of the FDA held a public hearing about the GED. Testimony was given not only by the FDA's own scientists, and representatives of the JRC, but also by those speaking for numerous advocacy organizations. These included APRAIS, TASH, and The Arc (all important advocacy groups for the rights of the disabled). Ari Ne'eman spoke movingly on behalf of ASAN:

As a child and into young adulthood, I self-injured, I was aggressive. I was removed from my neighborhood school because of behavioral problems and elopement. If I had been born in a different place or to a different family, the years I spent graduating high school and college and building and running an organization could have been spent subject to a treatment that the United Nations has rightly deemed torture. If I had been slightly less lucky, instead of serving as a presidential appointee and working on public policy, I could be living a life in which not a single moment would be free from the threat of pain.[54]

The hearing concluded without any resolution of the issue. But the Neurological Devices panel were clearly disturbed by what they had learned.[55]

Advocates kept up the pressure as the FDA slowly mulled over the GED question. Finally, in 2016, the FDA proposed a ban on Israel's devices, arguing that their use posed significant psychological and physical dangers. "These devices," one official wrote, "are dangerous and a risk to public health."[56] But a proposed ban was not an actual ban, and autistic advocates worried one wouldn't be enacted before President Barack Obama left office. They feared the next president would be less supportive. (The election of Donald Trump proved them right.) Vigorous advocacy continued for another four years, until finally, in March, 2020, the FDA banned any new use of electric shock devices to prevent self-injury or aggression. People already being shocked would continue to suffer while an appropriate "transition plan" was put into place.[57] Nevertheless, this represented a victory.

Sadly, a short-lived one. In July 2021, the Court of Appeals in the District of Columbia vacated the ban, on the grounds that while the FDA had the right to disallow specific devices for all purposes, it had no right to ban their use only for specific ones. Since the FDA allowed the use of mild shocks for treating things like smoking addiction, it could not stop monstrous shocks for the treatment of autism. Denying only the Judge Rotenberg Center the right to give electric shocks would mean the FDA was "interfering with the practice of medicine," which it had no statutory right to do. Sri Srinivasan, the chief judge of the court did dissent from his colleagues' decision, arguing that there was precedent for the FDA's action in banning a device for one purpose, while allowing it for others.[58] Nevertheless, the majority ruled, and the Judge Rotenberg Center returned to business as usual.

Yet the battle continues, now in the states. Proposed legislation in New York, known as "Andre's Law" in honor of Andre McCollins, would prevent the use of state funds to support institutions that use aversives. (New York State sends more people to the JRC than any other state.) In the meantime, autistic advocates still seek the closure of the JRC. They demand, at the very least, the end of its abusive practices:

> *To all the residents of JRC I say, I see you. Your community of disabled people sees you. You matter. Your lives mean more than what you have been led to believe when you are tortured and shocked, and treated as less than human. You are a person worthy of all the best that life has to offer, and you have a community that will continue to fight for your freedom from the torture you are currently forced to endure.*[59]

The battle continues.

CHAPTER TWELVE

Filicide

When children are killed by parents or caregivers, society's response is visceral. The murderer needs to be locked up for life, they say. The actions were utterly disgusting, and the killer needs to pay the price for what they did. Society is unequivocally hostile toward the murderer. However, society's views often shift a little when autism or disability comes into the picture. The response of news reporters, judicial bodies, and the general public is sympathy toward the person who committed the crime. The narrative changes from "cold-blooded murderer" to "loving parent who suffered and snapped under the burden of caregiving" or sometimes even "doting caregiver who killed because the other options were too unbearable." The term "mercy killing" is, surprisingly, commonly used. Those who are convicted often face less severe sentences.[1]

E very year, on March 1, the disability community holds a day of mourning for disabled people murdered by relatives or caretakers. Candlelight vigils are held all around the country. The names of the dead are read aloud, followed by a moment of silence in their honor. Every year the list expands so much that typically only those killed within the last twelve months are mentioned. Over 550 individuals with disabilities have faced the ultimate betrayal in the past five years alone.[2] Their lives have been taken by the very people who should be protecting them.

Not all of those named during the Day of Mourning are autistic, of course. Because of this book's focus, I will limit the stories I tell here to those of autistic people. But we must never forget that hundreds of children, adults, and elders with other disabilities—Down Syndrome, cystic fibrosis, dementia, hearing loss, cerebral palsy, spina bifida, mental illness, heart disease, etc.—are murdered by their families every year in the United States.

Who Are the Victims?

Jax Ponomarenko, age 5, died March 25, 2021

Jax's father beat him to death with a baseball bat in Parma, Ohio. The father had mental health issues and claimed the beating occurred while he was "hearing voices." He was eventually indicted on two counts of aggravated murder, after the grand jury concluded he actually acted with "prior calculation and design."[3]

Thomas Valva, age 8, died January 17, 2020

When police in Long Island, New York, responded to a 911 call, they found young Thomas Valva unconscious. He was pronounced dead at the hospital. Physicians observed that the child was seriously emaciated and that his body temperature was only 76 degrees. They agreed that he had died of hypothermia. Home surveillance video later showed Thomas and his siblings regularly sleeping on the floor of the unheated garage, while temperatures outside were well below freezing. (In contrast, the family dog had a comfortable bed inside the house.) The kids were being punished for soiling their pajamas. Concerned teachers and school administrators had made at least a dozen calls to child protection hotlines between 2018 and 2020. They reported that Thomas and his siblings were much too thin, came to school in filthy clothes, and ate out of the garbage there. Nevertheless, the father—himself a police officer—had retained custody of the children he abused. [4]

Alejandro Ripley, age 9, died May 21, 2020

Alejandro's mother drove him to a canal near her Florida home and pushed him into the water. A bystander rescued the child, but later that evening she pushed him into another body of water where he drowned. The mother invented a story about how two "Black men" had abducted and killed the boy. Later, surveillance footage was found that showed her shoving her son into the water.[5]

Of course, many individuals without disabilities are also murdered by their relatives and caregivers. This is sadly commonplace in American society. But in the news media, these victims are usually depicted as real people, with real personalities, relationships, likes and dislikes. Their deaths are given the full weight of tragedy. In contrast, when family members or caregivers murder disabled people, the news media focus on the grisly details and the murderer's character. Much time is spent looking for motives. The victims themselves remain strangely transparent. We know very little about Jax, Thomas, and Alejandro. Did they love stuffed animals or eating macaroni and cheese? Did they play Minecraft? Was "Goodnight Moon" their favorite bedtime story? Did they rush to give their neurotypical sister a kiss to wake her each morning? We don't know.

After Alex Spourdalakis (age 14) was stabbed to death by his mother, the mother of another autistic child wrote:

> Where are the news articles discussing who this young man was? What did he love? What were his passions? What made him happy? What must it be like to not be able to speak? Did he communicate through typing? Did he read and write and if so what did he like to read? What was his favorite subject? Did he love music? Did he like animals? Was there something special he enjoyed doing?
>
> What about Alex?[6]

When disabled people are murdered, the media too often elide the fact that a human being, with feelings and thoughts like any other person, is dead. Typically, the victims of filicide become no more than dead bodies, envisioned as pathetic because of their disability, but nothing more. Not only their killers but the media dehumanize them. And this, in turn, makes it easier to explain away the theft of their lives.

Death from Abuse

Sometimes that theft occurs in particularly brutal ways.

Zeus Cox, age 3, died July 5, 2021

When Lafayette, Indiana police arrived at the house, they found Zeus's body lying on the bedroom floor. The mother and her boyfriend told the police the autistic toddler had tripped and fallen, and that somehow those injuries had caused his death. Later it was revealed that the boyfriend had punched Zeus repeatedly, breaking ribs, rupturing his intestines in several places, and rupturing his kidneys. The couple did not seek medical aid but left the three-year-old to die in agonizing pain over the course of hours. [7]

Yonatan Aguilar, age 11, died August 22, 2016

Yonatan's mother pulled him out of school three years before his death, because teachers were noticing signs of physical abuse, as well as how dirty and hungry he was. Other people had called hotlines and notified police that they believed he and his siblings were being abused. But neither the Los Angeles County Department of Children and Family Services nor the police did anything. After he left school, Yonatan's mother told relatives and neighbors that he had been sent to an institution in Mexico. In reality, the autistic child spent three years locked in a closet, sedated to keep him quiet, periodically beaten, and starved. At the time of his death, he weighed only 34 pounds, less than half of what a typical eleven-year-old weighs. He had lost most of his hair and showed signs of chronic dehydration.[8]

The media like to focus on cases like those of Zeus and Yonatan—autistic children who suffer horrific and prolonged deaths at the hands of abusive relatives. In these cases, blame is easy to assign. Not only the monstrous parents are at fault; so are the authorities who failed to protect the victim.

"Mercy Killings"

Sometimes, though, murderers claim that they acted out of "mercy," that they killed out of "kindness" because the victims' lives were "unbearable." The term "mercy killing" perpetuates the belief that it is better to be dead than disabled. But seldom does anyone provide proof that mercy was really involved.

Luke and Daniel Schlemmer, ages 3 and 6, died April 1 and April 5, 2014

A year before the brothers from McCandless, Pennsylvania died, their mother had already decided she wanted to "end their suffering," so she tied them up and drove over them several times with her car. The boys miraculously survived that attack, so in April 2014 she sat on top of them in the bathtub until they drowned, arguing that because they were disabled, they would be "better off in heaven."[9]

The boys had never been diagnosed with autism. Their mother decided on her own that they were autistic. And that they should die.

Jorden and Jaden Webb, age 8, died April 3, 2019

Dorothy Flood of Tucson, Arizona shot her twin grandsons to death early in 2019. Her first shot hit Jorden in the stomach, but then the gun jammed. After an online search, she figured out how to clear the gun chambers, which allowed her to shoot Jaden in the chest. Then she shot both boys again, in the head.[10]

During the grandmother's trial, her lawyer argued: "Mrs. Flood recognized the physical pain that both boys were in and her choice of place to shoot them reflected her desire to relieve them of their pain, not cause more."[11] Jorden struggled with the gastro-intestinal upsets so common in autistics, so she shot him in the stomach. Jaden had asthma, so she shot him in the chest. Most people with such problems learn to live with them. It's a pretty safe bet that Jorden and Jaden could have done the same. It was their grandmother who couldn't.

In such "mercy killings," the very nature of the crimes (running over children with a car? shooting them multiple times?) raises doubt that compassion was ever part of the equation.

Overwhelmed?

The most common defense offered by those who have tried or succeeded in murdering their autistic relatives is that they were "overwhelmed" and "acting out of desperation." Caring for an autistic relative was just so difficult, they couldn't stand it anymore.

London McCabe, age 6, died November 3, 2014

London's mother threw him from the Yaquina Bay Bridge in Oregon. He fell 133 feet, breaking bones when he hit the water and eventually drowning. His mother claimed at first that she was motivated by "voices" in her head, but it later turned out that she had spent a month researching different ways to kill her son and how to develop a plea of "innocent by reason of insanity."[12]

Like Jaden and Jorden's grandmother, London's mother used the "I was overwhelmed" claim. So did Kristina Petrie. In 2018, she actually tried to saw her son's head off, although he managed to escape with relatively minor injuries. Caring for her two autistic sons was just too hard, Petrie claimed. According to a court document, "she did not want her children to grow up to be a burden to society and that the children needed to die."[13] Certainly caring for autistic children and adults can be physically challenging. It can be financially harmful and emotionally draining. (It can also be breathtakingly joyful and fulfilling.) But in most other murder cases, stress is not accepted as a justification.

What really roils the autistic community, though, are the excuses our society makes for some of these killers. When Elizabeth Hodgins shot her 22-year-old George and then turned the gun on herself in 2012, the papers were full of sympathy for her:

> She said she was tired and was having a difficult time getting [George] into a program. She couldn't find one that would take him," neighbor Jacquie Jauch said Wednesday. "She was just tired, tired and very lonely. She said she just couldn't do it anymore — take care of him." Jauch described the son — the couple's only child — as low functioning and high maintenance, unable to speak and easily agitated, but fully mobile.[14]

Other parents wrote to the papers, repeating how hard it was to care for an autistic child, and expressing their sympathy. George's being "low functioning" (a meaningless term) and "high maintenance" somehow excused his killer. "Walk a mile in her shoes," Hodgins's defenders said. What a kick in the gut for autistic people. Maybe these people should try walking a mile in an autistic's shoes, one advocate retorted.[15]

Government officials, including those who are supposed to be acting on behalf of victims, sometimes commiserate with their murderers. When Barbara Busch shot her daughter Cynthia, and then turned the gun on herself, the local police chief said: "People do get to their breaking point, and get to the point where they just, they feel there's no other alternative for them. It's a sad outcome."[16] For Cynthia Busch, it was more than sad. Not a judge, not a jury, but her own mother decided she should die. Public officials lined up to defend the murderous mother, when Mindy Speck, age 21, was purposely given a fatal dose of insulin. Even the prosecutor in the case—the person tasked with seeking justice for the victim—suggested that caring for her daughter had just "overwhelmed" Sandra Speck.[17]

Can we murder American citizens just because they are "low functioning," "high maintenance," "unloving," "an overwhelming burden"? Are we allowed to shoot Fentanyl addicts because they don't "function" very well? Can we kill narcissists who are "high maintenance"? My own parents were not very "loving." Would it have been acceptable for me to stab them to death? Corrupt politicians and oil company executives are suffocating our democracy and our planet. Does that make them a "burden?" Can we assassinate them with impunity?

In 2014, after London McCabe's death, NBC news interviewed Dee Shepherd-Look. A psychologist at California State University, Northridge, Shepherd-Look placed the blame for the murder squarely on the victim's shoulders. "Quite frankly," she proclaimed, "I am surprised this doesn't happen more often." She elaborated:

> These [i.e., autistic] children are really unable to be in a reciprocal relationship and the moms don't really experience the love that comes back from a child — the bonding is mitigated . . . That is one of the most difficult things for mothers.[18]

And that makes murder OK.

The Lives of Disabled People

As I said in Chapter One: autistic and other disabled people are just as human as everyone else. Let me add here: the lives of disabled people are just as valuable as the lives of non-disabled people. But too many Americans persist in seeing disabled people as "less than human," as nothing but a bundle of deficits. If you can euthanize unwanted kittens, why not an autistic child?

> For some reason, in our warped culture, being autistic somehow means you don't count – you are not considered human being enough to count even after someone tries to murder you! In fact, you will likely not even be part of the story after the first few sentences.[19]

If disability advocates get worked up about this issue, they have a very good reason. It is all too easy to imagine the horrors they describe happening to themselves. In a moving speech on the 2015 Day of Mourning, Ari Ne'eman put it this way:

> Had our lives been different, had we been born to or placed under the power of those who saw us as life unworthy of life, we might not be here today, except as another name on that list. It could have been us, there instead of here. Taken before our time with our deaths more celebrated than our lives ever were. It could have been us.[20]

The campaign to stop the killings continues tirelessly, with vigils, with protests, with personal statements. People who refuse to see their own ableism, who apply a double standard to disabled and non-disabled people, may push back.[21] But advocates won't stop speaking their truth:

> When journalists call murderers "loving and devoted parents," . . . when parents normalize murder by saying that all special-needs parents have murderous thoughts, the result is an environment in which these murders are seen as acceptable. Media coverage like this sends a message that homicide is a normal, understandable response to any discomfort one might experience while parenting a disabled child . . .[22]

> I need you — and judges and reporters everywhere — to understand that, however difficult it may be for families to support their disabled loved ones, murder is never excusable. There are always other options. Always.[23]

And slowly—agonizingly slowly—progress is being made. According to Zoe Gross of the Autistic Self-Advocacy Network, the media are now paying more attention to the victims of filicide and are somewhat less likely to show sympathy for their murderers. Heavier sentences are sometimes being imposed on those who kill disabled relatives.[24]

Autistic attorney Haley Moss lays out an agenda for the advocacy campaign in her law review article, "A Life Worth Living: Fighting Filicide Against Children with Disabilities." Moss argues that parents who kill the disabled should be prosecuted vigorously and given the same sentences as murderers of non-disabled people. She further argues that attacks on the disabled should be treated as hate crimes.[25] Unfortunately, this can't happen until more states pass hate crime laws that protect the disabled. As things now stand, the murder of a disabled person is only elevated to the status of a federal hate crime if it affects interstate commerce.[26] (This logic is hard to comprehend.) Moss also emphasizes that media reports must focus on the victims rather than the killers, so that the latter are no longer viewed so sympathetically: "By refusing to 'understand' or justify the killing of a disabled child, these filicides will be treated just as any other murder would be."

Finally, Moss challenges the public to become less ignorant about disabled people's humanity. Because ultimately what lies behind the crime of filicide and all the excuses for it is a refusal to accept that disabled people are human beings. The right not to be murdered is at the very core of our criminal justice system. It is enshrined in the Declaration of Independence and in the Universal Declaration of Human Rights, to which the United States is a signatory. And yet people with disabilities still find themselves begging for a security they, as human beings, should automatically enjoy.

We are asking to not be murdered.
We are asking: don't murder disabled people.
Some people tell us this is too much to ask.[27]

No. No, it's not too much to ask.

CONCLUSION

Holding on to Hope

I f you take anything away from this book, let it be hope.

As poet Nathan Spoon puts it, in "A History of Leaves," "we are waiting for tomorrow to give us what today withholds."[1] Today still withholds from autistic people the human dignity to which they are entitled. It enables shocking abuses. We have seen small children subjected to treatment intended to erase who they are, kids denied the chance to learn, locked in closets, and handcuffed by the police. We have learned how hard autistic people must struggle to find, let alone keep a job, and their limited options if they can't find one. We have seen autistics misdiagnosed, overmedicated, and denied life-saving care. And others locked away in psych wards because no one knows how to help them. We have seen people with autism victimized by the police, by "behavioral research" institutions, by their own families. It is easy to look at what happens in America today and fall into despair.

But that is not the end of the story, nor even the most critical part of it. Just as important is autistic people's ongoing struggle to reclaim their human rights. If much of this book has been devoted to darkness, this conclusion is devoted to courage, to action, and to hope. As more and more activists stand up and shout and fight and triumph, change is happening. More of us are becoming informed about autism and about autistic lives. More children—although not nearly enough—are being shielded from abusive early intervention, inadequate teaching, and violent school discipline. While autistic employment is still ridiculously low, it is nevertheless on the rise. Doctors and mental health practitioners are slowly beginning to acknowledge the gaps in their knowledge of autism. And the campaigns against state, institutional, and familial violence are gaining power.

It is my belief that eventually autistics will attain the same rights other Americans enjoy. It may not be in my lifetime, for I am an old woman. Success will come only slowly, with great labor, and despite many setbacks. But we can still hope that "tomorrow" will finally bring about true acceptance of autistic people's humanity.

And on those dark days when you feel beaten down, know I will hold onto your hope for you. Likewise, I will need you to hold onto my hope for me during my times of bleakness, until I can once again pick up that hope and walk forward. This is how we will be stronger together.[2]

Notes

Notes to Introduction

1 Jennifer Sarrett, "Autism Human Rights: A Proposal," *Disability Studies Quarterly* 32:4 (2012), open access.

2 The CDC currently estimates that 1 out of every 36 children in the United States is autistic: Centers for Disease Control and Prevention, "Data and Statistics on Autism Spectrum Disorder," April 4, 2023: https://www.cdc.gov/ncbddd/autism/data.html.

3 Centers for Disease Control and Prevention, "CDC Releases First Estimates of the Number of Adults Living with Autism Spectrum Disorder in the United States," April 7, 2022: https://www.cdc.gov/ncbddd/autism/features/adults-living-with-autism-spectrum-disorder.html.

4 Of course, some of those lawyers, doctors and tourists are autistic themselves.

5 Sabrina Rubin Erdely, "The Entrapment of Jesse Snodgrass," *Rolling Stone*, February 26, 2014: https://www.rollingstone.com/culture/culture-news/the-entrapment-of-jesse-snodgrass-116008/.

6 Matt Vasilogambros, "Thousands Lose Right to Vote Under 'Incompetence' Laws," *Pew Charitable Trust: Stateline*, March 21, 2018: https://www.pewtrusts.org/en/research-and-analysis/blogs/stateline/2018/03/21/thousands-lose-right-to-vote-under-incompetence-laws.

7 National Council on Disability, "Rocking the Cradle: Ensuring the Rights of Parents with Disabilities and Their Children," September 27, 2012: https://www.ncd.gov/sites/default/files/Documents/NCD_Parenting_508_0.pdf.

8 Susan Eileen Walz, "Universalizing Human Rights: The Role of Small States in the Construction of the Universal Declaration of Human Rights," *Human Rights Quarterly* 23:1 (2001): 44–72.

9 Kristina Ash, "U.S. Reservations to the International Covenant on Civil and Political Rights: Credibility Maximization and Global Influence," *Northwestern Journal of International Human Rights* 7:3 (2005): https://scholarlycommons.law.northwestern.edu/cgi/viewcontent.cgi?article=1018&context=njihr.

10 Lisa Herndon, "Why Is Racial Injustice Still Permitted in the United States?: An International Human Rights Perspective on the United States' Inadequate Compliance with the International Convention on the Elimination of All Forms of Racial Discrimination," *Wisconsin International Law Journal* 31:2 (2013), 322-351.

11 Isaac Linnartz, "The Siren Song of Interrogational Torture: Evaluating the U.S. Implementation of the U.N. Convention Against Torture," *Duke Law Journal* 57:5 (2008), 1485-1516.

12 United Nations Office of the High Commissioner on Human Rights, "Status of Ratification Interactive Dashboard": https://indicators.ohchr.org/. See also Marie Wilken, "U.S. Aversion to International Human Rights Treaties," *Global Justice Center*, June 22, 2017: https://globaljusticecenter.net/blog/773-u-s-aversion-to-international-human-rights-treaties.

13 Jamil Dakwar, "UN Issues Scathing Assessment of US Human Rights Record," *American Civil Liberties Union*, May 15, 2015: https://www.aclu.org/blog/human-rights/human-rights-and-criminal-justice/un-issues-scathing-assessment-us-human-rights.

14 Eric Garcia, *We Are Not Broken: Changing the Autism Conversation* (New York: Houghton Mifflin Harcourt, 2021), location 111.

15 This comes from a 2009 interview with Shore, no longer available online.

Notes to Chapter One

1 Judy Endow, "I Already Am a Human Being," *Aspects of Autism Translated*, November 2, 2013: http://www.judyendow.com/advocacy/i-already-am-a-human-being/., November 2, 2013: http://www.judyendow.com/advocacy/i-already-am-a-human-being/.

2 Nicholette Zeliadt, "Autism Genetics, Explained," *Spectrum,* June 27, 2017, revised version May 28, 2021: https://www.spectrumnews.org/news/autism-genetics-explained/.

3 Michael Lombardo, Lai Meng-Chuan, and Simon Baron-Cohen, "Big Data Approaches to Decomposing Heterogeneity across the Autism Spectrum," *Nature: Molecular Psychiatry* 24 (2019), 1435-50; these researchers have suggested using the term "the autisms" instead of "autism."

4 Ben VanHook has written a blistering attack on this common claim, in a post on *LinkedIn*: https://www.linkedin.com/posts/ben-vanhook-970041168_actuallyautistic-asd-stigma-activity-7028358289037881344-73EJ/?utm_source=share&utm_medium=member_ios. He says, "Statements like these are extremely disrespectful and harmful to our community. To say 'we are "all autistic"' IS NOT empathy. Instead, it is dehumanising, degrading, insensitive, and dangerous."

5 Broad Autism Phenotype studies generally focus on autism traits in relatives of autistic individuals. However, studies are now emerging on the prevalence of "subthreshold autism traits" in the general population. See, for example, Stephen M. Kanne, Jennifer Wang, and Shawn E. Christ, "The Subthreshold Autism Trait Questionnaire (SATQ): Development of a Brief Self-Report Measure of Subthreshold Autism Traits," *Journal of Autism and Developmental Disorders* 42 (2012), 769-80

6 American Psychiatric Association, *Diagnostic and Statistical Manual of Mental Disorders*, 5th ed. (Arlington, Virginia: American Psychiatric Association, 2013).

7 On the problematic nature of this "deficit view, see Janette Dinishak, "The Deficit View and Its Critics," *Disability Studies Quarterly* 36:4 (2016), open access.

8 Simon Baron-Cohen, *Mindblindness: An Essay on Autism and Theory of Mind* (Cambridge, MA: MIT Press, 2001).

NOTES

9 Simon Baron-Cohen, "Theory of Mind in Normal Development and Autism," *Prisme* 34 (2001), 174-83.

10 Here is one autistic person's critique of his work: Sarah Boon, "A Brief Overview Of Simon Baron-Cohen's Autism Research," *Sarah Boon*, February 13, 2022: https://autisticallysarah.com/2022/02/13/a-brief-overview-of-simon-baron-cohens-autism-research/.

11 Rosanna Edey, et al., "Interaction Takes Two: Typical Adults Exhibit Mind-Blindness towards those with Autism Spectrum Disorder," *Journal of Abnormal Psychology* 125:7 (2016), 879-85; Morton Ann Gernsbacher and Melanie Yergeau, "Empirical Failures of the Claim That Autistic People Lack a Theory of Mind," *Archives of Scientific Psychology* 7 (2019), 102-18.

12 Morton Ann Gernsbacher and Melanie Yergeau, "Empirical Failures of the Claim That Autistic People Lack a Theory of Mind," *Archives of Scientific Psychology* 7 (2019), 102-18.

13 Steven Pinker, *The Blank Slate: The Modern Denial of Human Nature* (New York: Viking, 2002), p. 62.

14 Mike Falcon and Stephen Shoop, "Stars CAN-Do About Defeating Autism," *USA Today*, April 10, 2002: https://usatoday30.usatoday.com/news/health/spotlight/2002/04/10-autism.htm.

15 And elsewhere, e.g.: Jenny Bergenmar, et al., "Autism and the Question of the Human," *Literature and Medicine* 33:1 (2015), 202-221.

16 Morton Ann Gernsbacher, "On Not Being Human," *Association for Psychological Science Observer* 20:2 (2007). Gernsbacher criticized efforts to de-humanize people generally, as well as autistic people specifically.

17 Autistic scientists have played an important role in this turnaround. See Rachel Nuwer, "Meet the Autistic Scientists Redefining Autism Research," *Spectrum*, June 10, 2020: https://www.spectrumnews.org/features/deep-dive/meet-the-autistic-scientists-redefining-autism-research/.

18 Steven Silberman, *Neurotribes: The Legacy of Autism and the Future of Neurodiversity* (New York: Penguin, 2015), p. 450-68, describes the development and spread of the concept within the autism community.

19 Judy Singer, *Neurodiversity: The Birth of an Idea* (self-published on Amazon Kindle, 2016). Even Simon Baron-Cohen has come around to using the term in a positive sense: "The Concept of Neurodiversity Is Dividing the Autism Community. It Remains Controversial, But It Doesn't Have to Be," *Scientific American* April 30, 2019: https://blogs.scientificamerican.com/observations/the-concept-of-neurodiversity-is-dividing-the-autism-community/.

20 Harvey Blume, "Neurodiversity: The Neurological Underpinnings of Geekdom," *The Atlantic,* September, 1998: https://www.theatlantic.com/magazine/archive/1998/09/neurodiversity/305909/.

21 Maureen Bennie, "The Positives of Autism," *Autism Awareness Centre* (Canada), March 25, 2019: https://autismawarenesscentre.com/the-positives-of-autism/.

22 Justin Robbins, "Autistic People Don't Need to Be Cured," *Stairway to STEM*, July 20, 2018: https://www.stairwaytostem.org/autistic-people-dont-need-to-be-cured/.

23 As first reported by KATC television, an ABC affiliate in Denham Springs, Louisiana, August 18,

NOTES

2015. The television station has removed the story from its website, but it can still be found online: https://www.rawstory.com/2015/08/louisiana-school-threatens-to-boot-first-grader-from-school-over-autistic-behaviors/.

24 Autistic people have sometimes used this language themselves, especially when describing victories over neurotypicals. For example, a Reddit group calling itself the "Autistic Retards" successfully "weaponized autism" to inflate the stock value of a struggling video game company: Christopher Caldwell, "Opinion: Are GameStop's 'Degenerates' Just Getting Started?" *New York Times* February 4, 2021.

25 Marie Bristol, et al, "State of the Science in Autism: Report to the National Institutes of Health," *Journal of Autism and Developmental Disorders* 26 (1996), 124.

26 Eric Fombonne, "Epidemiology of Autistic Disorder and Other Pervasive Developmental Disorders," *Journal of Clinical Psychiatry* 66 (2005): 3-8.

27 Jon Baio, "Prevalence of Autism Spectrum Disorder Among Children Aged 8 Years," Centers for Disease Control and Prevention, *Surveillance Summaries*, March 28, 2014: https://www.cdc.gov/mmwr/preview/mmwrhtml/ss6302a1.htm?s_cid=ss6302a1_w.

28 Michelle Dawson, et al., "The Level and Nature of Autistic Intelligence," *Psychological Science* 18 (2007), 657-62. This study is discussed by Temple Grandin and Richard Panek, *The Autistic Brain: Helping Different Kinds of Mind Succeed* (New York, 2013). See also Isabelle Soulieres, et al., "The Level and Nature of Autistic Intelligence II: What About Asperger Syndrome?" *PLOS/One*, September 28, 2011, open access; Valerie Courchesne, et al., "Autistic Children at Risk of Being Underestimated: School Based Pilot Study of a Strength-Informed Assessment," *Molecular Autism* 6 (2015): open access; Valerie Courchesne, et al., "Assessing Intelligence at Autism Diagnosis: Mission Impossible? Testability and Cognitive Profile of Autistic Preschoolers," *Journal of Autism and Developmental Disorders* 49:3 (2019), 845-856.

29 jojobean, in the "Your IQ as a Child vs. Your IQ as an Adult" discussion, *Wrong Planet*, September 13, 2010: https://wrongplanet.net/forums/viewtopic.php?t=137652.

30 Horus, in the "Your IQ as a Child vs. Your IQ as an Adult" discussion, *Wrong Planet* , September 13, 2010: https://wrongplanet.net/forums/viewtopic.php?t=137652.

31 Kerri Nowellf, et al., "Cognitive Profiles in Youth with Autism Spectrum Disorder: An Investigation of Base Rate Discrepancies using the Differential Ability Scales—Second Edition, "*Journal of Autism and Developmental Disorders*, 45 (2015), 1978-1988.

32 Valerie Courchesne, et al., "Autistic Children at Risk of Being Underestimated: School-Based Pilot Study of a Strength-Informed Assessment," *Molecular Autism* 6 (March, 2015), open access; Olga Khazan, "Autism's Hidden Gifts," *The Atlantic*, September 23, 2015: https://www.theatlantic.com/health/archive/2015/09/autism-hidden-advantages/406180/; Emily Sohn, "The Blurred Line Between Autism and Intellectual Disability," *Spectrum*, April 15, 2020: https://www.spectrumnews.org/features/deep-dive/the-blurred-line-between-autism-and-intellectual-disability/.

33 Julia Bascom, "The Obsessive Joy of Autism," *Just Stimming*, April 5, 2011: https://juststimming.wordpress.com/2011/04/05/the-obsessive-joy-of-autism/.

NOTES

34 Melissa Conrad Stoppler, "Impaired Social Skills and Lack of Emotion," *MedicineNet*, February 19, 2021: https://www.medicinenet.com/impaired_social_skills_and_lack_of_emotion/multisymptoms. htm.

35 Carter Carcione and Joshua Berg, "Asperger's Syndrome," *Prezi*, April, 2016: https://prezi. com/7nmzsborbhrl/aspergers-syndrome/.

36 "How Should I Deal with Being Called an Emotionless Robot If You Have Autism," *Quora*, July, 2018: https://www.quora.com/How-should-I-deal-with-being-called-an-emotionless-robot-if-you-have-autism.

37 At least two organizations (Families of Adults Affected by Aspergers Syndrome and The Neurotypical Site) actively promote these negative stereotypes, claiming that neurotypical romantic partners are traumatized by relationships with unloving autistic people, while neurotypical parents suffer because their autistic children don't show affection. Consider this passage from the "About Us" section of *The Neurotypical Site*: "*Naturally, there is a negative impact on the neurotypical who lives with someone on the Spectrum, which, unintentionally arises out of the developmental deficits of ASD*": https:// www.theneurotypical.com/about_us.html. Even though "unintentionally" suggests no direct blame for the autistic partner, autism is still treated as the reason for the failure of the relationship.

38 See, for example, the "Being a Hermit" discussion *Wrong Planet*, September, 2011: https:// wrongplanet.net/forums/viewtopic.php?f=23&t=173510&start=0.

39 Felicity Sedgewick, et al., "Gender Differences in the Social Motivation and Friendship Experiences of Autistic and Non-Autistic Adolescents," *Journal of Autism and Developmental Disorders* 46 (2016), 1297-1306; Sandra Strunz, et al., "Romantic Relationships and Relationship Satisfaction Among Adults With Asperger Syndrome and High-Functioning Autism," *Journal of Clinical Psychology* 73:1 (2017), 113-25; Giorgia Sala, et al., "Romantic Intimacy in Autism: A Qualitative Analysis," *Journal of Autism and Developmental Disorders* 50:11 (2020), 4133-4147.

40 Michael Ellermann (of the Swedish Autism and Asperger Association), "Interview with Jim Sinclair," January 11, 2016: https://studylib.net/doc/18125680/interview-with-jim-sinclair.

41 Sandra Strunz, et al., "Romantic Relationships and Relationship Satisfaction Among Adults with Asperger Syndrome and High-Functioning Autism," *Journal of Clinical Psychology* 73:1 (2017), 113-25.

42 Erin, "Thinking Unthinkable Thoughts: The Fear Of Losing My Mum," *Queerlyautistic*, February 5, 2018: https://queerlyautistic.com/thinking-unthinkable-thoughts-the-fear-of-losing-my-mum/.

43 BazoQ, in the "Guys, how do you keep your NT wife/girlfriend happy?" discussion, *Wrong Planet*, October 15, 2007: https://wrongplanet.net/forums/viewtopic.php?t=46160.

44 "Mama Pineapple," "#AutismAcceptance/#AutismAppreciation Doodles 'n' Scribbles, no. 14: Being an Autistic Parent (PART 2)," *The Misadventures of Mama Pineapple*, April 14, 2018: https:// mamapineappleblog.wordpress.com/2018/04/14/autismacceptance-autismappreciation-doodles-n-scribbles-no-14-being-an-autistic-parent-part-2/.

45 poppabirdsky, in the "Applying For Ssdi For The First Time" discussion, *Wrong Planet*, March 31, 2018: https://wrongplanet.net/forums/viewtopic.php?t=362215.

46 VegetableMan, in the "Caregiver Stress" discussion, *Wrong Planet*, June 16, 2014: https://wrongplanet.net/forums/viewtopic.php?t=261347.

47 DJFester, in the "Can an Aspie be a caregiver? Bad idea.....?" discussion, *Wrong Planet*, April 20, 2012: https://wrongplanet.net/forums/viewtopic.php?t=196172.

48 Catherine, "Inconsistence and Other Crap," *Ability to be Different*, July 21, 2019: https://abilitytobedifferentblog.wordpress.com/2019/07/21/inconsistence-other-crap/.

49 This refers to "spoon theory," a concept developed by Christine Miserandino, which posits that people with chronic illnesses and disabilities have only limited "spoonfuls" of energy on any given day, and that when they "run out of spoons" they need to stop what they are doing, rest and recover.

50 Erin, "Forced Socialisation (and the toilet-door graffiti that saved me from it)," *Queerly Autistic*, January 26, 2018: https://queerlyautistic.com/2018/01/26/forced-socialisation-and-the-toilet-door-graffiti-that-saved-me-from-it/.

51 Sandra Strunz, et al., "Romantic Relationships and Relationship Satisfaction Among Adults With Asperger Syndrome and High-Functioning Autism," *Journal of Clinical Psychology* 73:1 (2017), 113-25.

52 Metalgear29, in the "Being a Loner" discussion, *Wrong Planet*, September 20, 2014: https://wrongplanet.net/forums/viewtopic.php?t=267374.

53 E.g., C2V, in the "Do you feel better being alone?" discussion, *Wrong Planet*, July 25, 2017: https://wrongplanet.net/forums/viewtopic.php?t=351661; Charloz, in the "Being a Loner" discussion, *Wrong Planet*, September 21, 2014: https://wrongplanet.net/forums/viewtopic.php?f=3&t=267374&start=15.

54 Mother's report of her child's statement, quoted in Sasha Zeedyk, et al., "Perceived Social Competence and Loneliness Among Young Children with ASD: Child, Parent and Teacher Reports," *Journal of Autism and Developmental Disorders* 46 (2016), 436-49.

55 Lynne Soraya, "Loneliness," *The Aspie Life*, December 29, 2007: http://aspielife.blogspot.com/search?q=loneliness. See also Slw1990, in the "Are Aspies Perpetually Lonely?" discussion, *Wrong Planet*, August 4, 2015: https://wrongplanet.net/forums/viewtopic.php?t=290783.

56 Only recently has a group of scientists noticed the link between loneliness and suicidality in the autistic population: Darren Hedley, et al., "Understanding Depression and Thoughts of Self-Harm in Autism: A Potential Mechanism Involving Loneliness," *Research in Autism Spectrum Disorders* 46 (2018), 1-7; Darren Hedley, et al., "Risk and Protective Factors Underlying Depression and Suicidal Ideation in Autism Spectrum Disorder," *Depression and Anxiety* 35:7 (2018), 648-657.

57 Attributed to Temple Grandin by John Elder Robison, "Autism and Fear: Don't Let Your Life Be Ruled by Fear and Anxiety," *Psychology Today*, February 8, 2011: https://www.psychologytoday.com/us/blog/my-life-aspergers/201102/autism-and-fear.

58 Francisca van Steesel, et al., "Anxiety Disorders in Children and Adolescents with Autism Spectrum Disorders: A Meta-Analysis," *Clinical Child and Family Psychology Review* 14:3 (2011), 302-17.

59 Maxfield Sparrow (formerly Rose Sparrow Jones), "Anxiety and Mental Health Accessibility," *Unstrange Mind*, May 5, 2016: https://unstrangemind.wordpress.com/2016/05/05/anxiety-and-

mental-health-accessibility/.

60 Jeffrey Wood and Kenneth Gadow, "Exploring the Nature and Function of Anxiety in Youth with Autism Spectrum Disorders," *Clinical Psychology: Science and Practice* 17:4 (2010), p. 286.

61 The "amygdala theory of autism" was first put forward by Simon Baron-Cohen, et al., "The Amygdala Theory of Autism," *Neuroscience and Biobehavioural Reviews* 24 (2000), 355-364. Baron-Cohen suggested that unusual development of the amygdala played a role in the "social deficits" he observed among autistic people. More recently, neuroscientists have focused on the unusual way in which the autistic amygdala processes emotions, especially fear: J. Herrington, et al., "Anxiety and Social Deficits Have Distinct Relationships with Amygdala Function in Autism Spectrum Disorder," *Social, Cognitive, and Affective Neuroscience*, 11: 6 (2016), 907-914.

62 Tito Mukhopadhyay, *How Can I Talk If My Lips Don't Move? Inside My Autistic Mind* (New York: Arcade Publishing, 2008), p. 29.

63 Pawan Sinha, et al., "Autism as a Disorder of Prediction," *Proceedings of the National Academy of Sciences* 111:42 (2014), 15220-15225; J. Goris, "The Relation Between Preference for Predictability and Autistic Traits," *Autism Research* 12 (2019); Ye In Hwang, et al., "Understanding Anxiety in Adults on the Autism Spectrum: An Investigation of Its Relationship with Intolerance of Uncertainty, Sensory Sensitivities and Repetitive Behaviours," *Autism* 24:2 (2020), 411-22.

64 An eloquent expression of this anxiety can be found in Iain Kohn's poem "Terrified of People," *The Mighty*, January 13, 2016: https://themighty.com/2016/01/why-i-am-terrified-of-people-as-an-autistic-teen/

65 Judy Endow, "Fear, Anxiety, and Autistic 'Behavior," *Aspects of Autism Translated*, December 10, 2015: http://www.judyendow.com/advocacy/fear-anxiety-and-autistic-behavior/. Endow notes: "Because we do not have a way to predict if, when or how our bodies will serve us (or not!) it is quite common for autistic people to have some level of ongoing fear and/or anxiety."

66 Hal Dardick, "Council Settles Chicago Police Suit Involving Autistic Boy for $525,000," *Chicago Tribune*, January 18, 2012.

67 See below, Chapter Ten.

68 Geraldine Dawson, quoted in "From People with Autism, Lessons for Scientists on Love, Compassion," *Spectrum*, December 22, 2017: https://www.spectrumnews.org/features/special-report/people-autism-lessons-scientists-love-compassion/.

69 For more on the "empathy and autism" problem, see Patrick McDonagh, "Autism in an Age of Empathy: A Cautionary Critique," in Joyce Davidson and Michael Orsini, eds., *Worlds of Autism: Across the Spectrum of Neurological Difference* (Minneapolis: University of Minnesota Press, 2013), location 650-1067

70 Geraldine Dawson, "Brief Report: Neuropsychology of Autism: A Report on the State of the Science," *Journal of Autism and Developmental Disabilities* 26:2 (1996), 179-84.

71 Simon Baron-Cohen and Sally Wheelwright, "The Empathy Quotient: An Investigation of Adults with Asperger Syndrome or High Functioning Autism, and Normal Sex Differences," *Journal of Autism and Developmental Disorders* 34:2 (2004), 163-75.

NOTES

72 Mia, in the "Autism & Empathy" discussion, *Autism Forums*, March 4, 2020: https://www.Autism Forums.com/threads/autism-empathy.32725/.

73 Greg Love, "Being a Dad on the Autism Spectrum," *Medium*, August 12, 2016: https://medium. com/autistic-community/being-a-dad-on-the-autism-spectrum-c13afa61bf5#.6vv9p1bdi.

74 Kamila Markram and Henry Markram, "The Intense World Theory – a unifying theory of the neurobiology of autism," *Frontiers in Human Neuroscience* 4:224 (2010), open access. The Markrams posited that the input from other people's emotional states is so strong in autistic people that it forces them to withdraw from social interactions. See also Chunyan Meng, et al., "Processing of Expressions by Individuals with Autistic Traits: Empathy Deficit or Sensory Hyper-Reactivity?" *PLosOne* 15:7 (2021), open access.

75 Edenthiel, in the "HyperEmpathy and High Functioning Autistic?" discussion, *Wrong Planet*, April 30, 2016: https://wrongplanet.net/forums/viewtopic.php?t=304240.

76 Nex, in the "Autism & Empathy" discussion, *Autism Forums*, March 4, 2020: https://www.Autism Forums.com/threads/autism-empathy.32725/; wrongcitizen, in the "Do You Lack Empathy?" discussion, *Wrong Planet* (May 11, 2019): https://wrongplanet.net/forums/viewtopic.php?t=376082.

77 Isabel Dziobek, et al., "Dissociation of Cognitive and Emotional Empathy in Adults with Asperger Syndrome Using the Multifaceted Empathy Test (MET)," *Journal of Autism and Developmental Disorders* 38:3 (2008), 464-473; Adam Smith, et al., "The Empathy Imbalance Hypothesis of Autism: A Theoretical Approach to Cognitive and Emotional Empathy in Autistic Development," *Psychological Record* 59:3 (2009), 489-510.

78 For example, autistic subjects actually felt the embarrassment of people who had to perform in front of an audience more deeply than neurotypical controls: Noga Adler, et al., "Empathic Embarrassment Accuracy in Autism Spectrum Disorder," *Autism Research* 8:3 (2015), 241-49.

79 Pistachio, in the "Autism & Empathy" discussion, *Autism Forums*, March 25, 2020: https://www. Autism Forums.com/threads/autism-empathy.32725/page-2.

80 I. Santiesteban, et al., "Individuals with Autism Share Others' Emotions: Evidence from the Continuous Affective Rating and Empathic Responses (CARER) Task," *Journal of Autism and Developmental Disorders* 51:2 (2021), 391-404.

81 Geoffrey Bird, et al., "Empathic Brain Responses in Insula Are Modulated by Levels of Alexithymia but Not Autism," *Brain* 133 (2010), 1515-25; Amandine Lassalle, et al., "Influence of Anxiety and Alexithymia on Brain Activations Associated with the Perception of Others' Pain in Autism" *Social Neuroscience* 14:3 (2019), 359-377.

82 Sue Fletcher-Watson and Geoffrey Bird, "Autism and Empathy: What Are the Real Links?" *Autism* 24:1 (2020), 3-6.

83 Andrew Solomon, "The Myth of the Autistic Shooter," *New York Times*, October 12, 2015.

84 David DesRoches, "For a Teen with Autism, Being Different Was Seen as Being Dangerous," *WNPR Radio* (Darien, CT), September 10, 2018: https://www.wnpr.org/post/teen-autism-being-different-was-seen-being-dangerous.

85 Cited in Stephen White, et al., "Autism Spectrum Disorder and Violence: Threat Assessment

Issues," *Journal of Threat Assessment and Management* 4:3 (2017), 144-63.

86 David Im, "Template to Perpetrate: An Update on Violence in Autism Spectrum Disorder," *Harvard Review of Psychiatry* 24:1 (2016), 14-35; C.S. Allely, et al., "Violence is Rare in Autism: When It Does Occur, Is It Sometimes Extreme?" *Journal of Psychology* 151:1 (2017), 49-68.

87 Vicki Gibbs, Jennie Hudson and Elizabeth Pellicano, "The Extent and Nature of Autistic People's Violence Experiences During Adulthood: A Cross-sectional Study of Victimisation," *Journal of Autism and Developmental Disorders* 52 (2022), open access.

88 Jill Del Pozzo, et al., "Violent Behavior in Autism Spectrum Disorders: Who's at Risk?" *Aggression and Violent Behavior* 39 (2018), 53-60.

89 Julia Bascom, "The Obsessive Joy of Autism," *Just Stimming*, April 5, 2011: https://juststimming.wordpress.com/2011/04/05/the-obsessive-joy-of-autism/.

90 "On Stimming and Why 'Quiet-Hands'-ing an Autistic Person is Wrong," *The Caffeinated Autistic*, February 10, 2013: https://thecaffeinatedautistic.wordpress.com/2013/02/10/on-stimming-and-why-quiet-handsing-an-autistic-person-is-wrong/. See also the beautiful and disturbing poem by Julia Bascom, "Quiet Hands" *Just Stimming*, October 5, 2011: https://juststimming.wordpress.com/2011/10/05/quiet-hands/.

91 For example, the website for Golden Care Therapy, a company that provides ABA therapy for autistic kids: "The goal is to promote appropriate behaviors and discourage inappropriate behaviors" (https://www.goldencaretherapy.com/aba-therapy/). See Chapter Three below on ABA therapy.

92 Comment by "NothingsWrongWithMe", October 7, 2010, to "Understanding Hand-Flapping and What to Do (Or Not Do) About It," *Aspiring Dad*, January 30, 2008: https://aspiringdad.wordpress.com/2008/01/30/understanding-hand-flapping-and-what-to-do-or-not-do-about-it/.

93 Cynthia Kim, "At the Intersection of Gender and Autism—Part 3," *Musings of an Aspie*, December 4, 2014: https://musingsofanaspie.com/tag/girlhood/.

94 Grace, "Joyous Sensory Stimming," *Autistic Empath*, July 23, 2020: https://autisticempath.com/joyous-sensory-stimming/; Maxfield Sparrow, "Stimming: What it is and why Autistic people do it," *Neuroclastic,* February 11, 2021: https://neuroclastic.com/stimming-what-it-is-and-why-autistic-people-do-it/; Amelia Blackwater, "How I Experience Autistic Joy," *The Mighty*, March 29, 2023: https://themighty.com/topic/autism-spectrum-disorder/how-i-experience-autistic-joy/.

95 Steven Kapp, et al., "'People Should Be Allowed to Do What They Like': Autistic Adults' Views and Experiences of Stimming," *Autism* 23:7 (2019), 1782-92.

96 Eilidh Cage, et al., "Understanding, Attitudes and Dehumanisation Towards Autistic People," *Autism* 23:6 (2019), 1373-83. See also Elle Loughran, "The Rampant Dehumanization of Autistic People," *Neuroclastic,* January 6, 2020: https://neuroclastic.com/the-rampant-dehumanization-of-autistic-people/.

Notes to Chapter Two

1 Victory Fiorillo, "Philly Mom Gets Nasty Anonymous Letter About Her Son with Autism," *Philly Life and Culture*, April 12, 2016: https://www.phillymag.com/news/2016/04/12/philly-mom-gets-

NOTES

nasty-anonymous-letter-about-her-autistic-son/.

2 An early source of this identification in the United States was Bruno Bettelheim's article, "Feral Children and Autistic Children," *American Journal of Sociology* 64:5 (1959), 455-467. On comparison with animals as a form of dehumanization, see Nick Haslam, "Dehumanization: An Integrative Review," *Personality and Social Psychology Review* 10:3 (2006), 252-64.

3 Before the inclusion of people with "Aspergers Syndrome" in the general category of autism, it was reported that about 50% of autistics "do not acquire speech as a primary mode of communication": Barry Prizant, "Issues for Persons with Autism Who Are Non-Speaking or Who Have Limited Speech," *Journal of Autism and Developmental Disorders* 26:2 (1996), 173-178. With the addition of Aspergians—who by definition are verbally fluent—to the category, the percentage of "minimally verbal" autistics has dropped to about 25%: Jo Saul and Courtenay Norbury, "A Randomized Case Series Approach to Testing Efficacy of Interventions for Minimally Verbal Autistic Children," *Frontiers in Psychology*, May 24, 2021, open access.

4 People without autism often make similar noises, but we tend to ignore them. See below, Chapter Five.

5 A.M. Baggs, "In My Language," *Youtube* video, 8:36 minutes, January 14, 2007: https://www.youtube.com/watch?v=JnylM1hI2jc.

6 Diego Pena, *Anatomy of Autism: A Pocket Guide for Educators, Parents, and Students* (Self-published, 2017), p. 9.

7 There is a high rate of comorbidity between autism and apraxia of speech: Cheryl Tierney, et al., "How Valid Is the Checklist for Autism Spectrum Disorder When a Child Has Apraxia of Speech?" *Journal of Developmental and Behavioral Pediatrics* 36:8 (2015), 569-574. On apraxia, see the National Organization for Rare Diseases, *Rare Disease Database*: https://rarediseases.org/rare-diseases/apraxia/.

8 "Apraxia of Speech," *National Institute of Deafness and Other Communication Disorders*: https://www.nidcd.nih.gov/health/apraxia-speech#apraxia_01.

9 Ido Kedar, *Ido in Autismland* (Self-published, 2012), p. 54.

10 Daniel Cardinal and Mary Falvey, "The Maturing of Facilitated Communication: A Means Toward Independent Communication," *Research and Practice for Persons with Severe Disabilities* 39:3 (2014), 189-94.

11 For Ido Kedar, see Thomas Curwen, "Breaking the Silence: In the 'Silent Prison' of Autism, Ido Kedar Speaks Out," *Los Angeles Times,* December 21, 2013; see also Kedar's video presentation at the United Nations World Autism Awareness Day conference on "Assistive Technologies, Active Participation": https://www.un.org/en/events/autismday/assets/pdf/2019_Programme_WAAD. pdf. The text is available as "My Presentation at the UN World Autism Day on AAC and Communication Rights," *Ido in Autismland*, April 3, 2019: http://idoinautismland.com/?p=825. On Diego Pena, see Alicia Doyle, "Camarillo boy, 10, Shares His Story of Autism with Ventura College Students," *Ventura County Star* (Oxnard, CA), April 12, 2018; Mike Brown, "Nine-Year-Old Non-Speaking Boy Writes Bestseller Book about Autism," *Medium*, May 29, 2020: https://medium.com/@mikebrown_99013/nine-year-old-non-speaking-boy-writes-bestseller-book-

NOTES

about-autism-for-educators-the-art-of-b0f7700863f9.

12 Vanessa Hus Bal, et al., "Understanding Definitions of Minimally Verbal Across Instruments: Evidence for Subgroups within Minimally Verbal Children and Adolescents with Autism Spectrum Disorder," *Journal of Child Psychology and Psychiatry* 57:12 (2016), pp. 1424-1433.

13 For more on the many jobs and social roles autistics can fill, see Chapter Six below.

14 IACC Membership Roster: https://iacc.hhs.gov/about-iacc/members/roster/.

15 Ron Suskind, *Life Animated: A Story of Sidekicks, Heroes, and Autism* (Los Angeles and New York: Kingswell, 2014). The book was later turned into a documentary film with the same title.

16 Barry Prizant, *Uniquely Human: A Different Way of Seeing Autism* (New York: Simon and Schuster, 2015), p. 46.

17 SaveFerris, in the "Selective Mutism" discussion, *Wrong Planet*, February 12, 2017: https://wrongplanet.net/forums/viewtopic.php?t=337061.

18 Monachopia, in the "Selective mutism" discussion, *Autism Forums*, October 2, 2018: https://www.AutismForums.com/threads/selective-mutism.26728/#post-538911.

19 dragonfire42, in the "Dragon Greetings" discussion, *Autism Forums*, August 7, 2019: https://www.AutismForums.com/threads/dragon-greetings.30721/#post-634595.

20 Cited in Elissa Ball and Jaclyn Jeffrey-Wilenski, "Why Autism Training for Police Isn't Enough," *Spectrum*, November 26, 2020: https://www.spectrumnews.org/news/why-autism-training-for-police-isnt-enough/.

21 S. Chahboun, et al., "Can You Play with Fire and Not Hurt Yourself? A Comparative Study in Figurative Language Comprehension Between Individuals With and Without Autism Spectrum Disorder," *PLoS One*, 11:12 (December 30, 2016), open access; Agustin Vicente and Ingrid Falkum, "Accounting for the Preference for Literal Meanings in Autism Spectrum Conditions," *Mind & Language* 38:1 (2023), 119-40.

22 Gail Alvares, "The Misnomer of 'High Functioning Autism': Intelligence is an Imprecise Predictor of Functional Abilities at Diagnosis," *Autism* 24:1 (2020), 221-232.

23 Romana Tate, "What's the Difference Between High Functioning and Low Functioning Autism?" *Autistic Women and Nonbinary Network*, October 19, 2014: https://awnnetwork.org/whats-the-difference-between-high-functioning-and-low-functioning-autism/.

24 Alyssa Hillary, "Functioning Labels," *Yes, That Too*, May 3, 2012: http://yesthattoo.blogspot.com/2012/05/functioning-labels.html; Cynthia Kim, "Decoding the High Functioning Label," *Musings of an Aspie*, June 26, 2013: https://musingsofanaspie.com/?s=functioning+label;

25 Kat Williams, "The Fallacy of Functioning Labels," *National Centre for Mental Health, Wales*, April 4, 2019: https://www.ncmh.info/2019/04/04/fallacy-functioning-labels/.

26 For more on "burnout," see Chapter Six below.

27 Much has been written about the harm functioning labels cause for autistic people. Here are just a few recent examples: Finn Gardiner, "The Problems with Functioning Labels," *The Thinking Person's Guide to Autism*, March 23, 2018: http://www.thinkingautismguide.com/2018/03/the-problems-

with-functioning-labels.html; David Clements, "Autistic Functioning Labels and the Silencing of Autistics," *Medium*, April 4, 2019: https://medium.com/@waterprinciple/autistic-functioning-labels-and-the-silencing-of-autistics-7d142a37f2f9; "Functioning Labels Harm Autistic People," *Autistic Self-Advocacy Network*, December 9, 2021: https://autisticadvocacy.org/2021/12/functioning-labels-harm-autistic-people/; Jessica Penot, "Why Many People With Autism Dislike Functioning Labels," *Psychology Today* August 23, 2022: https://www.psychologytoday.com/us/blog/the-forgotten-women/202208/why-many-people-autism-dislike-functioning-labels.

28 Lydia Z. K. Brown, "Why Do I Think I'm Autistic . . .," *Autistic Hoya*, December 12, 2015: https://www.autistichoya.com/2015/12/why-do-i-think-im-autistic.html.

29 Ingo Kennerknecht, et al., "First Report of Prevalence of Non-Syndromic Hereditary Prosopagnosia (HPA)," *American Journal of Medical Genetics* 140:A (2006), 1617-1622; Regan Fry, et al., "Investigating the Influence of Autism Spectrum Traits on Face Processing Mechanisms in Developmental Prosopagnosia," *Journal of Autism and Developmental Disorders*, preprint, September 29, 2022.

30 Emily Sohn, "Abuse Marks the Lives of Autistic People," *Spectrum*, February 5, 2020: https://www.spectrumnews.org/features/deep-dive/how-abuse-mars-the-lives-of-autistic-people/.

31 Paul Ekman, "Universals and Cultural Differences in Facial Expressions of Emotion," *Nebraska Symposium on Motivation*, 19 (1971), pp. 207-82; Paul Ekman, Wallace Friesen, et al., "Universals and Cultural Differences in the Judgments of Facial Expressions of Emotion," *Journal of Personality and Social Psychology* 53 (1987), 712-17.

32 Paul Ekman and Erika Rosenberg, *What the Face Reveals: Basic and Applied Studies of Spontaneous Expression Using the Facial Action Coding System (FACS)*, 2nd ed. (Oxford, 2005), describes the development and use of these systems.

33 Karsten Wolf, "Measuring Facial Expression of Emotion," *Dialogues in Clinical Neuroscience* 17 (2015), 457-62.

34 The program is still available: https://resources.autismcentreofexcellence.org/p/mindreading-all-level-bundle.

35 Estelle Ryan, *The Gauguin Connection* (Self-published, 2012), and other books in the series.

36 Ofer Golan, et al., "The Cambridge Mindreading (CAM) Face-Voice Battery: Testing Complex Emotion Recognition in Adults with and without Asperger Syndrome," *Journal of Autism and Developmental Disorders* 36 (2006), 169-83; see also Ofer Golan, et al., "The Cambridge Mindreading Face-Voice Battery for Children (CAM-C): Complex Emotion Recognition in Children with and without Autism Spectrum Conditions," *Molecular Autism* 6 (2015), open access.

37 See the many studies reviewed in M. Uljarevic and A. Hamilton, "Recognition of Emotions in Autism: A Formal Meta-Analysis," *Journal of Autism and Developmental Disorders* 43 (2013), 1517–1526. An interesting recent study looked at the recognition of emotions during the Covid-19 pandemic, when people were wearing masks: Sarah McCrackin, et al., "Face Masks Impair Basic Emotion Recognition: Group Effects and Individual Variability," *Social Psychology* 54:1/2 (2023), 4-15.

38 Dominic Trevisan, et al., "Facial Expression Production in Autism: A Meta-Analysis," *Autism*

Research 11:12 (2018), 1586-1601.

39 Ido Kedar, *Ido in Autismland* (Self-published, 2012), p. 13.

40 Bob Christian, "Resting Bitch Farce," *The Ramblings of Bob Christian*, September 3, 2018: https://
bob-christian.com/2018/09/03/resting-bitch-farce/. See also Karen Schmitt and Jeffrey Cohn,
"Human Facial Expressions as Adaptations: Evolutionary Questions in Facial Expression Research,"
American Journal of Physical Anthropology 44, Supplement: *Yearbook of Physical Anthropology* (2001),
3-24—see especially pg. 15 on the social difficulties of those who display flat affect.

41 "Cynthia Kim, "You Scare Me," *Musings of an Aspie*, October 10, 2012: https://musingsofanaspie.
com/?s=you+scare+me.

42 Kim Kaplan, "Social Cues or Facial Expressions for Kids with Autism – Part 2," *ModernMom*,
August 13, 2012: https://www.modernmom.com/ee91278c-3b3d-11e3-be8a-bc764e04a41e.html.

43 Kim Kaplan, "Social Cues or Facial Expressions for Kids with Autism – Part 2," *ModernMom*,
August 13, 2012: http://www.modernmom.com/ee91278c-3b3d-11e3-be8a-bc764e04a41e.html.

44 Eileen Lamb, "Asperger's: What it's like for me to have autism," *the autism café*, October 6, 2019:
https://theautismcafe.com/aspergers/. See also an anonymous comment on "Traits of ASD Level 1
That Parents Should Be Aware Of," *My Aspergers Child*: https://www.myaspergerschild.com/2018/08/
traits-of-high-funtioning-autism-that.html.

45 Mark Hutten, "Students on the Autism Spectrum: Strategies that Can Guarantee Their Academic
Success," *My Aspergers Child*: http://www.myaspergerschild.com/2018/12/students-on-autism-
spectrum-strategies.html.

46 Lynn Abbott, "Making Faces," *Virginia Tech Department of Electrical and Computer Engineering
News*, April 26, 2016: https://ece.vt.edu/news/articles/2016/Making-faces1636660033239.html. See
also Charline Grossard, "Teaching Facial Expression Production in Autism: The Serious Game
JEMImE," *Creative Education* 10:11 (2019), 2347-2366.

47 Dominic Trevisan, et al., "Facial Expression Production in Autism: A Meta-Analysis," *Autism
Research* 11 (2018), 1586-1601.

48 In general, people seek to distance themselves from "affective deviants" (those whose faces express
emotions differently), often viewing them with moral outrage: Lauren Sczcurek, et al., "The Stranger
Effect: The Rejection of Affective Deviants," *Psychological Science* 23:110 (2012), 1105-1111.

49 Rosanna Edey, et al., "Interaction Takes Two: Typical Adults Exhibit Mind-Blindness towards
Those with Autism Spectrum Disorder," *Journal of Abnormal Psychology* 125:7 (2016), 879-85. This
article actually looked not at facial expressions, but at how "typical" adults failed to read autistic
body movements. On facial expressions, specifically, see Rebecca Brewer, Federica Biotti, et al., "Can
Neurotypical Individuals Read Autistic Facial Expressions? Atypical Production of Emotional Facial
Expression in Autism Spectrum Disorders," *Autism Research* 9:2 (2016), 262-71; A.J. Lampi, et al.,
"Non-Autistic Adults Can Recognize Posed Autistic Facial Expressions: Implications for Internal
Representations of Emotion," *Autism Research*, May 12, 2023, preprint.

50 Steven Stagg, et al., "Does Facial Expressivity Count? How Typically Developing Children
Respond Initially to Children with Autism," *Autism*, 18:6 (2014), 704-11.

NOTES

51 A really excellent introduction to these issues can be found in the 8-part series by Judy Endow, "Autism and the Sensory System," *Aspects of Autism Translated*, October-December, 2019: http://www.judyendow.com/sensory-solutions/autism-and-the-sensory-system-part-1-of-8/.

52 J. Neufeld, et al. "Is Synesthesia More Common in Patients with Asperger Syndrome?," *Frontiers in Human Neuroscience* 7 (December, 2013), open access. This group found that up to 31% of the autistic people in their small sample had a form of synesthesia, compared to only 1-2% in the general population. See also J. Ward, et al. "Atypical Sensory Sensitivity as a Shared Feature between Synaesthesia and Autism," *Scientific Reports*, 7:1 (2017), pp. 1-9; Tessa Van Leeuwen, et al., "Perceptual Processing Links Autism and Synesthesia: A Co-Twin Control Study," *Cortex* 145 (2021), 236-49.

53 Jack Dutton, "The Surprising World of Synaesthesia," *The Psychologist* 28:2 (February, 2015), 106-09; Bec Crew, "Scientists Have Identified a Weirdly Common Form of Synaesthesia," *Science Alert*, January 19, 2017: https://www.sciencealert.com/scientists-have-identified-a-weirdly-common-form-of-synaesthesia.

54 F. Van Hecke, et al., "Vestibular Function in Children with Neurodevelopmental Disorders: A Systematic Review," *Journal of Autism and Developmental Disorders* 49:8 (2019), 3328-3350.

55 C. T. Fuentes, et al., "No Proprioceptive Deficits in Autism Despite Movement-Related Sensory and Execution," *Journal of Autism and Developmental Disorders* 41:10 (2011), 1352–1361. Fuentes insisted that autistics had strong proprioceptive senses, despite his subjects' assertions that they didn't. More recent research supports autistic self-reports: Cortney Armitano-Lago, et al., "Lower Limb Proprioception and Strength Differences Between Adolescents with Autism Spectrum Disorder and Neurotypical Controls," *Perceptual and Motor Skills* 128:5 (2021), 2132-2147. Proprioception may be more of an issue for female than for male autistics: J. Tang, et al., "Presenting Age and Features of Females Diagnosed with Autism Spectrum Disorder," *Journal of Paediatrics and Child Health* 57:8 (2021), 1182-1189.

56 The Autlaw, "What It's Like Living With Sensory Processing Disorder," *Medium*, August 3, 2022: https://medium.com/@smcnett/what-being-autistic-is-like-for-me-part-one-sensory-issues-dc067f009a29.

57 Emma, "Body Image and Autism: A personal reflection," *Undercover Autism*, July 20, 2020: https://undercoverautism.org/2020/07/20/body-image-and-autism-a-personal-reflection/.

58 L. Fiene, et al., "The Interoception Sensory Questionnaire (ISQ): A Scale to Measure Interoceptive Challenges in Adults," *Journal of Autism and Developmental Disorders* 48:10 (2018), 3354-66. Fiene, et al. found that 74% of autistic adults reported "interoceptive confusion." See also E.R. Palser, et al., "Dissociation in How Core Autism Features Relate to Interoceptive Dimensions: Evidence from Cardiac Awareness in Children," *Journal of Autism and Developmental Disorders* 50 (2020), 572-82. Other researchers have claimed that while autistic children struggle with interoception, most adults have learned to compensate: Toby Nicholson, et al., "Interoception is Impaired in Children, But Not Adults, with Autism Spectrum Disorder," *Journal of Autism and Developmental Disorders* 49:9 (2019), 3625-37. Many autistic adults would disagree.

59 Cynthia Kim, "Interoception: How Do I Feel?" *Musings of an Aspie*, July 3, 2013: https://musingsofanaspie.com/2013/07/03/interoception-how-do-i-feel/.

60 Hence the title of John Elder Robison's autobiography, *Look Me in the Eye: My Life with Aspergers* (New York: Three Rivers Press, 2008).

61 Bloodheart, in the "Describe what happens when you try and make eye contact" discussion, *Wrong Planet*, January 25, 2011: https://wrongplanet.net/forums/viewtopic.php?t=149878.

62 Lucy Clapham, quoted in "16 People With Autism Describe Why Eye Contact Can Be Difficult" on *The Mighty Tumblr* account, February 10, 2016: https://themightysite.tumblr.com/post/139085053373/16-people-with-autism-describe-why-eye-contact-can.

63 Jennifer Msumba, *Shouting at Leaves* (Self published, 2021), p. 158. See also the "Describe what happens when you try and make eye contact" discussion, *Wrong Planet*, January, 2011: https://wrongplanet.net/forums/viewtopic.php?t=149878.

64 Amethyst Schaber, "Ask an Autistic #21--What About Eye Contact?" *Youtube* video, 9:40 minutes, November 20, 2014: https://www.youtube.com/watch?v=QXM9Mj5Zd7I. *Ask an Autistic* is a valuable resource, both for autistics, and for neurotypical people who want to understand them.

65 RiverSong, in the "Job Interview Anxiety, Overload & Shutdown?" discussion, *Autism Forums*, June 1, 2017: https://www.Autism Forums.com/threads/job-interview-anxiety-overload-shutdown.20317/#post-392659. See also Helixstein, in the "Describe what happens when you try and make eye contact" discussion, *Wrong Planet*, January 25, 2011: https://wrongplanet.net/forums/viewtopic.php?t=149878.

66 Quincy Hansen, "What Does Listening Look Like?" *Speaking of Autism . . .* , July 27, 2019: https://speakingofautismcom.wordpress.com/?s=eye+contact.

67 GiantHockeyFan, in the "Job Interviews Unfair and Insulting to People Like Us" discussion, *Wrong Planet*, October 7, 2013: https://wrongplanet.net/forums/viewtopic.php?t=242149.

68 Kevin L., in the "Body Language and Job Interviews" discussion, *Autism Forums*, June 27, 2018: https://www.Autism Forums.com/threads/body-language-and-job-interviews.25976/#post-520297.

69 Catherine, "April 30th: What Being Autistic Means to Me," *Ability to Be Different*, April 30, 2019: https://wordpress.com/read/blogs/126598048/posts/87.

70 Temple Grandin and Tony Attwood, *Different . . . Not Less: Inspiring Stories of Achievement and Successful Employment from Adults with Autism, Asperger's, and ADHD* (Arlington, Texas: Future Horizons, 2012).

71 Julia Bascom, "Foreword," in Julia Bascom, ed., *Loud Hands: Autistic People, Speaking* (Washington, DC: Autistic Self-Advocacy Network, 2012).

Notes to Chapter Three

1 Julie Roberts, "Neurodiversity-Affirming Therapy: Positions, Therapy Goals, and Best Practices," *Therapist Neurodiversity Collective*, April 4, 2022: https://therapistndc.org/neurodiversity-affirming-therapy/.

2 R. Larkin Taylor-Parker, "Be Yourself. Anything Else Is A Waste Of Time," *Medium*, September 28, 2016: https://medium.com/autistic-community/be-yourself-anything-else-is-a-waste-of-time-e992e539cfc5.

NOTES

3 Autism Society of America, "Resources: Interventions and Therapies": https://autismsociety.org/resources/intervention-and-therapies/.

4 National Institute of Mental Health, "Autism: Treatments and Therapies": https://www.nimh.nih.gov/health/topics/autism-spectrum-disorders-asd/index.shtml#part_145441.

5 Centers for Disease Control, "Autism Case-Training Curriculum: Early Intervention and Education": https://www.cdc.gov/ncbddd/actearly/autism/curriculum/documents/early-intervention-education_508.pdf.

6 Lonnie Zwaigenbaum, et al., "Early Identification of Autism Spectrum Disorder: Recommendations for Practice and Research," *Pediatrics* 136, Supplement 1 (2015), S10-S40.

7 John Summers, "As Private Equity Comes to Dominate Autism Services…It's Time to Ask Ourselves How Long We Want to Keep Rewarding Bad Behavior," *The Nation*, April 2, 2021: https://www.thenation.com/article/society/private-equity-autism-aba/.

8 The idea of an autistic "spectrum" was first posited by English researchers Lorna Wing and Judith Gould, "Severe Impairments of Social Interaction and Associated Abnormalities in Children: Epidemiology and Classification", *Journal of Autism and Developmental Disorders*, 9, (1979) 11–29. Asperger's Syndrome was first described by the Austrian psychiatrist, Hans Asperger, back in the 1940s. His work was largely unknown until it was translated into English and disseminated in Europe and later the United States in the 1980s and 1990s: Lorna Wing, "Asperger's Syndrome: A Clinical Account," *Psychological Medicine* 11:1 (1981), 115-29; Uta Frith, "Asperger and His Syndrome," in Uta Frith, ed., *Autism and Asperger Syndrome* (Cambridge: Cambridge University Press, 1991), pp. 1-36. On all these developments, see Steve Silberman, *Neurotribes: The Legacy of Autism and the Future of Neurodiversity* (New York: Random House, 2016), pp. 348-51.

9 At the beginning it was always children—only years later did adults with autism finally begin to receive diagnoses.

10 Centers for Disease Control and Prevention, "Data and Statistics on Autism Spectrum Disorder," April 4, 2023: https://www.cdc.gov/ncbddd/autism/data.html).

11 See, for example, Hal Arkowitz and Scott Lillienfeld, "Is There Really an Autism Epidemic?" *Scientific American*, August 1, 2012: https://www.scientificamerican.com/article/is-there-really-an-autism-epidemic/.

12 Eric Fombonne, "The Epidemiology of Autism: A Review," *Psychological Medicine* 29 (1999), 769–86.; Margot Prior, "Annotation: Is There an Increase in the Prevalence of Autism Spectrum Disorders?" *Journal of Paediatrics and Child Health* 39 (2003), 81–82; Paul Shattuck, "The Contribution of Diagnostic Substitution to the Growing Administrative Prevalence of Autism in U.S. Special Education," *Pediatrics* 117:4 (2006), 1028–37; Helen Coo, et al., "Trends in Autism Prevalence: Diagnostic Substitution Revisited." *Journal of Autism and Developmental Disorders* 38 (2008),1036–46; Peter Bearman and Marissa King, "Diagnostic Change and the Increased Prevalence of Autism." *International Journal of Epidemiology* 38:5 (2009), 1224–34; Ka-Yuet Liu, et al., "Social Influence and the Autism Epidemic," *American Journal of Sociology* 115:5 (2010), 1389–1434.

13 Autism Speaks has become not only the largest autism organization in the United States, but also the one most hated by the autistic community.

NOTES

14 U.S. Food and Drug Administration, "Consumer Update: Be Aware of Potentially Dangerous Products and Therapies that Claim to Treat Autism" (n.d.): https://www.fda.gov/consumers/consumer-updates/be-aware-potentially-dangerous-products-and-therapies-claim-treat-autism.

15 U.S. Department of Justice, Office of Public Affairs, "Seller of "Miracle Mineral Solution" Sentenced to Prison for Marketing Toxic Chemical as a Miracle Cure," October 28, 2015: https://www.justice.gov/opa/pr/seller-miracle-mineral-solution-sentenced-prison-marketing-toxic-chemical-miracle-cure.

16 Mark Grenon, "Leader of Fake Church Peddling Bleach as Covid-19 Cure Sought Trump's Support. Instead, He Got Federal Charges," *Washington Post*, July 9, 2020.

17 Autism Science Foundation, "Beware of Non-Evidence-Based Treatments" (n.d.): https://autismsciencefoundation.org/what-is-autism/beware-of-non-evidence-based-treatments/.

18 Federal Trade Commission, "Marketers of One-on-One 'Brain Training' Programs Settle FTC Charges That Claims about Ability to Treat Severe Cognitive Impairments Are Unsupported," March 18, 2016: https://www.ftc.gov/news-events/press-releases/2016/05/marketers-one-one-brain-training-programs-settle-ftc-charges.

19 "Brain Training for Autism," *Learning Rx*: https://www.learningrx.com/who-we-help/autism-spectrum/.

20 See, for example, James Herbert and Lynn Brandsma, "Applied Behavior Analysis for Childhood Autism: Does the Emperor Have Clothes?" *The Behavior Analyst Today* 3:1 (2002), 45-50; Zachary Warren, et al., "A Systematic Review of Early Intensive Intervention for Autism Spectrum Disorders," *Pediatrics* 127:5 (2011), 1303-11. Both note that researchers have not been able to replicate Ivar Lovaas's research findings, and that they cannot support claims of ABA's spectacular success. Other articles questioning ABA efficacy studies include: Mark Rodgers, et al., "Intensive Behavioural Interventions Based on Applied Behaviour Analysis for Young Children with Autism: An International Collaborative Individual Participant Data Meta-Analysis," *Autism* 25:4 (2021), 1137-53; Mojgan Gitimoghaddam, et al., "Applied Behavior Analysis in Children and Youth with Autism Spectrum Disorders: A Scoping Review," *Perspectives on Behavior Science* 45 (2022), 521-57

21 The most important academic journal in the field, *The Journal of Applied Behavior Therapy*, regularly publishes articles about training dogs as well as autistic children.

22 Michelle Dawson, "The Misbehaviour of Behaviourists," *No Autistics Allowed*, 2004: https://www.sentex.ca/~nexus23/naa_aba.html. Dawson's list of ethical concerns is not quite the same as mine, but equally valid.

23 A number of fields use ABA principles: on management, see the *Journal of Organizational Behavior Management*; on purchasing decisions, see the *Journal of Marketing*; on politics, see the *Journal of Political Marketing*.

24 Some scientists are beginning to recognize this as a problem: Aileen Sandoval-Norton, et al., "How Much Compliance is Too Much Compliance: Is Long-Term ABA Therapy Abuse?" *Cogent Psychology* 6:1 (2019) (open access).

25 The annual Applied Behavior Analysis International conference is attended by both those who

NOTES

work with autistic children and those who work with dogs or other animals.

26 Bob Christianson, "Alleged Cures," *The Ramblings of Bob Christianson*, May 30, 2018: https://bob-christian.com/2018/05/30/alleged-cures-podcast-may-7th/.

27 Steve Silberman, *Neurotribes: The Legacy of Autism and the Future of Neurodiversity* (New York: Random House, 2016), pp. 140-86.

28 Leo Kanner, "Autistic Disturbances of Affective Contact," *The Nervous Child* 2 (1943), 217-50.

29 Steve Silberman, *Neurotribes: The Legacy of Autism and the Future of Neurodiversity* (New York: Random House, 2016), pp. 261-74. For an example of this approach, see A.H. Chapman, "Early Infantile Autism: A Review," *Journal of Diseases of Children* 99 (1960), 783-786. The pre-eminent journal in the field, *The Journal of Autism and Developmental Disorders*, established in 1971, was originally called *The Journal of Autism and Childhood Schizophrenia*.

30 E.g., K. A. Doyle-Thomas, et al., "Metabolic Mapping of Deep Brain Structures and Associations with Symptomatology in Autism Spectrum Disorders," *Research in Autism Spectrum Disorders* 8:1 (2014), 44-51; Sophie Volk, et al., "Multicenter Mapping of Structural Network Alterations in Autism," *Human Brain Mapping* 36:6 (February, 2015), 2364; Daniel Yang, et al., "Cortical Morphological Markers in Children with Autism: A Structural Magnetic Resonance Imaging Study of Thickness, Area, Volume, and Gyrification," *Molecular Autism* 7:11 (2016), open access.

31 E.g., Yasser Ghambari, et al., "Joint Analysis of Band-Specific Functional Connectivity and Signal Complexity in Autism," *Journal of Autism and Developmental Disorders* 45:2 (February, 2015), 444-460; Oana Gurao, et al., "How Useful is Electroencephalography in the Diagnosis of Autism Spectrum Disorders and the Delineation of Subtypes: A Systematic Review," *Frontiers in Psychiatry* 8 (2017), open access; Jonathan Harvey, "Cortical Functional Connectivity during Praxis in Autism Spectrum Disorder," *Proceedings of the 41st Annual International Conference of the IEEE* (July, 2019), 333-36.

32 Most of the earlier research is summarized in Rosa Marotta, et al., "The Neurochemistry of Autism," *Brain Sciences* 10:3 (2020), open access.

33 Leo Kanner, "Autistic Disturbances of Affective Contact," *The Nervous Child* 2 (1943), 217-50; George Jervis, "The Mental Deficiencies," *Annals of the American Academy of Political and Social Science, 286: Mental Health in the United States* (1953), 25-33.

34 Michael Rutter, "The Influence of Organic and Emotional Factors on the Origins, Nature and Outcome of Childhood Psychosis," *Developmental Medicine and Child Neurology* 7:5 (1965), 520-21; M. DeMyer, et al., "The Measured Intelligence of Autistic Children," *Journal of Autism and Childhood Schizophrenia* 4:1 (1974), 42-60; E. Ritvo and B. Freeman, "Current Research on the Syndrome of Autism: Introduction," *Journal of the American Academy of Child Psychiatry* 17:4 (1978), 565-75.

35 An article in *Life* magazine described the children Lovaas worked with as "mental cripples," and talked about how one such child was "tamed" in his lab: "Screams, Slaps & Love: A Surprising, Shocking Treatment Helps Far-Gone Mental Cripples," *Life*, May 7, 1965. The text is available online at https://blogs.uoregon.edu/autismhistoryproject/archive/screams-slaps-and-love-a-surprising-shocking-treatment-helps-far-gone-mental-cripples-1965/. Another behaviorist, Charles Ferster, locked a child up alone in his lab daily for an entire year, "successfully" eliminating her tantrums:

NOTES

Charles Ferster, "Positive Reinforcement and Behavioral Deficits of Autistic Children," *Child Development* 32 (1961), 437-56.

36 Paul Chance, "Interview with O. Ivar Lovaas," *Psychology Today* 7 (1974), pp. 76-84..

37 Programs were established at Indiana University, the University of Washington, the University of Kansas, etc. However, the use of extreme aversives became less common in these programs during the 1980s, as public revulsion tempered behaviorist enthusiasm: Patrick Kirkham, "'The Line between Intervention and Abuse'– Autism and Applied Behaviour Analysis," *History of the Human Sciences* 30:2 (2017), 107-26. The National Society for Autistic Children (now the Autism Society of America) officially rejected the use of physical aversives under most circumstances in 1988. But many ABA practitioners still support aversives, including the use of electric shocks: see Chapter Eleven below.

38 J. Moore and G. Shook, "Certification, Accreditation, and Quality Control in Behavior Analysis," *The Behavior Analyst* 24:1 (2001), 45-55.

39 John LaRose, "Huge Untapped Demand in the $4+ Billion U.S. Autism Treatment Centers Market," *Market Research*, September 12, 2022: https://blog.marketresearch.com/huge-untapped-demand-in-the-4-billion-u.s.-autism-treatment-centers-market.

40 "Franchise Success on the Spectrum," *Franchising America*, July 10, 2020: https://franchisesamerica.com/franchise/success-on-the-spectrum-4408.

41 thatsrobrageous, in the "Applied Behavior Analysis" discussion, *Wrong Planet*, August 6, 2019: https://wrongplanet.net/forums/viewtopic.php?t=379090.

42 livingwithautism, in the "Applied Behavior Analysis" discussion, *Wrong Planet*, August 7, 2019: https://wrongplanet.net/forums/viewtopic.php?t=379090.

43 DrHouseHasAspergers, in the "Do You Hate ABA?" discussion, *Wrong Planet*, June 23, 2015: https://wrongplanet.net/forums/viewtopic.php?t=288266..

44 Connie Kasari, "How Much Behavioral Therapy Does an Autistic Child Need?" *Spectrum*, August 27, 2019: https://www.spectrumnews.org/opinion/viewpoint/how-much-behavioral-therapy-does-an-autistic-child-need/. Kasari notes that, given the heterogeneity of the autistic population, insisting on a certain number of hours per week for every child makes little sense.

45 Max Sparrow, "ABA," *Unstrange Mind*, October 7, 2014: http://unstrangemind.com/aba/.

46 Kat, "Autistics Against ABA," *Cerebrations of Kat*, May 2, 2020: https://www.cerebrationofkat.co.uk/home-page/autistics-against-aba/.

47 One estimate is that 89% of ABA practitioners work with autistic or intellectually disabled clients: "10 Things You Can Do with an ABA Degree Other Than Work with Kids with ASD," *Applied Behavior Analysis.Edu*: https://www.appliedbehavioranalysisedu.org/10-things-you-can-do-with-an-aba-degree-other-than-work-with-kids-with-asd/.

48 Capella University, an online, for-profit educational institution, graduates a large number of people in the field of ABA. To get a Ph.D. in ABA at Capella, no course on autism is required, but you can take one as an elective: https://www.capella.edu/online-degrees/phd-behavior-psychology/courses/. At Southern Illinois University, a traditional institution, no course on autism is required for

NOTES

a master's degree in ABA: https://gradcatalog.siu.edu/programs/bat/#req.

49 Researchers in this field also demonstrate ignorance about autism, as evidenced by an article in a major ABA journal: Tina Dass, et al., "Teaching Children with Autism Spectrum Disorder to Tact Olfactory Stimuli," *Journal of Applied Behavior Analysis* 51:3 (2018), 538-52. The article focuses entirely on the techniques used to get children to recognize odors, without ever mentioning the differences between neurotypical and autistic sensory experience.

50 The word "meltdown" occurs in the text of only two out of the thousands of articles in the *Journal of Applied Behavior Analysis*; in each case, the word is placed in quotation marks, to indicate that this is a word parents use, not one the researchers would use themselves. They prefer "tantrum."

51 On meltdowns, see Chapter Five below.

52 Emily Sohn, "Low Standards Corrode Quality of Popular Autism Therapy," *Spectrum*, October 28, 2020: https://www.spectrumnews.org/features/deep-dive/low-standards-corrode-quality-popular-autism-therapy/.

53 Alexander, "On Hurling Myself Into Traffic to Get out of ABA Therapy," *Neuroclastic*, January 27, 2020: https://neuroclastic.com/2020/01/27/on-hurling-myself-into-traffic-to-get-out-of-aba-therapy/.

54 Greg Hanley, "A Perspective on Today's ABA from Dr. Greg Hanley," *Practical Functional Assessment*, June 4, 2020: https://practicalfunctionalassessment.com/2020/06/04/a-perspective-on-todays-aba-by-dr-greg-hanley/.

55 Jo Ram, "I Am a Disillusioned BCBA: Autistics are Right about ABA," *Neuroclastic*, June 2, 2020: https://neuroclastic.com/2020/06/02/i-am-a-disillusioned-bcba-autistics-are-right-about-aba/.

56 Compass ABA's "ready to learn" skills include sitting at a table, looking at the "instructor," and not grabbing materials being presented: https://www.compassaid.com/aba-therapy. The Place for Children with Autism teaches "tolerance for staying seated during academic tasks": https://theplaceforchildrenwithautism.com/applied-behavior-analysis-for-autism/common-aba-treatment-outcomes/school-readiness-skills. Most youngsters of any neurotype at the targeted age would have a lot of trouble with these skills.

57 Steph, "Why I Left ABA," *Socially Anxious Advocate*, May 22, 2015: https://sociallyanxiousadvocate.wordpress.com/2015/05/22/why-i-left-aba/.

58 Shira Karpel, "Teaching Compliance with First/Then (Premack Principle)," *How to ABA*, April 2, 2018: https://howtoaba.com/teaching-compliance-first-premack-principle/.

59 "Our Preschool Program," *Newmeadow: Educating Young Children for Success*: https://newmeadow.org/classroom-instruction/.

60 Yaz Aboul, "HOW TO: Deal with Non-Compliant Behavior in Children with Autism (for Parents)," *AnimateBehavior,* July 10, 2015: https://animatebehavior.com/aba-news/how-deal-non-compliant-behavior-children-autism-parents/. Compare Amy Nielson, "How to Increase Compliance in Kids with Autism," *Big Abilities*, September 10, 2019: https://bigabilities.com/2019/09/10/3tipsforcompliance/.

61 Amelia Dalphonse, "Compliance Training," *Accessible ABA*: https://accessibleaba.com/blog/

— 318 —

compliance-training.

62 Amythest Schraber, "A Few Words on Compliance Training and Child Abuse," *Ask an Autistic*, *Youtube* video, 1:54 minutes, June 26, 2014: https://www.youtube.com/watch?v=c_ETWtD1_Dk.

63 Meg Murry, "The Importance of No," *Respectfully Connected*, March 2, 2016: https://respectfullyconnected.com/2016/03/the-importance-of-no/.

64 Aileen Sandoval-Norton, et al., "How Much Compliance is Too Much Compliance: Is Long-Term ABA Therapy Abuse?" *Cogent Psychology* 6:1 (2019), open access.

65 Daniel Wilkenfeld and Allison McCarthy, "Ethical Concerns with Applied Behavior Analysis for Autism Spectrum 'Disorder,'" *Kennedy Institute of Ethics Journal* 30:1 (2020), 31-69.

66 Greg Hanley, "A Perspective on Today's ABA from Dr. Greg Hanley," *Practical Functional Assessment*, June 4, 2020: https://practicalfunctionalassessment.com/2020/06/04/a-perspective-on-todays-aba-by-dr-greg-hanley/.

67 Beth Ryan, "touch nose, gummi bear: ABA in our family," *Love Explosions*, September 13, 2013: https://loveexplosions.net/2013/09/13/touch-nose-gummi-bear-aba-in-our-family/.

68 Philip Reyes, "World Autism Awareness Day 2015," *Faith, Hope, and Love . . . with Autism*, April 2, 2015: https://faithhopeloveautism.blogspot.com/2015/04/world-autism-awareness-day-2015.html.

69 Manuela Schuetze, et al., "Reinforcement Learning in Autism Spectrum Disorder," *Frontiers in Psychology* 8 (2017), open access.

70 Hila Harris, et al., "Perceptual Learning in Autism: Over-Specificity and Possible Remedies," *Nature: Neuroscience* 18:11 (2015), open access. Their conclusion: "Our results suggest that repetition, a technique widely used in intervention and education for ASD, may lead to inflexibility. The adverse consequences of repetition may apply to an even greater degree as the complexity of learning and behavior increases, such as in the domain of social behavior. Counterintuitively, reducing stimulus repetition may enhance learning and foster generalization in ASD."

71 Ido Kedar, "Motor Difficulties in Severe Autism," *Ido in Autismland*, November 3, 2015: http://idoinautismland.com/?p=376.

72 Julia Bascom, "Quiet Hands," *Just Stimming*, October 5, 2011: https://juststimming.wordpress.com/2011/10/05/quiet-hands/.

73 See, for example, the training video on "Learner Readiness," *Florida Institute of Technology, Scott Center for Autism*: https://www.thescottcenter.org/advisor/tool-kits/aba-basics-foundation-skills?page=3. Compare C. L. Lynch, "Invisible Abuse: ABA and the Things Only Autistic People Can See," *Neuroclastic*, March 28, 2019: https://neuroclastic.com/2019/03/28/invisible-abuse-aba-and-the-things-only-autistic-people-can-see/.

74 A very distressed toddler can be observed in "Teaching Eye Contact," *Coyne and Associates ABA*: https://vimeo.com/53015542. See also Mom Maauw Mayum, *alwaysabeautifullife*, Tumblr, 2017: https://alwaysabeautifullife.tumblr.com/post/156933695227/abuse-ableism-tw-yesterday-i-visited-a.

75 NextLevelNaps, in the "Differing approaches during refusals and tantrums" discussion, *Reddit* (n.d.): https://www.reddit.com/r/ABA/comments/9pv38h/differing_approaches_during_refusals_

NOTES

and_tantrums/.

76 Mary Barbera, "Autism and ABA Ethics: Using a Physical Prompt for Children with Autism," *Dr. Mary Barbera*, July 11, 2018: https://marybarbera.com/?s=physical+prompting; and see Greg Hanley, "A Perspective on Today's ABA from Dr. Greg Hanley," *Practical Functioning Assessment*, June 4, 2020: https://practicalfunctionalassessment.com/2020/06/04/a-perspective-on-todays-aba-by-dr-greg-hanley/.

77 Meredith K. Ultra, "I'm Sorry But That's Not Earning Your Token, *Ink & Daggers, Tumblr*, March 19, 2015: https://ink-and-daggers.tumblr.com/post/112076858794/im-sorry-but-thats-not-earning-your-token.

78 Tameika Meadows, "Instructional Control: Who's the Boss?" *I Love ABA*, January, 2013: https://www.iloveaba.com/2013/01/instructional-control-whos-boss.html.

79 A. Stout, "Be Careful — Some ABA Therapy Situations Can Become Traumatic or Abusive," *The Autism Site* (n.d.): https://blog.theautismsite.greatergood.com/aba-therapy-controversy/; Ruti Regan, "ABA Therapy is not like typical parenting," *Real Social Skills*, June 3, 2015: https://www.realsocialskills.org/blog/aba-therapy-is-not-like-typical-parenting. Regan describes how ABA practitioners determine what the best reinforcers will be, and how they draw up "reinforcement inventories."

80 Arionquin, "What an ABA session looks like," *How You Should Be Parenting Your Autistic Child*, January 24, 2016: https://autisticparenting.wordpress.com/2016/01/24/what-an-aba-session-looks-like/.

81 Ruti Regan, "Nice Lady Therapists," *Real Social Skills*, August 6, 2014: https://www.realsocialskills.org/blog/nice-lady-therapists.

82 Alexander, "On Hurling Myself Into Traffic to Get out of ABA Therapy," *Neuroclastic*, January 27, 2020: https://neuroclastic.com/2020/01/27/on-hurling-myself-into-traffic-to-get-out-of-aba-therapy/.

83 Freya Rumball, et al., "Experience of Trauma and PTSD Symptoms in Autistic Adults: Risk of PTSD Development Following DSM -5 and Non-DSM -5 Traumatic Life Events," *Autism Research* 13 (2020), 2122-2132.

84 Henny Kupferstein, "Evidence of Increased PTSD Symptoms in Autistics Exposed to Applied Behavior Analysis," *Advances in Autism* 4:1 (2018), 19-29.

85 Jo Ram, "I am a disillusioned BCBA: Autistics are right about ABA," *Neuroclastic*, June 2, 2020: https://neuroclastic.com/2020/06/02/i-am-a-disillusioned-bcba-autistics-are-right-about-aba/.

86 Amethyst Schaber, response to a question from lesmis5, *Neurowonderful, Tumblr*, December 6, 2014: http://neurowonderful.tumblr.com/post/104511295106/lesmis5-so-my-sister-just-threw-the-biggest.

87 Heather Gilmore, "Examples of Goals to Address in ABA (Applied Behavior Analysis)," *Reflections on Applied Behavior Analysis*, October 6, 2019: https://pro.psychcentral.com/child-therapist/2019/10/examples-of-goals-to-address-in-aba-applied-behavior-analysis/.

88 Ivaar Lovaas, "Behavioral Treatment and Normal Educational and Intellectual Functioning in

Young Autistic Children," *Journal of Consulting and Clinical Psychology*, 55 (1987), 3-9.

89 Molly Helt, et al., "Can Children with Autism Recover? If So, How?" *Neuropsychology Review*, 18(4) (2008), 339–366.

90 Here are just a few examples of ABA company advertisements that citing Lovaas' 1987 article, using the term "indistinguishable from their peers": *Steinberg Behavior Solutions*, https://www.sbsaba.com/aba-the-most-effective-treatment-for-autism/ *The Place for Children with Autism*, https://theplaceforchildrenwithautism.com/blog/what-makes-aba-therapy-effective/ *ChildsPlayPlus*, http://childsplayautism.com/how-much-aba-is-enough/ *Spectrum Autism Services*, http://sas-aba.com/what-is-aba.html *Blossom Center for Children*, https://blossomcenterforchildren.com/aba-therapy. In other words, many of today's ABA companies are still marketing themselves as potentially making autistic kids "normal."

91 Scott Morizot, "Optimal Outcome for Whom?" *Faith and Food*, August 12, 2017: http://faithandfood.morizot.net/2017/08/12/optical-outcome-for-whom/. He writes, "When I peel back the layers of hurt and pain, my deepest experience and understanding of my place in relation to the world was that something was fundamentally wrong with me. And I was driven to hide it."

92 For example, "EyeDash" reports "I seldom notice bladder fullness until it's really full . . ." in the "Question about Interoception DiscriminationDisorder" discussion, *Wrong Planet*, April 23, 2019: https://wrongplanet.net/forums/viewtopic.php?t=375532; Warmheart says "I don't always know when I am thirsty, hungry, in pain, or need to pee. You can imagine the drama this adds to life" in the "Does anyone else ever feel disconnected from your body?" discussion, *Autism Forums*, December 31, 2015: https://www.autismforums.com/threads/does-anyone-else-ever-feel-disconnected-from-your-body.14524/#post-276243.

93 Siri Carpenter, "The Children Who Leave Autism Behind," *Spectrum*, September 7, 2015: https://www.spectrumnews.org/features/deep-dive/children-who-leave-autism-behind/. For a discussion of "recovery" discourse, see Alicia Broderick, "Autism, "'Recovery (to Normalcy),' and the Politics of Hope," *Intellectual and Developmental Disabilities* 47:4 (2009), 263-81.

94 Ruth Padawer, "The Kids Who Beat Autism," *New York Times*, August 3, 2014: https://www.nytimes.com/2014/08/03/magazine/the-kids-who-beat-autism.html. But see Steven Kapp, "A Critical Response to 'The Kids Who Beat Autism'," *The Thinking Person's Guide to Autism*, August 11, 2014: http://www.thinkingautismguide.com/2014/08/a-critical-response-to-kids-who-beat.html. See also Elle Loughran, "Why is there not a cure for autism?" *Neuroclastic*, January 17, 2020: https://neuroclastic.com/2020/01/17/why-is-there-no-cure-for-autism/.

95 E.g., Mary Barbera, "Is Recovery From Autism Possible?" *Dr. Mary Barbera*, August 2, 2017: https://marybarbera.com/autism-recovery/?wickedsource=google&wtm_term=&wtm_campaign=10189701284&wtm_content=101131383119&wickedplacement=&wickedkeyword=; Ronal Leaf and John McEachin, "Recovery," *Autism Partnership*: https://www.autismpartnership.com/recovery-autism.

96 Wendy Katz Erwin, "The Great Behavior Fallacy: Why The New York Times Is Wrong To Think That ABA Can Treat Autism," *Neuroclastic*, January 13, 2020: https://neuroclastic.com/the-great-behavior-fallacy-why-the-new-york-times-is-wrong-to-think-that-aba-can-treat-autism/.

NOTES

97 A call for more studies that look at neurological outcomes: Poustka, L., Brandeis, D., Hohmann, S., et al., "Neurobiologically Based Interventions for Autism Spectrum Disorders: Rationale and New Directions," *Restorative Neurology and Neuroscience* 32 (2014), 197-212; Katherine Stavapoulos, "Using Neuroscience as an Outcome Measure for Behavioral Interventions in Autism Spectrum Disorders (ASD): A Review," *Research in Autism Spectrum Disorders* 35 (2017), 62-73.

98 "Autism Recovery – The Joe Mohs Story," *Autism Recovery Foundation*, October 15, 2012: https://www.autismrecoveryfoundation.org/news/autism-recovery-the-joe-mohs-story. The Foundation appears to be run by a group of ABA practitioners. Joe Moh's own 2009 video, "Recovery from Autism: The Joe Mohs Story," is no longer available.

99 Leya, "My Story," *And See Where It Takes You* (n.d.): https://andseewhereittakesyou.tumblr.com/mystory.

100 Anonymous, "You Might Not Believe That I Recovered from Autism" *Witty Profiles*, (n.d.): http://www.wittyprofiles.com/q/4696258.

101 Cheyenne Thornton, "ABA for Creating Masking Black Autistics," *Neuroclastic* April 18, 2021: https://neuroclastic.com/aba-for-creating-masking-black-autistics/.

102 Laura Anderson, "Autistic Experiences of Applied Behavior Analysis," *Autism* 27:3 (2023), 737-50.

103 Felicity Sedgewick, Laura Hull, and Helen Ellis, *Autism and Masking: How and Why People Do It, and the Impact It Can Have* (London: Jessica Kingsley, 2022), p. 16.

104 Kieran Rose, "Masking: I am not OK," *The Autistic Advocate*, July 24, 2018: https://theautisticadvocate.com/2018/07/masking-i-am-not-ok/.

105 magz, in the "What is Masking?" discussion, *Wrong Planet*, April 2, 2019: https://wrongplanet.net/forums/viewtopic.php?f=3&t=374847.

106 Judy Endow, "Autistic Burnout," *Aspects of Autism Translated*, July 7, 2015: http://www.judyendow.com/advocacy/autistic-burnout/. See also Kit Mead, "The Pitfalls of Passing and Not Passing," *Think Inclusive*, February 4, 2016: https://www.thinkinclusive.us/the-pitfalls-of-passing-and-not-passing/.

107 Max Jones, "ABA," *Unstrange Mind* , first published October 7, 2014; republished October 20, 2016: https://unstrangemind.wordpress.com/2014/10/07/aba/.

108 Eilidh Cage and Zoe Troxell-Whitman, "Understanding the Reasons, Contexts and Costs of Camouflaging for Autistic Adults," *Journal of Autism and Developmental Disorders* 49:5 (2019), 1899-1911.

109 Larkin Taylor-Parker, "Passing: How to Play Normal," *Think Inclusive*, January 27, 2016: http://www.thinkinclusive.us/passing-how-to-play-normal/.

110 Jocelyn Eastman, "Looking Autistic: The Positives and Pitfalls of Passing," *Art of Autism*, December 20, 2015: http://the-art-of-autism.com/looking-autistic-the-positives-and-pitfalls-of-passing/.

111 Nicole Wildhood, "What Does It Mean to 'Look Autistic'?" *The Atlantic,* March 24, 2016: http://www.theatlantic.com/health/archive/2016/03/what-does-it-mean-to-look-autistic/475287/.

112 Eilidh Cage and Zoe Troxell-Whitman, "Understanding the Reasons, Contexts and Costs of Camouflaging for Autistic Adults," *Journal of Autism and Developmental Disorders* 49:5 (2019), 1899-1911; Felicity Sedgewick, Laura Hull and Helen Elllis, *Autism and Masking: How and Why People Do It, and the Impact It Can Have* (London: Jessica Kingsley, 2022), pp. 171-177.

113 Masking/disclosing in the workplace will be discussed in Chapter Six below.

114 Joe90, in the "Disclosure" discussion, *Wrong Planet*, January 29, 2020: https://wrongplanet.net/forums/viewtopic.php?t=384453&p=8441306&utm_source=feedburner&utm_medium=feed&utm_campaign=Feed%3A+asperger+%28*Wrong+Planet+-+Autism+Forums*%29&utm_content=Google+Feedfetcher#p8441306.

115 Michelle Dawson, "The Misbehaviour of Behaviourists," *No Autistics Allowed*, 2004: https://www.sentex.ca/~nexus23/naa_aba.html.

116 NTania Melnyczuk, for example, wants to ban all ABA: "Why activists want to ban Applied Behaviour Analysis (ABA) for autistic people," *Youtube* video, 22.32. min., June 28, 2022: https://www.youtube.com/watch?v=UIjGGtTFdGY. I respect this perspective.

Notes to Chapter Four

1 Julia Bascom, quoted in Sara Luterman, "Autistic People Have Been Excluded from Advocacy Conversations. Julia Bascom Is Changing That," *The 19th News*, April 29, 2022: https://19thnews.org/2022/04/julia-bascom-asan-autism-advocacy/.

2 A detailed account of how these legal rights came into being can be found in three posts on my blog, *That Bloody Cat*, February 8, 2017, February 19, 2017, and April 9, 2017: https://thatbloodycat.com/2017/02/08/the-education-of-autistic-children-1950-1975/; https://thatbloodycat.com/2017/02/19/the-education-of-autistic-children-1975-1990/; https://thatbloodycat.com/2017/04/09/educational-legislation-1986-2004/.

3 Referring to Section 504 of the Rehabilitation Act of 1973.

4 Laid out in the Individuals with Disabilities Education Act (IDEA) of 1990.

5 "Romana Tate," "What's the Difference Between High Functioning and Low Functioning Autism?", *Autistic Women and Nonbinary Network*, October 19, 2014: https://awnnetwork.org/whats-the-difference-between-high-functioning-and-low-functioning-autism/.

6 "The Fish We Do Not Fry," *Autism Sparkles*, January 29, 2017: https://autismsparkles.wordpress.com/2017/01/29/the-fish-we-do-not-fry/.

7 See, for example, Dianne Berkell, "Instructional Planning: Goals and Practice," in Dianne Berkell, ed., *Autism: Identification, Education, and Treatment* (Hillsdale, NJ: Lawrence Erlbaum Associates, 1992), pp. 99-100, which emphasizes teaching "functional academics" such as the ability to count coins and read signs.

8 National Research Council's Committee on Educational Interventions for Children with Autism, *Educating Children with Autism* (Washington, DC: National Academy Press, 2001), pp. 90-91.

9 Even autistic students with "high support needs" get greater academic benefits from being

NOTES

placed in inclusive classrooms: "The Segregation of Students with Disabilities," *National Council on Disability*, February 7, 2018: https://ncd.gov/sites/default/files/NCD_Segregation-SWD_508.pdf.

10 Emma Zurcher-Long, "Can Speech Challenged Students Get an Appropriate Education?" *Emma's Hope Book*, February 9, 2016: https://emmashopebook.com/2016/02/09/can-speech-challenged-students-get-an-appropriate-education/.

11 "Communication Device Opens Up the World to Nonverbal Autistic Boy, *Buffalo Evening News*, December 3, 2015.

12 Philip Reyes, "Handwriting," *Faith, Hope, and Love...With Autism* , April 24, 2020: https://faithhopeloveautism.blogspot.com/2020/04/handwriting.html.

13 Ido Kedar, "Motor Difficulties in Severe Autism," *Ido in Autismland*, November 3, 2015: http://idoinautismland.com/?p=376. See also Emma Zurcher-Long's, "Can Speech Challenged Students Get an Appropriate Education?" *Emma's Hope Book*, February 9, 2016: https://emmashopebook.com/?s=can+speech+challenged

14 Jennifer Kurth and Ann Mastergeorge, "Individual Education Plan Goals and Services for Adolescents with Autism: Impact of Age and Educational Setting," *Journal of Special Education* 44:3 (2010), 149.

15 Sara Witmer and Summer Ferreri, "Alignment of Instruction, Expectations and Accountability Testing for Students with Autism Spectrum Disorder," *Focus on Autism and Other Developmental Disabilities* 29: 3 (2014), 136-38.

16 Gary Mcabee, "US Supreme Court Decision May Improve Individual Educational Programs for Children with Special Needs," *Journal of Child Neurology* 32:12 (2017), 973-74.

17 Paula Kluth, *You're Going to Love This Kid: Teaching Students with Autism in the Inclusive Classroom*, 3rd ed. (Baltimore, Maryland: Brookes Publishing, 2023).

18 The myth that all autistics are mathematical/technological geniuses is just that—a myth.

19 Ann, "Autism, School, Exclusion. What's Fair?" *Ann's Autism Blog*, August 15, 2018: http://annsautism.blogspot.com/2018/08/autism-school-exclusion-whats-fair.html.

20 Despite the demeaning deficit language, these problems are well-presented in Ana Gentil-Gutierrez, Et Al., "Implication of the Sensory Environment in Children with Autism Spectrum Disorder: Perspectives from School," *International Journal of Environmental Research and Public Health* 18:14 (2021), open access.

21 Judy Endow, "We Are Not in Our Own World," *Aspects Of Autism Translated*, September 14, 2014: http://www.judyendow.com/autistic-behavior/we-are-not-in-our-own-world/.

22 Elizabeth Jones, et al., "Distraction, Distress and Diversity: Exploring the Impact of Sensory Processing Differences on Learning and School Life for Pupils with Autism Spectrum Disorders," *Research in Autism Spectrum Disorders* 72 (2020), open access; Fiona Howe, "How Sensory Experiences Affect Adolescents with an Autistic Spectrum Condition within the Classroom," *Journal of Autism and Developmental Disorders* 46 (2016), 1656-1668. There are now many studies of sensory experience in autism more generally: see those reviewed in J. He, et al., "A Working Taxonomy for Describing the Sensory Differences of Autism," *Molecular Autism* 14:1 (2023), open access.

23 P. Dawes, et al., ["Profile and Aetiology of Children Diagnosed with Auditory Processing Disorder (APD)," *International Journal Of Pediatric Otorhinolaryngology*, 72 (2008), 483–89], found that about 9% of children referred to a clinic specializing in auditory processing disorders also had a diagnosis of autism; this suggests that autistic children are more likely to have an APD than neurotypical children.

24 Leslie Broun, "Teaching Students with Autistic Spectrum Disorders to Read," *Teaching Exceptional Children* 36 (2004), 36-40. See also Joanne Arciuli and Benjamin Bailey, "Review Article: The Promise of Comprehensive Early Reading Instruction for Children with Autism and Recommendations for Future Directions," *Language, Speech, And Hearing Services In Schools* 52:1 (2021), 225-238; Shuai Zhang, et al., "Using Construction-Integration Theory to Interpret Reading Comprehension Instruction for Students with Autism Spectrum Disorder: A Systematic Review and Meta-Analysis," *Reading Research Quarterly* 58:1 (2023), 126-59. It is remarkable how much research on literacy instruction for autistic kids still conflates autism and intellectual disability.

25 Unfortunately, the scientific study of visual processing issues in autism is still in its infancy. Even quite recent articles often fail to look beyond the most basic issues of face and pattern recognition: e.g., Klara Kovarski, "Visual Responses to Implicit Emotion Faces," in F. Volker, et al., eds., *Encyclopedia of Autism Spectrum Disorders*, 2nd ed. (New York: Springer, 2020). Experienced teachers may offer more reliable information on how visual issues affect schoolwork: e.g., Olga Bogdashina, *Sensory Perceptual Issues in Autism* (London: Jessica Kingsley, 2003).

26 Rachel Coulter, "Understanding the Visual Symptoms of Individuals with Autism Spectrum Disorder (ASD)," *Optometry and Vision Development* 40:3 (2009), 164-75.

27 Amanda Ludlow and Arnold Wilkins, "Atypical Sensory Behaviours in Children With Tourette's Syndrome and in Children with Autism Spectrum Disorders," *Research in Developmental Disabilities* 56 (2016), 108-16.

28 The Irlen method of using colored overlays and glasses to treat these individuals remains highly controversial but has proved life-changing for some autistic individuals. A famous example is that of the late Donna Williams, the Australian writer and autism activist.

29 Jennifer Kurth, "Educational Placement of Students with Autism," *Focus on Autism and Other Developmental Disabilities* 30 (2015), Pp. 249-56.

30 U.S. Department of Education, Office of Special Education and Rehabilitative Services, "Questions and Answers on Least Restrictive Environment (LRE) Requirements of the IDEA," *Wrightslaw*, November 23, 1994: https://www.wrightslaw.com/info/lre.osers.memo.idea.htm.

31 See Chapter Five below.

32 *Congressional Record* 146:55, Senate Section, S3569, May 8, 2000: https://www.congress.gov/congressional-record/2000/5/8/senate-section.

33 E.g., "Autism and IEPs and Grizzly Mommas . . . Oh My!!" *Autism Sparkles*: https://autismsparkles.wordpress.com/2013/02/22/autism-and-ieps-and-grizzly-mommas-oh-my/. These ferocious parents are not always right—sometimes the mainstream classroom is simply intolerable for their children, who would be better served as home (if possible), or in a special education classroom with additional academic programming to suit their needs.

NOTES

34 U.S. Department of Education, *Digest of Education Statistics*: "2022 Tables and Figures," 219.90: https://nces.ed.gov/programs/digest/d22/tables/dt22_219.90.asp?current=yes.

35 "Certificate Instead of a HS Diploma? No Way!" *Wrightslaw*, February 19, 2020: http://www.wrightslaw.com/blog/certificate-instead-of-a-diploma-is-this-ok/.

36 In 2018, only 41% of teens with autism reported enjoying excellent health, compared with 61% of all teens in general education classes; among autistic teens whose families were at or below the federal poverty line, only 29% enjoyed excellent health. In addition, 38% of autistic teens whose families were at or below the federal poverty line had trouble accessing health care, while 27% of all black autistic teens had unmet health care needs. See Paul Shattuck, et al., *National Autism Indicators Report: High School Students on the Autism Spectrum* (Philadelphia, PA: Life Course Outcomes Program, A.J. Drexel Autism Institute, Drexel University, 2018).

37 Quincy Hansen, "They Were Wrong," *Speaking Of Autism . . .*, July 22, 2020: https://speakingofautismcom.wordpress.com/2020/07/22/they-were-wrong/. Quincy graduated from high school in the summer of 2020—as class valedictorian.

38 Ariane Zurcher, "An Interview with an Autistic Teacher Who Teaches Autistic Students," *Emma's Hope Book*, February 4, 2013: https://emmashopebook.com/2013/02/04/an-interview-with-an-autistic-teacher-who-teaches-autistic-students/.

39 Sarah Butrymowicz and Jackie Mader, "Almost All Students with Disabilities Are Capable of Graduating on Time. Here's Why They're Not," *The Hechinger Report*, November 4, 2017: https://hechingerreport.org/high-schools-fail-provide-legally-required-education-students-disabilities/.

40 U.S. Department of Education, *Digest of Education Statistics*: "2022 Tables and Figures," 219.90: https://nces.ed.gov/programs/digest/d22/tables/dt22_219.90.asp?current=yes.

41 U.S. Department of Education, *Digest of Education Statistics*: "2022 Tables and Figures," 219.55 (https://nces.ed.gov/programs/digest/d19/tables/dt19_219.55.asp?current=yes) and 219.90 (https://nces.ed.gov/programs/digest/d19/tables/dt19_219.90.asp?current=yes).

42 Melissa Kearney and Phillip Levine, "Income Inequality, Social Mobility, and the Decision to Drop Out of High School," *Brookings Papers on Economic Activity* (Spring, 2016), 333-380.

43 Christen Bradley and Linda Renzulli, "The Complexity of Non-Completion: Being Pushed or Pulled to Drop Out of High School," *Social Forces* 90:2 (2011), 521-45.

44 Richard Reeves, et al., "The Unreported Gender Gap in High School Graduation Rates," *The Brookings Institution*, January 12, 2021: https://www.brookings.edu/blog/up-front/2021/01/12/the-unreported-gender-gap-in-high-school-graduation-rates/.

45 Elana McDermott, et al., "Why Do Students Drop Out? Turning Points and Long-Term Experiences," *Journal of Educational Research* 112:2 (2019), 270-82.

46 U.S. Department of Education, *Digest of Education Statistics*: "2022 Tables and Figures," 219.90: https://nces.ed.gov/programs/digest/d22/tables/dt22_219.90.asp?current=yes.

47 U.S. Department Of Education, *The Condition Of Education, 2020*, "Employment and Unemployment Rates by Educational Attainment" (updated May, 2020): https://nces.ed.gov/

programs/coe/indicator_cbc.asp; see also the section on "Annual Earnings."

48 Richard Cebula and Gigi Alexander, "Economic and Non-Economic Factors Influencing Geographic Differentials in Homelessness: An Exploratory State-Level Analysis," *American Journal of Economics and Sociology* 79:2 (2020), 511-40.

49 In 2018, 29% of those incarcerated in federal prisons had no high school diploma: U.S. Department of Justice, Bureau of Justice Statistics, "Data Collected Under The First Step Act, 2019," March, 2020: https://www.bjs.gov/content/pub/pdf/dcfsa19.pdf.

50 Rita Hamad, et al., "Educational Attainment and Cardiovascular Disease in the United States: A Quasi-Experimental Instrumental Variables Analysis," *PloS Medicine* 16:6 (2019), open access; Malerie Lazar and Lisa Davenport, "Barriers to Health Care Access for Low Income Families: A Review of Literature," *Journal of Community Health Nursing* 35:1 (2018), 28-37. An older study showed that people who earn GEDs tend to have poorer health outcomes, closer to the outcomes of high school dropouts than to those of people with diplomas: Anna Sajacova, "Health in Working-Aged Americans: Adults with High School Equivalency Diploma Are Similar to Dropouts, Not High School Graduates," *American Journal of Public Health* 102, Supplement 2 (2012), S284-S290.

51 See Parts Three and Four below.

52 Aspychata, in the "Can ASD People Also Have A Learning Disability?" discussion, *Autism Forums*, February 12, 2019: https://www.autismforums.com/threads/can-asd-people-also-have-a-learning-disability.32869/#post-681473.

53 U/DVREX, "Sometimes I Feel Like I Won't Be Able To Achieve Anything Later In Life," post on *R/Autism* subreddit, *Reddit*, June, 2020: https://www.reddit.com/r/autism/comments/gr7cvn/sometimes_i_feel_like_i_wont_be_able_to_achieve/.

54 Kristen Bottema-Beutel, et al., "High School Experiences and Support Recommendations of Autistic Youth," *Journal of Autism and Developmental Disorders* 50 (2020), 3397–3412.

55 Misery, in the "Did Or Do You Have A Teacher At School You Really Like/Liked?" discussion, *Autism Forums*, July 12, 2018: https://www.autismforums.com/threads/did-or-do-you-have-a-teacher-at-school-you-really-like-liked.26156/#post-525596.

56 Mia, in the "Compliments For The Other Side" discussion, *Autism Forums*, June 29, 2019: https://www.autismforums.com/threads/compliments-for-the-other-side-3.30343/#post-625149.

57 Cassandra Crosman, "A Neurodivergent Vision for the Future of Special Education," *In The Loop About Neurodiversity*, October 16, 2019: https://intheloopaboutneurodiversity.wordpress.com/2019/10/16/a-neurodivergent-vision-for-the-future-of-special-education/.

Notes to Chapter Five

1 Jennifer Richards, Jodi Cohen, and Lakeidra Chavis, "The Quiet Rooms: Children Locked Away in Illinois Schools," *ProPublica Illinois/Chicago Tribune,* November 19, 2019: https://features.propublica.org/illinois-seclusion-rooms/school-students-put-in-isolated-timeouts/.

2 Hannah Rappleye and Liz Brown, "Thirteen-year-old Activist with Autism Wants to Close Seclusion Rooms at Schools," *NBC News*, November 23, 2018: https://www.nbcnews.com/news/

education/thirteen-year-old-activist-autism-wants-close-seclusion-rooms-schools-n935356.

3 Jeanne Davide-Rivera, *Twirling Naked in the Streets and No One Noticed: Growing Up with Undiagnosed Autism* ([David and Goliath Publishing, 2013), p. 34.

4 Sadly, there remain so-called "experts" who assume that these children are making a choice to misbehave: e.g., Charles Wood, et al., "Stopping Behavior Before It Starts," *Teaching Exceptional Children* 50:6 (2018), 356-363. Compare Brooke Moore, "Revealing the Ideology of Normal: Using CHAT to Explore the Activity of School," *Sage Open* 12:2 (2022), open access.

5 Davide-Rivera, *Twirling Naked in the Streets*, p. 36.

6 Consider the case of Laura, described by Paula Kluth, *You're Going to Love This Kid: Teaching Students with Autism in the Inclusive Classroom*, 2nd ed. (Baltimore: Paul H. Brookes Publishing, 2010), p. 202.

7 See the post by WAautistic guy in the "What Are Your Worst Experiences at School" discussion, *Wrong Planet*, March 27, 2014: http://wrongplanet.net/forums/viewtopic. php?f=14&t=166310&start=30.

8 Emma Duerden, Hannah Oatley, Kathleen Mak-Fan, et al., "Risk Factors Associated with Self-Injurious Behaviors in Children and Adolescents with Autism Spectrum Disorders," *Journal of Autism and Developmental Disorders* 42 (2012), 2460-70.

9 Gnakub Soke, Steven Rosenberg, Richard Hamman, et al., "Brief Report: Prevalence of Self-Injurious Behaviors among Children with Autism Spectrum Disorder: A Population-Based Study," *Journal of Autism and Developmental Disorders* 46 (2016), 3607-14.

10 Stephen Kanne and Micah Mazurek, "Aggression in Children and Adolescents with ASD: Prevalence and Risk Factors," *Journal of Autism and Developmental Disorders* 41 (2011), 926-37.

11 Stephen Kanne and Micah Mazurek, "Aggression in Children and Adolescents with ASD: Prevalence and Risk Factors," *Journal of Autism and Developmental Disorders* 41 (2011), 926-37; Emma Duerden, et al., "Risk Factors Associated with Self-Injurious Behaviors in Children and Adolescents with Autism Spectrum Disorders," *Journal of Autism and Developmental Disorders* 42 (2012), 2460-70; Micah Mazurek and Kristin Sohl, "Sleep and Behavioral Problems in Children with Autism Spectrum Disorders," *Journal of Autism and Developmental Disorders* 46 (2016), 1906-15; G. Soke, et al., "Factors Associated with Self-Injurious Behaviors in Children with Autism Spectrum Disorders: Findings from Two Large National Samples," *Journal of Autism and Developmental Disorders* 47 (2017), 285-96; C.Laverty, et al., The 10-Year Trajectory of Aggressive Behaviours in Autistic Individuals," *Journal of Intellectual Disability Research* (January 18, 20223), open access; "Giulia Bresciani, et al., "Gastrointestinal Disorders and Food Selectivity: Relationship with Sleep and Challenging Behavior in Children with Autism Spectrum Disorder," *Children* 10:2 (2023), open access.

12 Sally, in the "About Hating Touch.." discussion, *Wrong Planet*, November 19, 2007: http://wrongplanet.net/forums/viewtopic.php?t=48437.

13 Lost_dragon, in the "Biggest Pet Peeve" discussion, *Wrong Planet*, August 14, 2017: https://wrongplanet.net/forums/viewtopic.php?f=3&t=338252&start=16.

NOTES

14 bluecurry, in the "What Were You Like in Elementary School" discussion, *Wrong Planet*, March 16, 2013: https://wrongplanet.net/forums/viewtopic.php?t=226220.

15 Felinesaresuperior, in the "Odd Things That Make You Feel Irrationally Angry" discussion, *Wrong Planet*, February 11, 2012: https://wrongplanet.net/forums/viewtopic.php?t=189358.

16 Radiofixr, in the "Did Anyone Else LIKE Being Bullied?" discussion, *Wrong Planet*, June 24, 2010: http://wrongplanet.net/forums/viewtopic.php?t=129369.

17 Tambourine-Man, in the "What Not to Do During a Meltdown—From an Autistic Adult" discussion, *Wrong Planet*, November 11, 2011: https://wrongplanet.net/forums/viewtopic. php?t=180194.

18 This mistake is also common among ABA practitioners, and even scientists—who really should know better. For example, Fred Volkmar, ed., *The Encyclopedia of Autism*, 2nd ed. (New York: Springer Nature, 2021) contains an article on "temper tantrums," but not on meltdowns. See also Rachel Goldin, et al., A Comparison of Tantrum Behavior Profiles in Children with ASD, ADHD, and Comorbid ASD and ADHD," *Research in Developmental Disabilities* 34 (2013), 2669-2675; Abigail Issarraras and Johnny Matson, "Treatment Approaches to Aggression and Tantrums in Children with Developmental Disabilities," in Johnny Matson, ed., *Handbook of Child Psychopathology and Developmental Disabilities Treatment* (Cham, Switzerland: Springer, 2017), pp. 257-68

19 Dr. Clarissa Kripke, "Understanding Autism, Aggression, and Self-Injury: Medical Approaches and Best Support Practices," *The Thinking Person's Guide to Autism*: http://www.thinkingautismguide. com/2016/08/when-autistic-children-are-aggressive.html.

20 Geoff Colvin and Martin Sheehan, *Managing the Cycle of Meltdowns for Students with Autism Spectrum Disorder* (Thousand Oaks, CA: Corwin, 2012), p. 145.

21 "*As a child I used to have violent and out-of-control meltdowns, but now I don't have those anymore*": Sofisol612, in the "What Does a Meltdown Look Like in an Adult Woman" discussion, *Wrong Planet*, September 20, 2017: https://wrongplanet.net/forums/viewtopic.php?t=337317.

22 Antisocial Butterfly, in the "Meltdowns? Fall Asleep/Tired Or Biting Meltdowns?" discussion, *Wrong Planet*, January 26, 2018: https://wrongplanet.net/forums/viewtopic. php?f=3&t=63131&start=15.

23 Rhi, "Meltdown," *Autism and Expectations*, November 24, 2018: https://autistrhi.com/2018/11/24/ meltdown/.

24 crouton, in the "Anyone Else Feel Embarrassed/ashamed After A Meltdown?" discussion, *Wrong Planet*, June 4, 2011: https://wrongplanet.net/forums/viewtopic.php?t=140790.

25 Callista, in the "Anyone Else Feel Embarrassed/ashamed After A Meltdown?" discussion, *Wrong Planet*, October 19, 2010: https://wrongplanet.net/forums/viewtopic.php?t=140790.

26 Grafton Integrated Health Care, a for-profit behavioral health organization, has claimed that its proprietary "Ukeru model" has reduced incidents of restraint by 99% and incidents of seclusion by 100% over the course of 14 years (2003-2016), in community as well as institutional settings. They claim that staff injuries from restraint have declined by 100% in community settings, and 97% in institutions: Jason Craig and Kimberly Sanders, "Evaluation of a Program Model for Minimizing

Restraint and Seclusion," *Advances in Neurodevelopmental Disorders* 2 (2018), 344-352. The authors of this paper are affiliated with Grafton, and I have not been able to discover any corroborating analyses conducted by unaffiliated scientists.

27 Judy Endow, *Outsmarting Explosive Behavior: A Visual System of Support and Intervention for Individuals with Autism Spectrum Disorders* (Shawnee Mission, KS: Autism Publishing Company, 2009); Deborah Lipsky and Will Richards, *Managing Meltdowns: Using the S.C.A.R.E.D. Calming Technique with Children and Adults with Autism* (London: Jessica Kingsley, 2009); Deborah Lipsky, *From Anxiety to Meltdown: How Individuals on the Autism Spectrum Deal with Anxiety, Experience Meltdowns, Manifest Tantrums, and How You Can Intervene Effectively* (London: Jessica Kingsley, 2011); Geoff Colvin and Martin Sheehan, *Managing the Cycle of Meltdowns for Students with Autism Spectrum Disorder* (Thousand Oaks, CA: Corwin, 2012).

28 Colvin and Sheehan, *Managing the Cycle of Meltdowns*, pp. 27-50. Compare Lipsky, *From Anxiety to Meltdown*, p. 127; Endow, *Outsmarting Explosive Behavior*, pp. 11-46.

29 Lipsky, *From Anxiety to Meltdown*, p. 229.

30 Colvin and Sheehan, *Managing the Cycle of Meltdowns*, pp. 63-108. Discussion of potential triggers is a particular strength of Lipsky, *From Anxiety to Meltdown* , pp. 161-214.

31 Colvin and Sheehan, *Managing the Cycle of Meltdowns*, p. 39.

32 Colvin and Sheehan, *Managing the Cycle of Meltdowns*, pp. 40-43.

33 Colvin and Sheehan, *Managing the Cycle of Meltdowns*, pp. 109-22.

34 The phrase "point of no return" is used by Judy Endow, *Outsmarting Explosive Behavior*, pp. 35-40. She uses it to emphasize that once a child has reached this point they are no longer in control of their behavior. A meltdown inevitable, and no disciplinary actions will stop it.

35 Lipsky and Richards, *Managing Meltdowns*; Lipsky, *From Anxiety to Meltdown*, pp. 216-22; Colvin and Sheehan, *Managing the Cycle of Meltdowns*, pp. 135-36

36 Lipsky, *From Anxiety to Meltdown*, p. 221.

37 Colvin and Sheehan, *Managing the Cycle of Meltdowns*, p. 123-41; compare Lipsky, *From Anxiety to Meltdown*, p. 221.

38 Lipsky, *From Anxiety to Meltdown*, pp. 110, 126, 141.

39 Colvin and Sheehan, *Managing the Cycle of Meltdowns*, pp. 142-53.

40 Colvin and Sheehan, *Managing the Cycle of Meltdowns*, pp. 49-51, 154-68.

41 "Education Access: We've Turned Classrooms Into a Hell for Neurodivergence," *Stimpunks*, 2022: https://stimpunks.org/access/education/ . The question "What is school like for autistic people?" was posted on *Quora* in 2017; A remarkable number of the responses contained the word "hell": https://www.quora.com/What-is-school-like-for-autistic-people.

42 SchrodingersMeerkat, in the "Is Suspension Really a Punishment" discussion, *Autism Forums*, November 29, 2017: https://www.autismforums.com/threads/is-suspension-really-a-punishment.22893/#post-455520.

43 "Is Suspension Really a Punishment?" discussion, *Wrong Planet*, 2012: http://wrongplanet.net/ forums/viewtopic.php?t=194004; "Anyone Ever Threatened with Suspension?" *Wrong Planet*, 2015: http://wrongplanet.net/forums/viewtopic.php?f=14&t=148672; "Is Suspension Really a Punishment", *Autism Forums*, November-December, 2017: https://www.autismforums.com/threads/is-suspension-really-a-punishment.22893/#post-455520.

44 Erik Drasgow, et al., "The IDEA Amendments of 1997: A School-Wide Model for Conducting Functional Behavioral Assessments and Developing Behavior Intervention Plans," *Education and Treatment of Children* 22:3 (1999), 244-66; Cynthia Dieterich, Nicole Snyder and Christine Villani, "Functional Behavior Assessment and Behavior Intervention Plans: Review of the Law and Recent Cases," *Brigham Young University Education and Law Journal* (2017), 195-217.

45 On functional assessment of behavior in a clinical setting, see Pamela Neidert, et al., "Functional Analysis of Problem Behavior," in Derek Reed, et al., eds., *Handbook of Crisis Intervention and Developmental Disabilities* (New York: Springer, 2013), pp. 147-67. On FBA as actually practiced in schools, see George Noell and Kristin Gansle, "Introduction to Functional Behavior Assessment," in Angeleque Akin-Little, et al., eds., *Behavioral Interventions in Schools: Evidence-based Positive Strategies* (Washington, DC: American Psychological Association, 2009), pp. 43-58; Alison Bruhn, et al., "Assessing and Treating Stereotypical Behaviors in Classrooms Using a Functional Approach," *Behavioral Disorders* 41 (2015), 21-37.

46 Nancy Stockall and Lindsay Dennis, "Stop the Running: Addressing Elopement in Young Children with Disabilities," *Young Exceptional Children* 19 (2016), 3-13.

47 Michael Couvillon, Lyndal Bullock and Robert Gable, "Tracking Behavior Assessment Methodology and Support Strategies: A National Survey of How Schools Utilize Functional Behavioral Assessments and Behavior Intervention Plans," *Emotional and Behavioural Difficulties* 14 (2009), 215-28; Lindsay Oram, Sarah Owens and Melissa Maras, "Functional Behavior Assessment and Behavior Intervention Plans in Rural Schools: An Exploration of the Need, Barriers and Recommendations," *Preventing School Failure* 60 (2016), 305-10. Many schools have no trained psychologist available to conduct FBAs. In 2021 the National Association of School Psychologists estimated that nationally there was only 1 psychologist for every 1,211 students: "Shortage of School Psychologists": https://www.nasponline.org/research-and-policy/policy-priorities/critical-policy-issues/shortage-of-school-psychologists.

48 Lauren Collins and Perry Zirkel, "Functional Behavior Assessments and Behavior Intervention Plans: Legal Requirements and Professional Recommendations," *Journal of Positive Behavior Interventions* 19 (2017), 180-90.

49 U.S. Department of Education, Office for Civil Rights, "Civil Rights Data Collection, 2017-18: The Use of Restraint and Seclusion on Children with Disabilities in K-12 Schools": https://www2.ed.gov/about/offices/list/ocr/docs/restraint-and-seclusion.pdf.

50 Erin Jordan, "Senators Ask Federal Probe of School Seclusion Reporting," *The Gazette* (Cedar Rapids, IA), June 3, 2018: https://www.thegazette.com/subject/news/education/senators-ask-federal-probe-of-school-seclusion-reporting-20180603.

51 Jenny Abamu, "Children Are Routinely Isolated in Some Fairfax County Schools. The District Didn't Report It," *WAMU Radio* (Washington, DC), updated March 13, 2019: https://wamu.org/

story/19/03/13/children-are-routinely-isolated-in-some-fairfax-county-schools-the-district-didnt-report-it/.

52 Jennifer Richards, Jodi Cohen, and Lakeidra Chavis, "The Quiet Rooms: Children Locked Away in Illinois Schools," *ProPublica Illinois/Chicago Tribune,* November 19, 2019: https://features.propublica. org/illinois-seclusion-rooms/school-students-put-in-isolated-timeouts/.

53 Jenny Abamu, "U.S. Schools Underreport How Often Students Are Restrained or Secluded, Watchdog Says," *National Public Radio, All Things Considered,* June 18, 2019: https://www.npr. org/2019/06/18/731703500/u-s-schools-underreport-how-often-students-are-restrained-or-secluded-watchdog-s.

54 Alex Putterman, "CT Students Restrained, Secluded Thousands of Times Causing Dozens of Injuries: 'Something Is Not Working,'" *CT Insider,* October 27, 2022; updated November 1, 2022: https://www.ctinsider.com/news/article/connecticut-schools-restraint-seclusion-injuries-17474991. php; see also Emilie Munson and Ying Zhao, "Teachers and Police Restrained Thousands of Kids in 22 New York Schools," *Times Union* (New York City), October 27, 2022; updated October 28, 2022: https://www.timesunion.com/news/article/new-york-student-restraint-seclusion-17474997.php.

55 U.S. Department of Education, Office for Civil Rights, "Civil Rights Data Collection, 2017-18: The Use of Restraint and Seclusion on Children with Disabilities in K-12 Schools": https://www2. ed.gov/about/offices/list/ocr/docs/restraint-and-seclusion.pdf. The Department of Education typically focuses on how discipline affects students served under IDEA. Some students, though, are accommodated under Section 504 of the Rehabilitation Act of 1973. The Department recently released some guidance on these students: U.S. Department of Education, Office for Civil Rights, "Supporting Students with Disabilities and Avoiding the Discriminatory Use of Student Discipline under Section 504 of the Rehabilitation Act of 1973," July, 2022: https://www2.ed.gov/about/offices/list/ocr/docs/504-discipline-guidance.pdf.

56 Andrea Kadlec, et al., "Coming Into the Light: An Examination of Restraint and Isolation Practices in Washington Schools," *Disability Rights Washington/ACLU of Washington,* February, 2023: https://www.disabilityrightswa.org/wp-content/uploads/2023/02/Restraint-and-Isolation-Report-dist.pdf.

57 Susan Ferriss, "Virginia Tops Nation in Sending Students to Cops, Courts: Where Does Your State Rank?" *The Center for Public Integrity,* April 10, 2015; revised February 19, 2016: https:// publicintegrity.org/education/virginia-tops-nation-in-sending-students-to-cops-courts-where-does-your-state-rank/; Susan Ferriss, "Virginia Drops Felony Charges Against Sixth-Grade Boy with Autism," *The Center for Investigative Reporting: Reveal,* March 15, 2016: https://www.revealnews.org/ article/virginia-drops-felony-charges-against-sixth-grade-boy-with-autism/.

58 U.S. Department of Education, "Restraint and Seclusion: A Resource Document," 2012: https:// www2.ed.gov/policy/seclusion/restraint-and-seclusion-resource-document.html.

59 Jessica Butler, "How Safe is the Schoolhouse?: An Analysis of State Seclusion and Restraint Laws and Policies," *Autism National Committee,* 2017; updated July, 2019: https://www.autcom.org/pdf/ HowSafeSchoolhouse.pdf.

60 There were earlier stories about this, but the full video of the events is included in Caitlyn Jones,

NOTES

"Denton Family of Special Needs Child Wants Third-Party Probe after Body Camera Footage Surfaces," *Denton Record-Chronicle*, August 14, 2018: https://dentonrc.com/education/denton_isd/denton-family-of-special-needs-child-wants-third-party-probe-after-body-camera-footage-surfaces/article_b300ed5a-515a-5890-83a4-3f56742dfc76.html.

61 Jennifer Richards, Jodi Cohen, and Lakeidra Chavis, "The Quiet Rooms: Children Locked Away in Illinois Schools," *ProPublica Illinois/Chicago Tribune* November 19, 2019: https://features.propublica.org/illinois-seclusion-rooms/school-students-put-in-isolated-timeouts/.

62 U.S. Department of Education, "Restraint and Seclusion: A Resource Document," 2012: https://www2.ed.gov/policy/seclusion/restraint-and-seclusion-resource-document.html.

63 Jessica Butler, "How Safe is the Schoolhouse?: An Analysis of State Seclusion and Restraint Laws and Policies," *Autism National Committee*, 2017; updated July, 2019: https://www.autcom.org/pdf/HowSafeSchoolhouse.pdf.

64 Associated Press, "Indiana Couple: School Strapped Autistic Daughter to Chair", July 27, 2018: https://www.apnews.com/6c1bf5670c23465c9d48ce4a77634131.

65 Jessica Butler, "How Safe is the Schoolhouse?: An Analysis of State Seclusion and Restraint Laws and Policies," *Autism National Committee*, 2017; updated July, 2019: https://www.autcom.org/pdf/HowSafeSchoolhouse.pdf.

66 Sawsan Morrar and Phillip Reese, "School Where Student with Autism Collapsed and Later Died Violated Restraint Rules, California Regulators Find," *Sacramento Bee*, December 8, 2018: https://www.sacbee.com/latest-news/article222799470.html.

67 Silas Allen, "Boulevard Heights Staff Used Illegal Restrain in Student Death," *Fort Worth Star-Telegram*, November 10, 2022.

68 Jennifer Richards, Jodi Cohen, and Lakeidra Chavis, "The Quiet Rooms: Children Locked Away in Illinois Schools," *ProPublica Illinois/Chicago Tribune* November 19, 2019: https://features.propublica.org/illinois-seclusion-rooms/school-students-put-in-isolated-timeouts/.

69 See, for example, the case of Jessica and Ronnie Kecman's son, described by Debbie Truong, "A Photo Emerges and a VA School System's Use of Seclusion Comes Under Scrutiny," *Washington Post*, May 26, 2018.

70 Jennifer Richards, Jodi Cohen, and Lakeidra Chavis, "The Quiet Rooms: Children Locked Away in Illinois Schools," *ProPublica Illinois/Chicago Tribune* November 19, 2019: https://features.propublica.org/illinois-seclusion-rooms/school-students-put-in-isolated-timeouts/.

71 On suicidality, see, among many other possibilities, P.J. Randhawa, "Mom Blames School's Use of Isolation Rooms after 8-Year-Old Attempts Suicide," *KSDK Television News* (St. Louis, MO), March 1, 2019; Chantalle Edmunds, "The Isolation Room: Local Parents Share Horror Stories about School System's Treatment of Students with Special Needs," *Loudoun Times-Mirror* (Loudoun, VA), February 15, 2018; on completed suicides, see the case of Jonathan King, which received national attention: Ashley Frantz, "Children Forced Into Cell-Like School Seclusion Rooms," *CNN Television News*, December 17, 2008: http://www.cnn.com/2008/US/12/17/seclusion.rooms/; Alan Judd, "Death Highlights Lack of Regulation at Georgia 'Psychoeducational' Schools," *Atlanta Journal-Constitution*, July 27, 2009;

NOTES

72 Anonymous, "Seclusion as Punishment," *We Always Liked Picasso Anyway*, October 3, 2013: https://autistictimestwo.blogspot.com/search?q=seclusion.

73 Hannah Grieco, "Restraining Students with Disabilities is Harmful," *Baltimore Sun*, April 22, 2019: https://www.baltimoresun.com/opinion/op-ed/bs-ed-op-0423-disabilities-restraints-20190417-story.html.

74 Rob Manning and Jenny Abamu, "Desperation And Broken Trust When Schools Restrain Students or Lock Them in Rooms," *National Public Radio, Morning Edition*, June 5, 2019: https://www.npr.org/2019/06/05/726519409/desperation-and-broken-trust-when-schools-restrain-students-or-lock-them-in-room.

75 U.S. Department of Education, "Restraint and Seclusion: A Resource Document," 2012: https://www2.ed.gov/policy/seclusion/restraints-and-seclusion-resources.pdf.

76 Nina Agrawal, "California Expands Ban on 'Willful Defiance' Suspensions in Schools," *Los Angeles Times*, September 10, 2019.

77 Morgan Craven et al., "Suspended Childhood: An Analysis of Exclusionary Discipline of Texas' Pre-K and Elementary School Students, Updated with 2015-16 Data," *Texas Appleseed*, November, 2015; updated March, 2017: http://stories.texasappleseed.org/suspended-childhood-updated.

78 Jessica Oh, "Child with Autism Locked out of School," *Kiro 7 Television* (Seattle, WA), January 23, 2019: https://www.kiro7.com/news/local/child-with-autism-locked-out-of-school/908564250/.

79 "Teacher Files Charges Against 8-Year-Old Student Who Hit Her," *KQRE Television* (Albuquerque, NM), April 14, 2018: https://abc13.com/education/teacher-files-charges-against-8-year-old-student-who-hit-her/3344462/. This incident was also widely reported.

80 David M. Perry, "America Keeps Criminalizing Autistic Children," *Pacific Standard*, June 12, 2017: https://psmag.com/education/america-keeps-criminalizing-autistic-children.

81 Agent Smirnoff, in the "Is Suspension Really a Punishment?" discussion, *Wrong Planet*, October 15, 2012: https://wrongplanet.net/forums/viewtopic.php?t=194004.

82 See "'Autistics Aren't Welcome Here': The Bullying of Autistic Students in America's Schools," *That Bloody Cat*, March 4, 2022: https://thatbloodycat.com/2022/03/04/autistics-arent-welcome-here-the-bullying-of-autistic-students-in-americas-schools/.

83 tlc, in the "Things You Hated About School" discussion, *Autism Forums*, March 30, 2018: https://www.autismforums.com/threads/things-you-hated-about-school.22361/#post-443119. See also dragoncat, in the "Things You Hated About School" discussion, *Autism Forums*, October 28, 2017: https://www.autismforums.com/threads/things-you-hated-about-school.22361/#post-443119. This topic elicited four pages of posts.

84 SchrodingersMeerkat, in the "Things You Hated About School" discussion, *Autism Forums*, October 27, 2017: https://www.autismforums.com/threads/things-you-hated-about-school.22361/#post-443119.

85 Aristophanes, in the "Why School Sucked" discussion, *Wrong Planet*, January 2, 2018: https://wrongplanet.net/forums/viewtopic.php?f=3&t=357585&start=60.

NOTES

86 The Musings of the Lost, in the "Why School Sucked" discussion, *Wrong Planet*, January 2, 2018: https://wrongplanet.net/forums/viewtopic.php?f=3&t=357585&start=60.

87 Elizabeth Rosner and Chris Perez, "Autistic Student Suspended for Standing Up to Bullies, $5M Suit Claims," *New York Post*, August 17, 2018: https://nypost.com/2018/08/17/autistic-student-suspended-for-standing-up-to-bullies-5m-suit-claims/.

88 Max Londberg, "Suit: Winton Woods Officials Allowed Bullying of Student with 'Significant Autism' for Years," *Cincinnati Enquirer* August 19, 2019.

89 Ed Williams, "Criminalizing Disability," *Searchlight New Mexico*, May 7, 2019: https://searchlightnm.org/criminalizing-disability/ .

90 deog, in the "I'm So Done!!!!" discussion, *Autism Forums*, October 9, 2018: https://www.autismforums.com/threads/im-so-done.27361/#post-552380.

91 IDEA, part B, subpart E, sections 300.530-300.536: https://sites.ed.gov/idea/regs/b/e.

92 IDEA, part B, subpart E, section 300.536: https://sites.ed.gov/idea/regs/b/e.

93 Bill Brownley, "Handling a Manifestation Determination Review (MDR): A 'How To' for Attorneys," *Wrightslaw*, December 10, 2018: https://www.wrightslaw.com/info/discipl.mdr.strategy.htm.

94 Robert Tudisco, "Can the School Give my Child with an IEP 'Unofficial' Suspensions?'" *Understood.org* (n.d.): https://www.understood.org/en/school-learning/your-childs-rights/basics-about-childs-rights/can-the-school-give-my-child-with-an-iep-unofficial-suspensions; see also Cristina Novoa and Rasheed Malik, "Suspensions Are Not Support: The Disciplining of Preschoolers With Disabilities," *Center for American Progress*, January 17, 2018: https://www.americanprogress.org/issues/early-childhood/reports/2018/01/17/445041/suspensions-not-support/.

95 "Pushed Out; Kicked Out: Stories from Families with Special Education Students in Washington," *Washington State ACLU*: https://www.aclu-wa.org/pages/pushed-out-kicked-out-stories-families-special-education-students-washington.

96 Cristina Novoa and Rasheed Malik, "Suspensions Are Not Support: The Disciplining of Preschoolers With Disabilities," *Center for American Progress*, January 17, 2018: https://www.americanprogress.org/issues/early-childhood/reports/2018/01/17/445041/suspensions-not-support/.

97 U.S. Department of Education, Office of Civil Rights, "School Climate and Safety," (based on the 2015-16 Civil Rights Data Collection), 2018: https://www2.ed.gov/about/offices/list/ocr/docs/school-climate-and-safety.pdf. The disparity begins in preschool: Cristina Novoa and Rasheed Malik, "Suspensions Are Not Support: The Disciplining of Preschoolers With Disabilities" (Report from the Center for American Progress, January 17, 2018: https://www.americanprogress.org/issues/early-childhood/reports/2018/01/17/445041/suspensions-not-support/. See Taylor Mirfenderefski and Sharon Frame, "Washington Special Needs Students Disciplined More Than Twice as Often as General Education Peers," *King 5 Television* (Seattle, WA), October 25, 2018; updated December 18, 2018: https://www.king5.com/article/news/local/washington-special-needs-students-disciplined-more-than-twice-as-often-as-general-education-peers/281-608161669.

98 Nicholas Gage, et al., "National Analysis of the Disciplinary Exclusion of Black Students with and

without Disabilities," *Journal of Child and Family Studies* 28:7 (2019), 1754-64.

99 U.S. Department of Education, Office of Special Education and Rehabilitative Services, "Racial and Ethnic Disparities in Special Education: A Multi-Year Disproportionality Analysis by State, Analysis Category, and Race/Ethnicity" (2016): https://www2.ed.gov/programs/osepidea/618-data/LEA-racial-ethnic-disparities-tables/index.html.

100 [No author], "Washington Special Needs Students Disciplined More Than Twice as Often as General Education Peers," *King 5 Television* (Seattle, WA), October 25, 2018; updated December 18, 2018: https://www.king5.com/article/news/local/washington-special-needs-students-disciplined-more-than-twice-as-often-as-general-education-peers/281-608161669.

101 Amity Noltemeyer, et al., "Relationship Between School Suspension and Student Outcomes: A Meta-Analysis," *School Psychology Review* 44 (2015), 224-40; Susan Faircloth, "Factors Impacting the Graduation and Dropout Rates of American Indian Males with Disabilities," in Susan Faircloth, Ivory Toldson, and Robert Lucio, eds., *Decreasing Dropout Rates for Minority Male Youth with Disabilities from Culturally and Ethnically Diverse Backgrounds* (Clemson, SC: National Dropout Prevention Center for Students with Disabilities, 2014), pp. 8-9.

102 Max Sparrow, *No You Don't: Essays from an Unstrange Mind* (Self-published, 2013), p. 51

103 Abigail Novak, "The Association Between Experiences of Exclusionary Discipline and Justice System Contact: A Systematic Review," *Aggression and Violent Behavior* 40 (2018), 73-82; Amity L. Noltemeyer, et al., "Relationship Between School Suspension and Student Outcomes: A Meta-Analysis," *School Psychology Review* 44: 2, (2015): 224-24; A.E. Cuellar and S. Markowitz, "School Suspension and the School-to-Prison Pipeline," *International Review of Law and Economics* 43 (2015), 98-106.

104 Ambra Green, et al., "Common Misconceptions of Suspension: Ideas and Alternatives for School Leaders," *Psychology in the Schools* 55:4 (2018), 419-28.

Notes to Chapter Six

1 Erin Clemens, "When I Say I'm Struggling as an Adult on the Autism Spectrum," *The Mighty*, November 6, 2022: https://themighty.com/topic/autism-spectrum-disorder/asking-for-help-for-my-struggles-as-an-adult-on-the-autism-spectrum/.

2 Erin McKinney, "What Working Means to Me as an Autistic Person," *The Mighty*, February 3, 2017: https://themighty.com/2017/02/autism-and-employment/?fbclid=IwAR0v3ZVh9olzCxobf4KNBTYvQWfn8CY-WpUclB0pPrFBwKHvUTjuXcMZcNU.

3 "No one is ever more than temporarily able-bodied": Carol Breckenridge and Candace Vogle, "The Critical Limits of Embodiment: Disability's Criticism," *Public Culture* 13:3 (2001), 349-57.

4 Keir Martin and Sylvia Yanagisako, "States of Dependence: Introduction," *Social Anthropology* 28:3 (2020), 646-56. The universality of dependence has been particularly important in feminist ethical studies: Jennifer Nedelsky, "Reconceiving Autonomy: Sources, Thoughts and Possibilities," *Yale Journal of Law and Feminism* 1:7 (1989), 7-36; Laura Back, "Private Dependence, Public Personhood: Rethinking 'Nested Obligations'," *Hypatia* 30:1 (2015), 115-31. It is also important in disability

NOTES

studies: Jennifer Sarrett, "Autistic Human Rights: A Proposal," *Disability Studies Quarterly* 32:4 (2012), open access; Charlie Platts, "An A to Z of Unemployment," *Medium*, April 9, 2021: https://charlieplatts.medium.com/an-a-to-z-of-unemployment-2b4ba24603b1. See especially the section called "D is for Dependent."

5 On the unexpected independence of people with intellectual disabilities, see now Patrick McKearney (2021) "What Escapes Persuasion: Why Intellectual Disability Troubles 'Dependence' in Liberal Societies," *Medical Anthropology*, 40:2 (2021), 155-168.

6 Nicky Rogge and Juliette Janssen, "The Economic Costs of Autism Spectrum Disorder: A Literature Review," *Journal of Autism and Developmental Disorders* 49:7 (2019), 2873-2900.

7 IDEA, Part B, Subpart A, Section 300.43: https://sites.ed.gov/idea/regs/b/a/300.43.

8 U.S. Department of Education, Office of Special Education and Rehabilitative Services, "A Transition Guide to Postsecondary Education and Employment for Students and Youth with Disabilities," 2017; revised August, 2020: https://sites.ed.gov/idea/files/postsecondary-transition-guide-august-2020.pdf.

9 squishy_pimple_battery, in the "How to figure out where to go to college" discussion, *Wrong Planet*, August 11, 2018: https://wrongplanet.net/forums/viewtopic.php?t=367063.

10 Jennifer Chen, et al., "Parents' Future Visions for their Autistic Transition-Age Youth: Hopes and Expectations," *Autism* 23:6 (2019), 1363-72

11 Susan Hetherington, et al., "The Lived Experiences of Adolescents with Disabilities and Their Parents in Transition Planning," *Focus on Autism and Other Developmental Disabilities* 25:3 (2010), 163-72; Megan Griffin, et al., "Involvement in Transition Planning Meetings Among High School Students with Autism Spectrum Disorders," *Journal of Special Education* 47:4 (2014), 256-64.

12 Cited in Elizabeth Munsell and Ariel Schwartz, "Youth Experiences of the IDEA-Mandated Transition Planning Process: A Metasynthesis of Youth Voices," *Review Journal of Autism and Developmental Disorders* 9 (May, 2022), 438-451.

13 Susan Hetherington, et al., "The Lived Experiences of Adolescents with Disabilities and Their Parents in Transition Planning," *Focus on Autism and Other Developmental Disabilities* 25:3 (2010), 163-72.

14 Jennifer Chen, et al. ("Parents' future visions for their autistic transition-age youth: Hopes and expectations," *Autism* 23:6 [2019], 1363-72) note that transition planning tends to be most successful with White, higher income autistic students.

15 Lusa Lo and Oanh Bui, "Transition Planning: Voices of Chinese and Vietnamese Parents of Youth with Autism and Intellectual Disabilities," *Career Development and Transition for Exceptional Individuals* 43:2 (2020), 89-100.

16 Government Accounting Office, "Youth with Autism: Federal Agencies Should Take Additional Action to Support Transition-Age Youth," May, 2017: https://www.gao.gov/products/gao-17-352.

17 Workforce Investment and Opportunity Act, Title 1, Chapter 2, Section 129.2.C: https://www.congress.gov/113/bills/hr803/BILLS-113hr803enr.pdf. See also U.S. Department of Education, Rehabilitative Services Administration, "Regulations Implementing the Rehabilitation Act of 1973,

NOTES

as Amended by the Workforce Innovation and Opportunity Act" (n.d.): https://www2.ed.gov/about/
offices/list/osers/rsa/wioa/transition-of-students-and-youth-with-disabilities-from-school-to-
postsecondary-education-and-employment.pdf.

18 Claire Snell-Rood, et al., "Stakeholder Perspectives on Transition Planning, Implementation, and
Outcomes for Students with Autism Spectrum Disorder," *Autism* 24:5 (2020), 1164-1176.

19 For these problems as related especially to autistics, see Anne Roux, et al., "Employment Policy
and Autism: Analysis of State Workforce Innovation and Opportunity Act (WIOA) Implementation
Plans," *Journal of Vocational Rehabilitation* 51 (2019), 285-98.

20 nick007, in the "Starting vocational rehab...any advice?" discussion, *Wrong Planet*, May 19, 2018:
https://wrongplanet.net/forums/viewtopic.php?t=363984.

21 Anne Roux, et al., "Employment Policy and Autism: Analysis of State Workforce Innovation and
Opportunity Act (WIOA) Implementation Plans," *Journal of Vocational Rehabilitation* 51 (2019),
285-98

22 Carol Schall, et al., "Competitive Integrated Employment for Youth and Adults with Autism:
Findings from a Scoping Review," *Child and Adolescent Psychiatric Clinics of North America* 29:2
(2020), 373-399.

23 fifasy, in the "Poverty is Harder with Aspergers" discussion, *Wrong Planet*, October 13, 2017:
https://wrongplanet.net/forums/viewtopic.php?t=355217.

24 U.S Bureau of Labor Statistics, "Employment Status of the Civilian Noninstitutional Population
by Disability Status and Selected Characteristics, 2022 Annual Averages," last modified February 23,
2023: https://www.bls.gov/news.release/disabl.t01.htm.

25 Anne Roux, et al., "National Autism Indicators Report: Transition into Young Adulthood," *A.J.
Drexel Autism Institute, Drexel University*, 2015: https://drexel.edu/~/media/Files/autismoutcomes/
publications/National%20Autism%20Indicators%20Report%20-%20July%202015.ashx.

26 Anne Roux, et al. "National Autism Indicators Report: Employment and Other Day Activities," *A.J.
Drexel Autism Institute, Drexel University*, 2017: https://drexel.edu/autismoutcomes/publications-and-
reports/publications/National-Autism-Indicators-Report-Developmental-Disability-Services-and-
Outcomes-in-Adulthood/.

27 Anne Roux, et al. "Employment and Other Day Activities" in *National Autism Indicators Report:
Developmental Disability Services and Outcomes in Adulthood*, Philadelphia: Drexel University Autism
Institute, 2017: https://drexel.edu/autismoutcomes/publications-and-reports/publications/National-
Autism-Indicators-Report-Developmental-Disability-Services-and-Outcomes-in-Adulthood/.

28 Julie Lounds Taylor, et al., "Sex Differences in Employment and Supports for Adults with Autism
Spectrum Disorder," *Autism* 23:7 (2019), 1711-1719.

29 Anne Roux, et al., "Employment Outcomes of Young Adults on the Autism Spectrum," in *National
Autism Indicators Report: Transition into Young Adulthood* (Philadelphia, PA: A.J. Drexel Autism
Institute at Drexel University, 2015): https://drexel.edu/autismoutcomes/publications-and-reports/
publications/Employment-Outcomes-of-Young-Adults-on-the-Autism-Spectrum/.

30 Anna Remington, "Why Employing Autistic People Makes Good Business Sense," *The*

NOTES

Conversation, April 14, 2015: https://theconversation.com/why-employing-autistic-people-makes-good-business-sense-39948. See also Rosie and Anna Remington, "The Strengths and Abilities of Autistic People in the Workplace," *Autism in Adulthood* 4:1 (2022), 22-31.

31 Anna Remington, "Why Employing Autistic People Makes Good Business Sense," *The Conversation*, April 14, 2015: https://theconversation.com/why-employing-autistic-people-makes-good-business-sense-39948; Peter Wong, et al., "Positive Autism: Investigation of Workplace Characteristics Leading to a Strengths-Based Approach to Employment of People with Autism," *Review of International Comparative Management* 19:1 (March, 2018), 15-30: http://rmci.ase.ro/no19vol1/02.pdf;

32 See especially James Richards, "Examining the exclusion of employees with Asperger syndrome from the workplace," *Personnel Review* 41:5 (2012), 630-46. While this study was done in the U.K., many of the same issues arise in the United States as well.

33 Xueqin Qian, et al., "Exploring Correlates of Paid Early Work Experiences for Youth with Autism Using NLTS2012 Data," *Focus on Autism and Other Developmental Disabilities* 36:1 (2021), 14-24.

34 Clyde, in the "No Experience and Need Job" discussion, *Wrong Planet*, December 7, 2010: https://wrongplanet.net/forums/viewtopic.php?f=18&t=145240&sid=75d64319150c4fb929ae11082f78c65b.

35 ResilientBrilliance, in the "How do Aspies make it very far since we suck at networking?" discussion, *Wrong Planet*, August 30, 2016: https://wrongplanet.net/forums/viewtopic.php/viewtopic.php?f=18&t=326866.

36 Rachel Silverman and James Williams, "Two Autistic Perspectives on the Workforce" on James Williams' website: http://www.jamesmw.com/employment.htm.

37 "Soft skills consist of an individual's communication skills, social skills and personal attributes. Interview questions on soft skills allow you to explain personality traits that you can showcase in the workplace": "10 Soft Skills Interview Questions and Answers," in the Career Guide section of the *Indeed.com* website, December 7, 2020: https://www.indeed.com/career-advice/interviewing/soft-skills-interview-questions; "If done effectively, the interview enables the employer to determine if an applicant's skills, experience and personality meet the job's requirements. It also helps the employer assess whether an applicant would likely fit in with the corporate culture," Society for Human Resource Management toolkit, ""Interviewing Candidates for Employment": https://www.shrm.org/resourcesandtools/tools-and-samples/toolkits/pages/interviewingcandidatesforemployment.aspx. .

38 Aaliyah Holt, "One of the Things That Keeps Autistic Adults Out of Jobs: Interviews," *The Lone Aspie*, March 31, 2020: https://theloneaspie.com/one-of-the-things-that-keeps-autistic-adults-out-of-jobs-interviews/; Katie Maras, et al., "Ameliorating the disadvantage for autistic job seekers: An initial evaluation of adapted employment interview questions," *Autism* 25:4 (2021), 1060-1075; Connie Anderson, et al., "Young Adults on the Autism Spectrum and Early Employment-Related Experiences: Aspirations and Obstacles," *Journal of Autism and Developmental Disorders* 51:1 (2021), 88-105.

39 Chris Bonnello, "Finding employment as an autistic person" *Autistic Not Weird*, July 22, 2019: https://autisticnotweird.com/employment/.

40 On the autistic need for predictability, see Chapter 1 above.

NOTES

41 Tori0326, in the "Hard Time Finding Work Due to Aspergers" discussion on the *Wrong Planet* website, May 19, 2018: https://wrongplanet.net/forums/viewtopic.php?t=363351.

42 Brandy Beshears, in the "Why Can't Some People with Aspergers Hold Paid Jobs?" *Quora*, September 6, 2020: https://www.quora.com/Why-cant-some-people-with-Aspergers-hold-paid-jobs. See also NothingToSeeHere, in the "Deathly Job Interviews" discussion, *Autism Forums*, March 3, 2020: https://www.autismforums.com/threads/deathly-job-interviews.32713/#post-678797

43 Katie Maras, et al., "Ameliorating the Disadvantage for Autistic Job Seekers: An Initial Evaluation of Adapted Employment Interview Questions," *Autism* 25:4 (2021), 1060-75.

44 Rebecca Knight, "7 Practical Ways to Reduce Bias in Your Hiring Process" *Harvard Business Review* (June 12, 2017), 2-7; "Interviewing Your Applicant With Autism": https://hireautism.org/resource-center/interviewing-your-applicant-with-autism; Amber Biela-Weyenberg, "5 Tips to Make Your Interview Process Autism-Friendly," *Oracle Fusion Cloud Human Capital Management*, March 31, 2022: https://blogs.oracle.com/oraclehcm/post/5-tips-to-make-your-interview-process-autism-friendly.

45 Cited in Jennifer Sarrett, "Interviews, Disclosures, and Misperceptions: Autistic Adults' Perspectives on Employment Related Challenges," *Disability Studies Quarterly* 37:2 (2017), open access.

46 On the relationship between finding someone "likeable" and sharing personal characteristics with them, see Elizabeth Tenney, et al., "Being Liked is More Than Having a Good Personality: The Role of Matching," *Journal of Research in Personality* 43:4 (2009), 579-85.

47 On "likeability" and bias in the hiring process, see John Cotton, et al., "The "Name Game": Affective and Hiring Reactions to First Names," *Journal of Managerial Psychology* 23:1 (2008), 18-39; Linda Nguyen and Michelle Hebl, "Discrimination toward Asian Job Applicants on the Basis of their Accents," *Academy of Management Annual Meeting Proceedings* 2016:1 (2016), 1; Jeffrey Pinto, et al., ""The Aura of Capability": Gender Bias in Selection for a Project Manager Job," *International Journal of Project Management* 35:3 (2017), 420-31; Corinne Moss-Racusin and Helena Rabasco, "Reducing Gender Identity Bias Through Imagined Intergroup Contact," *Journal of Applied Social Psychology* 48:8 (2018), 457-74; Asia Eaton, et al., "How Gender and Race Stereotypes Impact the Advancement of Scholars in STEM: Professors' Biased Evaluations of Physics and Biology Post-Doctoral Candidates," *Sex Roles* 82: 3-4 (2020), 127-41. Research on the relationship between "likeability" and disability is in its infancy, but it seems clear that disabled people in general, and autistic people in particular, tend to be considered "unlikeable" by employers. See, for example, Mason Ameri, et al., "The Disability Employment Puzzle: A Field Experiment on Employer Hiring Behavior," *ILR Review* 71:2 (2018), 329-64.

48 An autistic adult brought an anti-discrimination case after being denied a job. In response, the employer actually emphasized the importance of interviews in screening for "weirdness": Wendy Hensel, "People with Autism Spectrum Disorder in the Workplace: An Expanding Legal Frontier," *Harvard Civil Rights-Civil Liberties Law Review* 52:1 (2017), 73-102, see p. 88, note 114.

49 Sarah Butcher, "Where Autistic Candidates (and Others) Go Wrong in Job Interviews," *Efinancial Careers*, November 17, 2020: https://www.efinancialcareers.com/news/2020/11/autism-job-interviews.

NOTES

50 b-edward, in the "Job interviews unfair and insulting to people like us" discussion, *Wrong Planet*, October 8, 2013: https://wrongplanet.net/forums/viewtopic.php?t=242149.

51 Rasputin, in the "Deathly Job Interviews" discussion, *Autism Forums*, March 4, 2020: https://www. autismforums.com/threads/deathly-job-interviews.32713/#post-678797.

52 SunnyDay16 in the "Do I or don't I?" discussion, *Autism Forums*, March 4, 2018: https://www. autismforums.com/threads/do-i-or-dont-i.24323/page-2.

53 Cliodhna O'Connor, et al., "Diagnostic Disclosure and Social Marginalisation of Adults with ASD: Is There a Relationship and What Mediates It?" *Journal of Autism and Developmental Disorders* 50 (2020), 3367-3379.

54 Sally Lindsay, et al., "Disclosure and Workplace Accommodations for People with Autism: A Systematic Review," *Disability and Rehabilitation* 43:5 (2021), 597-610.

55 Tiffany Johnson and Aparna Joshi, "Dark Clouds or Silver Linings? A Stigma Threat Perspective on the Implications of an Autism Diagnosis for Workplace Well-Being," *Journal of Applied Psychology* 101:3 (2016), 430-49.

56 Gritches, in the "Autistic People in Demand" discussion, *Autism Forums*, October 17, 2017: https:// www.autismforums.com/threads/autistic-people-in-demand.22200/#post-439079.

57 ThisAdamGuy, in the "Suing for Disability Discrimination" discussion, *Wrong Planet*, July 29, 2015: https://wrongplanet.net/forums/viewtopic.php?f=18&t=290346&start=0.

58 Mason Ameri, et al. "The Disability Employment Puzzle: A Field Experiment on Employer Hiring Behaviour," *International Labor Review* 71:2 (2018), 329–364.

59 This is true of people with disabilities in general: Mary McLaughlin, et al., "Stigma and Acceptance of Persons with Disabilities: Understudied Aspects of Workforce Diversity," *Group & Organization Management*, 29:3 (2004), 302–333. However, autism carries a particularly strong stigma in our society, and this has negative effects on employment: James Richards, "Examining the Exclusion of Employees with Asperger Syndrome from the Workplace," *Personnel Review* 41:5 (2012), 630-646; Jennifer Sarrett, "Interviews, Disclosures, and Misperceptions: Autistic Adults' Perspectives on Employment Related Challenges," *Disability Studies Quarterly* 37:2 (2017), 1–22; Mason Ameri, et al. "The Disability Employment Puzzle: A Field Experiment on Employer Hiring Behaviour," *International Labor Review* 71:2 (2018), 329–364; David Nicholas, et al., "Evaluation of Employment-Support Services For Adults with Autism Spectrum Disorder," *Autism* 22:6 (2018), 693-702. See also the "Equal opportunities for disabled adults in employment - Do they just say it cos they have to?" discussion, *Autism Forums*, November 1, 2018: https://www.autismforums.com/ threads/equal-opportunities-for-disabled-adults-in-employment-do-they-just-say-it-cos-they-have-to.27688/#post-559910.

60 Philip Armour, et al., "Disability Saliency and Discrimination in Hiring," *American Economics Association, Papers and Proceedings* 108 (2018), 262-66.

61 Helen McArdle, "Scientist with Autism Leads Research Showing Brain Can Be "Retrained" to Overcome Condition," *The Herald* (Scotland) February 19, 2015: https://www.heraldscotland.com/ news/13202384.scientist-autism-leads-research-showing-brain-can-retrained-overcome-condition/.

NOTES

This deceptively-titled article was written while Cusack was working as a neuroscientist at the University of Aberdeen in Scotland; he next became Science Director at Autistica, and then, in 2020, CEO (Andy Ricketts, "Autistica Appoints First Openly Autistic Head of a Major Charity," *ThirdSector News*, July 7, 2020: https://www.thirdsector.co.uk/autistica-appoints-first-openly-autistic-head-major-charity/management/article/1688819.

62 Lydia X.Z. Brown, *C.V.*, *Autistica Hoya*: https://autistichoya.net/cv/.

63 Charlotte Alter, Suyin Haynes, and JustinWorland, "Greta Thunberg: 2019 Person of the Year," *Time*, December 23-30, 2019: https://time.com/person-of-the-year-2019-greta-thunberg/.

64 David Serpa, "Being Autistic in Real Estate. 11 Reasons Autistic People Should Consider a Career in Real Estate," *Labcoat Agents*, May 10, 2020: http://www.labcoatagents.com/blog/autistic-real-estate-11-reasons-autistic-people-consider-career-real-estate/.

65 Shane Stoddard, "Trains: How My Special Interest Became My Career," *Organization for Autism Research: News and Events*, May 8, 2019: https://researchautism.org/trains-how-my-special-interest-became-my-career/.

66 Dr. Eric Endlich, "The Good Enough Doctor," *Asperger/Autism Network* website, January 4, 2018: https://www.aane.org/good-enough-doctor/.

67 Alyssa Shanahan, "Meet Alyssa," *Simply Special Ed*: https://www.simplyspecialed.com/about/; Nina Moinni, "Autistic Teacher Praised for Work with Students," *NBC Television News*, May 22, 2012: https://www.nbcnews.com/video/autistic-teacher-praised-for-work-with-students-44436035775. There is even a (private) Facebook page for autistic teachers: https://www.facebook.com/AutisticTeachers/.

68 Rabbi Ruti Regan, https://www.rabbiregan.org/.

69 Julia, *autismthoughts*: https://autismthoughts.wordpress.com/.

70 There is even an international IT Consulting company, auticon, that hires only autistics.

71 Emily Paige Ballou, *Autistic Women and Non-Binary Network*: https://awnnetwork.org/directory/emily-paige-ballou/.

72 John Elder Robison, *Look Me in the Eye: My Life with Aspergers* (New York: Random House, 2007).

73 Meghan Holohan, "'More Visibility Is Needed': Pennsylvania State Rep One of Few with Autism," *NBC Television: The Today Show*, January 15, 2021, on State Representative Jessica Benham: https://www.today.com/health/pa-state-rep-jessica-benham-one-1st-politicians-autism-t205917.

74 Sarah Luterman, "Disclosure of Autism at Work Holds Risks and Benefits," *Spectrum*, September 18, 2018: https://www.spectrumnews.org/opinion/viewpoint/disclosure-autism-work-holds-risks-benefits/.

75 Wanderer03, in the "Do others experience this?" discussion, *Autism Forums*, March 19, 2016: https://www.autismforums.com/threads/do-others-experience-this.15723/#post-296611.

76 sybok, in the "Autism and Work Life" discussion, *Autism Forums*, March 2, 2020: https://www.autismforums.com/threads/autism-and-work-life.32708/#post-678744.

77 Jonathan Mitchell, "Gadfly approved for retirement social security," *Autism's Gadfly*, June 15, 2017:

NOTES

http://autismgadfly.blogspot.com/2017/06/gadfly-approved-for-retirement-social.html.

78 emmanique, "Autistic Friendly Employers – Fact or Fiction," *Cutting Cookies Circus*, March 18, 2019: https://thecuttingcookiescircus.wordpress.com/2019/03/18/autistic-friendly-employers-fact-or-fiction/.

79 Misery, in the "Anyone Else Here Never Have a Job?" discussion, *Wrong Planet*, September 5, 2016: https://wrongplanet.net/forums/viewtopic.php?t=328282.

80 Kay Lomas, "Why Working Is Harder Than It Looks for Many People with Autism," *Organization for Autism Research*, September 5, 2018: https://researchautism.org/why-working-is-harder-than-it-looks-for-many-people-with-autism/.

81 Yenn Purkis, "The Need for Sensory Accessibility and Understanding" *Yenn Purkis Autism Page*, November 6, 2020: https://yennpurkis.home.blog/2020/11/06/the-need-for-sensory-accessibility-and-understanding/.

82 Americans with Disabilities Act (1990, amended in 2008), Subchapter 1, 12112.5A: https://www.ada.gov/pubs/adastatute08mark.htm#12112b.

83 Lyric Holmans, "Autistic Sensory Processing Differences—Autism & Lighting Sensitivity," *Neurodivergent Rebel,* Podcast, 14:11 minutes, March 3, 2021: https://neurodivergentrebel.com/2021/03/03/autistic-sensory-processing-differences-autism-lighting-sensitivity/.

84 B.J. Forshaw, "Working with Aspergers," *My Autistic Dance*, August 5, 2011: https://myautisticdance.blog/2011/08/05/working-with-aspergers-on-about-com-guide-to-autism/.

85 DemonAbyss, in the "Sensory issues with professional attire" discussion, *Wrong Planet*, February 28, 2016: https://wrongplanet.net/forums/viewtopic.php?t=305922.

86 Sarsaparilla, in the "Don't connect well with people at the office" discussion, *Autism Forums*, January 30, 2015: https://www.autismforums.com/threads/dont-connect-well-with-people-at-the-office.10646/#post-188940.

87 Aaliyah Holt, "How Employers Can Make Autistic Lives Easier," *The Lone Aspie*, updated August 6, 2020: https://theloneaspie.com/how-employers-can-make-autistic-lives-easier/.

88 Julia, "Something Good- Day 77," *autismthoughts*, March 18, 2020: https://autismthoughts.wordpress.com/2020/03/18/something-good-day-77/.

89 Kay Lomas, "Why Working Is Harder Than It Looks for Many People with Autism," *Organization for Autism Research*, September 5, 2018: https://researchautism.org/why-working-is-harder-than-it-looks-for-many-people-with-autism/.

90 Angelika Anderson, et al., "A Systematic Review of Interventions for Adults with Autism Spectrum Disorder to Promote Employment," *Review Journal of Autism and Developmental Disabilities* (2017: 4), 26-38.

91 Marghalara Rashad, et al., "Building Employers' Capacity to Support Vocational Opportunities for Adults with Developmental Disabilities," *Review Journal of Autism and Developmental Disabilities* (2017:4), 165-73; Eric Patton, "Autism, Attributions and Accommodations: Overcoming Barriers and Integrating a Neurodiverse Workforce," *Personnel Review* 48:4 (2019), 915-934.

NOTES

92 Sonikku, in the "Workplace Bullying: How Did You Survive?" discussion, *Wrong Planet*, January 17, 2017: https://wrongplanet.net/forums/viewtopic.php?t=335722.

93 Suzanne in the "Bullied by Teenage Girl at Work," discussion, *AutismForums*, February 27, 2018: https://www.autismforums.com/threads/bullied-by-teenage-girl-at-work.24276/#post-483375.

94 On job coach bullying, see Summer_Twilight, in the "Workplace Bullying: How Did You Survive?" discussion, *Wrong Planet*, January 17, 2017: https://wrongplanet.net/forums/viewtopic.php?t=335722.

95 Hayley Peterson, "Target Workers Claim 'Walk of Shame' that Allegedly Led to a Suicide is a Widespread Practice," *Business Insider*, February 5, 2016: https://www.businessinsider.com/target-workers-claim-walk-of-shame-is-widespread-2015-2.

96 jacinto, in the "Bullied by Teenage Girl at Work," discussion, *Autism Forums*, February 26, 2018: https://www.autismforums.com/threads/bullied-by-teenage-girl-at-work.24276/#post-483375.

97 See the "Workplace Bullying" discussion, *Wrong Planet*, December 2019-April 2020: https://wrongplanet.net/forums/viewtopic.php?f=32&t=383123&start=32.

98 Kieran Rose, "Masking: I Am Not OK," *The Autistic Advocate*, July 24, 2018: https://theautisticadvocate.com/2018/07/masking-i-am-not-ok/. See also E. Perry, et al., "Understanding Camouflaging as a Response to Autism-Related Stigma: A Social Identity Theory Approach," *Journal of Autism and Developmental Disorders* 52 (2022), 800-810.

99 Laura Hull, et al., "'Putting on My Best Normal'": Social Camouflaging in Adults with Autism Spectrum Conditions," *Journal of Autism and Developmental Disorders* 47:8 (2017), 2519–2534; Eilidh Cage and Zoe Troxell-Whitman, "Understanding the Reasons, Contexts and Costs of Camouflaging for Autistic Adults," *Journal of Autism and Developmental Disorders* 49:5 (2019), 1899–1911.

100 Cassandra Crosman, "Disability Disclosure and Privacy Management," *In the Loop about Neurodiversity*, April 14, 2019: https://intheloopaboutneurodiversity.wordpress.com/2019/04/14/disability-disclosure-and-privacy-management/.

101 Francine Russo, "The Costs of Camouflaging Autism," *Spectrum*, February 21, 2018: https://www.spectrumnews.org/features/deep-dive/costs-camouflaging-autism/.

102 Kate, "Passing,"*The Thinking Person's Guide to Autism*, September 14, 2012: http://www.thinkingautismguide.com/2012/09/passing.html.

103 Judy Endow, "Losing an Autism Diagnosis," *Aspects of Autism Translated*, August 17, 2014: http://www.judyendow.com/autistic-behavior/losing-an-autism-diagnosis/.

104 Michael Scott Monje (Athena Michaels-Dillon), "Not That Autistic," originally published on *Shaping Clay* (http://www.mmonjejr.com/2013/01/not-that-autistic.html), but updated for publication in Michelle Sutton, ed., *The Real Experts: Readings for Parents of Autistic Children* (Fort Worth, TX: Autonomous Press, 2015).

105 Michael Scott Monje (Athena Michaels-Dillon), "Not That Autistic," originally published on *Shaping Clay* (http://www.mmonjejr.com/2013/01/not-that-autistic.html), but updated for publication in Michelle Sutton, ed., *The Real Experts: Readings for Parents of Autistic Children* (Fort Worth, TX: Autonomous Press, 2015).

NOTES

106 E.g., Barb Cook, "Workplace Social Skills: Challenging the Narrative for Autistic People," *Xceptional*, July 14, 2020: https://xceptional.io/employees/workplace-social-skills-challenging-narrative-autistic-people/; Utini, in the "Co-Worker Constantly wants to hang out and it's stressing me out" discussion, *Autism Forums*, August 22, 2018: https://www.autismforums.com/threads/co-worker-constantly-wants-to-hang-out-and-its-stressing-me-out.26756/#post-539713. See also Neuroguides, "An Unwanted Hill to Climb: The Challenges Autistic Adults Face in Social and Occupational Settings," *Neuroclastic*, October 10, 2020: https://neuroclastic.com/2020/10/10/an-unwanted-hill-to-climb-the-challenges-autistic-adults-face-in-social-and-occupational-settings/.

107 Julia Bascom, "Anatomy of an Autistic," in the archived version of her blog *Just Stimming*, originally published April 5, 2011: https://juststimming.wordpress.com/2011/04/05/.

108 Devon Price, "What Hiding My Autism Costs Me," *Medium*, April 28, 2020: https://humanparts.medium.com/what-hiding-my-autism-costs-me-333d7adc97d4.

109 "Anna," "Off the Spectrum: How Autistic Are You?" *Anonymously Autistic*, August 9, 2016: https://anonymouslyautistic.net/2016/08/09/off-the-spectrum-how-autistic-are-you/. On the long-term costs of passing, see also Emily Paige Ballou, "The Unrecovered," *The Thinking Person's Guide to Autism*, January 11, 2020: http://www.thinkingautismguide.com/2020/01/the-unrecovered.html.

110 Emily Paige Ballou, "I Identify as Tired," *The Thinking Person's Guide to Autism*, December 31, 2019: http://www.thinkingautismguide.com/2019/12/i-identify-as-tired.html. Ballou is using a phrase taken from autistic comedian Hannah Gadsby's "Nanette" show.

111 Kassiane Sibley, "The Tyranny of Indistinguishability: Performance," *Radical Neurodivergence Speaking*: http://timetolisten.blogspot.com/2013/11/the-tyranny-of-indistinguishability.html.

112 Ryan Boren, "Autistic Burnout: The Cost of Masking and Passing," *Ryan Boren*, January 26, 2017: https://boren.blog/2017/01/26/autistic-burnout-the-cost-of-coping-and-passing/.

113 Kieran Rose, "An Autistic Burnout," *The Autistic Advocate*, May 21, 2018: https://theautisticadvocate.com/2018/05/an-autistic-burnout/.

114 C.M. Condo, "what happened" *this great ape*, August 26, 2020: https://thisgreatape.com/2020/08/26/what-happened/.

115 Luna Corbden, "Autism and Shame," *Luna Corbden is Making You Think*, November 6, 2013: https://www.corbden.com/2013/11/autism-and-shame.html.

116 Anonomously Autistic, "Passing: The Problem with Autistic People Being Forced to Act Normal," *The Mighty*, October 22, 2016: https://themighty.com/2016/10/passing-the-problem-with-autistic-people-being-forced-to-act-normal/.

117 Autistic adults are generally more likely to experience shame than their neurotypical peers: Denise Davidson, et al., "Proneness to Self-Conscious Emotions in Adults with and without Autism Traits," *Journal of Autism and Developmental Disorders* 47:11 (November, 2017), 3392-22394. See also Gordon Gates, *Trauma, Stigma, and Autism: Developing Resilience and Loosening the Grip of Shame* (London: Jessica Kingsley, 2019); Asta Johannsdottir, et al., "What's Shame Got To Do with It? The Importance of Affect in Critical Disability Studies," *Disability and Society* 36:3 (2021), 342-357.

118 Jonathan Beck, et al., "Looking Good But Feeling Bad: "Camouflaging" Behaviors and Mental

NOTES

Health in Women with Autistic Traits," *Autism* 24:4 (2020), 809–821

Laura Hull L, et al. "Putting On My Best Normal": Social Camouflaging in Adults with Autism Spectrum Conditions," *Journal of Autism and Developmental Disorders* 47:8 (2017), 2519-2534; Jonathan Beck, et al., Looking Good But Feeling Bad: "Camouflaging" Behaviors and Mental Health in Women with Autistic Traits," *Autism* 24:4 (2020), 809–821; Laura Hull, et al., "Is Social Camouflaging Associated with Anxiety and Depression in Autistic Adults?" *Molecular Autism* 12:1 (2021), open access.

120 Professori, in the "Passing" discussion, *Autism Forums*, April 16, 2016: https://www. autismforums.com/threads/passing.16055/#post-305585.

121 Dora Raymaker, "'Having All of Your Internal Resources Exhausted Beyond Measure and Being Left with No Clean-Up Crew": Defining Autistic Burnout," *Autism in Adulthood* 2:2 (June, 2020), 132-43.

122 E.g., Sarah DeWeerdt, "Autistic Burnout, Explained," *Spectrum*, March 30, 2020: https://www. spectrumnews.org/news/autistic-burnout-explained/; Jane Mantzalas, et al., "A Conceptual Model of Risk and Protective Factors for Autistic Burnout," *Autism Research* 15:6 (2022), 976-87; Samuel Arnold, et al., "Confirming the Nature of Autistic Burnout," *Autism* 27 (2023), preprint online.

123 Eric Garcia describes his own experience of burnout in *We're Not Broken: Changing the Autism Conversation* (New York: Houghton Mifflin Harcourt, 2021), p. 74.

124 Dora Raymaker, "'Having All of Your Internal Resources Exhausted Beyond Measure and Being Left with No Clean-Up Crew": Defining Autistic Burnout," *Autism in Adulthood* 2:2 (2020), 132-43132-43.

125 "AinsleyHarte," in the "Autistic Burnout" discussion, *WrongPlanet*, April 16, 2013: https:// wrongplanet.net/forums/viewtopicphp?f=3&t=153352&sid=fd8394a8ef412b3562390350ea16c5fb &start=45.

126 Kieran Rose, "An Autistic Burnout," *The Autistic Advocate*, May 21, 2018: https:// theautisticadvocate.com/2018/05/an-autistic-burnout/.

127 Amethyst Schaber, response to question on the *Neurowonderful Tumblr* site, December 6, 2014: http://neurowonderful.tumblr.com/post/104511295106/lesmis5-so-my-sister-just-threw-the-biggest.

128 Maxfield Jones, "ABA," *Unstrange Mind*, October 7, 2014: https://unstrangemind.wordpress. com/2014/10/07/aba/.

129 Beth Winegarner, "'The Battery's Dead': Burnout Looks Different in Autistic Adults," *New York Times*, September 3, 2021: https://www.nytimes.com/2021/09/03/well/live/autistic-burnout-advice. html.

130 Elbowgrease says, "I've basically been going through a recurring cycle of burnout and recovery every 3-6 months for most of my life," in the "Burnout?" discussion, *Wrong Planet*, December 4, 2017: https://wrongplanet.net/forums/viewtopic.php?t=357341.

131 Mountain Goat, in the "Masking" discussion, *Wrong Planet*, March 17, 2021: https://wrongplanet. net/forums/viewtopic.php?t=395334.

NOTES

132 Shelly Willoughby, "Aspie Adulthood: The Tough Spot Between Being Unable to Work -and- Not Qualifying for Disability," *Neuroclastic*, April 28, 2019: https://neuroclastic.com/2019/04/28/aspie-jobs/.

133 Bether3, in the "Masking" discussion, *Wrong Planet*, March 17, 2021: https://wrongplanet.net/forums/viewtopic.php?t=395334.

Notes to Chapter Seven

1 Scott Luxor, "Employing Autistic Staff, Rising Tide Car Wash Plans Third Location," *South Florida Sun Sentinel*, December 30, 2020.

2 MeiMei Fox, "20-Year-Old with Autism and His Mother Open Bakery to Employ Others on Spectrum," *Forbes*, October 29, 2017.

3 U.S Commission on Civil Rights, *Subminimum Wages: Impacts on the Civil Rights of People with Disabilities*, September, 2020: https://www.usccr.gov/files/2020/2020-09-17-Subminimum-Wages-Report.pdf .

4 U.S. Social Security Administration, *Program Operations Manual System, RS 02101.270, A*: https://secure.ssa.gov/apps10/poms.nsf/lnx/0302101270.

5 Madison Hopkins, "Missouri Allows Some Disabled Workers to Earn Less than $1 an Hour. The State Says it's Fine if that Never Changes," *ProPublica/Kansas City Beacon*, November 15, 2022: https://www.propublica.org/article/missouri-sheltered-workshops-low-graduation-rate.

6 Robert Cimera, et al., "Do Sheltered Workshops Enhance Employment Outcomes for Adults with Autism Spectrum Disorder?" *Autism* 16:1 (2012), 87-94.

7 In Missouri as of 2022, 45% of workers had been in the sheltered workshop for a decade; another 20% had been there for two decades: Madison Hopkins, "Missouri Allows Some Disabled Workers to Earn Less than $1 an Hour. The State Says it's Fine if that Never Changes," *ProPublica/Kansas City Beacon*, November 15, 2022: https://www.propublica.org/article/missouri-sheltered-workshops-low-graduation-rate.

8 U.S Commission on Civil Rights, *Subminimum Wages: Impacts on the Civil Rights of People with Disabilities*, September, 2020: https://www.usccr.gov/files/2020/2020-09-17-Subminimum-Wages-Report.pdf.

9 U.S Commission on Civil Rights, *Subminimum Wages: Impacts on the Civil Rights of People with Disabilities*, September, 2020: https://www.usccr.gov/files/2020/2020-09-17-Subminimum-Wages-Report.pdf.

10 National Council on Severe Autism, "Position Paper: Vocational Options": https://www.ncsautism.org/vocational-options.

11 "Lane, et al., v. Brown, et al. Settlement Agreement," *Center for Public Representation*: https://www.centerforpublicrep.org/wp-content/uploads/2017/02/Lane_Settlement-Agreememt.executed.pdf.

12 U.S. Department of Labor, Office of Disability Employment Policy, "Employment First": https://www.dol.gov/agencies/odep/initiatives/employment-first.

13 "McMorris Rodgers, Scott Introduce Bill to Help Workers with Disabilities Access Competitive

and Meaningful Employment," *Representative Kathy McMorris Rodgers*, April 6, 2021: https://mcmorris.house.gov/mcmorris-rodgers-scott-introduce-bill-to-help-workers-with-disabilities-access-competitive-and-meaningful-employment/.

14 House Committee on Education and Labor, "Fact Sheet on the Transformation to Competitive Integrated Employment Act": https://edlabor.house.gov/imo/media/doc/2021-04-05%20TCIEA%20Fact%20Sheet.pdf.

15 Ekie, "October is Disability Employment Awareness Month," *I Know This Rose Will Open*, October 9, 2018: https://wordpress.com/read/blogs/80224270/posts/303.

16 wyvery, in the "SSI/Disability Benefits" discussion, *Autism Forums*, January 26, 2014: https://www.autismforums.com/threads/ssi-disability-benefits.5181/#post-78461. See also wanderer03, in the ""What Do I Need to Do to Win My SSDI Benefits?" discussion, *Autism Forums*, June 22, 2016: https://www.autismforums.com/threads/what-do-i-need-to-do-to-win-my-ssdi-benefits.16756/#post-321855; skibum, in the "Applying for SSDI in the US?" discussion, *Wrong Planet*, May 17, 2018: https://wrongplanet.net/forums/viewtopic.php?t=363909.

17 Jeffrey Hemmeter, "Supplemental Security Income Program Entry at Age 18 and Entrants' Subsequent Earnings," *Social Security Bulletin* 75:3 (2015): https://www.ssa.gov/policy/docs/ssb/v75n3/index.html.

18 An old study found that autistics tended to be more successful at re-establishing SSI benefits at age 18 than those in other disability categories: David Auxter, et al., "The Precarious Safety Net: Supplemental Security Income and Age 18 Redeterminations," *Focus on Autism and Other Developmental Disabilities* 14:4 (1999), 194-203.

19 kamiyu910, in the "What Is Your Income" discussion, *Wrong Planet*, April 20, 2013: https://wrongplanet.net/forums/viewtopic.php?f=3&t=228964&start=16. Compare C.M. Condo, "what doesn't kill me (isn't going to work)," *this great ape*, May 14, 2020: https://thisgreatape.com/2020/05/14/what-doesnt-kill-me-isnt-going-to-work/.

20 Kate Lang, "Apply, Deny, Appeal: The Difficult Process of Claiming Disability Benefits," *Generations* 43:4 (2019-2020), 18-24; Dara Lee Luca and Yonatan Ben-Shalom, "The Role of Nonattorney Representation in the SSDI Determination Process: A Case Study of One Prominent Intermediary," *Journal of Disability Policy Studies* (2020), 1-12.

21 Lila Rabinovitch, "A Pipeline of Unscrupulous Practices: Qualitative Study of Attitudes Toward the Social Security Disability Program," *Journal of Disability Policy Studies* 31:3 (2020), 173-80.

22 Albert Fang and Gregory Huber, "Perceptions of Deservingness and the Politicization of Social Insurance: Evidence from Disability Insurance in the United States," *American Politics Research* 48:5 (2020), 543-59.

23 This_Amoeba, in the "Staying on SSI for the rest of my life. any experience?" discussion, *Wrong Planet*, July 7, 2017: https://wrongplanet.net/forums/viewtopic.php?t=338631.

24 Quoted in Lila Rabinovitch, "A Pipeline of Unscrupulous Practices: Qualitative Study of Attitudes Toward the Social Security Disability Program," *Journal of Disability Policy Studies* 31:3 (2020), 173-80.

25 Charis Hill, "Applying for Disability Has Dehumanized Me," *Being Charis*, April 14, 2016: https://beingcharis.com/2016/04/14/applying-for-disability-has-dehumanized-me/.

26 U.S. Social Security Administration, Blue Book, Part A, Section 12.10: https://www.ssa.gov/disability/professionals/bluebook/12.00-MentalDisorders-Adult.htm#12_02.

27 U.S. Social Security Administration, "SSI Federal Payment Amounts for 2023": https://www.ssa.gov/oact/cola/SSI.html.

28 U.S. Social Security Administration, "Understanding Supplemental Security Income SSI Income — 2023 Edition": https://www.ssa.gov/ssi/text-income-ussi.htm.

29 Robin Hartill, "This Is the Maximum Social Security Disability Benefit in 2023," *The Motley Fool*, December 28, 2022: https://www.fool.com/retirement/2022/12/28/this-is-the-maximum-social-security-disability-ben/.

30 KagamineLen, in the "What I Hate About SSI" discussion, *Wrong Planet*, April 17, 2015: https://wrongplanet.net/forums/viewtopic.php?t=280140.

31 Psychostic, in the "Staying on SSI for the rest of my life. any experience?" discussion, *Wrong Planet*, April 20, 2018: https://wrongplanet.net/forums/viewtopic.php?t=338631.

32 workinclassantihero, "I need mental health care but can't afford it," on the r/AutisticPride subreddit, *Reddit*, March, 2021: https://www.reddit.com/r/AutisticPride/comments/lma12j/i_need_mental_health_care_but_cant_afford_it/.

33 Cara Ryan, "Disability Justice and Material Needs: Reflections on the Experiences of Autistic New Yorkers Living Under Covid-19," *Somatosphere* February 19, 2021: http://somatosphere.net/2021/disability-justice-and-material-needs.html/.

34 qawer, in the "What's the common reason for independence issues for aspies?" discussion, *Wrong Planet*, June 17, 2013: https://wrongplanet.net/forums/viewtopic.php?f=3&t=233312.

35 E.g., Michael Bernick and Richard Holden, *The Autism Job Club: The Neurodiverse Workforce in the New Normal of Employment* (New York: Skyhorse Publishing, 2015).

36 For The Arc's Employment Initiative, see: https://thearc.org/our-initiatives/employment/.

37 Corporations that have such programs include Walgreens, Microsoft, and Home Depot, among others.

Notes to Chapter Eight

1 Pete Wharmby, "How Can Autism Affect Your Health?" *Neuroclastic*, December 2, 2019: https://neuroclastic.com/how-can-autism-affect-your-health/

2 Mel Baggs, "We need real money badly," *Cussin' and Discuss,'* March 28, 2020: https://cussinanddiscussin.wordpress.com/2020/03/28/we-need-real-money-badly/.

3 Neil Genzlinger, "Mel Baggs, Blogger on Autism and Disability, Dies at 39," *New York Times*, April 29, 2020.

4 Mary Gerisch, "Health Care as a Human Right," *American Bar Association Human Rights Magazine*

NOTES

43:3 (August, 2018): https://www.americanbar.org/groups/crsj/publications/human_rights_magazine_home/the-state-of-healthcare-in-the-united-states/health-care-as-a-human-right/.

5 Cass Sunstein, *The Second Bill of Rights: FDR's Unfinished Revolution and Why We Need It More Than Ever* (New York: Basic Books, 2004).

6 Gabriel Zieff, et al., "Universal Healthcare in the United States of America: A Healthy Debate," *Medicina* 56:11 (2020).

7 Gordon Burtch and Jason Chan, "Investigating the Relationship Between Medical Crowdfunding and Personal Bankruptcy in the United States: Evidence of a Digital Divide," *MIS Quarterly* 43:1 (2019), 237-262.

8 Katherine Keisler-Starkey and Lisa Bunch, "Health Insurance Coverage in the United States: 2020," *U.S Census Bureau*, September 14, 2021: https://www.census.gov/library/publications/2021/demo/p60-274.html.

9 Rakesh Singh and Craig Palosky, "A Polling Surprise? Americans Rank Unexpected Medical Bills at the Top of Family Budget Worries," *Kaiser Family Foundation*, February 28, 2020: https://www.kff.org/health-costs/press-release/a-polling-surprise-americans-rank-unexpected-medical-bills-at-top-of-family-budget-worries/.

10 Amy Cha and Robert Cohen, "Problems Paying Medical Bills, 2018," *Centers for Disease Control and Prevention, National Center for Health Statistics Data Brief 357*, February, 2020: https://www.cdc.gov/nchs/data/databriefs/db357-h.pdf.

11 Jessica Rast, et al., *National Autism Indicators Report: Health and Health Care* (Philadelphia, PA: Life Course Outcomes Program, A.J. Drexel Autism Institute, Drexel University, November, 2020): https://iacc.hhs.gov/publications/general/2020/natl-autism-indicators-report-november-2020.pdf.

12 "Information about the health and healthcare experiences of autistic adults is much less robust than information about children and adolescents": Jessica Rast, et al., *National Autism Indicators Report: Health and Health Care* (Philadelphia, PA: Life Course Outcomes Program, A.J. Drexel Autism Institute, Drexel University, November, 2020): https://iacc.hhs.gov/publications/general/2020/natl-autism-indicators-report-november-2020.pdf.

13 Jessica Rast, et al., *National Autism Indicators Report: Health and Health Care* (Philadelphia, PA: Life Course Outcomes Program, A.J. Drexel Autism Institute, Drexel University, November, 2020): https://iacc.hhs.gov/publications/general/2020/natl-autism-indicators-report-november-2020.pdf.

14 Pia Bradshaw, et al., "How Can We Support the Healthcare Needs of Autistic Adults Without Intellectual Disability?", *Current Developmental Disorders Reports* 6 (2019), 45-56.

15 Teal Benevides, et al., "Racial and Ethnic Disparities in Benefits Eligibility and Spending Among Adults on the Autism Spectrum: A Cohort Study Using the Medicare Medicaid Linked Enrollees Analytic Data Source," *PLOS One* (May 25, 2021), open access.

16 Alena Hall, "Medicare Open Enrollment Is Extra Complicated This Year—Here's How Seniors Can Navigate It Successfully," *Forbes: Health*, November 2, 2021: https://www.forbes.com/health/healthy-aging/medicare-advantage-guide/.

17 "Medicare Coverage for People with Disabilities," *Center for Medicare Advocacy* (n.d.): https://

NOTES

medicareadvocacy.org/medicare-info/medicare-coverage-for-people-with-disabilities/.

18 Pats, in the "need to stop trying to do things myself to avoid having to talk to people" discussion, *Autism Forums*, December 19, 2019: https://www.autismforums.com/threads/need-to-stop-trying-to-do-things-myself-to-avoid-having-to-talk-to-people.32042/#post-663322.

19 There was also a Medicare Part E, but it has been phased out.

20 Dena Bunis, "Understanding Medicare's Options: Parts A, B, C and D," *American Association of Retired Persons*, January 1, 2021: https://www.aarp.org/health/medicare-insurance/info-01-2011/understanding_medicare_the_plans.html.

21 Maranda Russell, "Medicare Fees Mini Rant," *Maranda Russell*, March 11, 2020: https://marandarussell.com/2020/03/11/medicare-fees/.

22 invisibleboy, in the "Abilify / Aripiprazole to improve anxiety and socializing?" discussion, *Wrong Planet*, July 1, 2015: https://wrongplanet.net/forums/viewtopic.php?t=287946.

23 Robin Rudowitz, et a., "How Many Uninsured Are in the Coverage Gap and How Many Could be Eligible if All States Adopted the Medicaid Expansion?" *Kaiser Family Foundation*, March 31, 2023: https://www.kff.org/medicaid/issue-brief/how-many-uninsured-are-in-the-coverage-gap-and-how-many-could-be-eligible-if-all-states-adopted-the-medicaid-expansion/.

24 Larry Levitt, "The Inequity of the Medicaid Coverage Gap and Why It Is Hard to Fix It," *JAMA [Journal of the American Medical Association] Forum*, October 14, 2021: https://jamanetwork.com/journals/jama-health-forum/fullarticle/2785323.

25 The federal poverty guidelines are calculated by the Department of Health and Human Services every year, using information about housing and food costs, etc. to determine who should be considered "poor" and who should not.

26 Larry Levitt, "The Inequity of the Medicaid Coverage Gap and Why It Is Hard to Fix It," *JAMA Forum*, October 14, 2021: https://jamanetwork.com/journals/jama-health-forum/fullarticle/2785323.

27 Gideon Luken and Breanna Sharer, "Closing Medicaid Coverage Gap Would Help Diverse Groups and Narrow Racial Disparities," *Center on Budget and Policy Priorities*, revised June 14, 2021: https://www.cbpp.org/research/health/closing-medicaid-coverage-gap-would-help-diverse-group-and-narrow-racial

28 Eric Lopez, et al., "How Much More Than Medicare Do Private Insurers Pay? A Review of the Literature," *Kaiser Family Foundation*, April 15, 2020: https://www.kff.org/medicare/issue-brief/how-much-more-than-medicare-do-private-insurers-pay-a-review-of-the-literature/.

29 D. Casper, et al., "Medicaid Reimbursement for Common Spine Procedures: Are Compensation Rates Consistent?," *Spine* 44 (2019), 1585-90;

30 Nancy Ochieng, et al., "How Many Physicians Have Opted-Out of the Medicare Program?" *Kaiser Family Foundation*, October 22, 2020: https://www.kff.org/medicare/issue-brief/how-many-physicians-have-opted-out-of-the-medicare-program/.

31 Christian Boccuti, et al., "Primary Care Physicians Accepting Medicare: A Snapshot," *Kaiser Family Foundation*, October 30, 2015: https://www.kff.org/medicare/issue-brief/primary-care-

physicians-accepting-medicare-a-snapshot/.

32 In one such program, which was designed to encourage conversations about transition, only about half of the pediatricians actually raised the issue with their patients: Jill Harris, et al., "Development and Implementation of Health Care Transition Resources for Youth with Autism Spectrum Disorders within a Primary Care Medical Home, *Autism* 25:3 (2021), 753-66.

33 Jill Harris, et al., "Development and Implementation of Health Care Transition Resources for Youth with Autism Spectrum Disorders within a Primary Care Medical Home, *Autism* 25:3 (2021), 753-66; Nancy Cheak-Zamora, et al., "Provider Perspectives on the Extension of Community Healthcare Outcomes Autism: Transition to Adulthood Program," *Journal of Developmental and Behavioral Pediatrics* 42:2 (2021), 91-100.

34 Jean Hall and Noelle Kurth, "A Comparison of Health Disparities Among Americans with Intellectual Disability and/or Autism Spectrum Disorder and Americans with Other Disabilities," *Inclusion* 7 (2019), 160-68.

35 Rae Morris, et al., "Healthcare Providers' Experiences with Autism: A Scoping Review," *Journal of Autism and Developmental Disorders* 49 (2019), 2374-2388.

36 Cited in Marji Warfield, et al., "Physician Perspectives on Providing Primary Medical Care to Adults with Autism Spectrum Disorders (ASD)," *Journal of Autism and Developmental Disorders* 45 (2015), 2209-2217.

37 Hector Perez, et al., "Chaos in the Clinic: Characteristics and Consequences of Practices Perceived as Chaotic," *Journal for Healthcare Quality* 39 (2017), 43-53; Seth Freedman, et al., "Docs with their Eyes on the Clock? The Effect of Time Pressures on Primary Care Productivity," *Journal of Health Economics* 77 (2021), online/not open access.

38 Autistic doctors must also struggle with these systems. And yes, there are autistic doctors, and not just on television. Here is a website devoted to their concerns: https://theautisticdoctors.com/.

39 Elizabeth Weir, et al., "Autistic Adults Have Poorer Quality Healthcare and Worse Health Based on Self-Report Data," *Molecular Autism* 13:23 (2022), open access.

40 Christina Nicolaidis, et al., "Development and Psychometric Testing of the AASPIRE Adult Autism Healthcare Provider Self-Efficacy Scale," *Autism* 25 (2021), 767-73.

41 Ousseny Zerbo, et al., "A Study of Physician Knowledge and Experience with Autism in Adults in a Large Integrated Healthcare System," *Journal of Autism and Developmental Disorders* 45 (2015), 4002-14.

42 Eric Garcia, *We're Not Broken: Changing the Autism Conversation* (Boston and New York: Houghton Mifflin Harcourt, 2021), p. 124.

43 Anonymous, *The Uninspirational*, August 30, 2020: https://theuninspirational.wordpress. com/2020/08/30/living-and-dying/.

44 Hertfordshire Purple, in the "Needle Phobia and Autism" discussion, *R/autism* subreddit, *Reddit*, 2021: https://www.reddit.com/r/autism/comments/oxpetv/needle_phobia_and_autism/.

45 Elizabeth Weir, et al., "Autistic Adults Have Poorer Quality Healthcare and Worse Health Based on

Self-Report Data," *Molecular Autism* 13.23 (2022), open access.

46 Ousseny Zerbo, et al., "A Study of Physician Knowledge and Experience with Autism in Adults in a Large Integrated Healthcare System," *Journal of Autism and Developmental Disorders* 45 (2015), 4002-4014; Rae Morris, et al., "Healthcare Providers' Experiences with Autism: A Scoping Review," *Journal of Autism and Developmental Disorders* 49 (2019), 2374-2388; Gerard McCormack, "Primary Care Physicians' Knowledge of Autism and Evidence-Based Interventions for Autism: A Systematic Review," *Review Journal of Autism and Developmental Disorders* 7 (2020), 226-41; Kirsten Corden, et al., "A Systematic Review of Healthcare Professionals' Knowledge, Self-Efficacy and Attitudes Towards Working with Autistic People," *Review Journal of Autism and Developmental Disorders* (2021), open access. On pediatric residents' knowledge of autism, see Sarabeth Broder-Fingert, et al., "Residents' Knowledge and Comfort with Caring for Children with Autism Spectrum Disorder," *Clinical Pediatrics* 53 (2014), 1390-92.

47 Quoted in Ousseny Zerbo, et al., "A Study of Physician Knowledge and Experience with Autism in Adults in a Large Integrated Healthcare System," *Journal of Autism and Developmental Disorders* 45 (2015), 4002-14.

48 Ousseny Zerbo, et al., "A Study of Physician Knowledge and Experience with Autism in Adults in a Large Integrated Healthcare System," *Journal of Autism and Developmental Disorders* 45 (2015), 4002-14.

49 Christina Nicolaidis, et al., "Comparison of Healthcare Experiences in Autistic and Non-Autistic Adults: A Cross-Sectional Online Survey Facilitated by an Academic-Community Partnership," *Journal of General Internal Medicine* 28 (2013), 761-769; Marji Warfield, et al., "Physician Perspectives on Providing Primary Medical Care to Adults with Autism Spectrum Disorders (ASD)," *Journal of Autism and Developmental Disorders* 45 (2015), 2209-2217; Leah Duker, et al., "Examining Primary Care Health Encounters for Adults With Autism Spectrum Disorder," *American Journal of Occupational Therapy* 73 (2019), online/not open access; Rae Morris, et al., "Healthcare Providers' Experiences with Autism: A Scoping Review," *Journal of Autism and Developmental Disorders* 49 (2019), 2374-2388; David Mason, et al., "A Systematic Review of What Barriers and Facilitators Prevent and Enable Physical Healthcare Services Access for Autistic Adults," *Journal of Autism and Developmental Disorders* 49 (2019), 3387–3400.

50 Christina Nicolaidis, et al., "'Respect the Way I Need to Communicate with You': Healthcare Experiences of Adults on the Autism Spectrum," *Autism* 19 (2015), 824–831.

51 B19, in the "Barriers to good health care for autistic women" *Wrong Planet*, May 23, 2015: https://wrongplanet.net/forums/viewtopic.php?t=286363.

52 Noca, in the "Do You Feel Like Nobody Listens?" discussion, *Wrong Planet*, February 14, 2016: https://wrongplanet.net/forums/viewtopic.php?t=306085.

53 Ashariel, in the "Autism-friendly/-aware family doctors" discussion, *Wrong Planet*, April 5, 2016: https://wrongplanet.net/forums/viewtopic.php?f=3&t=309379&start=16.

54 Rae Morris, et al., "Healthcare Providers' Experiences with Autism: A Scoping Review," *Journal of Autism and Developmental Disorders* 49 (2019), 2374-2388

55 Christina Nicolaidis, et al., "Comparison of Healthcare Experiences in Autistic and Non-Autistic

NOTES

Adults: A Cross-Sectional Online Survey Facilitated by an Academic-Community Partnership," *Journal of General Internal Medicine* 28 (2013), 761-769; Laura Holmes, et al., "Addressing Sexuality in Youth with Autism Spectrum Disorders: Current Pediatric Practices and Barriers," *Journal of Developmental and Behavioral Pediatrics* 35 (2014), 172-78. Gynecological care is problematic for women with disabilities of all sorts: Laura Taouk, et al., "Provision of Reproductive Healthcare to Women with Disabilities: A Survey of Obstetrician–Gynecologists' Training, Practices, and Perceived Barriers," *Health Equity* 2 (2018), 207-215; David McConnell and Shanon Phelan, "The Devolution of Eugenic Practices: Sexual and Reproductive Health and Oppression of People with Intellectual Disability," *Social Science and Medicine* 298 (2022), online/not open access.

56 Natalie Badgett, et al., "Emergency Department Utilization Among Youth with Autism Spectrum Disorder: Exploring the Role of Preventive Care, Medical Home, and Mental Health Access," *Journal of Autism and Developmental Disorders* 53 (2023), 2274–2282; Britanny Hand, et al., "Specialized Primary Medical Home: A Positive Impact on Continuity of Care Among Autistic Adults," *Autism* 25:1 (2021), 258-265; Nancy Cheak-Zamora, et al., The Impact of the Medical Home on Access to Care for Children with Autism Spectrum Disorders, *Journal of Autism and Developmental Disorders*, 45:3 (2015), 636–644.

57 kx250rider, in the "EEG Test" discussion, *Wrong Planet*, April 24, 2013: https://wrongplanet.net/forums/viewtopic.php?t=229389.

58 Bolletje, in the "Medicine don't work on me the way they are supposed to" discussion, *Autism Forums,* November 16, 2020: https://www.autismforums.com/threads/medicine-dont-work-on-me-the-way-they-are-supposed-to.34756/#post-729175.

59 Gerrit Schalkwyk, et al., "Varieties of Misdiagnosis in ASD: An Illustrative Case Series," *Journal of Autism and Developmental Disorders* 45 (2015), 911-918. Several studies have found that about one third of autistic individuals have been prescribed psychotropic medications without any psychiatric disorder being present: see Chantel Ritter, et al., "Psychotropic Polypharmacy Among Children and Youth with Autism: A Systematic Review," *Journal of Child and Adolescent Psychopharmacology,* 31:4 (2021), 244–258,

60 WittyAspie, in the "Long term use of anti-depressants equals severe withdrawal symptoms" discussion, *Autism Forums,* June 11, 2018: https://www.autismforums.com/threads/long-term-use-of-anti-depressants-equals-severe-withdrawal-symptoms.25718/#post-514379.

61 Ronald Marcus, et al., "A Placebo-Controlled, Fixed-Dose Study of Aripiprazole in Children and Adolescents With Irritability Associated With Autistic Disorder," *Journal of the American Academy of Child and Adolescent Psychiatry* 48 (2009), 1110-1119; Gonzalo Salazar de Pablo, et al., "Systematic Review and Meta-analysis: Efficacy of Pharmacological Interventions for Irritability and Emotional Dysregulation in Autism Spectrum Disorder and Predictors of Response," *Journal of the American Academy of Child and Adolescent Psychiatry* 62:2 (2023), 151-168.

62 L.R. Charlot, et al., "Psychotropic medications use and side effects of individuals with intellectual and developmental disabilities," *Journal of Intellectual Disability Research* 64:11 (2020), 852-63; Gonzalo Salazar de Pablo, et al., "Systematic Review and Meta-analysis: Efficacy of Pharmacological Interventions for Irritability and Emotional Dysregulation in Autism Spectrum Disorder and Predictors of Response," *Journal of the American Academy of Child and Adolescent Psychiatry* 62:2

(2023), 151-168.

63 Sinead Brophy, et al., "Characteristics of Children Prescribed Antipsychotics: An Analysis of Routinely Collected Data," *Journal of Child and Adolescent Psychopharmacology* 28:3 (2018), 180-91.

64 Erin Henneberry, et al., "Decades of Progress in the Psychopharmacology of Autism Spectrum Disorder," *Journal of Autism and Development Disorders* 51 (2021), 4370-4394; Jeffrey Goltz, et al., "Second Generation Anti-Psychotic-Induced Weight Gain in Youth with Autism Spectrum Disorders: A Brief Review of Mechanisms, Monitoring Practices, and Indicated Treatments," *International Journal of Developmental Disabilities* 67:3 (2021), 159-67.

65 S. Brophy, et al., "Characteristics of Children Prescribed Anti-Psychotics: Analysis of Routinely Collected Data," *Journal of Child and Adolescent Psychopharmacology* 28:3 (2018), 180-191. See also Chantel Ritter, et al., "Psychotropic Polypharmacy Among Children and Youth with Autism: A Systematic Review," *Journal of Child and Adolescent Psychopharmacology*, 31:4 (2021), 244–258.

66 Wayne Ray, et al., "Association of Anti-psychotic Treatment with Risk of Unexpected Death Among Children and Youths," *JAMA Psychiatry* 76:2 (2019), 162-171.

67 Amy Esler, et al., "Psychotropic Medication Use for Adults with Autism Spectrum Disorder Who Receive Services and Supports Through Adult Developmental Disability Services in the United States," *Journal of Autism and Developmental Disorders* 49 (2019), 2291–2303.

68 Greta Bushnell, et al., "Trends in Anti-psychotic Medication Use in Young Privately Insured Children," *Journal of the American Academy of Child and Adolescent Psychiatry* 60:7 (2021), 877-886; David Lohr, et al., "Anti-psychotic Medications for Low-Income Preschoolers: Long Duration and Psychotropic Medication Polypharmacy," *Psychiatric Services* 73:5 (2022), 510-17.

69 Su Young Park, et al., "Anti-Psychotic Use Trends in Youth with Autism Spectrum Disorder and/ or Intellectual Disability: A Meta-Analysis," *Journal of the American Academy of Child and Adolescent Psychiatry*, 55:6 (2016), 456-468. Johanna Lake, et al., "Medical Conditions and Demographic, Service and Clinical Factors Associated with Atypical Anti-psychotic Medication Use Among Children with An Autism Spectrum Disorder," *Journal of Autism and Developmental Disorders* 47 (2017), 1391-1402 found slightly lower rates of use: about 17% of adolescents were prescribed anti-psychotics. Marina Sarris, "Anti-psychotics and Autism: Weighing the Benefits, Eyeing the Risks," *Kennedy Krieger Institute: Interactive Autism Network*, December 13, 2016: https://iancommunity.org/ssc/anti-psychotics-and-autism-weighing-benefits-eyeing-risks.

70 Wyverary, in the "Medication Experiences" discussion, *Autism Forums*, February 3, 2014: https://www.autismforums.com/threads/medication-experiences.5377/#post-82505.

71 Southern Discomfort, in the "meltdowns and medications" discussion, *Autism Forums*, September, 26, 2017: https://www.autismforums.com/threads/meltdowns-and-medication.21932/#post-432322.

72 WittyAspie, in the "Violent 10yo" discussion, *Autism Forums*, September 22, 2018: https://www.autismforums.com/threads/violent-10yo.27030/#post-548124.

73 BuyerBeware, in the "Abilify / Aripiprazole to improve anxiety and socializing?" discussion, *Wrong Planet*, July 21, 2015: https://wrongplanet.net/forums/viewtopic.php?t=287946.

74 AliB2409, in the "Dysphoria as side effect of Seroquel and Seroquel XR" discussion, *Wrong Planet*,

NOTES

August 22, 2018: https://wrongplanet.net/forums/viewtopic.php?t=301224.

75 Donna Spencer, et al., "Psychotropic Medication Use and Polypharmacy in Children with Autism Spectrum Disorders," *Pediatrics* 132:5 (2013): 833–840; Jeffrey Goltz, et al., "Second Generation Anti-Psychotic-Induced Weight Gain in Youth with Autism Spectrum Disorders: A Brief Review of Mechanisms, Monitoring Practices, and Indicated Treatments," *International Journal of Developmental Disabilities* 67:3 (2021), 159-67. One Canadian study found that an increase in the prescription of anti-psychotics to autistic children in the second decade of our century, and the development of guidelines for monitoring drug effects, led to little or no increase in monitoring for side effects: Imaan Kara and Melanie Penner, "Impact of Anti-psychotic Guidelines on Laboratory Monitoring in Children with Neurodevelopmental Disorders," *Journal of Child and Adolescent Psychopharmacology*, 31: 1 (2021), 79-83. Another study found that parents, rather than physicians, were responsible for monitoring the effects psychotropic medications were having on their children: Johanna Lake, et al., "Parent Perspectives on Psychotropic Medication Use and Interactions with Prescribing Health Care Providers Among Adolescents and Adults with an Autism Spectrum Disorder," *Focus on Autism and Other Developmental Disabilities* 30:3 (2015), 165-173; Alison Knopf, "Insurance-Funded Study Finds Inadequate Monitoring of Young Patients on SGAs [Second Generation Anti-Psychotics]," *Brown University Child and Adolescent Psychopharmacology Update* 22:3 (2020), 5-6.

76 Pura Ballester, et al., "The Challenge of Detecting Adverse Events in Adults with Autism Spectrum Disorder who Have Intellectual Disability," *Autism Research* 15:1 (2022), 192-202.

77 Evan Taniguchi, et al., "Retrospective Chart Review of Psychotropic Prescribing Patterns and Polypharmacy Rates for Youth with Autism Spectrum Disorder (ASD)," *Journal of the American Academy of Child & Adolescent Psychiatry* 60, Supplement 10 (2021), S164.

78 Richard Houghton, et al., "Psychiatric Comorbidities and Use of Psychotropic Medications in People with Autism Spectrum Disorder in the United States," *Autism Research* 10 (2017), 2037-2047.

79 Rini Vohra, et al., "Prescription Drug Use and Polypharmacy Among Medicaid-Enrolled Adults with Autism: A Retrospective Cross-Sectional Analysis," *Drugs—Real-World Outcomes* 3 (2016), 409-425; Richard Houghton, et al., "Psychiatric Comorbidities and Use of Psychotropic Medications in People with Autism Spectrum Disorder in the United States," *Autism Research* 10 (2017), 2037-2047.

80 Aliya Feroe, et al., "Medication Use in the Management of Comorbidities Among Individuals With Autism Spectrum Disorder From a Large Nationwide Insurance Database," *JAMA Pediatrics* 175:9 (2021), 957-965

81 existentialterror, in the "Do you find the world cold, inhospitable and cruel?" discussion, *Wrong Planet*, March 11, 2015: https://wrongplanet.net/forums/viewtopic.php?t=278189.

82 Shira Stein, "Organ Transplant Disability Bias Gets Second Look Under Trump," *Bloomberg: Law*, March 29, 2019: https://news.bloomberglaw.com/health-law-and-business/organ-transplant-disability-bias-gets-second-look-under-trump.

83 Center for Dignity in Healthcare for People with Disabilities, "Organ Transplant Protections for People with Disabilities," *Kennedy Krieger Institute*, updated February 4, 2021: https://www.kennedykrieger.org/sites/default/files/library/documents/community/maryland-center-for-developmental-disabilities-mcdd/MCDD_OTFactSheet031121.pdf.

NOTES

84 "Organ Donation and Transplantation," *Cleveland Clinic Health Library*, last reviewed May, 2021: https://my.clevelandclinic.org/health/articles/11750-organ-donation-and-transplantation.

85 Timothy Shriver, "The Discriminatory Reason Doctors Won't Give a Baby the Heart She Needs," *Washington Post*, April 8, 2016.

86 Christopher Richards, et al., "Use of Neurodevelopmental Delay in Pediatric Solid Organ Transplant Listing Decisions: Inconsistencies in Standards Across Major Pediatric Transplant Centers," *Pediatric Transplantation* 13:7 (2009), 843-50.

87 "Severely Autistic Boy Needs New Heart: 'He Typed that He was Scared to Die,'" *KVAL Television News* (Eugene, Oregon), December 17, 2012: https://kval.com/news/local/severely-autistic-boy-needs-new-heart-he-typed-that-he-was-scared-to-die; "Organ Transplant Discrimination Against People with Disabilities," *National Council on Disability*, September 25, 2019: https://ncd.gov/sites/default/files/NCD_Organ_Transplant_508.pdf.

88 Mindy Statter, et al., "Policy Statement: Children with Intellectual and Developmental Disabilities as Organ Transplantation Recipients," *Pediatrics* 145:5 (2020), 1-9.

89 Mindy Statter, et al., "Children with Intellectual and Developmental Disabilities as Organ Transplantation Recipients," *Pediatrics* 145:5 (2020), 1-9; Aaron Wightman, et al., Prevalence and Long-Term Outcomes of Solid Organ Transplant in Children with Intellectual Disability," *Journal of Pediatrics* 235 (2021), 10-21.

90 Michael Killian, "Psychosocial Predictors of Medication Non-Adherence in Pediatric Organ Transplantation: A Systematic Review," *Pediatric Transplantation* 22:4 (2018), 1-15.

91 "WHOQOL: Measuring Quality of Life," *World Health Organization*: https://www.who.int/tools/whoqol.

92 Mindy Statter, et al., "Children with Intellectual and Developmental Disabilities as Organ Transplantation Recipients," *Pediatrics* 145:5 (2020), 1-9

93 Matthew Crocker, et al., "Assessing the Relative Importance of Key Quality of Life Dimensions for People With and Without A Disability: An Empirical Ranking Comparison Study," *Health and Quality of Life Outcomes* 19 (2021), open access. One group of researchers found that autistic people with depression rated their own life quality as poor, but those without depression rated their life quality as highly as neurotypicals: Bethany Oakley, et al., "How Do Core Autism Traits And Associated Symptoms Relate To Quality Of Life? Findings from the Longitudinal European Autism Project," *Autism* 25:2 (2021), 389-404. Another group found that being employed, having social supports, and being in a relationship greatly improved autistic people's self-ratings of quality of life: David Mason et al., "Predictors of Quality of Life for Autistic Adults," *Autism Research* 11:8 (2018), 1138-47.

94 "Organ Transplants for People with Disabilities: A Guide for Clinicians," *Autistic Self-Advocacy Network*, March 8, 2014: https://autisticadvocacy.org/wp-content/uploads/2014/03/OrganTransplantationClinicianGuide_final.pdf.

95 For more details on the scoring systems used to determine patient priority under Crisis Standards of Care, see "On Covid, Crisis Standards of Care, and Autism," *Megan McLaughlin Writing*, September

NOTES

27, 2021: https://meganmclaughlinwriting.com/?page_id=105.

96 See the problems discussed in the American Medical Association's "Crisis Standards of Care: Guidance from the AMA Code of Medical Ethics," updated April 5, 2020: https://www.ama-assn. org/delivering-care/ethics/crisis-standards-care-guidance-ama-code-medical-ethics.

97 Samuel Bagenstos, "Who Gets the Ventilator? Disability Discrimination in COVID-19 Medical-Rationing Protocols," *Yale Law Journal, Forum*: May 27, 2020: https://www.yalelawjournal.org/forum/who-gets-the-ventilator.

98 Office of Civil Rights, Department of Health and Human Services, "News Release: OCR Resolves Complaint with Utah After it Revised Crisis Standards of Care to Protect Against Age and Disability Discrimination," August 20, 2020: https://public3.pagefreezer.com/content/HHS.gov/31-12-2020T08:51/https://www.hhs.gov/about/news/2020/08/20/ocr-resolves-complaint-with-utah-after-revised-crisis-standards-of-care-to-protect-against-age-disability-discrimination.html.

99 Disability Rights Pennsylvania, "Press Release: COVID-19 Civil Rights Complaint Filed Against Pennsylvania's Medical Treatment Rationing Guidelines," April 6, 2020: https://www.disabilityrightspa.org/newsroom/covid-19-civil-rights-complaint-filed-against-pennsylvanias-medical-treatment-rationing-guidelines/.

100 Autistic Self-Advocacy Network, et al., "Examining How Crisis Standards of Care May Lead to Intersectional Medical Discrimination Against Covid-19 Patients," February 12, 2021: https://autisticadvocacy.org/wp-content/uploads/2021/02/FINAL-Intersectional-Guide-Crisis-Care-2-10-21.pdf.

101 This can happen when doctors use the "Glasgow Coma Scale" to evaluate brain function/damage in triage situations.

102 Arun Karpur, et al., "Brief Report: Impact of COVID-19 in Individuals with Autism SpectrumDisorders: Analysis of a National Private Claims Insurance Database," *Journal of Autism and Developmental Disorders* 52 (2022), 2350-2356.

103 Editorial, "The Hidden Inequalities of Covid-19," *Autism* 24:6 (2020), 1309-1310.

104 Press conference held in Chicago on March 25, 1966, in connection with the annual meeting of the Medical Committee for Human Rights.

105 Josh Serchen, et al., "A Comprehensive Policy Framework to Understand and Address Disparities and Discrimination in Health and Health Care: A Policy Paper from the American College of Physicians," *Annals of Internal Medicine* 174:4 (2021), 529-532.

106 Joe Fassler, "How Doctors Take Women's Pain Less Seriously," *The Atlantic*, October 15, 2015: https://www.theatlantic.com/health/archive/2015/10/emergency-room-wait-times-sexism/410515/; Laura Kiesel, "Women and Pain: Disparities in Experience and Treatment," *Harvard Health Blog*, October 9, 2017: https://www.health.harvard.edu/blog/women-and-pain-disparities-in-experience-and-treatment-2017100912562 ; Dan Schoenfeld, et al., "Disparities in Care Among Patients Presenting to the Emergency Department for Urinary Stone Disease," *Urolithiasis* 48:3 (2020), 217-25.

107 Bree Andrews, et al, "Black Women and Babies Matter," *American Journal of Bioethics* 21:2 (2021),

NOTES

93-95; Ambria Mahomes, "'You Should Have Said Something': Exploring the Ways that History, Implicit Bias, and Stereotypes Inform the Current Trends of Black Women Dying in Childbirth," *University of San Francisco Law Review* 55:1 (2020), 17-29; Donna Hoyert, "Maternal Mortality Rates in the United States, 2020," *National Center for Health Statistics Health E-Stats*, February, 2022: https://www.cdc.gov/nchs/data/hestat/maternal-mortality/2020/maternal-mortality-rates-2020.htm.

108 "When Health Care Isn't Caring," *Lambda Legal Fund*, 2010: https://www.lambdalegal.org/sites/default/files/publications/downloads/whcic-report_when-health-care-isnt-caring.pdf; Jean Hall, et al., "Health Disparities Among Sexual and Gender Minorities with Autism Spectrum Disorder," *Journal of Autism and Developmental Disorders* 50 (2020), 3071-3077.

109 Johnny Profane, "This #AutisticElder Begins… to Worry… about Dementia," *AutisticAF*, May 15, 2021: https://autisticaf.me/2021/05/15/this-autisticelder-begins-to-worry-about-dementia/.

110 James Cusack, et al., "Personal Tragedies, Public Crisis: The Urgent Need for a National Response to Early Death in Autism," *Autistica*, 2017: https://www.autistica.org.uk/wp-content/uploads/2016/03/Personal-tragedies-public-crisis.pdf.

111 Diana Schendel, et al., "Association of Psychiatric and Neurologic Comorbidity with Mortality Among Persons with Autism Spectrum Disorder in a Danish Population," *JAMA Pediatrics* 170:3 (2016), 243-250. A Finnish study had roughly the same results: Elina Jokiranta-Olkoniemi, et al., "Risk for Premature Mortality and Intentional Self-Harm in Autism Spectrum Disorders," *Journal of Autism and Developmental Disorders* 51 (2021), 3098–3108.

112 Ilhom Akobirshoev, et al., "In-Hospital Mortality Among Adults with Autism Spectrum Disorder in the United States: A Retrospective Analysis of US Hospital Discharge Data," *Autism* 24:1 (2020), 177-89.

113 Leann Smith DaWalt, et al., "Mortality in Individuals with Autism Spectrum Disorder: Predictors Over a 20-Year Period," *Autism* 23:7 (2019), 1732–1739.

114 T. Hirvikoski, et al., "Premature Mortality in Autism Spectrum Disorder" *The British Journal of Psychiatry* 208:3 (2016), 232–238.

115 Jamie Reilly, et al., "Coupling of Autism Genes to Tissue-Wide Expression and Dysfunction of Synapse, Calcium Signalling and Transcriptional Regulation," *PLoS ONE*, December 18, 2020, open access.

116 Angelica Tiotiu, et al., "Impact of Pollution on Asthma Outcomes," *International Journal of Environmental Research and Public Health* 17:17 (2020), 6212.

117 Michelle Failla, et al., "Using Phecode Analysis to Characterize Co-Occurring Medical Conditions in Autism Spectrum Disorder," *Autism* 25:3 (2021), 800-811; Elizabeth Weir, et al., "Increased Prevalence of Non-Communicable Physical Health Conditions Among Autistic Adults," *Autism* 25:3 (2021), 681-694.

118 Joseph Guan and Guohua Li, "Injury Mortality in Individuals with Autism," *American Journal of Public Health* 107:5 (2017), 791-93.

119 On higher rates of suicidality in autistics, see Paige Cervantes, et al., "Suicidal Ideation and Intentional Self-Inflicted Injury in Autism Spectrum Disorder and Intellectual Disability: An

Examination of Trends In Youth Emergency Department Visits in the United States from 2006 to 2014," *Autism* 27:1 (2023), 226-43; Victoria Newell, et al., "A Systematic Review and Meta-Analysis of Suicidality in Autistic and Possibly Autistic People without Co-Occurring Intellectual Disability," *Molecular Autism* 14:12 (2023), open access. On the link between bullying and suicidality, see Rachel Holden, et al., "Investigating Bullying as a Predictor of Suicidality in a Clinical Sample of Adolescents with Autism Spectrum Disorder," *Autism Research* 13:6 (2020), 988-997. On the link between masking and suicidality see S. Cassidy, et al., "Is Camouflaging Autistic Traits Associated with Suicidal Thoughts and Behaviours? Expanding the Interpersonal Psychological Theory of Suicide in an Undergraduate Student Sample," *Journal of Autism and Developmental Disorders* 50 (2020), 3638-3648; Felicity Sedgewick, Lauren Hull and Helen Ellis, *Autism and Masking: How and Why People Do It and the Impact It Can Have* (London: Jessica Kingsley, 2022), p. 175.

120 Barbara Kornblau, "The Case for Designating People with Intellectual and Developmental Disabilities as a Medically Underserved Population," *Autistic Self-Advocacy Network*, April 2014: https://autisticadvocacy.org/wp-content/uploads/2014/04/MUP_ASAN_PolicyBrief_20140329.pdf. .

121 Alice Kuo, et al., "The Autism Intervention Research Network on Physical Health (AIR-P) Research Agenda," *Pediatrics* 149, Supplement 4 (April, 2022), S1-S3.

122 The AIR-P home page can be found here: https://airpnetwork.ucla.edu/; a list of their research publications can be found here: https://airpnetwork.ucla.edu/publications/research-publications.

Notes to Chapter Nine

1 Neuroguides, "Mental Health Carnage: the Relentless Misunderstanding of Autistic Persons," *Neuroclastic*, May 7, 2019: https://neuroclastic.com/mental-health-carnage-the-relentless-misunderstanding-of-autistic-persons/.

2 David Popovic, et al., "Childhood Trauma in Schizophrenia: Current Findings and Research Perspectives," *Frontiers in Neuroscience* 13 (2019), open access.

3 Teal Benevides, et al., "Listening to the Autistic Voice: Mental Health Priorities to Guide Research and Practice in Autism from a Stakeholder-Driven Project," *Autism* 24:4 (2020), 822-33.

4 Jeremy Veenstra-VanderWeele, "Recognizing the Problem of Suicidality in Autism Spectrum Disorder," *Journal of the American Academy of Child and Adolescent Psychiatry* 57:5 (May, 2018), 302-03; L. Dell'Osso, et al., "Mood Symptoms and Suicidality Across the Autism Spectrum," *Comprehensive Psychiatry* 91 (2019), 34-38; Tatja Kirvikoski, et al., "Individual Risk and Familial Liability for Suicide Attempt and Suicide in Autism: A Population-Based Study," *Psychological Medicine* 50:9 (2020), 1463-1474.

5 Tatja Hirvikoski, et al., "Premature Mortality in Autism Spectrum Disorder," *British Journal of Psychiatry* 208: 3 (2016), 232-38.

6 Sarah Cassidy, et al., "Risk Markers for Suicidality in Autistic Adults," *Molecular Autism* 9:42 (2018), open access; Sarah Cassidy, et al., "Is Camouflaging Autistic Traits Associated with Suicidal Thoughts and Behaviours? Expanding the Interpersonal Psychological Theory of Suicide in an Undergraduate Student Sample," *Journal of Autism and Developmental Disorders* 50:10 (2020), 3638-3648; Jonathan Beck, et al., "Looking Good but Feeling Bad: 'Camouflaging' Behaviors and Mental Health in Women

NOTES

with Autistic Traits," *Autism* 24:4 (2020), 809-821.

7 Nicole Stadnick, et al., "Service Use by Youth with Autism within a System-Driven Implementation of Evidence-Based Practices in Children's Mental Health Services," *Autism* 24 (2020), 2094-2103.

8 K. Cooper, et al., "Adapting Psychological Therapies for Autism," *Research in Autism Spectrum Disorders* 45 (2018), 43-50;Jeffrey Wood, et al., "Cognitive Behavioral Treatments for Anxiety in Children with Autism Spectrum Disorder: A Randomized Clinical Trial," *JAMA Psychiatry* 77:5 (2020), 474-83; Naomi Fisher, et al., "Using Eye Movement Desensitisation and Reprocessing (EMDR) with Autistic Individuals: A Qualitative Interview Study with EMDR Therapists," *Psychology and Psychotherapy: Theory, Research, and Practice* 95:4 (2022), 1071-1089.

9 Eric Youngstrom, "Editorial: Stepping Up Care to Reach More Families," *Journal of the American Academy of Child and Adolescent Psychiatry* 61 (2022), 972-73.

10 Lenny Bernstein, "This is Why it's So Hard to Find Mental Health Counseling Right Now," *Washington Post*, March 6, 2022.

11 Brenna Maddox, et al., "'I Wouldn't Know Where to Start': Perspectives from Clinicians, Agency Leaders, and Autistic Adults on Improving Community Mental Health Services for Autistic Adults," *Autism* 24 (2020), 919-930; Nicole Ginn Dreiling, et al., "Mental health Project ECHO Autism: Increasing Access to Community Mental Health Services for Autistic Individuals," *Autism* 26 (2022),434-445.

12 Brenna Maddox, et al., "'I Wouldn't Know Where to Start': Perspectives from Clinicians, Agency Leaders, and Autistic Adults on Improving Community Mental Health Services for Autistic Adults," *Autism* 24 (2020), 919-930.

13 Dawn Adams and Kate Young, "A Systematic Review of the Perceived Barriers and Facilitators to Accessing Psychological Treatment for Mental Health Problems in Individuals on the Autism Spectrum," *Review Journal of Autism and Developmental Disorders* 8 (2021), 436-453.

14 bunnyb, in the "Barriers to good health care for autistic women" discussion, *Wrong Planet*, October 26, 2017: https://wrongplanet.net/forums/viewtopic.php?f=27&t=286363&start=48.

15 On the deadly misdiagnosis of "excited delirium," see Chapter Ten below.

16 I am grateful to Professor Howard Berenbaum of the University of Illinois for clarifying this distinction.

17 Quoted in Sheena Au-Yeung, et al., "Experience of Mental Health Diagnosis and Perceived Misdiagnosis in Autistic, Possibly Autistic and Non-Autistic Adults," *Autism*, 23 (2019), 1508–1518. For another first-hand account, see Beth, "How mental health misdiagnosis affects me," *Just a Square Peg*, February 25, 2022: https://justasquarepeg.com/how-mental-health-misdiagnosis-affects-me.

18 Sheena Au-Yeung, et al., "Experience of Mental Health Diagnosis and Perceived Misdiagnosis in Autistic, Possibly Autistic and Non-Autistic Adults," *Autism*, 23 (2019), 1508–1518.

19 Louise Camm-Crosbie, et al., "'People Like Me Don't Get Support': Autistic Adults' Experiences of Support and Treatment for Mental Health Difficulties, Self-Injury and Suicidality," *Autism* 23 (2019), 1431-1441.

20 xxZeromancerLovexx, in the "Does Therapy Work" discussion, *Wrong Planet*, August 5, 2020: https://wrongplanet.net/forums/viewtopic.php?t=389348.

21 Louise Camm-Crosbie, et al., "'People Like Me Don't Get Support': Autistic Adults' Experiences of Support and Treatment for Mental Health Difficulties, Self-Injury and Suicidality," *Autism* 23 (2019), 1431-1441.

22 Andreia Costa, et al., "Suicidality in Adults with Autism Spectrum Disorder: The Role of Depressive Symptomatology, Alexithymia, and Antidepressants," *Journal of Autism and Developmental Disorders* 50:10 (2020), 3585-3597; E. Gormley, et al., "Alexithymia is Associated with Emotion Dysregulation in Young People with Autism Spectrum Disorder," *Journal of Physical and Developmental Disabilities* 34:1 (2022), 171-186; Bethany Oakley, et al., "Alexithymia in Autism: Cross-Sectional and Longitudinal Associations with Social-Communication Difficulties, Anxiety and Depression Symptoms," *Psychological Medicine* 52:8 (2022), 1458-1470.

23 Bethany Oakley, et al., "Alexithymia in Autism: Cross-Sectional and Longitudinal Associations with Social-Communication Difficulties, Anxiety and Depression Symptoms," *Psychological Medicine* 52:8 (2022), 1458-1470.

24 Quoted in K. Cooper, et al., "Adapting Psychological Therapies for Autism," *Research in Autism Spectrum Disorders* 45 (2018), 43-50.

25 GameCube, in the "Does Therapy Work" discussion, *Wrong Planet*, August 10, 2020: https://wrongplanet.net/forums/viewtopic.php?t=389348.

26 Brenna Maddox, et al., "'I Wouldn't Know Where to Start': Perspectives from Clinicians, Agency Leaders, and Autistic Adults on Improving Community Mental Health Services for Autistic Adults," *Autism* 24 (2020), 919-30.

27 Angnix, in the "'You Need To Go To The Hospital'" discussion, *Wrong Planet*, August 9, 2019: https://wrongplanet.net/forums/viewtopic.php?f=3&t=379088&view=next.

28 DatoVanSmurf, in the "To any autistic person here who has been put in a psych ward against your will I'm so sorry and I know your pain" discussion, *R/autism* subreddit, *Reddit*, 2021: https://www.reddit.com/r/autism/comments/p2u3kv/to_any_autistic_person_here_who_has_been_put_in_a/.

29 Most of the research focuses on children: Sarah Lytle, et al., "Youth with Autism Spectrum Disorder in the Emergency Department," *Journal of Clinical Psychiatry* 79:3 (2018), online/not open access; Kelly McGuire and Matthew Siegel, "Psychiatric Hospital Treatment of Youth with Autism Spectrum Disorder in the United States: Needs, Outcomes, and Policy," *International Review of Psychiatry* 30:1 (2018), 110-15; Gagandeep Rana, et al., "A 6-Year Retrospective Review of Psychiatric Emergency Service Utilization by School-Age Children," *Clinical Child Psychology and Psychiatry* (May, 2022) .

30 Sarah Lytle, et al., "Youth with Autism Spectrum Disorder in the Emergency Department," *Journal of Clinical Psychiatry* 79:3 (2018), online/not open access

31 Leo Zed, in the "Male Aspies and Masking" discussion, *Autism Forums*, September 27, 2022: https://www.autismforums.com/threads/male-aspies-and-masking.41363/#post-897686.

32 FinleyT, "Day 79: Why I've Been Gone," *FinleyT*, May 15, 2022: https://finleyt.blog/2022/05/15/

day-79-why-ive-been-gone/.

33 Timothy Shea, et al., "Racial and Ethnic Inequities in Inpatient Psychiatric Civil Commitment," *Psychiatric Services*, 73:12 (2022), 1322-1329.

34 Celline Cole, et al., "Patient Communication Ability as Predictor of Involuntary Admission and Coercive Measures in Psychiatric Inpatient Treatment," *Journal of Psychiatric Research* 153 (2022), 11-17.

35 Kim Mulford, "New Jersey 'Ill-Equipped' to Treat Patients with Autism and Mental Illness," *Courier Post* (Cherry Hill, NJ), December 11, 2019.

36 SusanLR, in the "I can see why some people hate meds" discussion, *Autism Forums*, July 7, 2022: https://www.autismforums.com/threads/i-can-see-why-some-people-hate-meds.40354/.

37 FireBird, in the "Have You Ever Been in Hospital?" discussion, *Wrong Planet*, May 16, 2014: https://wrongplanet.net/forums/viewtopic.php?f=3&t=259071&start=16.

38 DissolvedGirl, in the "Hello! Recently self-diagnosed, excited and confused" discussion, *Autism Forums*, June 27, 2018: https://www.autismforums.com/threads/hello-recently-self-diagnosed-excited-and-confused.25983/#post-520560.

39 Jeffrey Rothschild, et al., "Medication Safety in a Psychiatric Hospital," *General Hospital Psychiatry* 29:2 (2007), 156-162.

40 Anonymous, "An Open Letter in Response to 'I Am Adam Lanza's Mother,'" *The Platform*, December 23, 2012: https://platformonline.uk/posts/an-open-letter-in-response-to-i-am-adam-lanzas-mother.

41 dcj123, in the "I just got out of the psych ward" discussion, *Wrong Planet*, September 24, 2016: https://wrongplanet.net/forums/viewtopic.php?f=3&t=296446&view=previous.

42 u/spiritualnarc, "sensory over stimulation driving me insane lately," in the *R/Aspergers* subreddit, *Reddit*, 2021: https://www.reddit.com/r/aspergers/comments/q5z3bn/sensory_over_stimulation_driving_me_insane_lately/.

43 "Shannon" quoted in Paul Maloret, *Mental Health Inpatient Experience of Patients with Autism Spectrum Conditions: A phenomenological study* (Ph.D. Dissertation, Department of Health Research, University of Herefordshire, June, 2019), p. 90: https://uhra.herts.ac.uk/bitstream/handle/2299/23058/97007242%20MALORET%20Paul%20Final%20Version%20of%20DHRes%20Submission.pdf?sequence=1&isAllowed=y.

44 One research review reported that different studies have found that between 9 and 91% of all autistic children suffer from gastrointestinal issues, many of which are food-related: Geraldine Leader and Arlene Mannion, "Gastrointestinal Disorders," in Johnny Matson, ed., *Comorbid Conditions Among Children with Autism Spectrum Disorders* (Cham: Springer, 2016), pp. 257-81.

45 Anonymous, "An Open Letter in Response to 'I Am Adam Lanza's Mother,'" *The Platform*, December 23, 2012: https://platformonline.uk/posts/an-open-letter-in-response-to-i-am-adam-lanzas-mother.

46 See, for example, Astrid, "Time-Out Rooms, Comfort Rooms, Snoezelen Rooms," *A Multitude of*

Musings, October 4, 2021: https://astridetal.com/tag/seclusion/.

47 Yenn Purkis, "Autism and hospital – why things need to improve," *Yenn Purkis Autism Page*, August 6, 2022: https://yennpurkis.home.blog/2022/08/06/autism-and-hospital-why-things-need-to-improve/.

48 "Delta," quoted in Paul Maloret, *Mental Health Inpatient Experience of Patients with Autism Spectrum Conditions: A phenomenological study* (Ph.D. Dissertation, Department of Health Research, University of Herefordshire, June, 2019), p. 100: https://uhra.herts.ac.uk/bitstream/handle/2299/23058/97007242%20MALORET%20Paul%20Final%20Version%20of%20DHRes%20Submission.pdf?sequence=1&isAllowed=y.

49 See, for example, Pro Publica, "A Patient in a Psychiatric Ward Was Seen on Video Possibly Being Sexually Assaulted. No One Reported It," *Pro Publica*, November 23, 2021: https://www.propublica.org/article/a-patient-in-a-psychiatric-ward-was-seen-on-video-possibly-being-sexually-assaulted-no-one-reported-it.

50 E.g., Jessica Chaffkin, et al., "Characteristics of Assaultive Patients Whom Inpatient Psychiatric Staff Report to Law Enforcement," *Psychiatric Services* 73:7 (2022), 768-773; Elke Ham, et al., "Workplace Stressors and PTSD among Psychiatric Workers: The Mediating Role of Burnout," *International Journal of Mental Health Nursing* 31:5 (2022), 1151-1163.

51 Eric Wright, et al., "Institutional Capacity to Respond to the Ethical Challenges of Patient Sexual Expression in State Psychiatric Hospitals in the United States," *Journal of Ethics in Mental Health* 7 (2012), 1-5.

52 Beth Hundsdorfer and Molly Parker, "A Disabled Young Patient Was Sent to Get Treatment. He Was Abused Instead. And He Wasn't the Last," *ProPublica* , September 2, 2022 : https://www.propublica.org/article/illinois-choate-mental-health-abuse-beatings.

53 This_Space_Intentionally_Left_Blank, in the "Psych Wards and Autism" discussion, *Wrong Planet*, May 12, 2016: https://wrongplanet.net/forums/viewtopic.php?t=219819.

54 Quoted in Paul Maloret, *Mental Health Inpatient Experience of Patients with Autism Spectrum Conditions: A phenomenological study*, (Ph.D. Dissertation, Department of Health Research, University of Herefordshire, June, 2019) p. 89: https://uhra.herts.ac.uk/bitstream/handle/2299/23058/97007242%20MALORET%20Paul%20Final%20Version%20of%20DHRes%20Submission.pdf?sequence=1&isAllowed=y.

55 lostonearth35, in the "Psych Wards and Autism" discussion, *Wrong Planet*, May 11, 2016: https://wrongplanet.net/forums/viewtopic.php?t=219819.

56 For example, CuddleHug, in the "Have You Ever Been in Hospital?" discussion, *Wrong Planet*, May 16, 2014: https://wrongplanet.net/forums/viewtopic.php?f=3&t=259125&view=previous.

57 David Gray-Hammond, "My Experience Of Restraint in a Psychiatric Hospital: This is Not a Love Story," *Neuroclastic* March 18, 2020: https://neuroclastic.com/my-experience-of-restraint-in-a-psychiatric-hospital-this-is-not-a-love-story/.

58 International Coalition Against Restraint and Seclusion, "A Child in a Straight Jacket," *Neuroclastic*, January 27, 2020: https://neuroclastic.com/a-child-in-a-straight-jacket/.

NOTES

59 Jacqueline Klein, "A Theory of Punishment: The Use of Mechanical Restraints in Psychiatric Care," *Southern California Review of Law and Social Justice* 21:1 (2011), 47-72.

60 Mister Anonymity, in the "Has anyone been failed by the mental health system?" discussion, *Autism Forums*, March 27, 2022: https://www.autismforums.com/threads/has-anyone-been-failed-by-the-mental-health-system.39243/.

61 Marie Chieze, et al., "Effects of Seclusion and Restraint in Adult Psychiatry: A Systematic Review," *Frontiers in Psychiatry* 10 (2019), open access.

62 Pauline Cusack, et al., "An Integrative Review Exploring the Physical and Psychological Harm Inherent in Using Restraint in Mental Health Inpatient Settings," *International Journal of Mental Health Nursing* 27 (2018), 1162-76

63 Carol Vidal, et al., "Risk Factors for Seclusion in Children and Adolescents: The Role of Demographic Characteristics, Clinical Severity, Life Experiences and Diagnoses," *Child Psychiatry and Human Development* 51 (2020), 648-55; Samuel Dotson, et al., "Demilitarizing Hospital Restraints: Recognizing the Stones in Our Glass Houses," *Psychiatric Services* 73:1 (2022), 100-102.

64 Vincent Staggs, "Predictors of Seclusion and Restraint Following Injurious Assaults on Psychiatric Units," *Journal of Patient Safety* 17 (2021), 562-567.

65 "Trauma and Violence," *Substance Abuse and Mental Health Services Administration*, August 2, 2022: https://www.samhsa.gov/trauma-violence.

66 Vincent Staggs, "Trends in Use of Seclusion and Restraint in Response to Injurious Assault in Psychiatric Units in U.S. Hospitals, 2007–2013," *Psychiatric Services* 66:12 (2015), 1369-1372.

67 Charles Dike, et al., "Implementing a Program to Reduce Restraint and Seclusion Utilization in a Public-Sector Hospital: Clinical Innovations, Preliminary Findings, and Lessons Learned," *Psychological Services* 18:4 (2021), 663-70.

68 Sarah Ailey, et al., "Evaluation of Factors Related to Prolonged Lengths of Stay for Patients with Autism with or without Intellectual Disability," *Journal of Psychosocial Nursing and Mental Health Services* 57:7 (2019), 17-22. This article focuses on length of stay for psychiatric patients, but autistics tend to have longer stays for all kinds of hospitalization: C. McLaughlin, et al., "Adult Trauma Patients with Autism Spectrum Disorder: A Case-Control Study to Evaluate Disparities After Injury," *Injury* 52:11 (2021), 3327-3333; A. Koyama, et al., "Severe Outcomes, Readmission, and Length of Stay Among COVID-19 Patients with Intellectual and Developmental Disabilities," *International Journal of Infectious Diseases* 116 (2022), 328-330.

69 Warmheart in the "Under Lock and Key" discussion, *Autism Forums*, February 25, 2017: https://www.autismforums.com/threads/under-lock-and-key.19165/#post-369475.

70 Erin Ward-Ciesielski and Shireen Rizvi, "The Potential Iatrogenic Effects of Psychiatric Hospitalization for Suicidal Behavior: A Critical Review and Recommendations for Research," *Clinical Psychology: Science and Practice* 28:1 (2021), 60-71.

71 Hattie, in the "22 yr old girl, just diagnosed" discussion, *Autism Forums*, April 5, 2017: https://www.autismforums.com/threads/22-yr-old-girl-just-diagnosed.19659/.

72 Jocelyn Carter, et al., "Brief Report: Meeting the Needs of Medically Hospitalized Adults with

Autism: A Provider and Patient Toolkit," *Journal of Autism and Developmental Disorders* 47 (2017), 1510-1529.

73 Robin Gabriels, et al., "Improving Psychiatric Hospital Care for Pediatric Patients with Autism Spectrum Disorders and Intellectual Disabilities," *Autism Research and Treatment* (2012), 1-7.

74 Yenn Purkis, "My own quiet rage against the machine—thoughts on institutional care," *Yenn Purkis Autism Page*, December 16, 2021: https://yennpurkis.home.blog/2021/12/17/my-own-quiet-rage-against-the-machine-thoughts-on-institutional-care/.

75 dcj123, in the "I Just Got Out Of The Psych Ward" discussion, *Wrong Planet*, September 23, 2016: https://wrongplanet.net/forums/viewtopic.php?f=3&t=296446&view=previous.

76 John Pring, "Ten years on from Winterbourne View Scandal, Activists Ask: Why Has So Little Changed?" *Disability News Service* (UK) May 27, 2021: https://www.disabilitynewsservice.com/ten-years-on-from-winterbourne-view-scandal-activists-ask-why-has-so-little-changed/; Lucy Adams, et al., "The Patients Locked in Secure Hospitals for Decades," *BBC News*, August 15, 2022: https://www.bbc.com/news/uk-scotland-62477095.

77 Jenisautistic, in the "psyche ward mac n cheese" discussion, *Autism Forums*, May 16, 2020: https://www.autismforums.com/threads/psyche-ward-mac-n-cheese.33176/page-3.

Notes to Chapter Ten

1 Lydia X. Z. Brown, "Introduction: Notes from the Field (Not the Ivory Tower)," in Lydia X.Z. Brown, E. Ashkenazy, and Morenike Giwa Onaiwu, eds., *All the Weight of Our Dreams: On Living Racialized Autism* (Location Unknown: Dragonbee Press, 2017), p. 7.

2 Jonathan Smith, et al., "Investigation Report and Recommendations, City of Aurora, Colorado, Pursuant to a City Council Resolution Approved July 20, 2020," February 22, 2021, p. 22: https://cdnsm5-hosted.civiclive.com/UserFiles/Servers/Server_1881137/File/News%20Items/Investigation%20Report%20and%20Recommendations%20(FINAL).pdf. The material in this section of the chapter is all taken from this report.

3 David Perry and Lawrence Carter-Long, "The Ruderman White Paper on Media Coverage of Law Enforcement Use of Force and Disability: A Media Study (2013-2015) and Overview," *Ruderman Foundation*, March, 2016: https://rudermanfoundation.org/wp-content/uploads/2017/08/MediaStudy-PoliceDisability_final-final.pdf.

4 Michael Sierra-Arevalo, "The Commemoration of Death, Organizational Memory, and Police Culture," *Criminology* 57 (2019), 632-658. The FBI estimates that there are almost one million law enforcement officers working in the U.S.: https://ucr.fbi.gov/crime-in-the-u.s/2017/crime-in-the-u.s.-2017/tables/table-74. In 2022, 60 of these officers were killed by gunfire and another 14 by vehicular assault; in comparison, 81 died of Covid-19: *The Officer Down Memorial Page* for 2022: https://www.odmp.org/search/year/2022.

5 Tim Hrenchir, "Youth's Mother Questions Why Officer Took Him to the Ground," *Topeka Capital-Journal* October 23, 2020.

6 Laura Ly and Eric Levenson, "Rochester Police Officers Handcuff and Pepper-Spray a 9-Year-

Old Girl After Call of 'Family Trouble'," *CNN Television News*, February 2, 2021: https://www.cnn.com/2021/02/01/us/rochester-police-pepper-spray-child/index.html.

7 Zaz Hollander, "A Wasilla Special Needs Student Was Pepper-Sprayed by a Trooper as His Parents Watched in Shock," *Anchorage Daily News*, April 8, 2022.

8 Jonathan Smith, et al., "Investigation Report and Recommendations, City Of Aurora, Colorado, Pursuant to a City Council Resolution Approved July 20, 2020," February 22, 2021: https://cdnsm5-hosted.civiclive.com/UserFiles/Servers/Server_1881137/File/News%20Items/Investigation%20Report%20and%20Recommendations%20(FINAL).pdf.

9 Ibram X. Kendi, "Compliance Will Not Save Me," *The Atlantic*, April 19, 2021: https://www.theatlantic.com/ideas/archive/2021/04/compliance-will-not-save-my-body/618637/. Kendi describes the death of a 13-year-old who complied with police orders and was shot anyway.

10 Samantha Simon, "Training for War: Academy Socialization and Warrior Policing," *Social Problems* 68, (September 12, 2021), 1-23.

11 Andres Jauregui, "NYPD Officers Accused Of Beating Teen With Autism Assumed He 'Was Up To No Good': Lawyer," *Huffington Post,* July 8, 2015.

12 Stephen Rex Brown, Leo Vartorella, and Bill Hutchinson, "Autistic Teen Beat Up by Cops in the Bronx: Suit," *New York Daily News*, July 8, 2015.

13 "Crisis in Our Communities: Racial Disparities in Community Living, Part 4: The Criminal Legal System," *Autistic Self-Advocacy Network*, February 2022: https://autisticadvocacy.org/criminal-legal-system/.

14 Cited in Susan Stonecypher-Hawkins, "Disability Justice Advocate Neli Latson Joins White House Black History Month Event," *The Arc* blog, February 23, 2023: https://thearc.org/blog/disability-justice-advocate-neli-latson-joins-white-house-black-history-month-event/.

15 Becky Schlickerman, et al., "Teen with Autism Shot to Death," *Chicago Tribune*, February 2, 2012; Joseph Erbentrout, "Stephon Watts Lawsuit: Mother Of Autistic Teen Fatally Shot By Calumet City Cops Sues," *Huffington Post*, April 26 2012; Adrienne Hurst, "Black, Autistic, and Killed by Police," *Chicago Reader*, December 17, 2015.

16 Rachel Treisman, "13-Year-Old Boy With Autism Disorder Shot By Salt Lake City Police," *National Public Radio*, September 9, 2020: https://www.npr.org/2020/09/09/910975499/autistic-13-year-old-boy-shot-by-salt-lake-city-police.

17 Pam Katz, "Advocates Applaud Full Pardon for Neli Latson, A Young Black Man with Disabilities, After Decade of Injustice," *The Arc*, June 22, 2021: https://thearc.org/blog/advocates-applaud-full-pardon-of-neli-latson/.

18 Osagie Obasogie, "Excited Delirium and Police Use of Force," *Virginia Law Review* 107:8 (2021), 1545-1620.

19 Cited in Terry McGuinness and Maurice Lipsedge, "'Excited Delirium', Acute Behavioural Disturbance, Death and Diagnosis," *Psychological Medicine* 52:9 (2022), 1601-11.

20 American Psychiatric Association, "Position Statement on Concerns About Use of the Term

"Excited Delirium" and Appropriate Medical Management in Out-of-Hospital Contexts," December, 2020: https://www.psychiatry.org/File%20Library/About-APA/Organization-Documents-Policies/Policies/Position-Use-of-Term-Excited-Delirium.pdf.

21 American Medical Association, "Press Release: New AMA Policy Opposes "Excited Delirium" Diagnosis," June 14, 2021: https://www.ama-assn.org/press-center/press-releases/new-ama-policy-opposes-excited-delirium-diagnosis.

22 Altaf Saadi, et al., "End the Use of "Excited Delirium" as a Cause of Death in Police Custody," The Lancet 399 (March 12, 2022), 1028-1030.

23 Wetlie cited in Altaf Saadi, et al., "End the Use of "Excited Delirium" as a Cause of Death in Police Custody," The Lancet 399 (March 12, 2022), 1028-1030

24 Osagie Obasogie, "Excited Delirium and Police Use of Force," Virginia Law Review 107:8 (2021), 1591.

25 Yue Yu, et al., "Young Adults with Autism Spectrum Disorder and the Criminal Justice System," Journal of Autism and Developmental Disorders 51 (2021), 3624–3636; Charlotte Blackmore, et al., "Adults with Autism Spectrum Disorder and the Criminal Justice System: An Investigation of Prevalence of Contact with the Criminal Justice System, Risk Factors and Sex Differences in a Specialist Assessment Service," Autism 26:8 (2022), 2098-2107.

26 Julianna Rava, et al., "The Prevalence and Correlates of Involvement in the Criminal Justice System Among Youth on the Autism Spectrum," Journal of Autism and Developmental Disorders 47:2 (2017), 340-46.

27 Dylan Cooper, et al., "Policy Gaps and Opportunities: A Systematic Review of Autism Spectrum Disorder and Criminal Justice Intersections," Autism 26:5 (2022), 1014-1031.

28 Both Onaiwu and Gardner are cited in Elyssa Ball and Jaclyn Jeffrey-Wilenski, "Why Autism Training for the Police Isn't Enough," Spectrum, November 26, 2020: https://www.spectrumnews.org/news/why-autism-training-for-police-isnt-enough/.

29 Lauren Gardner and Jonathan Campbell, "Law Enforcement Officers' Preparation for Calls Involving Autism: Prior Experiences and Response to Training," Journal of Autism and Developmental Disorders 50:12 (2020), 4221–4229

30 Lauren Gardner, et al., "Law Enforcement Officers' Interactions with Autistic Individuals: Commonly Reported Incidents and Use of Force," Research in Developmental Disabilities 131 (2022), online/not open access.

31 Melissa Sreckovic, et al., Autism Training for Law Enforcement Officers: A Scoping Review," Journal of Autism and Developmental Disorders 50 (2020), 4221-4229.

32 Scott Wolfe, et al., "Social Interaction Training to Reduce Police Use of Force," Annals of the American Academy of Political and Social Science 687:1 (2020), 124-45; Robin Engel, et al., "Does De-Escalation Training Work? A Systematic Review and Call for Evidence in Police Use-of-Force Reform," Criminology and Public Policy 19:3 (2020), 721-759; Lauren Gardner and Jonathan Campbell, "Law Enforcement Officers' Preparation for Calls Involving Autism: Prior Experiences and Response to Training," Journal of Autism and Developmental Disorders 50:12 (2020), 4221–4229;

Robin Engel, et al., "De-Escalation Training Receptivity and First-Line Police Supervision: Findings from the Louisville Metro Police study," *Police Quarterly* 25:2 (June, 2022), 201-226.

33 Lauren Gardner, et al., "Law Enforcement Officers' Interactions with Autistic Individuals: Commonly Reported Incidents and Use of Force," *Research in Developmental Disabilities* 131 (2022), online.

34 On the subject of George Floyd's murder: "Quickshot—Baby Steps to Justice," *Cambria's Big Fat Autistic Blog*, June 6, 2020: https://cambriaj1977.wordpress.com/2020/06/06/quickshot-baby-steps-to-justice/.

35 See the varying opinions expressed in the "Cop to autistic "I will blow your f***** head off, ni***r&q," discussion on the Wrong Planet website, 2010-2011: https://wrongplanet.net/forums/viewtopic.php?f=3&t=129613.

36 AFeralWolfChild, "Don't Copsplain to me: On surviving the NYPD while Autistic & Black," *Neuroclastic*, June 6, 2020: https://neuroclastic.com/dont-copsplain-to-me-on-surviving-the-nypd-while-autistic-black/.

37 "Disability Justice Solidarity in Fighting White Supremacy and State Violence," *Autistic Women and Non-Binary Network*, June 1, 2020: https://awnnetwork.org/disability-justice-solidarity-in-fighting-white-supremacy-and-state-violence/;

38 Finn Gardiner, Manuel Diaz, and Lydia X.Z. Brown, "Charles Kinsey's Story Is About Race. It's Also About Ableism," *Sojourner*, July 27, 2016: https://sojo.net/articles/charles-kinseys-story-about-race-its-also-about-ableism; also in Lydia X.Z. Brown, E. Ashkenazy, and Morenike Giwa Onaiwu, eds., *All the Weight of Our Dreams: On Living Racialized Autism* (Location Unknown: Dragonbee Press, 2017).

39 https://autisticadvocacy.org/wp-content/uploads/2020/06/PL-Police-Violence-Toolkit.pdf.

Notes to Chapter Eleven

1 nirrti_rachelle, in the "Autistic Boy Tortured" discussion, *Wrong Planet*, June 18, 2012: https://wrongplanet.net/forums/viewtopic.php?f=3&t=201439&start=16. This chapter draws very heavily on the materials compiled by Lydia X.Z. Brown in her *Judge Rotenberg Center Living Archive*: https://autistichoya.net/judge-rotenberg-center/, and on the superb history of the center presented in Jan Nisbet and Nancy Weiss, *Pain and Shock in America: Politics, Advocacy, and the Controversial Treatment of People with Disabilities* (Waltham, MA: Brandeis University Press, 2021. I am very grateful to Brown, Nisbet, and Weiss, as well as to Shain Neumeier, for equally important work as a writer, attorney and advocate against the JRC.

2 See her website at https://www.jennifermsumba.com/.

3 Jennifer Msumba, *Shouting at Leaves* (Self-published, 2021), p. 101.

4 Jennifer Msumba, "Escaping the Judge Rotenberg Center," video, 14:06 minutes, *Youtube, 2018*: https://www.youtube.com/watch?v=A7hklHN-qqY.

5 Anna Werner, "Extended Interview with Jennifer Msumba, on *CBS Television News*, August, 2014; now part is available as a video, 4:02 minutes, *Youtube*, 2015: https://www.youtube.com/

watch?v=oFYae6WyTWs.

6 Former JRC staffer Greg Miller, in the comments section of Jane Meredith Adams, "Controversial Psychologist Found Working at Special Ed Schools," *EdSource*, August 27, 2015: https://edsource. org/2015/state-suspends-certification-tobinworld-matthew-israel-aversive-therapy/85342.

7 Matthew Israel, "Aversive Therapy Saves Lives," *Washington Post*, October 9, 2010.

8 Cited in Richard Meislin, "Disturbed State Children are Spanked at Institute," *New York Times*, December 19, 1978.

9 Jennifer Gonnerman, "Matthew Israel, Interviewed by Sarah Gonnerman," *Mother Jones Magazine*, August 20, 2007.

10 "XXX" (anonymous survivor), "Judge Rotenberg Center Survivor's Letter," *Judge Rotenberg Center Living Archive*, January 15, 2013: https://www.autistichoya.com/2013/01/judge-rotenberg-center-survivors-letter.html.

11 Terri Du Bois, quoted in Heather Morrison, "This Controversial Massachusetts Facility is the Last in the Country to Use Electric Shock on Students," *Mass.Live News*, July 22, 2016; updated October 28, 2021: https://www.masslive.com/news/2016/07/inside_judge_rotenberg_center.html#incart_river_home%23incart_m-rpt-1.

12 Anonymous resident, quoted in U.S. Food and Drug Administration, "Proposal to Ban Electrical Stimulation Devices Used to Treat Self-Injurious or Aggressive Behavior," April 25, 2016: https://www.federalregister.gov/documents/2016/04/25/2016-09433/banned-devices-proposal-to-ban-electrical-stimulation-devices-used-to-treat-self-injurious-or.

13 Nisbet, and Weiss, *Pain and Shock in America,* pp. 58, 48, 60.

14 "It is Mind and Body Torture," *Adapt* (n.d.): https://adapt.org/it-is-mind-and-body-torture-jennifer-msumba-survivor-of-jrc/.

15 Mitchell Zuckov, "Autistic Man Dies After 'White Noise" Therapy,' *Associated Press News*, July 26, 1985: https://apnews.com/article/a9daa8c5b61ea71abf10e73a6943818d.

16 JayJay Mudridge, JRC survivor, cited in Sarah Rose, "ABA and Relics of The Past," *Capilano Courier* (Capilano University, Vancouver, British Columbia) January 1, 2021: http://www.capilanocourier.com/2021/01/01/aba-autism/.

17 There is some uncertainty about the power of the GED-4. The JRC itself says it delivers 41 milliamperes: https://www.judgerc.org/assets/understanding_the_electrical_parameters_of_the_ged.pdf. Engineer James Eason told the Food and Drug Administration that he had examined the device and found it delivers more like 90 mA: Food and Drug Administration, "Proposal To Ban Electrical Stimulation Devices Used To Treat Self-Injurious or Aggressive Behavior," *The Federal Register* April 25, 2016: https://www.federalregister.gov/documents/2016/04/25/2016-09433/banned-devices-proposal-to-ban-electrical-stimulation-devices-used-to-treat-self-injurious-or.

18 "FDA Proposes Ban on Skin-Shock Devices to Punish Misbehavior in Children," *Citizens Commission on Human Rights International*, April 28, 2016: https://www.cchrint.org/2016/04/28/fda-proposes-ban-on-skin-shock-devices/; Lydia Brown, "The Moral and Legal Bases For Banning Aversive Conditioning Devices Used for Contingent Electric Shock," comments submitted to the

NOTES

Neurological Devices Panel of the Food and Drug Administration, April, 2014, *Judge Rotenberg Center Living Archive*: https://autistichoya.files.wordpress.com/2014/05/the-moral-and-legal-bases-for-banning-aversive-conditioning-devices-used-for-contingent-electric-shock-lydia-brown.pdf.

19 Jennifer Gonnerman, "Matthew Israel Interviewed by Sarah Gonnerman," *Mother Jones Magazine*, August 20, 2007: https://www.motherjones.com/politics/2007/08/matthew-israel-interviewed-jennifer-gonnerman/.

20 Ed Pilkington, "Shock Tactics: Treatment or Torture?" *Guardian*, March 11, 2011: https://www.theguardian.com/society/2011/mar/12/electric-shock-school-matthew-israel.

21 Msumba, *Shouting at Leaves*, p. 109.

22 U.S. Food and Drug Administration, "FDA Takes Rare Step to Ban Electrical Stimulation Devices for Self-Injurious or Aggressive Behavior," March 4, 2020: https://www.fda.gov/news-events/press-announcements/fda-takes-rare-step-ban-electrical-stimulation-devices-self-injurious-or-aggressive-behavior.

23 See the introduction to her video here: https://www.youtube.com/watch?v=A7hklHN-qqY.

24 Nisbet and Weiss, *Pain and Shock in America*, pp. 255-256.

25 Ed Pilkington, "Shock Tactics: Treatment or Torture?" *Guardian*, March 11, 2011: https://www.theguardian.com/society/2011/mar/12/electric-shock-school-matthew-israel.

26 Nisbet and Weiss, *Pain and Shock in America*, pp. 207, 225.

27 Cited in Nisbet and Weiss, *Pain and Shock in America*, p. 32.

28 Letter from Charlene Harrington, California Department of Health, to Matthew Israel, January 17, 1977, cited in Nisbet and Weiss, *Pain and Shock in America*, p. 43.

29 Nisbet and Weiss, *Pain and Shock in America*, pp. 41-43

30 David Wharton, "After a Troubled Past, Autistic Home Reopens, *Los Angeles Times*, August 14, 1986.

31 Nisbet and Weiss, *Pain and Shock in America*, p. 64.

32 Nisbet and Weiss, *Pain and Shock in America*, p. 265.

33 Barbara Hawes, "Report to the New York State Office of Mental Retardation and Developmental Disabilities Concerning the Behavior Research Institute in Providence, Rhode Island," January 11, 1979, *Judge Rotenberg Center Living Archive*: https://autistichoya.net/judge-rotenberg-center/#stategovt.

34 Rusty Kindlon, et al., "Observations and Findings of Out-of-State Program Visitation, Judge Rotenberg Educational Center," 2006, *Judge Rotenberg Center Living Archive*: https://autistichoya.files.wordpress.com/2014/05/nysed-2006-report.pdf.

35 Nisbet and Nancy Weiss, *Pain and Shock in America*, p. 262.

36 Videos of Andre's nightmarish experience are available, but I would like to offer a very strong trigger warning. They are truly horrible to watch.

NOTES

37 Shain Neumeier, "The Judge Rotenberg Center on Trial, Part 1," *Autistic Self-Advocacy Network*, April, 2012: https://autisticadvocacy.org/2012/04/the-judge-rotenberg-center-on-trial-part-one/. The other six parts can also be viewed on the website.

38 Here is the APRAIS website: https://www.stophurtingkids.com/aprais.

39 Quentin Davies, "'Prisoners of the Apparatus': The Judge Rotenberg Center," *Autistic Self-Advocacy Network*, August 9, 2014: https://autisticadvocacy.org/2014/08/prisoners-of-the-apparatus/.

40 Nisbet and Weiss, *Pain and Shock in America*, pp. 270-71, 276.

41 Vince Cestone, "Antioch Special Needs School Tobinworld Connected with Controversial Doctor" *KRON Television News* (San Francisco), May 25, 2016: https://www.kron4.com/news/in-depth-antioch-special-needs-school-tobinworld-connected-with-controversial-doctor/; Vince Cestone, "In Depth: More Allegations of Abuse at Antioch Special Needs School Tobinworld Surface," *KRON Television News*, May 24, 2016: https://www.kron4.com/news/in-depth-more-allegations-of-abuse-at-antioch-special-needs-school-tobinworld-surface/; Corey Hunt, "Tobinworld II Closes its Doors," *The Press* (Brentwood, CA), July 13, 2016; Kevin Smith, "Tobinworld Special Needs School in Glendale to Close Dec. 20," *Los Angeles Daily News,* November 7, 2019. Corey Hunt, "Tobinworld II Closes its Doors," *The Press* (Brentwood, CA), July 13, 2016. The permanent closure of Tobinworld III is mentioned in a State of California document, the "Worker Adjustment and Retraining Notification," July 1, 2019: https://edd.ca.gov/siteassets/files/jobs_and_training/warn/WARN_Report_for-7-1-2019_to_02-25-2020.pdf

42 Nisbet and Weiss, *Pain and Shock in America*, pp. 277-78.

43 "Torture, Not Treatment: Electric Shock and Long-Term Restraint in the United States on Children and Adults with Disabilities at the Judge Rotenberg Center," *Disability Rights International*, 2010: https://www.driadvocacy.org/work/our-reports-publications/.

44 Juan Mendez, "Report of the Special Rapporteur on Torture and Other Cruel, Inhuman or Degrading Treatment or Punishment," *United Nations Human Rights Council*, 2013: https://www.ohchr.org/sites/default/files/Documents/HRBodies/HRCouncil/RegularSession/Session22/A-HRC-22-53-Add4_EFS.pdf.

45 Amy Sequenzia, "The Reality Behind Those Walls," *Ollibean* , November 10, 2016: https://ollibean.com/reality-walls/.

46 "APRAIS calls for immediate action to cease funding of the Judge Rotenberg Center," *TASH*, January 22, 2013: https://tash.org/aprais-issues-letter-on-judge-rotenberg-center/.

47 *Judge Rotenberg Center Living Archive*: https://autistichoya.net/judge-rotenberg-center/.

48 Susan Mizner, "Shocking Kids into Compliance," *American Civil Liberties Union*, April 25, 2014: https://www.aclu.org/news/disability-rights/shocking-kids-compliance.

49 "Letter to Members of the Conference Committee of the State Senate and House of Representatives," *Human Rights Watch*, June 21, 2012: https://www.hrw.org/news/2012/06/21/us/massachusetts-protect-children-disabilities.

50 Nisbet and Weiss, *Pain and Shock in America*, p. 273.

51 Nisbet and Weiss, *Pain and Shock in America*, p. 275.

52 Nisbet and Weiss, *Pain and Shock in America*, pp. 291-92.

53 Nisbet and Weiss, *Pain and Shock in America*, pp. 284-89.

54 Ari Ne'eman testimony, U.S. Food and Drug Administration Neurological Devices Panel, April 24, 2014, *Judge Rotenberg Center Living Archive*: https://autistichoya.files.wordpress.com/2016/04/fda-neuro04-24-14-final.pdf.

55 Nisbet and Weiss, *Shock and Pain in America*, pp. 295-300.

56 Nisbet and Weiss, *Shock and Pain in America*, pp. 301-02.

57 Nisbet and Weiss, *Shock and Pain in America*, pp. 312-13.

58 The court's decision (and the dissent) can be read here: https://www.cadc.uscourts.gov/internet/opinions.nsf/C32A7577ED02127D8525870A00555511/$file/20-1087-1905079.pdf.

59 Sharon DaVanport, cited in "ASAN Endorses New York Bill to Stop The Shock," *Autistic Self-Advocacy Network*, May 4, 2022: https://autisticadvocacy.org/wp-content/uploads/2022/05/ASAN-press-release-andre-mccollins.pdf.

Notes to Chapter Twelve

1 A. Stout, "Caregivers That Kill Autistic Children Need To Be Viewed And Charged As The Murderers They Are," *The Autism Site* blog (n.d.): https://blog.theautismsite.greatergood.com/caregiver-murder/.

2 "2023 Anti-Filicide Toolkit," *Autistic Self-Advocacy Network*: https://autisticadvocacy.org/anti-filicide/.

3 Cory Shaffer, "Parma man accused of beating his 5-year-old son to death indicted on charges that carry death penalty," *cleveland.com* (Cleveland, OH), July 30, 2021: https://www.cleveland.com/court-justice/2021/07/parma-man-accused-of-beating-his-5-year-old-son-to-death-indicted-on-charges-that-carry-death-penalty.html;

4 Kim Bellware, "8-Year-Old Son of NYPD Officer Died After Being Forced to Sleep in Freezing Garage, Police Say," *Washington Post*, January 6, 2020; Sarah Maslin Nir, "A Dozen Calls to Child Abuse Hotline Did Not Save 8-Year-Old Boy," *New York Times*, February 23, 2020; Chris Harris, "NYPD Cop's Dog Slept in Heated Room While Son, 8, Froze to Death in Garage: Housekeeper," *People Magazine*, May 19, 2021.

5 "Florida Woman Accused of Killing Autistic Son Faces Death Penalty," *Associated Press News*, October 30, 2020: https://apnews.com/article/virus-outbreak-miami-florida-crime-77158bdb8a A952785cff1157bc82b136; "National Digest: Miami Woman Accused of Faking Her Autistic Son's Abduction after Drowning Him," *Washington Post*, May 23, 2020.

6 Ariane Zurcher, "But What About Alex?" *Emma's Hope Book*, June 12, 2013: https://emmashopebook.com/2013/06/12/but-what-about-alex/. Zurcher is the neurotypical parent of an autistic young woman; she chronicled her daughter's struggles and triumphs on her blog until Emma was old enough to type for herself. I don't usually cite autism parents in this book, but I have not

been able to find any such eloquent statement of erasure by an autistic person.

7 "Lafayette Couple Charged with the Murder of a Toddler,"*Exponent* (Purdue University, Lafayette, IN), August 18, 2021; Ron Wilkins, "Mother Guilty of Murdering and Neglecting Her 3-Year-Old Son," *Lafayette Journal and Courier*, May 19, 2022. Family members suspected Zeus was autistic, but he had not been formally evaluated: "Zeus Cox," *Autism Memorial*, July 5, 2021: https://autismmemorial.wordpress.com/2021/07/05/zeus-cox/.

8 Hailey Branson-Potts and Richard Winton, "Boy, 11, Found Dead in Echo Park Closet Weighed Just 34 Pounds," *Los Angeles Times*, September 14, 2016; Derek Hawkins, "Woman Allegedly Locked 11-Year-Old Son in Closet for Three Years," *Washington Post*, October 28, 2016; "LA Mom Accused in Death of Special-Needs Son Kept in Closet," *Associated Press New*, June 19, 2019: https://apnews.com/article/6b78c0e259f8478eb460be61343af102. A similar case recently occurred in Michigan, when parents took their 8-year-old son out of school and starved him to death. Paige Barnes, "Parents Charged With Murdering 8-Year-Old In St. Joseph Were 'Sick Of Having CPS' [Child Protection Services] Called On Them," *WSBT Television News* (Mishiwaka, IN), June 3, 2022: https://wsbt.com/news/local/parents-charged-with-murdering-8-year-old-in-st-joseph-were-sick-of-having-cps-called.

9 Associated Press, "Drowning Case in Pennsylvania Takes Tragic Turn," *CBS Television News*, April 5, 2014: https://www.cbsnews.com/news/daniel-schlemmer-dies-after-allegedly-held-underwater-by-mother/; the "tragic turn" was when Daniel, who had lingered for several days, was finally taken off life support. See also "Husband: Tub Drowning Suspect Said She Drove Over their Sons," *Associated Press News*, March 9, 2017: https://apnews.com/article/a608c87e9c4d4599893205bdaf20036c; "Mom Sentenced To 30 To 80 Years In Prison For Sons' Bathtub Drownings," *KDKA Television News* (Pittsburgh, PA), September 13, 2017: https://www.cbsnews.com/pittsburgh/news/mom-sentenced-prison-sons-bathtub-drownings/.

10 "The Latest: Police: Woman Killed Twin Grandsons," *Associated Press News*, April 5, 2019: https://apnews.com/article/41f618e859884913b1e4061685a9791b; "Police: Woman Admitted to Killing Special Needs Grandsons," *KOLD Television News* (Tucson, Arizona), April 8, 2019: https://www.kold.com/2019/04/08/documents-dorothy-flood-admitted-killing-grandsons-tucson-home/.

11 Jacob Geanous, "Grandmother Says She is 'So Sorry' She Shot Her Autistic 8-Year-Old Grandsons Dead," *Metro* (England), January 31, 2020: https://metro.co.uk/2020/01/31/grandmother-says-sorry-shot-autistic-8-year-old-grandsons-dead-12161103/#.

12 The cases mentioned below are all drawn from the Disability Day of Mourning website: https://disability-memorial.org/. However, in each case I have also checked media accounts of what happened. On London McCabe, see: Cassandra Vinograd and Tracy Connor, "Jillian McCabe Accused of Throwing Autistic Son Off Oregon Bridge," *NBC Television News*, November 4, 2014: https://www.nbcnews.com/news/us-news/jillian-mccabe-accused-throwing-autistic-son-oregon-bridge-n240606; "DA: Mom Planned Son's Death Before Throwing Him Off the Yaquina Bay Bridge," *KPIC Television News* (Roseburg, Oregon), February 23, 2016: https://kpic.com/news/local/da-mom-planned-sons-death-before-throwing-him-off-the-yaquina-bay-bridge; Tracy Connor, "Jillian McCabe Gets Life for Throwing Her Autistic Son Off Bridge," *NBC Television News*, February 24, 2016: https://www.nbcnews.com/news/us-news/jillian-mccabe-gets-life-throwing-her-autistic-son-

bridge-n524506.

13 Crystal Bonvillian, "'Overwhelmed' Mom Accused of Trying to Decapitate Son with Bow Saw," *Atlanta Journal-Constitution*, March 28, 2018. Compare what police said about the murder of Nicholas Richett in 2015: https://autisticadvocacy.org/2015/06/statement-on-the-murder-of-nicholas-richett/.

14 Lisa Fernandez, "Sunnyvale Police: Mother Killed 22-Year-Old Autistic Son, Then Herself," *The Mercury News* (San Jose, CA), March 7, 2012.

15 Kassiane Sibley, "Here, try on some of my shoes," *Radical Neurodivergence Speaking*, September 9, 2013: http://timetolisten.blogspot.com/2013/09/here-try-on-some-of-my-shoes.html.

16 Karin Johnson, "Mother in Murder-Suicide was 'Struggling, Depressed,' Friends Say," *WLWT Television News* (Cincinnati, OH), March 11, 2016: https://www.wlwt.com/article/mother-in-murder-suicide-was-struggling-depressed-friends-say/3563229#.

17 "Prosecutor: Mom Confessed to Killing Disabled Adult Daughter," *Associated Press News*, August 31, 2016: https://apnews.com/article/1cbf5005eb974b7688814b65545bb94e.

18 Susan Donaldson James and Cassandra Vinograd, "Jillian McCabe Was 'Overwhelmed' Before Autistic Son's Fatal Plunge," *NBC Television News*, November 5, 2014: https://www.nbcnews.com/health/mental-health/jillian-mccabe-was-overwhelmed-autistic-sons-fatal-plunge-n241176.

19 Judy Endow, "Murdering Autistics is WRONG," *Aspects of Autism Translated*, May 29, 2020: http://www.judyendow.com/advocacy/murdering-autistics-is-wrong/.

20 Ari Ne'eman, "On Our Backs, We Will Carry Them," *Autistic Self-Advocacy Network*, February 27, 2015: https://autisticadvocacy.org/2015/02/on-our-backs-we-will-carry-them/.

21 Arielle Silverman, "This Wasn't a Vigil About Jack: My Hometown's Reaction to a Disability Day of Mourning Vigil," *Disability Wisdom Consulting*, April 2, 2021: https://www.disabilitywisdom.com/2021/04/02/this-wasnt-a-vigil-about-jack-my-hometowns-reaction-to-a-disability-day-of-mourning-vigil/.

22 Zoe Gross, "Killing Words," *Autistic Self-Advocacy Network*, April 10, 2012: https://autisticadvocacy.org/2012/04/killing-words/.

23 Shannon des Roches Rosa, "Untwisting Perceptions: Autism, Parenting, and Victimhood," *The Thinking Person's Guide to Autism*, March 2, 2017: https://thinkingautismguide.com/2017/03/untwisting-perceptions-autism-parenting.html.

24 Interview with Zoe Gross, January 25, 2023. I am grateful to Ms. Gross for the opportunity to talk to her.

25 Haley Moss, "A Life Worth Living: Fighting Filicide Against Children with Disabilities," *Florida A & M University Law Review* 14 (2019), 57-78.

26 "Frequently Asked Questions About Filicide" section of the "2023 Anti-Filicide Toolkit", *Autistic Self-Advocacy Network*, January, 2023: https://autisticadvocacy.org/wp-content/uploads/2015/01/ASAN-Anti-Filicide-Toolkit-FAQ.pdf.

27 Amy Sequenzia, "'Please Don't Murder Us' Shouldn't Be Controversial," *Autistic Women and Non-*

Binary Network, November 11, 2014: https://awnnetwork.org/please-dont-murder-us-shouldnt-be-controversial/.

Notes to Conclusion

1 Nathan Spoon, "A History of Leaves," *Wordgathering* 14:1 (March, 2020): https://wordgathering.com/vol14/issue1/poetry/spoon/.

2 Judy Endow, "Why the Disability Community Is Grieving," *Ollibean*, November 9, 2016: https://ollibean.com/disability-community-grieving/.

INDEX

neurodiversity model of, 15-17
prevalence in U.S., 1, 60-61
"recovery" from, 89-91
treatment industry, 61-63, 69

Autism Speaks, 26, 61, 94, 282

"autisms," 11, 103

autistic people,
as caregivers, 24-25
health needs, 210, 229
prejudice against, 48, 167-169
rates of criminality among, 31-32, 265
stereotypes of, 5, 22, 31-32
voices of, 6-7

autistic pride, 54-55

Autistic Self-Advocacy Network (ASAN),
7, 223, 226, 267, 278, 282,

Autistic Women and Non-Binary
Network (AWN), 7, 267

aversives, 68-69, 81-83, 269, 270-284
working to stop use of, 279-281

Baggs, Amanda (Mel), 36, 199

Bascom, Julia, 32, 55, 80

Behavior Research Institutes, see Judge
Rotenberg Center

bleach, use in "treating" autism, 62

Blume, Harvey 15

Brown, Lydia X. Z., ix, 43-44, 168, 267,
281

bullying, 229
in schools, 112, 114, 132-133, 135,
143-144
on the job, 171, 175-177

burnout, 183-185

Busch, Cynthia, 292

Cameron, Linden, 262-263

camouflaging, see masking

Campbell, Alex, 117-118

Canales, Troy, 261

communication, 36-41, 100-101
ability to speak and intelligence, 36-39,
41, 100-101
echolalia, 39-40, 41
facilitated communication, 38
loss of speaking ability, 39-40
non-speaking autistics, 36-39,
non-verbal aspects of
communication, 41

compliance, 29, 74-76, 243-245, 257, 260
dangers of, 76

Cornelison, Linda, 274

Covid, 224-229
crisis standards of care, 225-226
discrimination against the disabled
in, 225-227
disproportionate effect on autistics, 227
triage, 224-225

Cox, Zeus, 288-289

Crosman, Cassandra, 115-116

Dawson, Michelle 7, 19

INDEX

INDEX

physical costs of, 180-181
psychological costs of, 93-95, 182-183
self-hatred and, 93-95

McCabe, London, 291

McClain, Elijah, 255-258, 261

McCollins, Andre, 277-279, 284
"Andre's Law," 284

Medicaid, 204-206, 282
race/ethnicity and, 205

medical needs, autistic, 213

Medicare, 202-204

medication, 213-220
hypersensitivity, 214
paradoxical reactions, 213-14
see also, atypical antipsychotics,
psychotropic medications

meltdowns, 126-132, 208, 236, 247, 260,
262-263
beyond conscious control, 127-129
confused with temper tantrums, 72,
126-127
effective teacher responses to, 129-132
stages of, 129-30

Mendez, Juan, U.N. Special Rapporteur
on Torture, 280-281

Mental Disability Rights International
(MDRI), 280
now Disability Rights International
(DRI), 280
mental illness, rates in autistics, 231-232

"mercy killings," 285, 289-291

mind-blindness, see theory of mind

Miracle Mineral Solution, see bleach

Monje, Michael Scott, 178-179

mortality rates, autistic, 228-230

Moss, Haley, 295

Msumba, Jennifer, 269-270, 272, 274

Ne'eman, Ari, 283, 294

Neumeier, Shain, 278

neurodiversity, 15-17

non-speaking autistics, see
communication

parenting, 2-3

"passing," see masking

Pena, Diego, 36, 38

physicians,
communication with, 209-213
ignorance about autism, 210-211
monitoring medications, 218-220
reluctance to accept patients on
Medicaid, Medicare, 206
reluctance to accept autistic patients,
206-207

police,
abuse by, 1-2
autistics and "criminal profiling" by, 261
violence, 28-29, 255-268
race/ethnicity and, 256-264
working to end, 266-268
see also, warrior policing

polypharmacy, 218-220
dangers of drug interactions, 219-220

Ponomarenko, Jax, 286

Post-Traumatic Stress Disorder (PTSD), 85-86

predictability, importance of, 27-28, 173-175

proprioception, 50-51, 104-105

psychiatric hospitals and wards, 237-251
abusive behaviors by staff in, 243
admission to, 237-238
race/ethnicity and, 237
forced compliance in, 243-245
ignorance of autism in, 250
increase mental health problems, 247-251
length of stay, 248-50
medication in, 238-239
reforming, 249-250
restraint and seclusion in, 245-248
race/ethnicity in, 247
sexual assaults in, 243
stressors for autistic patients in, 239-242
violence in, 242-243
women in, 242

psychopaths, autistics not, 31-32

psychotropic medications, 214-220, 274
atypical antipsychotics, 215-218
dangers of, 216, 238-239
FDA approved for "behaviors," 215-218
in psychiatric hospitals and wards, 238-239

purposeful misbehavior, 132-133, 144

quality of life, 223

"quiet hands," 33

Regan, Ruti, 85

restraint and seclusion, 117-118, 136-140, 245-248

Ripley, Alejandro, 287

Schaber, Amethyst, 53, 184

Schlemmer, Luke And Daniel, 290

school discipline, 117-149
Behavior Intervention Plan (BIP), 134-136, 145
Functional Behavior Assessment (FBA), 133-136, 145
Manifestation Determination Review (MDR), 146
race/ethnicity and, 137-138, 141-142, 148
restraint and seclusion in schools, 117-118, 136-140
ineffectiveness of, 140
physical dangers of, 138-139
psychological dangers of, 140
working to end, 117-118, 136
suspension and expulsion, 141-149
ineffectiveness of, 148-149
rates of, 147-148
"unofficial" suspensions, 141, 147-148

school-to-prison pipeline, 148

schools, autistic students in, 98-116
certificates of completion, 111
disruptive behaviors, 109-110, 118-133
see also, aggression, meltdowns, purposeful misbehavior
dropping out, 112-113
race/ethnicity and drop-out rates, 112
graduation rates, 113
importance of teacher support, 114-115
low expectations, 98-103, 114

INDEX

mainstream classrooms, 108-110
placement, 108, 145-147
sensory processing issues, 105-108
special education classrooms, 100-101,
108, 110

senses, *see* auditory processing,
interoception, proprioception, vestibular
sense, visual processing, taste

sensory differences, 48-54

sensory processing, 49-50, 105-108

sensory sensitivity, 49, 103-105

sensory stress
in schools, 103-105
on the job, 171-173
in psychiatric hospitals and wards,
240-241, 250

sheltered workshops, 187-190

Shore, Stephen 7

Singer, Judy 15

social interactions, stress of, 25,

Social Security Disability Insurance
(SSDI), 190-191, 193-195, 202-203

Sparrow, Maxfield, 26-27

Speck, Mindy, 292

speech, *see* communication

Spoon, Nathan, vii, ix, 296

Spourdalakis, Alex, 288

Srinivasan, Hari, 39

stimming (self-stimulatory behaviors),
32-34, 95, 223, 233
as sign of agitation, 130
efforts to extinguish, 33, 73, 89

subminimum wage, 187-189

suicide, 140, 176, 185, 216, 229, 232
masking and, 232

"suicide attacks," 236-237

Supplemental Security Income (SSI),
190-195, 205

Suskind, Owen, 39

taste, sense of, 50

Taylor-Parker, Larkin, 93

theory of mind, 14-15
Baron-Cohen, Simon, and, 14

transplants, denial of, 220-223

transition to adulthood, 155-160
planning, as laid out in IDEA, 156-157
race/ethnicity in transition
planning, 158

Valva, Thomas, 286-287

vestibular sense, 50, 104

visual processing, 43, 54, 106-107

vocational rehabilitation services,
159-160

voting rights, loss of, 2

Webb, Jorden And Jaden, 290-291

Made in the USA
Monee, IL
18 August 2023

41242339R00221